Beauties and the Beasts

First published in October 2012

© Text and pictures - John Claridge

© Design - Mpress (media) Ltd

Editors: Rosie Barham and Terry Doe

ISBN number: 978-0-9572559-2-0

Unit Four, Ashton Gate, Harold Hill, Romford, RM3 8UF

Designed and published by m!press (Media) LTD.

I would like to dedicate this book to my wife, Lynn. You are my best friend, lover and soulmate and I'm so glad I found you in my life. Without your love and support I would never have had the confidence to write this book. Thank you for giving me five special children: Amber, Megan, Bobby, and my two little treasures, Isabelle and Benjamin. I love you all very much.

Acknowledgements

Firstly, I would like to thank Cliff Moulder at Mpress for having the faith and confidence in me to produce this book. Without his backing this huge project, for me, might never have got off the ground.

Thanks to Paul Moulder, for his massive efforts in laying out and designing this book. Also thanks to Terry Doe and Rosie Barham for dissecting my English grammar.

Big-up to my old pal, Lewis Read, for his foreword. I expected you to rip me big time with your weird and wonderful sense of humour but was honoured by your kind words.

To Kasey Ledger for her excellent maps and drawings, all done at short notice while sitting exams - no surprise on the A* in art!

To Dave Ellyatt for his advice, encouragement and positive vibes on the chapters within this book. A big thank you to Dave and Peter Drennan for the sponsorship from ESP over the years.

To all the companies that have supported me in one way or another in the past.

To all the magazine editors who have used my articles over the years. In particular, Marc Coulson who saw my potential and along with David Hall gave me the opportunity to become the proud editor of Advanced Carp Fishing.

Thanks to all the guys who have supplied their cherished trophy shots.

To all the mates I've made on this long journey and shared a brew with, especially the Yateley Massive. A big shout-out to all the boys.

To my big brother, Paul, and good friend, Lee Picknell, for getting me interested in fishing. God knows what I'd be doing otherwise.

To Mum and Dad for never stopping me from going fishing, and putting up with the stink of me making bait in the kitchen.

To my little princess Isabelle for making Daddy read bedtime stories and giving me the idea for the title of this book.

Last, but not least, is Lynn and the kids for always letting me go angling and supporting me to the hilt. I love you all.

Contents

Contents

Foreword

Many of you will have read about John's fishing exploits in one his regular features in the monthly magazines, but what these brief snapshots into the world of JC's big carp fishing don't fully convey is a real insight into the angler himself. The reader may not appreciate his dedicated mindset and the way that he goes about outwitting his scaly opponents with an apparently laid-back facade and consummate ease, and that doesn't necessarily truly showcase his talent, tactical knowledge, determination, enthusiasm and tactical prowess as a master of the art of carp catching.

I count myself extremely fortunate to have angled with JC on the Car Park Lake and enjoyed some truly memorable moments with him during my own extended stay on that great water. John's time on the lake was a little shorter and arguably a little more successful for the very simple reason that he has his own unique style. By combining those two essential personal attributes for long-term success as a top level carper, namely superb watercraft with a resolute determination to succeed, the outcome has been the downfall of some of the very finest carp this country has to offer.

Don't for one moment dare to pigeon-hole 'Nasty McChevin' as just another 'Yateley angler'! He is much much more than that, for despite his long association with the lakes at Yateley, his angling career has seen him visit and catch carp from a great many waters across the length and breadth of the south of England.

Yes, it is true he cut his angling teeth fishing the Yateley Lakes as a youngster. Can you imagine how exciting it must have been as a young angler, being raised in Yateley - fishing for the fantastic tench that the complex was once famed for? It's also hardly surprising that having been immersed in such a big fish culture, the eventual outcome would be that 'carp fever' would take a firm stranglehold on John and shape his future so dramatically.

By fishing and sharing his younger angling experiences with his clan, made up of brother Paul and close friend Lee Picknell, the three pooled their knowledge and experience – and all three soon evolved into superb carp anglers in their own right.

John's affair with Yateley had a temporary break in his mid-teens when his parents moved from Yateley to Gloucestershire, to take on a farm, but this only served to give John the opportunity to broaden his experience by fishing venues in a new area. When he came back to fish for the now famous big carp at Yateley he was more than mentally and tactically prepared to catch the fish of his dreams.

JC's living on a pig farm also naturally gave rise to the odd bit of banter, and the nickname of 'Rasher' has stuck with him ever since, despite Rasher Farm no longer being a working pig farm. Since when did facts get in the way of some well-meant piss-taking!

Personally, I preferred calling him 'Nasty McChevin'; a nickname eventually derived from two original jibes. The first being that his brother, Paul, was 'Nice Claridge' and John was 'Nasty Claridge' – although in reality, two more genuine and pleasant anglers you would be lucky to find set up on the side of any carp lake. The other part was John's amazing ability to catch the commons that live in the Car Park! These Redmire commons had been stocked much later than the mirrors and consequently looked like chub (Chevin) swimming next to the leviathan-sized originals, they're not so small any more.

I even had a little poster made with John's head superimposed on the body of the 'The Highlander' with the immortal words:
"I am Nasty McClaridge of the Clan McClaridge and I am the... Lowlander
There can be only one
Thank fuck"

I'm not sure if John can reproduce the very dodgy pixilated artwork, but it production represents perfectly the great camaraderie that the lake evoked among the friendly band of regulars. The sense of fun that the hard fishing forced us to adopt kept us sane – at least until the next hard-won opportunity arose and all the work of fish spotting and priming spots came to fruition once more.

It's amazing how a joke and a chat with a good mate can drag you through the bad times, with even the most downtrodden of spirits being lifted by a cup of hot water down a shoe or some equally childish prank, but these are the things that forge lifelong friendships.

These days, I don't have the pleasure of spending time on the banks with JC. John's own carp angling adventures have seen him go off on an alternative carp fishing journey, visiting a very different set of venues from my own, but I'm extremely lucky that I have stayed in regular contact with him while he worked in Colin's fishing shop in Chippenham – and latterly, since he has taken the opportunity to jump from humble feature writer to the key editorial role in one of the country's leading carp fishing monthlies.

So, here it is; John's first book!

Within its pages you will see that you don't have to be wasted to catch carp. You don't have to be single to be single-minded. You can be a successful angler, have a family, have a job and move on in life without angling in a manner that is detrimental to those around you – and most of all, you can enjoy yourself and have fun while you're doing it.

I'm absolutely certain that you will enjoy reading it and admiring the considerable portfolio of big carp captures that JC has amassed along the way. There's only one word to describe it – inspirational.

'Go Jonny, go Jonny, go Jonny......'

Introduction

As I sit behind the rods, penning this introduction, the stark realisation is that I've just written a whole book. I've written many magazine articles in the past, but never envisaged writing a book of my own, although I've often been asked when I would be doing so. I'd never felt that I'd caught enough big fish to fill an entire book, that would do me justice and live with the likes of Terry Hearn's 'Still Searching', but how many anglers can compare their results with Terry's captures? Certainly, having a full time job and enough children to fill a five-a-side team, I could never compete, but how many people can relate to a full-time angler? As you read these pages, I hope you will understand and appreciate the frustrations, and equally enjoy my successes, as a carp angler and a working man. There might not be dozens of 40s and 50s adorning these pages, but a 30-pounder has always been a big fish to me, and there are certainly some beauties, as well as a few proper beasts.

I was born and bred in the village of Yateley, where monsters swam nearby, but my first carp was a 2lb wildie caught on luncheon meat, a full quarter of a century ago. I started out at the age of five, tiddler bashing with my elder brother, Paul, and my very first fish was a little chub from the River Blackwater. Since that day, fishing has been my passion.

Apart from my dad's friend's farm lake, I fished the Yateley lakes as a junior, mainly for tench in the summer and pike in the winter. I was happy with my own company and I'd usually fish alone, keen on all things nature. I was content when sitting by the lake watching a float, but when I witnessed a monster 6lb mirror caught by an old boy at the farm lake one magical June 16th, I was smitten with the 'size' and beauty of its scattered scaling, and carp fishing soon occupied most of my thoughts. Although I never caught one of the farm carp, I tried hard, and once I'd caught that first wildie at Warren Hill, I was soon catching up to eight in one day.

I caught my first mirror and common carp from Firgrove Lake, in Yateley, all three to six-pounders, and as I was within walking distance by road and across fields, I could load up a pram frame with my tackle and get in a few after-school trips.

When I was 16 my parents moved to Gloucestershire and I soon got stuck into the carp in Gardners Pool at Saul, taking my first of 30-odd doubles that season and just as many singles, including the lake's one and only 20-pounder at 22lb 6oz. My confidence was rising dramatically as I caught twice as many as all the older anglers. I was on a learning curve and thirsty for knowledge, so I read all the material I could get my hands on.

I read the books of Rod Hutchinson and Rob Maylin over and over, in search of improvement, and the humour of both made their writing hugely enjoyable. In later years, Terry Hearn's books were among my favourites and fishing, or aspiring to fish, the same venues inspired me to go and catch some of the same fish. If this book can be half as inspiring and entertaining as the ones written by those three guys, then I will regard it as a job well done.

Around 90 per cent of this book has been written on the bank, using pen and paper. Fishing is the only time I get to write, but sitting behind the rods in peaceful, picturesque surroundings is when the words flow best. I hope you'll find that the stories do indeed flow, that each chapter reads well, and that it's not too hard going. Special thanks go to my wonderful wife, Lynn, who has done a sterling job typing up the whole book. I love you very much, babe.

I hope that the excellent maps will give you an insight into the make-up of the lakes I have written about, and I give a big thank you to the talented young artist, Kasey Ledger; at just 16 years of age I'm sure she will have a very bright future.

This book is my journey through good times and bad, the rough and the smooth of fishing busy circuit waters which, yes, you might have read about before, but each and every carp is a special one so I make no apologies.

The greater the challenge and the harder it is to come out the other side victorious when you feel sometimes you're beaten, then the sweeter the capture becomes.

So sit back, relax, and I hope you enjoy my story spanning two decades of my fishing life. Thanks for taking the time to read it.

John Claridge

The lake's one and only 20-pounder at 22lb 6oz.

Chapter 1 - Frampton - Ready for the challenge?

I threw my bike over the ditch and as I scrambled up the bank, I caught my first glimpse of sparkling blue water through the undergrowth. I was keen to get a closer look so I stashed the bike in the bushes and was soon on the path. There in front of me was a glorious expanse of gin-clear water and with the sun glinting on the ripples as a warm May wind blew gently into the margin, it was love at first sight.

Huge trees lay in the water along the bank on which I stood, and three large islands rose from a lake contained by a heavily tree-lined perimeter, except for one side which was fairly open, with a large field behind it that backed on to the Frampton Courthouse. In that May sunshine I was looking at the perfect lake and I didn't even know if it held any carp, let alone how many and how big they might be.

Not sure if I was allowed to walk round, I headed left, keeping to the more overgrown banks and away from the openness of the field bank. As I ventured closer, I could see more water through the trees on the other side, and at this point I didn't know if it was a different lake or the same one. As I was about to venture up what turned out to be a peninsular, I was sure I heard a carp crashing out. The noise had come from beyond another spit of land on the other side of this bay, and as I started to head in that direction, I heard it again. I went at full sprint in the hope of seeing what was making the commotion but as I got round and headed up the spit, I had to rein in my eagerness because the path was narrow, winding and uneven, and there were large holes in some nearby mounds, which appeared to be a badger sett.

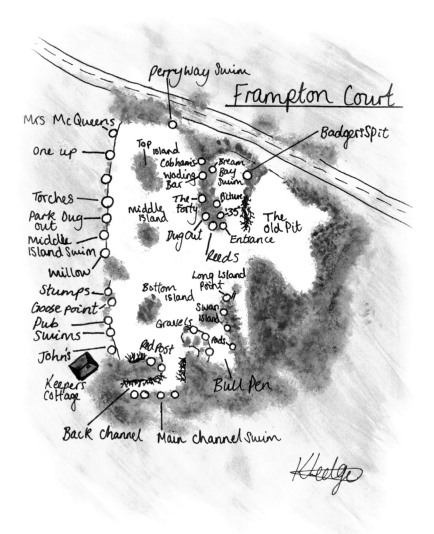

Perry Way Swim

Frampton Court

Mrs McQueens

Badgers Spit

One up

Top Island

Cobhams

Bream Bay Swim

Wading Bar

Torches

The Forty

Picture

Park Dug out

Middle Island

:35

The Old Pit

Middle Island Swim

Dug Out

Entrance

Willow

Reeds

Stumps

Long Island Point

Goose point

Bottom Island

Swan Island

Pub Swims

Gravels

John's

Red Post

Pads

Keepers Cottage

Bull Pen

Back channel   Main channel Swim

The Old Pit; scene of dozens of carp in full throes of passion.

The left-hand side of the spit was a reed-lined, shallow, weeded area with potamogeton beds that were being smashed to pieces. I'd hit the jackpot and as I stood there, in front of my eyes were dozens of carp in the full throes of passion, spawning in shallow water just yards from where I stood. I climbed a tree, and then another, keen to get a better look at the horny carp that were writhing in the water beneath me, but it was so overgrown and the water was churned up into chocolate soup, so it was hard to get a clear view.

From the ground, my best sighting of a carp came when one would virtually get thrown out of the water as the males were swarming round and rutting into the fat females. I sat and watched for ages. Now I was sure that this stunning lake held carp and judging by the evidence before me, quite a lot and far bigger than I could have dreamed. The carp god must have been looking after me. I grew up just a mile or so from the famous Yateley complex, and we'd moved a hundred miles into the depths of Gloucestershire, just three miles away from this fantastic lake. The next step was to find out how to obtain a fishing ticket, if indeed fishing was allowed.

After venturing up the main peninsular, I could see more of the lake and it just seemed to get better and better. I retraced my steps, recovered my bike from the bushes and headed round to the field bank, on the lookout for a sign or someone to ask about a ticket. As I was pushing my bike along the field bank, I met a local dog walker who informed me that the man I needed to speak to was a chap called John who lived in the keeper's cottage at the far end of the field, at the top end of the lake. He worked for the Court Estate so I'd probably catch him of an evening or weekend.

Saturday lunchtime saw me pestering my dad to give me a lift and fortunately, John was at home. I told him I'd just moved away from Yateley, was on the lookout for places to fish and that I was keen to fish the lake. John told me the lake had produced carp to 35lbs and that was music to my ears. He then assured me that there were bigger fish swimming out there and that made me even more excited than before. John picked up on my enthusiasm for the place and for carp fishing, and although the syndicate was full, he took my name and address and told me to come back and see him in a year's time, because he'd probably be able to sort me out for the following season.

A year later and John was true to his word. After handing over my £80, and getting a rundown on what had happened the previous season, I spent ages staring admiringly at all the photos of the fish that inhabited the Court. John offered to take me out in the boat later that week and I couldn't wait, but for now I'd have to make do with walking round.

Just before I left John's cottage, a chap called Steve Gratton turned up. He had been a member for several years and kindly offered to give me the guided tour. I accepted gratefully and from that day on Gratts became a good mate. I tried to absorb as much info as possible but with my head racing it was hard to take it all in and when I went out in the boat with John one evening that week, it was even harder to remember anything. I'd had the foresight to take a notepad, but because I was peering over the side of the boat the whole time, I didn't manage to log much in the way of features. I'd been given a great insight as to the make-up of the lake, though.

The last couple of weeks of the close season dragged a bit, but most evenings I'd get the bike out and ride the three miles to the lake. I was 17, still learning to drive and waiting impatiently for my test date to arrive. Once I had the independence of my own wheels, fishing would be easier and although I'd saved up and bought my own fishing wagon, an old Escort diesel van, I needed someone (my dad) to assist while the L-plates were still attached.

Working all week at the farm meant that my fishing time was confined to weekends only. My dad was working away, lorry driving, and I was reliant on him getting home on a Friday at a reasonable hour to drive me to the lake. Thanks dad, I did appreciate it!

Anyway, June 15th finally arrived and I was dropped off for a whole week on a lake with a difficult reputation, where most anglers only caught one or two a season. I'd certainly have my work cut out. After catching my first 20 the previous season from Gardners Pool at 22lbs 6oz, most Frampton fish would be a personal best.

John was true to his word, a Frampton ticket was mine.

I expect a lot of the older members felt I'd be out of my depth; a 17 year-old kid, with limited experience, but I'd outfished everyone on Gardners by a country mile and several Frampton members had fished there as well. Only time would tell, but I wasn't there to fail and I was ready for a challenge.

There were quite a few anglers there for the draw and as Gratts was the only one I knew, I hung about near him. John explained how it all worked; as your name was drawn, you simply had to name your preferred swim. There was a map of the lake so you could see what had already gone.

I came out about halfway through and although I was unsure where to go, I chose the Goose Point swim. This gave me the top island to fish to, and having marked the spots on my map when I'd been out in the boat, I had an idea where to cast. This is one of the shorter chucks to the island, so I felt I'd be able to cast comfortably to it.

Frampton was not only a big step up in difficulty but also in acreage, and I'd already had to purchase three new rods, 12-foot, 3lb Armalites, which I hoped would make good all-rounders and enable me to cast to most of the lake's spots, barring the really long chucks to the middle. Wading was allowed back then and some of the swims were shallow enough to wade out a bit before giving it the big one, so I'd be able to access most areas.

I managed to get two baits on gravel humps in the island margin and fished one in close, down to the left. This was the first water where I'd been able to use three rods so it had been an expensive time, not only upgrading my tackle but also having to buy in threes, as opposed to a pair of everything.

June the 16th 1990 dawned nice and sunny but the lake was quiet with no one having received any action. That was to change that evening, as word soon filtered round that Andy Buff had caught the big one down at the end of the far bank off the bottom island. I wound in quickly and legged it down there, keen to feast my eyes on the beast. An awesome creature it was too, and up half a pound from when Buffy had caught it the previous season, this time setting the lake record at 36lb 12oz. With renewed enthusiasm I returned to the Goose to recast the rods and fell asleep dreaming of that monster carp. A 36-pounder back in 1990 was just that, a monster, and even a 20-pounder was like catching a 30 today. Any water that held more than one 30 was very special, and a 40 – well, there was only a handful of those in the whole country!

Another couple of 20s were caught at that end of the lake the next morning and with quite a few anglers going because it was a Sunday, I fancied a move. With a new wind pushing down on the Perryway (road bank) and learning that Buffy was vacating the One Up from Mrs McQueen's swim, I made the move. This was long before the days of barrows and I had a week's supply of gear, so I collapsed into the swim after carrying it all. Buffy wished me luck and headed off leaving me to it. I'd got the impression from a few people that Buffy wasn't the most popular person on the lake, probably due to him being a bit of a Jack the lad, and the fact that he used to catch a few! However, I liked him and although he wasn't whiter than white, he was all right in my book. He took me slightly under his wing that first season, and as he certainly seemed to catch his share of the bigger fish, I always took notice of his advice.

The Parrot was christened from that day.

The wind was pushing down and creating a lovely flat spot in the lee of the island. So, with the left-hand rod cast on a gravel hump beneath a snag tree on the end of the island, the middle rod in front of the tree and the right one in a hole in the bushes further up the island margin, I managed to get 20 boilies around each of my hook baits, presented on the bottom with bent hook rigs. The previous season, I'd had success on my fishmeal boilies with lobster flavouring and I knew the carp liked it so I was sticking to it.

At a quarter to ten that evening I was taken totally by surprise. My left-hand rod was away and I was down the bank and on it as it tore off, holding firm until, slowly, I got it back to my side of the island. It once tried getting in the snag tree but I managed to hold on and soon it was coming toward me. All I could think was that I had a Frampton carp on and I must not stuff this up. The fight was unspectacular and I soon had my debut capture in the net. It looked a good fish and after getting someone to help me, I got this leathery grey carp out and on my mat. As I took my hook from its bottom lip, I noticed its parrot mouth and so the Parrot was christened from that day.

At 23lbs 6oz, not only had I caught a Frampton carp within 48 hours, I'd also beaten my personal best by a pound. That fish gave me the confidence that I could catch from Frampton, which was a good job because apart from a fish falling off later that week after just a few seconds of hooking it, Frampton became a steep learning curve over the next few weeks. I fished most weekends and tried to move round the lake a lot, fishing as many different swims as possible but it was all to no avail.

I turned up at the end of August and found a few carp milling about near a weedbed in front of the Log swim (soon afterwards to be known as the Dugout). This swim was rarely fished back then, but as it was toward the end of the peninsular it was ideal for intercepting fish as they moved from the bottom island to the Bream Bay/Old Pit and vice-versa. From the notes I'd made during my close season trip in the boat, I knew of a shallow hump to the left of the swim, and then a broken bar ran diagonally out toward the end of the bottom island.

It looked like a classic underwater road system and with fish already in the area about 70 yards out, I stepped out my baits along the bar. The weed was more prominent than at the start, so I'd changed to pop-ups. The one on the back of the shallow gravel hump to the left had a 1-inch pop-up on, but for the two fished further out near the weed bed, I'd fished one 5 inches up and one off the lead on a 9-inch hooklink, an effective method I'd employed the previous year fishing in bottom weed at Horseshoe Lake.

The shallow Bream Bay.

Mist was hanging on the water at dawn and I watched over the flat calm surface as the sun emerged from behind the trees. My left-hand rod lurched round and the baitrunner purred, picking up pace as it sped away, and for five minutes I prayed the fish would stay on as it ploughed up and down on a short line.

As a big mirror's nose kissed the spreader block, I lifted, and punched the air, eagerly peering in the net at a huge set of shoulders that backed on to a big, sloping head. With a huge scale on its gill plate and more along its back, it certainly looked like I'd started the day with another personal best. I wasn't disappointed and at a weight of 27lb 8oz, and I'd caught one of Frampton's jewels.

None of the guys recognised it but while looking through the album at John's cottage the following week, I recognised it as Mike Wilmott's first fish. He had caught it a couple of seasons previously, I believe, from the Badger Spit at 26lbs 2oz. This fish has since grown to be one of the biggest fish in the land and has topped 54lbs!

I had changed baits to Premier Baits' Fish Mix with Nodd Oil and Squiddly Diddly flavour so I had renewed confidence, and because No-Name (as the fish became known) had been nailed an inch inside his mouth, I was now converted to the pop-ups as well.

No-Name, one of Frampton's jewels.

Despite there being quite a few fish still in the area that day, no further action was forthcoming and although I was able to get in the same swim the following week, I failed to repeat my success.

Autumn was fast approaching and it was a good job I'd passed my driving test that September because it allowed me to get to the lake a bit earlier on a Friday. The nights were drawing in and the weed was fairly prominent so I needed a bit of extra time to get the rods sorted.

The water levels were very low and there was an abundance of swans on the lake, so I started to look at the deeper areas, and with the temperatures in decline, I started to give the channel some attention come the middle of October.

Fishing the Main Channel swim gave me a good amount of far bank tree line to cast to and I could get a rig off the end of the point, on a little gravel spot. A swan soon discovered my 1½-inch pop-up on the shallower spot so I moved it to the extreme edge of the white-leaved tree that hung over the shelf at the end of the bank opposite, in swan-safe depths.

On Sunday morning, I received a two-inch drop-back and was left a bit bemused as I hovered near the rod and nothing else happened. I wound in a couple of hours later and found that my rig was snagged solid so I ran round to John's house, there were no mobile phones in those days, and he fetched the boat. Reaching down he found my rig with the hook buried into a branch, a good six feet to the left of where I'd cast it. Done up like a kipper, and it just goes to show how insensitive the old monkey climbers were - I only had 30 yards of line out.

I was determined not to be beaten and to have the last laugh, so I pre-baited the spot midweek and returned on the Friday for revenge. Back in the Main Channel swim, I got the rigs nice and tight to the bushes, and baited with 25 boilies around each. I chose to use two rods because it was a bit tight in this swim and an extra line pinging across the channel was likely to do more harm than good. It was a warm night. I heard a good fish crash at 8pm on the far margin, so I found sleep hard to get and kept waking up.

At 6.25am, I had a short drop-back and after the previous week's occurrence, I was just about to strike when it flew up and I struck but felt nothing; a liner perhaps, that had initially pulled the lead down the shelf before taking line. I went round later and sat in the trees for 45 minutes but saw nothing. With the coots occasionally nicking my freebies, I topped up with 20 baits round each rig, after recasting at 4pm. At 6pm I noticed that the coots had disappeared from the channel, and I had a feeling that something was about.

Half an hour later, my feelings were confirmed as the bait fished in the hole in the trees opposite was picked up and the fish kited along the tree line to the right. As the carp got above the other bait, I managed to turn its head and lead it across the channel, into my margin where it powered about. Not a monster, this one, but after a couple of months of blanking, I was grateful for the 11lb 14oz common that had made a mistake that evening.

The following trip, again after baiting up in the week, produced a further two small fish, this time a mirror of 11lbs and a smaller common at just over 8lbs, bringing my tally to five.

With winter fast approaching, I managed a few more trips to the end of November; the only other action coming with a bit of pike fishing and one weekend I took nine snappers between 6 and 16lbs, but the carp seemed to have shut up shop. On reflection I was happy with my first season but now I had the long wait until the fish became active the next summer. Roll on June 16th!

After a couple of months blanking, I was grateful for an 11lb 14oz common.

Chapter 2 - Frampton
Treading water

After the comparative success of my first season on the Court Lake at Frampton, I was full of optimism and excitement with the onset of my second season, and this year the bonus of driving meant it was much easier for me to get to and from the lake.

I plucked up the courage to ask my dad for a week off; he reluctantly agreed and as I had all of the opening week to fish, I was confident I could get the season off to a flyer like the first year.

I had a bit of knowledge about the lake by now, so I was more clued up to where I wanted to start this year's campaign. I'd walked the lake every day the previous week and had even managed to get out in the boat once, and I felt the Dugout was the place to be. Once there were lots of lines out, I felt that the fish would move out of the shallow Bream Bay where they'd spent that last week and, as the Old Pit was too shallow, I thought they'd probably move en masse, out into the main lake between the islands. The Dugout's diagonal bar headed out to the bottom island which had quite a few snags on it, and I was sure that this would be their route.

Once again, the draw was held in John's garden and by the time the names went into the hat, it was mightily busy, with over 40 anglers willing their name to come out early. By the time my name came out I'd long given up hope of getting a good swim and when it did, about fifth from last, the only swim left down at the desired end was the Badger Spit. This was the swim where I'd first set eyes on Frampton carp, as they spawned behind the Old Pit, on my first recce trip to the lake, over two years before. If there was a carp in the area, I felt they wouldn't stay for long, so after setting up I wandered round to the peninsular to find out who was in the Dugout and how long they'd be stopping.

A new member, Barry Mills, was setting up and after a chat it transpired that Barry was only down for a couple of nights so I arranged to move in the Dugout when he vacated. Feeling a bit happier, I walked over the field to the Three Horseshoes pub where everyone was having a drink or six before returning for chucking out time at half past nine - that's chucking the rods out, not chucking out of the pub. I dare say a few stayed on until pub chucking out time, but I was too keen to get started.

This year, it seemed that Frampton was becoming a highly desirable lake. Some famous faces and very good anglers were now members, and people were travelling the length and breadth of the country in pursuit of the famous Frampton carp. Among the new faces were Bernie 'The Bus' Loftus, the Tomlinson brothers (Lee and Dave), Dave Lane, Dave 'Travolta' Brown, and Barry Mills who'd been on the Redmire syndicate in its heyday. Mike Willmott was back, too, and looking to fish a lot more than in previous years.

With my baits all fished in close along the potamogeton weed, I waited with great anticipation. I was up at first light and looked out over a lifeless piece of water; the Bream Bay my only view. A couple of anglers were going, because it was a Sunday, so I went off in search of a move and my only option, which I decided to take, was the Reeds. Although it only controlled the entrance of the Bream Bay water, at least I was closer to the main lake and being so close to the Dugout, I'd have an easy move when Barry went home on the Monday. As Barry had taken three fish on the opening day, I was gagging to get in there as soon as possible, but Barry was already making noises of perhaps staying longer, so I'd have to bide my time.

With only a liner to show for my time so far, and with Bernie disappearing back to Manchester on Monday morning, I got into the Harry's swim which was situated between the Reeds and the Dugout right on the end of the peninsular.

As I moved my gear in, I heard a shout from Bernie down the bank. Mike Willmott had a big fish on the mat behind the swim, halfway down the peninsular, so I legged it down there. I was sure it was Buffy's 36 but no one else seemed to recognise it. As it was hoisted onto the scales, a milestone for the lake was achieved.

Frampton's first 40-pounder.

There, hanging inside the sling, was Frampton's first 40-pounder, and at 43lb 8oz it had made it in some style. I think Mike, along with the rest of us, was a bit shell-shocked. She was slipped into a large sack and word filtered round the lake. John was fetched from the hut at the bottom of his garden, which is his very own swim and a productive paradise, to witness such an historic moment for the water. This was by far the largest carp I'd ever seen on the bank and the fact that it was such a nice, clean, very handsome fish made it all the more impressive.

Returning to my swim to get set up, I was understandably super-keen to catch one myself so with all three rods cast out, in close around the back of the shallow hump between Harry's and the Dugout, and a dozen baits over the top of each hook bait, I declined the offer of going over to the pub for Mike's celebrations. It certainly appeared that a good night was had by all, but not being a drinker, it sounded like it got a bit messy. Dave Fuidge had competed with two big Bristolian guys, known as 'The Animals', necking down raw eggs in yard of ale glasses, and all manner of other disgusting dares. Fair play to Dave, but I'd have been sick for a week.

Barry was still catching from the Dugout and had decided to stay for the week, so I was a bit deflated after having been promised the swim before the season had even kicked off. Imagine how I felt on the second evening, after helping Barry with yet another 20-pounder, when I walked the few yards back to my swim to find one of my spools half-empty.

The buzzer had packed up. There must have been 150 yards of line gone and on winding down, I found that my rig had been dumped out by the middle island with weed on the end, but no fish.

After a few days of north-westerlies and squally showers, the wind swung to the south-west, and the 19th turned out to the first warm, dry day. The Wading Bar produced a couple and it appeared the fish were starting to get on the move, so when the wind swung back to a strong north-north-westerly, and was pushing up to the channel, I upped sticks and went right up the other end, to the Main Channel swim, the scene of catching my three little ones last October.

I knew that these Frampton carp loved tiger nuts. Virtually all the fish caught so far had fallen to the growlers, so I fished nuts on all three rods in the channel. Trying to cast super-tight to the far bushes meant that I could leave the rigs out for as long as necessary without the need to recast, and if the nuts were picked up by a coot, I could be sure they hadn't been pulled off the hair. Fishing at close quarters, it was also easy to bait up prior to casting by simply throwing out a handful of tigers from the far bank. The showers returned and the wind pumped into the channel, and once again, I felt confident.

At half-past eight the next morning, the swinger on the middle rod pulled up and hung there. I struck instantly and the rod hooped over. As the carp kited away from the far bank trees, I was laughing as it swung away from danger, and I stepped out into the water as the fish headed into my margin, way up to the right. With only one branch overhanging on the surface, and now with a better angle and me standing out in the lake, it should be plain sailing.

My heart was in my mouth as a big fish swirled on the surface and all that was needed was to lead it down my margin, but with a sudden surge it bolted again, under and then into the overhanging branch, banging into it in the process, causing the hook to pop out. I couldn't believe it and just stood there up to my nuts in water, in utter disbelief. I felt like I'd been punched in the stomach. Things just got worse when the wind changed back to a south-westerly that pushed down the other end. Someone up there had it in for me!

The following day, heavy rain just compounded my gloomy mood, but after a wander round later that afternoon I headed back to my swim in a better frame of mind and re-baited, getting all three baits super-tight to the bushes. The right-hand rod landed about three inches off the end of the bush, and as it was shallower water I didn't bait this spot; I just fished two balanced tigers in isolation, on a short,

I registered my first 20lb common at 21lbs on the nose.

braided hooklink. It was on gravel and I hoped it might be enough to tempt any fish entering or exiting the channel.

At 4.30am, the middle rod registered a two-inch lift and as I pulled into it, it hooped over before instantly going straight again. I was hacked off now, and with the onset of rain and the thought of having to pack up that day, I dived back in the bag with my tail firmly between my legs.

At 10.25am, the right-hand rod rattled off and as I got to it, it dropped back. Initially, I felt nothing but as I quickly wound down, the rod suddenly hooped over. After the previous loss down the edge, there was no way I was letting it get near that overhanging branch. By not giving it any line, I had the fish zig-zagging as it came across the channel toward me, wallowing just below the surface. With socks off and trousers yanked up, I slipped into the margin and, as a good common gulped its first gobful of air, I lifted the net around it.

More and more anglers were fishing.

I was well pleased to have got one in the net, and then it suddenly dawned on me - I definitely had a new PB common. I carried her up to the mat and saw that the bent hook was firmly embedded in the bottom lip. As I looked her over I noticed that there was a chunk missing from the bottom lobe of the tail, and rolling the fish over revealed my conquest as One Eye, so named for obvious reasons. As the scales went past the magical 20 mark, I registered my first 20lb common at 21lbs on the nose. A 20lb common was quite a rare fish back in those days, and a perfect way to end a rather frustrating and difficult first week of the season. I was off the mark now, and with the lake producing lots of bites, I looked forward to catching more, and bigger, carp.

More and more anglers were fishing, so the weekends were becoming increasingly busy and I spent quite a few of them stuck frustrated at the bottom of the channel. I liked the channel and when fish were in there it was a good area to get a bite, because with the deeper water and tree cover, they would feed a bit more confidently. If they weren't in there, though, you could be an awful long way away from them.

I was using tiger nuts the majority of the time. Fishing at close range, I was using mini PVA bags full of nuts, which I'd dry out on a towel to prevent the bag melting before placing the whole rig in the bag. I was using multi-strand for a hooklink, and the suppleness of it could not be beaten for the hookbait to act naturally.

I decided Long Island Point was the swim I wanted.

Once sucked up, my rig would be hard to eject as I had two hairs coming off the shank with a single popped-up tiger nut on each and this was anchored with a normal tiger on a third, short hair at the eye end.

It was simple to tie as my hair was simply a loop on each end of a length of Dacron and passed through a length of shrink tube. The bottom hair being the doubled loop as it passed through the tube in one direction before being folded and passed back out. Teamed with a multi-strand hooklink, it would be a banker to tangle on a cast but the PVA bag meant it was always presented correctly. The number of nuts I put in the bag dictated the range I could cast it, but with about 15 nuts, which was plenty, I could get it out 75 yards, as long as it wasn't too windy.

With the luxury of a second week's holiday in the middle of August, I hoped to get a swim that would give me a better shot at the fish. A hot and sunny week had been forecast and I fancied one of the two end swims on Long Island Point. After finding Bernie was in the One Down and likely to be there for a few days, I decided that the Point was the swim I wanted, but I had to wait until the Sunday morning before it became free.

Fish were showing out on the bars, at between 70 and 100 yards range where the water was a bit deeper, and Bernie had caught fishing long from One Down, so I set up on Sunday full of anticipation. Week sessions had been good to me in the past, and I needed to catch before the summer passed me by.

I fished my right-hand rod over a few pouchfuls of nuts, across toward the Reeds swim, on the back of a bar where there was a deeper gap before it rose to another bar. The other two rods were fished out to the left, in the middle area of the lake. With lots of bars running horizontally across in front of me, it was bar, gully, bar, gully all the way, and the depth got deeper the further out you went. At about 75 yards, the gully was about four feet deep behind a two-foot bar, and this is where I cast my PVA bags loaded with tigers. A good cast with the bag would hit just the right range and the left-hand rod was aimed at the Court house, with the middle one toward the centre of the middle island. With fish showing in the area, I was on carp for once, and I hoped to get some early action.

Nothing showed at first light, but by 10 o'clock one or two started to show out near the long rods. At 11.45, I had an absolute screamer. I lifted into it and was immediately back-winding as it stripped 20 yards of line from me. As it stopped, it then came in and out across in front of me, heading toward the Bream Bay. Bernie had heard the take, was now by my side and after watching the fish whizzing about in the shallow water, he expertly scooped up my second common of the season. It wasn't a big one, but it was a start. We weighed it at 14lbs 12oz, took a few pics, slipped it back, and I made Bernie a celebratory cuppa. While I tied up a new multi-thread rig, a fish rolled right by the middle rod and then we saw a tail stick out of the water and give us a wave. Very matter of factly, Bernie told me that I would get another take in a minute because the fish only had to slip down the slope of the bar, and there was my little patch of nuts.

Bernie wasn't wrong and the middle rod was soon in meltdown. This one took even more line off me before kiting to the left and swinging out into Bernie's swim. It kited right into the margin and I steered it out from under the bushes, straight into the net, expertly manned by Bernie. He informed me that it was a 20lb mirror so things were certainly looking up. At 21lbs 10oz it was a solid-looking, clean fish and the old cliché of coming along like buses was true. Well, I did have Bernie 'The Bus' in the swim with me!

The following evening, Bernie suggested that I should come to the pub to celebrate the brace, which I agreed to; foolishly, on reflection, because I'm not a drinker and my companions for the evening consisted of Dave Lane, Dave 'Travolta' Brown and Bernie himself. I got my PVA bags all tied up with dry tigers and hung them from the rods in a bucket, all ready to cast out on my return.

Long Island common.

We all turned up at the Three Horseshoes. John Leadbeater was already there and chuckled at my choice of drinking partners, but the lager was flowing, we certainly had a good laugh and Bernie was on top form with his stories of Harefield and the like. Anyone who was brave enough to stand near the dartboard soon scarpered when we were playing because my eyes were struggling to see which board I was aiming at - one board often blurred into two.

As we staggered back to the lake after closing time, I was hanging and just wanted to collapse on my bed chair. Bernie was going back to Dave's for a brew but I declined and headed round to Long Island. It was quite a dark night but as most of the way was across the fields it was okay going, that was until I reached Long Island. The wide peninsular was full of tall pine trees which gave complete cover overhead; it was as black as your hat and I couldn't see a thing. Time and time again, I staggered off the winding path and blindly thrashed about in the ferns trying to find it. Eventually, I saw light at the end of the point, and my brolly. I was so relieved. Casting a bag 70-odd yards was just not going to happen and I crawled into my sleeping bag.

'Coming along like buses' was true.

Channel success but nothing big.

I awoke soon after first light and managed to get a cast out. Bernie appeared soon afterwards, looking fine, whereas my head was still banging but Bernie was a seasoned pro at this game. He asked me if anything had happened and I told him I'd only just put them out. He couldn't believe this and said I should have cast out when I'd got back from the pub. I told him that even if I'd been physically capable of casting out, I'd have wanted to know where I'd caught from, if I got lucky. Bernie said this was nonsense and that loads of fish got caught on pub casts. This was not for me, though, and hence I've never been one for going to the pub at night time and so wasting a night's fishing.

The fish moved off and there was no more action that week, or for that matter that autumn. I was getting into my football at the time and Saturday afternoon games really got in the way of fishing. My van was always overheating and was beginning to look a bit terminal and as I didn't have the money to get it repaired, that was the end of my second season.

The '92 season followed a similar pattern and I only fished the summer. Again, it was busy and weekend fishing had its downfalls because I could rarely get on fish. By fishing Long Island Point and the Main Channel swim, I was able to extract four commons out of the lake, but nothing big and it was all a bit disappointing.

The '93 season was to see changes as the numbers of the syndicate were cut. The 'undesirables' were not being invited to rejoin and with natural wastage the syndicate was drastically reduced. I hoped that this would give me the opportunity to angle properly on a regular basis, and I had high hopes for the forthcoming season.

Mark Jones with No-Name.

Chapter 3 - Frampton Haulinnn!

With the carp having taken a hammering on the tigers over the last couple of years, I felt it was time to get back on the boilies. I knew that John had caught a lot of fish in the autumn, from his tree at the end of his garden, using Mainline Strawberry Zest baits, so knowing they were partial to that flavour and that John had only ever fished the one swim, I felt the fruity route would be the way to go out on the main lake.

Ordering about 60kg of Essential Opal mix with the strawberry flavour in it gave me an improved bait. This fruity birdfood mix would be highly digestible and, I hoped, highly attractive. I started to bait up with a few kilos every other night at the start of June and as I was well in with John, I had permission to do it from the boat. This made the job much quicker. On one circuit of the lake, I could literally deposit the baits onto eight different spots with no wastage and thankfully, no sweat and no sore arm from having to use a throwing stick.

I concentrated my baiting around the bottom island, the snags on the end always receiving a good helping of the juicy strawberries. This was where I'd caught the Parrot from that first season, and it was where I hoped to get the draw. The syndicate numbers had been reduced, so I hoped this season would be more 'fruitful', and I'd get a better swim choice on a Friday afternoon.

On the day of the draw, the 15th, most of the fish appeared up at the northern end so my decision to concentrate my baiting at that end of the lake looked like a good one. Having such bad luck in the draws in previous years, I was due a good one and the gods were looking down favourably that day. I came out second, and with only the Gravels taken I got my first choice of One Up from Mrs McQueens. Well, I say I came out second, but really it was sixth because four swims had already been taken out of the draw. These were for the chosen bailiffs and the reasoning offered to the rest of the syndicate was that bailiffs would be around the lake to 'keep an eye' on everything. Firstly, the supposed rule breakers had already been denied membership and secondly, if this were the case, you'd assume the four swims would be dotted around the lake, not two next to each other on the end of Long Island Point, and the two main swims on the main peninsular, the Dugout and the Forty. Very peculiar; these were four of the best swims on the lake; funny that!

I was happy enough, though, because I'd secured the swim I wanted, but there were a lot of moans and groans among the rest of the syndicate, especially after we'd had a lecture on how things would be different this season. Basically, bailiffs would be keeping a close eye on everyone and any rule breakers would lose their tickets. What were we, a bunch of school kids or a group of paying, experienced carp anglers? God knows what any new members thought. They must have questioned what they'd let themselves in for.

My rigs were fairly simple, being bottom baits mounted onto size 4 Mustad 34021s, a straight-pointed, strong hook, and with about 8 inches of 25lb Silkworm hooklink coming off, line-aligner style. I was fishing these, helicopter-style on some looped, stemmed leads that I'd bought from Leslies. A soft bead went on the stern, then the rig swivel, and then a soft-tapered, stemmed tail rubber, the rig rotating on the metal stem. These would cast a lot better than an inline and with three tied up with Opal baits, I clipped up to the range. One was cast to the hole in the island bushes, one to the edge of the overhanging snags, and one to the gravel hump, a rod length off the end and level with the snag.

A couple of hours were spent socialising over at the pub and as the bailiffs were using the Three Horseshoes, a lot of the lads, certainly down at this end of the lake, went to the Bell. Well, it was closer, and it had a pool table! The rigs flew out just after 9pm and all went smoothly.

I sat up until midnight and the odd fish crashed out so I crawled into the bag, full of confidence. I hadn't been asleep for long before the left-hand rod was whizzing. I hit it and it kited left away from the island – brilliant! That was until the hook pulled out. I was gutted. I checked my watch and it was 1.15am. At least I knew they liked the bait and we were only just over an hour, officially, into the season. There was plenty of time yet.

By breakfast I was distraught after having lost a further three good carp; two to hooklinks parting, and one getting smashed up because despite being locked up to the island, it just flat-rodded me. It was unstoppable. The fish had spawned and so they were long, lean fighting machines, and I did wonder if my bait had steroids in it, such was the brute strength of these hard-battling demons I was latching on to. All four had felt like good fish and I could already have had my best season in just the first 12 hours. The pre-baiting was obviously paying dividends and I stuck out a load more, only to lose a fifth fish as my hooklink cut clean again.

Over the next few days, I lost a further four. Two hooks were straightened, and bear in mind that these were thick-gauged size 4 Mustads. When a fourth hooklink went, about 2" from the swivel, I could only assume that the braid was looping around the stemmed lead and cutting through itself. I changed the lead arrangement to an inline with 2mm silicone anti-tangle tubing and on the ninth take I got it away from the island. As I got it 20 yards out, it looked like I was winning, but then it just fell off.

In the 18 years since, I've never had such a bad run of luck and I was at such a low, thoroughly depressed and dejected. How can you lose nine fish on the trot? I believe it was just a freak run of bad luck – it wasn't as though I wasn't using strong gear. With nine takes in five days, all the other lads were queuing up to get in behind me and although everyone was offering sympathy at the time to my face, it became apparent several months later that one or two were slagging me off behind my back – but more of that later.

I went home for a couple of days to lick my wounds and returned on the 22nd for a work overnighter. I was determined to keep away from that bloody island and as the weather was hot and sticky, I chose to fish the shallow bars out from Long Island Point.

Fishing my usual spots at 80-100 yards, I baited with about 80, 20mm baits around each, and as it was such a warm night, I just laid the bed chair out and kipped under the stars. The relentless mozzies were buzzing round my head, and I was hot and sweaty from sticking out a couple of hundred baits, so sleep was hard to come by. Every time I nodded off, I could hear that that awful high-pitched whine as another bloodsucker landed on me. I must have drifted off, though, because I awoke startled by a screaming one-noter. Fishing open water allowed me to slacken the clutches and this fish was hurtling toward the middle of the lake. Never had I been so desperate to land a fish and I constantly told myself to keep calm and take my time. It certainly didn't want to help me out and constantly went on long runs, but in time the runs became shorter and less frequent.

As it came in close I waded into the margin, in my boxers, and was mightily relieved when it went into the net. I gave a 'haulinnn!' shout from the bottom of my lungs, but hadn't given much thought to how big it was. It was just a case of landing a Frampton carp and as I peered into the folds, there lay a big, long mirror with linear scaling - a fish I didn't recognise. At 26lbs, it was a cracker and must have been close to 30 pre-spawning.

14lb 6oz fully-scaled.

There lay a big, long mirror with linear scaling - a fish I didn't recognise.

Over the course of the next month, a lot of anglers fished the One-Up from Mrs McQueens and still not a single fish had been landed from there. Quite a few were hooked but all were lost, which made me look not quite such a noddy for losing nine.

Having had a little 14lb 6oz fully-scaled in this time, I decided to have another go in the newly named 'Jinxed' swim, one wet and windy Friday afternoon in mid-July. With a lovely flat spot off the end of the island it looked cock-on and after getting the rods out and a couple of pounds of boilies over the hook baits, I sheltered from the elements, tucked up in the bivvy.

At half past midnight, I put an end to the jinx and despite it only being a 14lb 2oz common, I'd shown that it was possible to land a fish from the swim. The icing on the cake, though, came at 4.30pm on the Saturday afternoon when after a spirited battle, I cradled in my arms one of the lake's beautiful, fully-scaled carp; at 26lbs 8oz, it was my second-biggest carp to date.

My next work overnighter produced another brace of fish, both mirrors, at 20lb 8oz and 12lb 4oz, in quick succession at first light, and this time from the Reeds swim. It was a busy night all round. My good mate, Brian Humphries, was next to me in Harry's and landed Kinky Tail at 26lbs 4oz among fish crashing at 2.30am. Working on the farm and doing hard manual work, and then fishing a work night with little sleep was killing me but now I was hitting some form I had to keep it going, at least until I had one or two of the big ones.

With Brian on a similar fruity birdfood boilie, it was obvious that the carp were loving their fruity sweets this summer. Bri had already clocked up about 14 fish, up to a spawned-out Rosie at 27lbs 6oz.

August was now upon us and a pattern of feeding behaviour became apparent. When the carp were in the heavy weed areas they seemed preoccupied on naturals and were

My next overnighter produced another brace.

I cradled in my arms one of the lake's beautiful, fully-scaled carp.

very hard to tempt, whereas in the sparsely weeded areas the fish could be tempted on the boilies and they'd happily trough on their sweeties. The clearer areas, and hence the prime swims, in my opinion, were the Reeds, Harry's and the Dugout on the end of the point, and the two end Long Island swims in the middle, shallower part of the lake.

On August the 1st I had a screamer off the end of Long Island but the fish slipped the hook after just a few seconds. I hoped this was just a blip and my bad luck wasn't going to return. The only other take that weekend was opposite, in Harry's, a low double, so at least my thinking on their location was confirmed.

The fish were still in the area the next weekend and after taking some pictures of Kinky Tail for a friend, Steve Cole, I moved in behind him into One Down from Long Island Point. I only had to wait until 7.15am the following morning when a three-inch lift on my left-hand rod signalled a pick-up and I was soon connected to a fish at 90 yards. A small 13lb common was the culprit and as I had to work this Saturday it had at least spared a blank.

I was still managing to do the odd work overnighter and on the Wednesday I chose to fish in the channel as the weather had taken a turn for the worse and was chilly and wet. The effort of doing a work night paid off once again and I caught an old adversary, the Parrot, my first Frampton fish, and despite it reaching 28lbs previously, it didn't look too well, and this time registered only three ounces over 20lbs.

The weekend was uneventful so I returned on Tuesday for a work night. The weather had turned back to hot and humid and I was relieved to find the Reeds vacant, and with the odd fish cruising about I got on with the job in hand. I cast two baits tight to the far reeds about 50 yards out, to spots that I'd caught on the last time I'd fished the swim.

I wanted to fish the third rod on my side and I'd seen a single good fish mooching about on the back of the gravel hump about 20 yards out, so I investigated this area with the marker rod. Brian turned up and suggested fishing the nearside of the hump but I'd found a cracking firm silt area in four feet of water just on the back, and as this was in the vicinity of where the fish had been mooching earlier, I decided to go for this spot. With a bottom bait cast tight to the back of the float and 50 baits dotted around it I made us both a tea.

Brian departed after wishing me luck and declaring that he felt I was going to catch a big'un. I hoped he was right and set about tidying up my swim which resembled a bomb site, with everything scattered about as I set up quickly. I still haven't changed to this day!

While I was sorting out my kit, the close-in rod's buzzer bleeped a few times and the swinger pulled up. I was straight on it and struck thin air - a liner. At least I knew fish were travelling through in-close. As I recast, on release of the line I spotted a fish about five yards to the right of my spot. The hook bait landed right on the money, and the carp didn't visibly spook, it just melted away from sight.

With the line sunk and slackened, I attached the swinger, flicked on the buzzer and turned my back to put the brolly up. On hearing a quick burst of bleeps, I spun round to see a bow wave heading left off the close-in spot. I instantly assumed the fish had swum into the line and spooked, until I looked down to see the tip bent round and the line bowstring tight. Stupidly, I hadn't slackened off the baitrunner after fishing up tight in the Channel the previous week. I quickly knocked off the anti-reverse and the fish soon made up for not taking line on the take by stripping about 40 yards off me as it powered out toward the Old Pit.

I managed to put the brakes on it and as it tired itself out from its energetic run, I soon pumped it back into my margin. I slipped off my shoes and socks and waded out with the net. It was now trying to get under the bushes to my left, but with steady side-strain the carbon subdued it and I turned its head, rolling it over just below the surface. It looked a really good one and after a couple of nervous minutes under the tip, it wallowed on the surface and with it coughing air its big gob was pulled up to the spreader block and a fine mirror was engulfed in my net. 'Hauuuulliinnnn!'

An impressive grey mirror lay beaten, and on checking its other flank I knew that the easily recognisable Two-Tone was mine. My first 30 was surely achieved as Two-Tone had gone mid-30 the previous season, but as the fish had spawned heavily that summer, only the scales could confirm it.

The big mirror was slipped into the wet, zeroed sling and now was the moment of truth. As the needle swung round it stopped at 29lbs and I lifted the fish, thinking that it wasn't completely off the mat, but 29lbs it was.

Of course, I'd rather it had recorded its normal 30lbs-plus but it was about the fish that I'd caught, not the weight, and the awesome Two-Tone secured a new PB so I was suitably made up. The Point was surprisingly empty and it was getting dark, so I slipped her into a big sack secured in deep water in the Dugout until daylight. That's not something I'd do these days, but apart from being a bit 'fresh' in the morning, she went off none the worse for wear after I'd got a few good slides of her in the sunshine.

It was around this time that we heard some very bad news. John Leadbeater had been taken into hospital with a heart attack. It appeared that John was going to be okay but we were told that he was not to be bothered from then on. The day-to-day running of the venue would be in the hands of the other bailiffs.

I was concerned for John's health as we'd become quite close over the last three years and had spent countless hours, either sitting on the garden wall outside his back door, or on his fishing platform at the end of his garden, chatting about the glorious Frampton carp. I didn't realise it at the time but from that day I had to be concerned with my own Frampton future. The more success I got on the lake, the more I became a marked man and without John as my main ally, it unfortunately became a slippery slope. How long could I keep my footing?

With John out of the picture and one of the other head bailiffs, Nigel Cobham, disappearing from the scene with no real explanation to the syndicate, this left the third head bailiff as head honcho. I'm not naming any names, but this bloke was a right berk. Those who fished Frampton will know who I'm talking about, but from now on he will be known as The Berk.

The awesome Two-Tone secured a new PB.

As is often the case with some people, power goes to their heads. Liberties were taken, the use of the boat being a prime example. Yes, I did use the boat in the close season but it was exactly that - closed. However, The Berk would have the boat out anytime of the day, looking for fish, spots, checking out other people's spots when they were out of their swims (very naughty) and even using it to move his gear - lazy git! The use of the boat was supposed to be for emergencies, such as snagged or weeded fish and none of the above could really be classed as an emergency.

Anyway, The Berk was in charge and felt he could do as he bloody well pleased, and anyone who didn't like it had to lump it. Charming. Also, his binoculars were not used for spotting fish, and the 'bailiffs keeping an eye on the members' certainly rang true, if you get my drift. Not a pleasant, relaxing experience casting your rods out when you can feel eyes staring at you from afar!

Back to the fishing, and that week I was shown some photographs of a stunning mirror carp that had been landed recently at 31lbs. For the record, it was a new 30-pounder for the lake and an unrecognised fish. I instantly fell in love with this long, scaly one, which is what it was christened. It had big, gold scales and deep, black markings along its lateral line; a true corker of a carp. This was the first carp I'd chosen to target on Frampton and I wouldn't rest until its picture was in my album.

The Long Scaly One brought the tally of Frampton 30-plus carp to nine. The biggest, the 40, had not been out since Lee Tomlinson had caught it back in '91, a couple of weeks after Mike Willmott had banked it at its top weight of 43lbs 8oz. Funny how both these guys were no longer members. The next in line were the Brown One, No-

Name, Rosie, Two-Tone, the scaly Yo-Yo, and the other two, which were 29 to 31 Four-Star and the classically-named, short, fat Look at the Length. Dave Gawthorn accidentally named it when he held the fish up to the video camera and commented proudly, "Look at the length of her, for such a short fish." Classic one-liner, mate. So I had a few to go at to get my first 30, despite having already caught two of them at lower weights. Hopefully, the Long Scaly One would slip up again and get me over the magical milestone.

The fish were still spending a lot of time in the same areas, despite water levels getting very low. I managed to sneak out a pretty little 14lb 2oz mirror on a Saturday night but I was starting to think that the big fish would not be comfortable in the very shallow water, so with the August bank holiday weekend looming, I felt that one of the more open water, slightly deeper areas would be a better bet at a good'un.

Living locally, I was taking advantage of the four-hour 'off the lake' rule, in that I would get to the lake at lunchtime, choose my swim and set up my gear before nipping back home, getting the afternoon feed done on the farm and with a quick shower and change be back on the lake within a couple of hours, well within my allotted time. Earlier in the season, no one had said anything but I was catching regularly now, and the moans and groans were going round, supposedly, so The Berk, head honcho, informed me that I was no longer allowed to do this. Apparently, I had an unfair advantage. Well, the whingers could always move closer if it was such a big deal!

Anyway, I managed to secure Long Island Point and with three nights ahead of me and buzzing with confidence, I felt I couldn't fail. The carp agreed with me and I was off to a great start by 11pm that Friday night with a scattered 18lb 2oz mirror off a new spot, fished a bit longer at 110 yards. A chilly north-westerly was blowing over the weekend but on the Sunday, that dropped, a fresh south-westerly sprung up and as the temperature climbed, so did my confidence.

My main hotspot was at 80 yards toward the estate house, so I positioned two hook baits there in close proximity and topped up with another 100 or so 20 millers. The other rig went back to the long spot from where I'd taken the 18-pounder. The wind blew itself out and the lake fell calm and quiet at dusk.

In the depths of the night I awoke to a couple of bleeps to the left-hand rod. I looked at the watch - 4.20am - and swung my legs out of the bag. Suddenly, the line was out of the clip and the reel was ticking away steadily. A solid resistance was felt and with the fish kiting right on the long line, I was soon gaining on it.

I secured Long Island Point.

The fish just plodded along, hugging the bottom. I slipped into the margins and the fish swung in under the rod tip. With it bobbing on the top I slid the net under it but the fish just rolled off. I lifted the net and could see the pigging mesh was flat tight like a giant tennis racket. I gave it a shake but it was having none of it. Typically, the up to now chilled-out carp, suddenly came to and started chugging off back out into the lake. With one hand playing the fish, I pulled the mesh about with the other, desperately trying to untangle it. I shouted out to John Price, who was in One Down, but there was no response. I was starting to panic a bit and then, as if by magic, I raised the net and to my relief the mesh fell down and I had a useable net again.

Concentrating fully on the fish, I led her back to the net and this time there was no drama as the mesh enclosed the jewel that lay within. I struggled up the bank with the fish, and with my head torch on, I peeled away the mesh to reveal my target fish. Wow! The Long Scaly One was even more stunning in the flesh than in the pictures. I slipped her into the sling, carried her down to John's swim and woke him up with the sight of a big fish cradled inches from his nose. I quickly returned to my swim and with John's help hoisted her up. My first 30 would have to wait a bit to be achieved as the scales told a different story but at 29lbs 13oz a second personal best in a fortnight had been achieved and I was proud that this fish was my PB.

Although September is regarded by many as the best fishing month, once again it proved fruitless for me. With the water levels extremely low in a lot of my prime areas and with the bird life expanding on a daily basis, the fishing became much harder as the carp moved out to extreme range. October followed a similar pattern; just the odd fish was getting nailed, the Long Scaly One making a third appearance and, you guessed it, back up to 31lbs! In November, the fish really shut up shop with Brian Humphries catching the only fish at 24lbs 4oz, this being Brian's 25th fish of the season.

I was now fishing singles at range, low pop-ups, or balanced baits and it was one of these that brought me further success come December. The fish were holed up in the middle, so I chose to fish on the field bank, 120 yards out with all three rods from the overhang on the left-hand side of the middle island, and stepped across in the zone between the middle and bottom island.

On the Saturday, the middle rod pulled up tight. There was no evidence of birds, so I bent into it and at last felt that satisfying lunge of a carp on the end. On a long line, it didn't do a lot and within a few minutes I'd landed number 13 for the season, after being stuck on a dozen for so long. A nice common of 19lbs was happily held up to the camera before being slipped back into the icy depths.

Two weeks later, and with the forecast of gale force south-westerlies, I set up in the Forty swim and got three baits cast tight to the big snags off the island. It was a very big cast for me at about 130 yards, and after seeing John Carver using it, I'd cast my baits out of a length of guttering. I propped up the five-foot length of guttering at 45 degrees and laid the lead and bait in it, with the tip at the top of the pipe. With the butt held high this gave a big casting arc, without the rig catching the ground and this could be cast accurately.

Anyway, I'd whacked out three rigs, two of them with pop-ups on a whisker rig that I'd seen in Rob Maylin's new book, which had two bristles coming off in a 'V'. The anti-eject qualities were such that the carp could suck it in, but on ejection the bristles would catch, forcing the hook to stick in the mouth.

The fish were holed up in the middle.

Brian's 25th fish of the season.

With three hook baits blasted out within a few feet of each other on the edge of the snags, I battened down the hatches as the wind started to build in strength. A gusty night followed and as it was blowing a hooligan there was no way I would be able to get the baits back out as well again, so with my baits tied on and them being buoyant enough to last 48 hours, I decided to leave them where they were.

My good mates, Humphs and Splodger, arrived at lunchtime and with Humphs dropping in next door and Splodge going behind him in the Bream Bay, I had some company in those horrendous conditions. Despite the hooligan winds it was quite mild and if this didn't stir the carp, then nothing would.

A few fish must have been blowing into the shallower Bream Bay because soon after dark, Splodge was called into action and that evening went on to catch three fish, the best being the lovely Four Star at 29lbs 4oz. What a fatty! And the fish was looking plump as well.

By Sunday morning the wind was so severe it was a job to stand up in it. All manner of twigs and branches were coming off the trees and the buzzers were bleeping constantly, despite the line being bowstring tight with the severe undertow. When Brian walked into my swim at about 10am and commented on the angle of my lines, I got out of the bivvy to have a look, telling him the undertow was bad.

However, instead of my lines pointing straight out, the two left-hand rods were about 35 degrees further to the left. I lifted the tip of the middle rod and it was pointing out toward the middle island, nowhere near where I'd cast it. I quickly wound down and the rod hooped over and I felt a lunge.
"I've only got one on!" I told Humphs, laughing.
The mono was singing in the wind, and I gained line immediately because the weed bed the carp was sitting in was dead and brittle. After pumping the fish in through the white-capped waves, a good mirror rolled under the tip and Humphs expertly netted it. I don't know how long it had been on, but I'd had a few bleeps about half an hour previously that I'd put down to a branch that was floating through at the time. At 28lb 4oz it was a mental capture in mental conditions.

Humphs had dropped the left-hand rod on the floor so that it was out of the way when landing the mirror, I picked it up to wind in because it was time to pack

A mental capture in mental conditions.

The fish was looking plump as well.

up anyway. The line on this one was pointing out to the same area where the mirror was sat, and jokingly, I said, "I've probably got one on here as well." I wound down and burst out laughing as the rod hooped over to a lunge. "Carp on!" I shouted.

I was called every name under the sun as Humphs picked up the net again. Soon, a long 17lb common was in the net and that brought my tally to 15 for the season. What a way to end a great weekend! Five December fish between us and shared in great company. Unlucky, Humphs, but you'd had your share that season!

My Christmas present had come a week early and now as keen as mustard, I got back in the Forty swim on Boxing Day afternoon but under very different conditions. Now it was calm and cold and there was a little bit of cat ice in the Bream Bay margins, but although a frost had been forecast, it was not supposed to be as cold as Christmas Day night. However, the useless sods got it wrong. It was bloody freezing and I woke up to a solid sheet of ice. Where I was fishing locked up at range my lines didn't touch the water until about 10 yards out and although I could wind back through the ice, the leader knots jammed and I was stuck fast. I found a few small rocks and hurled these at my lines but the ice was too thick and they just bounced off.

Barry Mills, who had recently been made a bailiff, turned up to fish but seeing my predicament decided to go straight back home, suggesting I go round to get the boat. I walked all the way around the lake to get the boat and smashed the ice with the oar but I soon turned back after 20 yards. It was an impossible task because I was miles away from my swim.

On return to my swim, I found that The Berk had arrived. He lobbed a pair of chesties at me, told me to get in to break the ice and as I stood on tiptoe smashing the ice with a bankstick, I received a lecture on how I should have been checking for ice every hour through the night. Then he told me that I was lucky not to be losing my ticket. Lucky! I didn't feel very bloody lucky, standing out in freezing water getting a bollocking just for being keen enough to fish. It wasn't my fault the bloody weatherman was about four degrees out, and the fact that both The Berk and Barry Mills had both turned up to fish, proved that I wasn't the only one the weather had sprung a surprise on.

The fish appeared to be holed up in the middle through the colder months, so it meant fishing extreme range most of the time. This led to the odd crack-off and these were to be reported to the bailiffs so that, by using the boat, lines and rigs could be picked up off the lakebed. It was a good idea, but not everyone was as honest as me and my group of mates. It appeared that the three guys who were there most weekends, and coincidentally were the three top rods that season, Humphs, Splodger and me, were getting the blame for the lion's share of crack-offs. I'd had four during

the season and had reported all of them, but rumours were flying round and I got to hear that apparently I'd had nine on the trot. This was utter bullshit! It later transpired that the nine fish on the trot, which I'd lost in the opening week, had got twisted to nine crack-offs! Bizarre.

Anyway, there was a bailiffs' meeting in the March and we were told that the three of us were to meet with one of the senior bailiffs, Kenny Sykes, to explain ourselves. At the meeting, Kenny told us on the level what was being said and as he was one of the sensible ones, he let us know what the score was and said it was being blown out of all proportion.

We explained that, as we were fishing more than most, and at longer ranges than most, it stood to reason we'd experience the odd crack-off. Also, we explained that if the people who honestly reported their crack-offs were being punished, then everyone would keep schtum and this would defeat the object of clearing lost tackle from the lake! Kenny said he'd report back on what we'd said, and that we'd agreed to use heavier, longer leaders.

This 'chat' gave a rather sour taste to the end of what had been an otherwise memorable season for me. I'd had 25 takes, with 15 landed, including two personal bests. What would next season bring? I hoped for that first Frampton 30, but would the grief continue if success followed?

"I've probably got one on here as well."

Chapter 4 - Frampton
The good, the bad and the ugly!

Once again, the close season dragged and by the time the infamous Frampton reunion arrived I had a freezer full of bait I'd rolled and was introducing to the lake in earnest. I'd switched over to Solar, as the Mainline that I'd been using the previous season I'd got from The Berk, head honcho, and as now I wasn't in his good books, I felt it wise to sort my own bait out.

Brian, Shaun and Dave Cole were all using Solar, so we decided to go in with the Dairy Cream Mix and chose to use different flavours. I wanted mine to be a little bit different so I was mixing the cream base mix 50/50 with the more fishy Neptune mix and added the proven mixture of Squid and Octopus flavour with the fruity Esterblend 12. To try to disguise my bait from the lake's vast birdlife, I'd dyed them green, hoping for them to blend in on the lake's bottom but at the same time, by their strong smell, alert the carp to their presence. I'd rolled the majority of the baits in 24mm size because not only could I stick these out a long way, but also when baiting up I could get a good amount of bait in much quicker; and it was a lot quicker to roll the bloody things - a laborious task at the best of times!

I'd baited a range of swims, focusing on the area I'd had success on the previous year - Long Island, Reeds and the Bottom Island. The draw for the start was to take place at the reunion in Frampton village hall a few days before the 16th, so we'd all know where we were for the start. Splodger and Humphs both had 28 fish the previous season and it seemed one of them would win the Angler of the Year cup, but for some reason it wasn't awarded that year. I can't think why!

My good luck of the previous year's draw didn't continue. I had to wait until about fifth from last and reluctantly had to settle for a swim in the Bull Pen. The season opened on the weekend and I hoped that a move on the Sunday would get me where I wanted to be and then my season could really begin.

I had nothing in front of me and was stuck in a corner so I packed up on the Saturday afternoon and moved on to the Long Pond. I'd been invited to join the small Long Pond syndicate the year before because the shallow pond was having to be dug out and funds were needed in order for the work to be done; three of us financed this excavation work to the tune of £500 each. As a Long Pond member, I had the Court Lake for nothing, and as the Court was more expensive than the annual Long Pond ticket, in a few years I'd have recouped my money. Of course, that was if it turned out to be a long term membership and, at the time, I had no reason to think that it wouldn't. How things can change!

The Long Pond was empty so I chose my swim, flicked out a couple of rigs to likely-looking spots and dosed the areas with the new bait. An hour later I had the biggest resident in my net; Pearly, a fish that I was told was 30lbs when I stumped up the cash, but at 24lb 4oz it fell woefully short! A double, and three lost fish completed the day's events and at first light I packed away and headed up to Long Island to secure the Point swim for my week's annual holiday.

A new member, Jerry Hall, was next door in One Down and although he was blonde, he was unfortunately not Jagger's leggy ex-missus, and on Tuesday morning he woke me to

say he'd landed a big leathery mirror that had bottomed his scales. He asked if he could borrow mine. Thinking he must have the 40, I told him that I only had 40lb Avons myself, but he said that his only went to 30lbs - a bit inadequate for Frampton. As he opened up the sack I recognised the fish as No-Name and she pulled my Avons round to 31lb 6oz. That was a brilliant result for Jerry and as he seemed unsure about what to do with himself after putting it back, I informed him he'd best stick the kettle on.

The weather was predicted to warm up as the week wore on, and I was quite confident. I had two rods on spots that I'd caught from last season and I moved the third about in the entrance to the Bream Bay. After spotting a couple of fish in the back channel behind Long Island Point, I moved this rod to a small hole in the weed a couple of yards off the overhang of the Alcatraz island, in the entrance of the back channel. The weed was quite fierce this year but with accuracy I could flick the rig into this small hole to land on the firm silty bottom. With my 24mm pop-up on a D-rig braided hooklink in the hole, I catapulted 30 baits on top. They all fell into the ripples of the previous one; those big baits are so much easier to bait up with!

That evening, I sat up quite late chatting with Jerry. He was keen to learn about all the different big fish that lived out in the depths in front of us and as we went through them one by one, I told him about setting myself a target fish last season - the Long Scaly One. When he asked me if I had a target for this year, I instantly declared it to be Yo-Yo, a certain 30-pounder, but I loved the scaly ones and Yo-Yo was certainly that. I say 'a certain 30' but Yo-Yo got its name from its inconsistent weights. It would fluctuate up and down like a yo-yo. I'd seen it in the close season, however, and it had looked in the 36-38lb class, so even if it spawned it should still be a good weight. It was getting late so I said goodnight and got into the bag, dreaming of big carp.

I awoke at 6.30am to a misty morning and a screaming Delkim, only to find a bloody pair of swans swimming away from my rod tips. As I shouted a few choice obscenities at them, it dawned on me that the swans were swimming out into the main lake but my tip was bent round to the right. I leapt down the step and with the tip plunged under I hung on as the carp was past the little island and I didn't want my line catching the overhanging branches. With the angle of the pull coming from beneath, the carp, which didn't feel very big, swirled on the surface. Now I knew where it was, I coaxed it back away from danger, raised the rod tip and played it out in the safety of my margins. As I said, initially I'd thought it was a small one but now it felt quite heavy and when I caught a glimpse of its scaly flanks, I had an eerie feeling that I knew what it was. The early morning mist shrouded the lake as I stood alone doing battle, the hunter and the hunted, and soon the silence was broken as I screamed 'Haulin!' across the glassy, calm lake.

At 24lb 4oz it fell woefully short!

The beautiful Yo-Yo lay beaten in my net and as Jerry ran into the swim, I announced, "Target achieved." Despite Jerry declaring that it certainly looked 30lbs, I wasn't counting my chickens just yet and with the odd mark on her flank it was evident she'd dropped pounds since I'd seen her a few weeks back. The needle hovered around the 30lb mark and neither of us was able to hold her steady, so we stuck a bank stick through the scales' handle and as the needle settled on 30lbs 1oz, I was over the moon. One ounce was good enough for me and after photos had been taken, I happily let her waddle off back under the misty surface.

That was the only action for the week but I packed up on the Saturday a happy chappy, and as my new target was the Brown Fish, which hadn't been out for a couple of years and had then weighed in at 33½lbs, I looked forward to another good season.

I returned on Wednesday for a one-nighter and as the lake was busy, I dropped into the bottom of the Bream Bay. I'd only just got all my rods out when I heard the familiar 'Haulin'!' shout from the direction of Splodge in One Up from Mrs McQueens. From behind me in The Wading Bar I could see Shaun with a fish in the net and I yelled across, "How Big?"

I heard the familiar 'Haulin'!' shout from the direction of Splodge.

Target achieved and 1oz over was good enough for me.

Shaun answered, "F***ing big! Can you come and do the honours?" There was a chap that was just up the bank in the Forty, so I asked him to look after my rods while I legged it round. Look At The Length had fallen foul of Splodge's Dairy Cream Scopex boilies, and at 30lb 10oz he was indeed right - it was f'ing big. I quickly rattled off a few shots and was back in my swim in five minutes. I thanked the guy for minding my rods, an uneventful night followed and it was Friday afternoon when I returned to find the shit from last season had been stoked up again.

As I began to set up, a couple of bailiffs arrived with the news that they had received an anonymous letter saying I'd left my rods unattended on Wednesday and that I had been seen in Splodger's swim on the other side of the lake. Yes, I was in Shaun's swim photographing his fish, but I told them my rods had not been left unattended because I had another member sitting with them. They said that The Berk had instructed them to take my ticket until further notice if the allegations were true, but if I denied it I could stay but would be banned for life if they found out later that it was true. They went off to check my story out with the chap who'd been looking after my rods, but the wind had completely been taken out of my sails. The knives were out and were being sharpened; they were after my blood. A while later, they returned admitting that my story checked out and telling me that I was in the clear but The Berk would be calling in on me the next day for a lecture. I couldn't wait!

After nipping home at lunchtime for some more bait, I returned to find that I'd missed my visitor but I had been summoned to the Almighty's swim. He told me this incident was not on; they were my rods and not anyone else's responsibility. However, it was now forgotten (not by me), and I was then treated to a lecture of how privileged I was to fish such a place and I should decide which route I should take and who I should side with. Basically, he was suggesting I should either come into the 'fold' with the bailiffs, or turn to the supposed 'dark side' and carry on fishing with my mates. I couldn't believe he was telling me who I could be mates with. Who did he think he was, my dad?

The statement, 'now you've caught a 30, something I've never had' and no 'well done on your 30' made it crystal clear that the green-eyed monster was doing its dirty business. He then instructed me to tell the other lads that we were no longer to shout 'Haulin'!' when we banked a fish. Apparently, it was causing offence to some members. My arse, it was. It was more likely that they couldn't catch anything and were jealous. I really felt victimised just for being keen and catching a few and at the age of 21 there was no way I going to be told who I should be friends with by a bailiff.

Shaun, Brian and Coley were all catching well on sweeter flavours, so I got myself a bottle of white chocolate and candy sweetener and, just using straight Dairy Cream mix, I made myself a big batch of 18mm baits. Because the weed was so bad there was no way I could fish at range, so the big 24s were not necessary. I soon had a couple of double-figure commons out of marginal swims, and one made me take an early morning dip as it snagged me up in a potamogeton weed bed off the Badger Spit swim.

When I arrived the following Friday afternoon, I found Coley in the Reeds and he told me that he'd seen a good fish head-and-shoulder just inside the Old Pit. With the rest of the lake busy, this would do me and as it was hot and humid, the shallow waters would have fish travelling backwards and forwards. I set up in the Mouth of the Old Pit swim and being just 18 inches deep, I would only be able to use hook baits as the swans would be on me otherwise. As is always the case, a hook bait in the right place is much better than a bed of bait in the wrong one.

As I was tying on my pop-ups I noticed a fish bow wave out of the Old Pit and down the edge of the potamogeton and reed beds. I sat and watched while another half-dozen fish patrolled the same route. Fish could also be seen in the Old Pit and so, full of confidence, I cast all three baits along their patrol route; one in the entrance, one on a known hotspot half-way along the weedbed, and one at the end of the weed where it met the reed bed. Unfortunately, I spooked the odd fish but they soon returned and seemed happy drifting backwards and forwards.

It was good to be fishing so close to Dave. The last thing we needed was word getting out that we were out of our swims but our brollies were almost back to back, such was the proximity of the two swims. I didn't have long to wait and at 8.15pm I was away. I managed to get the fish through the weedbeds, but a large lump of weed had accumulated around the inline lead, which had slid up the line and as a small common swung about behind the green stuff, I pulled it up to the drawstring, it swirled, and the hook pulled. At least it wasn't a big one.

I recast and as it was getting dark I stuck out a few baits dotted all the way along the weedbed. The same rod was away again at 10.15pm but by keeping the rod held high I teased the fish through the gaps in the weed. Then, leaning into it from the right, I made it pull down to the left into clearer water and away from the dense weedbed between me and Dave. A couple of minutes later, Dave did the honours and scooped up a nice chunky mirror. At 25lb 12oz it appeared to be one of the better fish in the area.

I only managed a tiny bit of broken sleep that night because another two takes were forthcoming in the early hours. Unfortunately, both fell off in the same large weedbed, but neither felt big and before it got light a lot of commotion was happening on the far bank. The carp were having another spawn, despite it being the 30th of July, so it looked like it was the smaller male fish that had been tempted to one of my sweet chocolates. I wound in, packed up, and left them to it, shattered but pleased to have got back in among the action. Four bites in a few hours was some going!

At 25lb 12oz it appeared to be one of the better fish in the area.

August had always been kind to me on Frampton and brimful of confidence I was pleasantly surprised to find a quiet lake come Friday afternoon. I found a few fish mooching about in open water in front of the Dugout, so with no hesitation I quickly set up camp. I had a plumb about and my normal spots still had a sparse amount of short weed on them so I fished my pop-ups a bit higher, 3-4 inches as opposed to the normal 1 inch.

The bright conditions didn't continue, Saturday brought in cooler temperatures and fish weren't on show. At 9.30am on Sunday, I was just taking the brolly down when the right-hand rod roared off. I couldn't do much with it as it tore out toward the middle. After the initial run, I coaxed it back and Travolta, who was fishing behind in the Entrance, waded out with the net in one hand and as he was still drinking his tea, a cup in the other. The carp looked like it might go straight into the net as it wallowed in, but Travolta was still sipping his tea. I commented that it looked like it was ready and with, "It's all under control, boy," Travolta tossed the cup on to the bank and scooped up the big mirror, all in one movement. Turning round he gave me a big grin and wink. Cheers mate, good job one of us was calm.

The mirror was a right minter and looked 26lb 'ish. I prided myself on knowing virtually all the fish in Frampton, but I didn't recognise this one and at 28lbs 4oz, it was a double surprise. Muttering a hushed, 'Haulin', I lifted her up for the shots as Splodge did the honours with the camera.

The following weekend, I couldn't believe my luck as I walked up the Point. The water in front of the Wading Bar was full of carp and all in close, 20-40 yards out. I soon had a bucket in there and found that our beloved leader had moved out of there that morning and gone up to the other end. What a Berk! I took the car round and while walking back to the Wading Bar, I stopped and chatted to the lads on the way. When I told them that I'd dropped in the Wader I was told that I'd be for the high jump if I bagged one after his lordship had vacated it. Good plan, I thought!

Once again, the spots were a bit dirty and sparsely weeded so with 4" pop-ups cast onto the clearest bits and tightly baited with 100 boilies, I helped myself to three fish that weekend. A pretty 21lb 4oz mirror and then an 18lb 5oz mirror on Saturday, and a chunky little 12lb 12oz common on Sunday.

A right minter.

I helped myself to three fish that weekend.

Most of the 30s had been caught a couple of times but the Brown One hadn't been out since June and I fancied that to be the next big one. Deciding to do a work night, I chose the Forty swim as the Wading Bar and Dug Out were both taken. I climbed a tree and spotted a handful of fish mooching about through the channels in the weed about 50 yards out. After a few casts I was satisfied my three baits were on good bottom, all between 40-60 yards out and sticking with the high pop-ups as they'd been so effective and different to everyone else's conventional 1 to 1½-inch ones. A six-egg mix of boilies over the three baits completed the traps.

At 1.45am, the left-hand rod tore off and from the moment I picked it up I had a feeling it was a really good one. Slow, deliberate, powerful runs ensued, and each time I gained line, the fish would take it back. This happened four or five times and just as it appeared to be tiring the hook pulled. I slumped back on my bed, really gutted and just hoped that it wasn't my target Brown Fish that had got away.

Word had got out that the lake was fishing well and so it was rammed the following week. I set up in the Stumps swim near the top island but it was really the other end I wanted to be, so I packed up early Saturday and went on the look about for some fish.

The fish were still in the Wading Bar area but that was taken. Trimmy informed me that he'd seen a good'un show close in front of the Perryway swim on the road bank so I legged it round, water bottle in hand to see if it was vacant. Relieved to see it free, I dropped my bottle and fetched the rest of my gear. By the time the gear was all set up it was lunchtime so a few of us nipped over to the Bell for a spot of lunch and to celebrate recent captures.

With Splodger 'the hustler' on the pool table, we all took him on and a good laugh was had by all. Now, I'm no drinker and after four pints of lager I was well merry, shall we say. So getting back to my swim, I had a big cup of water and had a little lie down. An hour's snooze and I felt a lot better and got on with getting some baits out.

Casting just a bare lead around, I found a tiny silt spot in a hole in the weed about 25 yards out and slightly to the left. This was an area where I'd seen them show when fishing the Wading Bar a couple of weeks before. Clipping the lead up, I cast back out, hitting the clip, and it slid along the bottom a couple of feet before locking up in weed. With a rig attached I got it back on the spot and accurately catapulted 50 baits on top. The other two went either side in the margins under the big trees that lay out in the water.

I slept like a log that night and didn't wake until 8am. Lying in the bag, I had one of those moments when you wake up and wonder why you haven't had a take. Just then, the middle alarm bleeped and as I looked out there was a huge vortex in the shallow water. I was up and on the rod as it pulled from the clip and as the fish I was attached to headed left, another big bow wave shot out toward the island. My hooked culprit had obviously been sharing his breakfast!

I'd fished the two rods in the margins and I'd put a backlead on this line, which now had a lump of weed attached to it and I couldn't get direct contact on the fish as it ploughed into a weedbed. As I wound down to the backlead, it lifted and some of the weed came off, and with the weed being brittle at this late summer stage, I got the fish moving toward me.

The carp had been unplugged from the sanctuary of the weedbed so it went for plan B of its escape and headed for the snag tree to my left. Fully clothed, I waded out and winched as much line on to the reel as possible and with my breath held, I just made it and turned its head at the last possible second. It then bogged in some weed but on such a short line among many bubbles fizzing on the surface, I drew her in. The weed was concentrated around the lead so I let the fish drift in and as soon as I could make out the bulk of the fish, I lifted the net around it and punched the air. I pulled the weed out and a real whacker lay there, gills pumping, angry that she'd been tripped up.

As the cameras whizzed I proudly held up my biggest-ever carp.

The penny dropped and I knew the big brown mirror was indeed my target - the Brown One

With a lot of effort, I heaved the monster onto the mat, and stared at it. In all the excitement, I couldn't fathom which fish it was. I slipped her into the wet sling and watched as the needle spun round; 10... 20... 30... and it kept going before settling at 34lb 8oz. It was one of the really big ones at last, and another personal best, but which one? As soon as I opened the sling, the penny dropped and I knew that the big brown mirror was indeed my target - the Brown One. Wadey, who was fishing the Wading Bar, shouted across, "How big then?" and loud enough so all could hear, I yelled out, "34lbs 8oz. The Brown One." Well, I hadn't shouted 'Haulin!' had I?!

I slipped her into a sack for a few minutes, Coley turned up on cue and after we'd had a brew and I'd relayed the whole fight to him, we carried her out to the field bank so that we had some decent light, and soon the cameras were whizzing as I proudly held up my biggest-ever carp.

The bank holiday was busy. Dave had caught a few, and after my capture of the Brown Fish we had a very enjoyable Saturday lunchtime over at the Bell. It got even funnier on the way back as I stopped off at Dave's swim, the Willow. Dave was fishing at extreme range; he was already a big caster and the added 'fuel' of the lager would enhance distance even more. With hook bait attached, Dave told me where it was going and with that, he picked up the rod, went down the slope to the water's edge and waded out a few feet to get a drop for a big cast.

Dave turned to me and started laughing. The silly sod had only forgotten to put his thigh waders on and was now standing fully clothed and up to his nuts in water. I was laughing so much, rolling about on his bedchair, that the leg on it collapsed and it had us both in hysterics for ages. The whole time, Dave just stood in the water and after composing himself, he lager-blasted his lead to the horizon and then trudged on to dry land, dripping with water. The look on Dave's face was priceless; some moments you never forget.

September saw me busy at work and also suffering with illness, so little angling was managed and with the darker evenings I'd stopped my midweek overnighters as well. I managed to witness a couple of big'uns on the bank as Splodger rang me a couple of times to go up and do photos for him in the week, both No-Name and Rosie at over 35lbs falling to his extreme-range tactics.

My next bite also came at range. On October 23rd, I dropped into the Wading Bar and eventually managed to get my baits along the island margin. After a pub lunch, I returned mid-afternoon and with the lager loosening me up, I had no problem whacking the baits out. One fell perfectly, right under a willow branch that overhung the hard gravel hump. I was well happy with that one and put a six-egg mix of 24mm sweeties around it with the stick. That job sweated the lager out a bit and the following morning I awoke to a take on that rod. It came in fairly easily and a pretty 21lb 2oz mirror was soon swimming back to its weedy home after having his picture taken.

November was as busy as any month had been. The fish were at good weights and everyone seemed keen to catch before the weather turned and they shut up shop for the winter. On Friday the 18th, I turned up not realising what was ahead of me. There was a mild south-westerly blowing as I walked up the point with my fingers crossed that the Wading Bar swim would be empty. My heart sank as I saw Pete just putting his gear into the swim. I'd missed out literally by seconds and when I learned that all the other point swims were taken, I felt a bit despondent.

Dave had caught a few.

I was well happy with the cast, the lager loosening me up.

Rosie falling to Splodger's extreme range tactics.

I stood in the Wading Bar and noticed that the wind was just starting to ripple into the Bream Bay behind me, so I wandered over and nipped up the tree for a better view. My mood suddenly lifted. I could see two fish below making their way down to the corner of the bay; not whackers, but one looked a good mid-20, and beggars can't be choosers, so I quickly grabbed my gear, before parking the car and legging it back before the daylight faded away from me.

With three, 3-inch pop-ups cast to firm spots, I set the house up in the dark and relaxed for the long night ahead. My sleep was interrupted a few times, but liners were the culprit. At least I was confident there were still fish in the bay.

Saturday lunchtime saw a few of us wind in and head over to the pub, which had several benefits. Away from the prying eyes of the bailiffs, we could enjoy a drink, and a bit of banter round the pool table, and there were a couple of particularly nice barmaids! With a few beers inside me, I plucked up the courage and asked one of them out but after getting a polite knock back, I headed back to the lake with my tail between my legs and repositioned the rods. The wind was pumping into the Bream Bay now, and the end bank looked good so I found the bar just off that margin, cast my pop-up onto it and put 30-40 baits around it.

After sulking for a bit that evening, I got my head down until I was awoken at 4.15am by what I thought was a liner, until the spool began to spin. I was out and on it and all thoughts of barmaids vanished as the fish kited right back out into the bay before weeding me up. I kept the pressure on and as the weed had died off, it all started to break through after about five minutes and I soon had it in close.

After an anxious few moments in the edge as I was forced to bury the rod under water and hang on as it tried to escape in the marginal snag, I breathed a sigh of relief as Pete lifted the net around my eleventh carp of the season. I didn't know it, but this short chunky 25lb 11oz mirror was to be the last Frampton carp I was to cradle in my arms. Sad, sour events were about to unfold.

The next weekend, I decided to fish the side of the middle island and as it was getting dark at half past four, it was all a bit of a rush. With three hookbaits tied on, I blasted two out with no hassle but as I thrashed out the third, a bird's nest somehow ballooned off the spool, the line snapped and the lead and leader landed about 40 yards out. Now, the rule on crack-offs was to report them to a bailiff so that they could be recovered, but as darkness was descending that would have to wait until the next day, so I retackled the rod and got it thrashed out to the middle.

I didn't know it but this chunky 25lb 11oz mirror was to be my last Frampton carp.

The next morning, Splodger wandered past. He'd just been made a bailiff so I told him that I'd cracked off, but Splodge being Splodge, he told me to tell Dave Jones over at the pub at lunchtime. Fair enough, it was only a couple of hours, I suppose. Shortly after, I got a message that Dave Cole had caught a 20lb common out of Cobhams and needed me to be cameraman, so knowing that he was off at lunchtime, I quickly packed down and arrived at Dave's with all my gear. I took the pics and then Phil Calloway, who was next door in the Wading Bar, had a 22lb mirror. At least I was more confident that I was in a better area.

Trimmy was moving into where I'd been, so I told him where my crack-off was, and he told me that it wouldn't interfere with where he was casting. We all went over to the pub and I told Dave Jones, who was a head bailiff, where the crack-off was and he said he'd have a look on the Sunday afternoon. No urgency then! That night proved to be my last and ended a 4½ year campaign on what is still one of the most picturesque lakes in the country, and which holds some of the best big fish as well.

Soon after arriving home at lunchtime, the home phone rang and it was Barry Mills, the newly-appointed head bailiff – yes, there was more than one! I was told in a very matter of fact way that due to cracking off on Friday and not reporting it until the Saturday, I was now suspended from fishing the lake until either John or The Berk said otherwise. I was not allowed to give an explanation and the fact that it was dark and they couldn't look for the rig was not a good enough reason. Well, if it was so

bloody urgent why still had the rig not been recovered 24 hours after I'd reported it? Apparently, The Berk had decided that this was the way to get rid of me and I was under strict instructions not to go to John, who I'm sure would have heard me out and seen it in a different light.

It was obviously a day for 'hanging' because no more than half an hour later, Humphs phoned me with the news that he'd just been banned as well. Brian's crime was casting too close to the island and snagging an underwater root, which he obviously couldn't see because it was, as I said, under water!

Two months later, we both got a phone call from The Berk who informed us that our punishment was a ban for the rest of the season, but we could reapply the following year. Yeah, thanks for that. I saw red and told him bluntly exactly what I thought of his childish, jealous actions and he confirmed this by laughing like a spoilt kid that had got his own way.

It was the end of an era for me, but I refuse to let him spoil some of the great memories of such a nice lake. I'd caught some cracking carp and made some good friends, but now a move had been forced upon me. Where to, though? Could I find another place I could feel at home on?

That night proved to be my last.

Chapter 5 - Pastures new

Now I had a thirst for 30-pounders, I needed to find myself a new venue which gave me a realistic chance of catching fish of that size. Unfortunately, Gloucestershire isn't a hotbed for big carp so travelling was going to become a necessity. With Brian being in the same boat as me and needing a new venue, we met up one Sunday at the start of December in Cirencester, along with another friend, Tim, who was a member of a small syndicate in the nearby Cotswold Water Park.

We planned to have a look at the syndicate water known as Farmhouse Lake before looking at a group of waters also on a very small syndicate, but these were more about rumour and the potential of holding decent-sized fish. We knew that Farmhouse definitely held at least a couple of 30-pounders, as well as a small head of back-up fish.

We met up with the old boy who ran the fishing syndicate, another John, and after seeing the photos of the fish that adorned his shed walls, I for one was keen on this water. John told us to have a look round the lake and if we liked what we saw, we could both have winter tickets.

We drove down a long gravel track and as we pulled up to the wooden gates, there lay the Farmhouse Lake. At about 23 acres it was a good size, considering that it only held about 23 carp, to our knowledge, and although it wasn't as mature and picturesque as Frampton, it was quiet and hassle free - exactly the tonic I needed after recent events!

After a lap of the lake and a chat with the only lad who was fishing, we headed back to the yard and handed over our money. We were now members of the Farmhouse syndicate and because of the abolition of the close season, our tickets weren't going to run out until the end of April. A bonus of the winter ticket was that we'd almost guaranteed our places for next season as well.

We had a quick look round the other complex of lakes, but with a hefty price tag and only vague rumours that there were carp in all of them, and despite one, Dairy Farm, having produced good carp in the past, I was a bit sceptical so we decided to pass on that one. I headed home with my Farmhouse ticket in my pocket, keen to get back angling after the Frampton debacle.

To rub salt into the wounds, I'd have to drive right past the Court Lake each time I went fishing, but I was determined not to be beaten. I'd go and catch from other lakes out there. As much as I loved the place and the carp it held, I now had no other option but to broaden my carp fishing horizons and try to succeed on other challenging waters.

Brian only had Saturday nights to fish, so it was going to be a bit of a solo mission to try to locate any carp. December is never the ideal time to start a campaign on a new water, but I had to, and so the following Friday I took the 40-minute drive to Farmhouse. Jamie had been there for a week, and was still there, so I wandered down the river bank to see if anything had occurred. Jamie was a Bristol guy and it soon became apparent that we had mutual friends, so we got chatting about various things and obviously, Frampton was a topic of conversation. Now we were on friendlier terms, I broached the subject and asked him if anything was happening. He told me that he'd already caught the Big Male at 33lb plus, if my memory serves me correctly. At least they were still feeding and I now knew that the lake definitely held at least one good 30.

Not wanting to tread on his toes during my first weekend on, I set up camp on the opposite side, the tree bank, in a wide swim about two-thirds of the way down. This gave me a good view of the lake and with the westerly wind blowing on to the bottom bank, got me 'on the wind', but comfortable as it wasn't directly in my face. With the forecast of gale force winds to come, I didn't fancy being in the teeth of it; it was mid-December after all!

Unsurprisingly, nothing happened that first night and when Brian arrived at lunch time on the Saturday I had nothing to report, apart from Jamie's fish. Bri dropped in a couple of swims up from me and after much thrashing of the water and

A bigger mirror this time, the Mug at 34lb 8oz was now a lake record.

whingeing about the weed that was still prolific, he came and joined me because the view of the lake was much better from my swim.

In the middle of the night, I awoke to someone calling out my name and as I stuck my head out of the bivvy, nearly getting it blown off in the process, there was a smiling Jamie in need of assistance. I fetched Brian and we headed round to Jamie's swim. After the success of catching the Male, he'd followed it up with a bigger mirror this time. A fish known as the Mug at 34lbs 8oz was a lake record, and just happened to equal my current PB.

Despite the unfortunate name, Jamie informed us that it hadn't been out for quite a while, which showed in its mint condition. Jamie had obviously got on the fish but little did we know at the time that Jamie was a master stroke-puller. He hadn't caught the fish from the 60 yards that he'd told us, it was, in fact, more like 160 yards. Jamie was a bit of a Captain Pugwash and after finding the fish with the aid of a lamp at night, he had dropped his tiger hookbaits on them and as the nuts didn't deteriorate, he could leave them out for as long as it took. The swim on the river bank being a bit of a blind alley meant he probably hadn't caught them too far off from where I was fishing on the opposite bank. Although he wasn't sticking to the rules, as I found out a long time after, you had to hand it to him as it was a good piece of angling to catch the two big ones in the middle of December.

The wind was still at gale force, so at least I now knew what good conditions were for the lake; a big, warmish westerly or south-westerly, always the best winter conditions on every lake I've fished.

On the back of a good season on Frampton, I stuck to my Dairy Cream boilies, with the White Chocolate and Ester Cream flavours. Braided pop-up rigs also formed part of my plan of attack and because the weed was very bad, it was a case of constant plumbing until I could find clear spots.

I started back after Christmas and as there was no one else fishing, I fished the river bank in the hope that the fish were still in that area. Throughout January, I started to work my way round the lake, learning the spots and finding areas where I hoped to land on the fish.

On my sixth trip at the start of February, I fished for the first time on the bottom bank and with the biggest snag tree to my right, I could fish both this feature and the open water. This bank received any west winds so I hoped the fish might be in this area. After plumbing the edge of the tree, I found that it wasn't as deep as I'd hoped for at only three feet. However, it was worth one rod and I put this on a clean spot on the edge of the branches and fished the other two at 45 and 60 yards out. With a light breeze pushing in, it wasn't too cold for a change and I felt quite confident as I snuggled down nice and warm in the sleeping bag.

The right-hand rod soon arched round and with the bobbin tight at the top, I leaned into it instantly. A fish was on but it didn't feel heavy and after a bit of splashing I soon had the culprit under my feet. Unsure what it was, I netted it and grabbing my head torch I shone it in the net. For a second I thought it was a little common but as I lifted it out I could see it was a bloody great chub. I weighed it because it looked huge, and at 5lbs 11oz was a big old specimen. I took a quick picture on the mat and

let him go. I got the rig back on the edge of the tree, had myself a cuppa and no sooner had I finished my tea than it was off again. A minute later, I had another big chub in my net and this one went 6lbs, and from that day I referred to the snag as the 'Chub Tree'.

The rest of the night remained quiet and the day dawned bright and sunny. While I enjoyed the first taste of spring-like sunshine that afternoon, I looked out to the right as the sun was setting behind the trees and a carp slid a good halfway out. A bar of gold silhouetted against the far bank. Was this spot hiding buried treasure? It was more in front of the swim the other side of the snag tree, so noting the spot from both swims, I launched a rig out to it.

At last there was a sign, and there was no one else fishing the lake at the time. I hoped I'd pinpointed the carp's winter hideaway and I was sure that fish wouldn't be alone. Despite having a rig in the area, that night the bobbin remained motionless but having been sunny all day, the temperature obviously dropped with such a clear sky. I had to leave mid-morning, but before I left I had a plumb in the area and found a couple of clearings in the weed wide enough to get one good pull back with the marker rod. I split my remaining bait between the two spots; one at 60 yards and the other at about 45 yards out. Now I just had to wait until Friday and hope that the weather would be favourable.

That week dragged by but when I woke on the Friday to find it wet and windy, I thanked the carp gods, ploughed on with my work and managed to get done by 2pm. With the Astra loaded, I toed it to the Water Park and as I dodged the potholes down the gravel track to the lake, I crossed my fingers; the bottom bank was empty.

As I pulled up to the gate I was relieved to see an empty lake and after parking up I donned the waterproofs, loaded up my wheelbarrow and headed down the river bank to my destination on the bottom bank.

The weather certainly wasn't pleasant. The westerly wind was blowing straight in my face, but for fishing conditions it was perfect, so I quickly chucked up the bivvy and got everything inside before it was drenched. Once all that was sorted I got on with getting the rods out.

I'd already had a cast about the previous week so the right-hand rod went out toward a tall tree, 60 yards to the right, the middle rod at 45 yards in line with a little stumpy tree, and as John never walked the bottom bank I put a third rod out on the Chub Tree.

A big old specimen.

Although the rules stated two rods, everyone used three and as John always came round in his big red van, you could see him coming. If you were on the river bank, all you had to do was take one off the rests and lay it on the floor when you heard the van coming because John couldn't see it from the other side of the river; he would seldom get out of the van.

The only place you were likely to get caught was on the point. Again, if you heard him coming you just wandered over to the van and even if he came over, if you had the third rod in the reeds, he'd be none the wiser. John's dog was more likely to find the rod as he jumped about in the undergrowth. On a couple of occasions he did clock the third rod, but all he'd said was, 'You'd better wind that in,' and a simple, 'Yeah, I'll do that,' was all that was required. It was a bit more relaxed than Frampton and, to be honest, there were so few people fishing Farmhouse I could have used six rods and not interfered with anyone.

With 30 boilies around each hookbait I got done with daylight to spare and sheltering from the persistent rain, I watched the water as darkness descended. No one else arrived so as usual I had the lake to myself, everyone else was obviously waiting for spring. With the pattering of the rain playing its tune on the bivvy, I soon fell asleep that evening.

At 5.15am a few bleeps had me slipping my trainers on and scurrying out of the bivvy door. The left-hand bobbin was tight against the rod and after the events last weekend I was pretty confident of the culprit. I wasn't wrong and another specimen chub

I soon rolled a common into the net.

slipped into the net. This one was of a similar stamp and a quick weigh confirmed its weight at 5lbs 11oz. As it was an easy cast, I flicked the rig back to the snag and threw a handful of baits around it.

Soon after daylight, the wind picked up and was blowing straight into my face. I was as confident as I'd been in my whole time on the lake so as I'd seen the carp show late afternoon, I planned to leave the rods out all day undisturbed. I watched the water intently all day, but time was getting on and I was starting to lose hope. I checked my watch at ten past four and decided to give it another hour before re-baiting.

I only had to wait for five minutes until the bobbin on the right-hand rod crept to the top and held tight. I bent into it and straightaway I felt more weight than a chub. I'd hooked my first carp post-Frampton, and desperately didn't want to stuff this up. Keeping the fish to the right-hand side of the swim and away from the chub tree, meant it all went smoothly and I soon rolled a common into the net.

The fish, though not huge, was pristine and fortunately there was a pike angler on the river bank and I rushed off to get him to take some photos for me. At 19lbs 8oz, it fell just short of the 20 mark but it was an early February bite, and now not only had I seen one in the area but I'd caught one as well, so if I could keep the 'action' under my hat, there was no reason that I couldn't get more, as long as the weather didn't take a turn for the worse.

After getting off the mark, I was understandably keen to get back the next weekend and after getting up early, I raced through my jobs, left home at lunchtime and got to the lake at 2pm. I raced round to the bottom bank and put all three rods out in the 'zone'. As I was putting up the bivvy, the left-hand rod burst into life and after a short battle, a lovely, fully-scaled mirror lay in the net.

There were three fully-scaled mirrors in Farmhouse, and as the largest one was a big long one I was guessing that this was the second-biggest because as it was a chunkier shape of mid-20 proportions. After taking my short pop-up rig out from his bottom lip, I weighed him at 24lb 14oz; a truly gorgeous carp to catch in February, so with no one else around I slipped him in a sack and when John came driving round, I legged it round to get him to do some photos.

John's health meant that he couldn't walk that far, so I had to carry the Fully round a couple of hundred yards to him in the sack. Unfortunately, the photos didn't do the fish justice but in the days of slides, of course, I didn't know that until I got them back.

A truly gorgeous carp to catch in February.

I was super-confident and with the wind still ruffling in from the west, I spent the Saturday afternoon fully expectant of another bite - mid/late afternoon appeared to be the hot time. I was a bit disappointed when nothing happened and the next two trips followed the same pattern. The weather had taken a turn for the worse and the first weekend of March resulted in a heavy frost on the Friday night, and when the snow came on Saturday I gave it until 4pm before departing for home.

I carried on fishing the weekends and set up facing the wind each time. At the end of March, I managed my third Farmhouse carp at 14lbs 4oz, and probably the smallest mirror in the lake. I was fishing the end of the river bank, and a cold north-westerly was blowing so it continued the pattern of the fish being on the wind. Well, the small ones were, but I was no closer to catching a big one.

They seemed to have eyes for the ginger one as Jamie doubled up on the Mug on Good Friday, well, it was good for him, down a tad at 33lbs, and then a fortnight later doubled up with the Male again at 32lb 12oz. My only end-of-season fish were chub of 6lbs 7oz and 6lbs 10oz, and a tench on the last weekend.

The Farmhouse had a closed month in May, so I dabbled with the odd worknight on Wickwater down the road, and kept my eye in with a few doubles but again, nothing big. I hoped that June would bear bigger fruit and with Brian and I getting a ticket for Patshull's Church Pool, perhaps a 30-pounder wasn't too far away.

June the 1st was opening day, so I'd managed to get a rare couple of days off work and with no one apparently allowed on the lake before midnight, I left home at 11pm. As I drove down the track, I expected to see cars at the gate but there were none. As I got closer, I could see that both car parks had motors in them and as I pulled through the gate I could see silhouettes of bivvies on the grassy point. Not only had everyone beat me, but they were already fishing, too. So much for 'no entry before midnight'!

I had a quick look round and with about a dozen already fishing, it was a case of just dropping in, so I set up at the start of the river bank in the deep bay, but after seeing a couple show on the bottom bank that morning, I packed up and moved to the right-hand side of the Chub Tree at noon.

The two big ones seemed to have eyes only for the ginger one.

I was off the mark! 21lbs 4oz.

The sun came out and with a rod on the side of the plateau, my Cream and Scopex pop-up was picked up and the spool went into meltdown. This fish really fought well and I willed it to be a big one. It certainly was a lovely fish but again, one of the smaller ones at 21lbs 4oz. Anyway, I was off the mark.

Adam, who was fishing the other side of the Chub Tree, took my pictures and I returned the favour for him that night when he caught one of the best-looking fish I'd seen, in the shape of the Linear. At 32lb 8oz it was now big as well as beautiful. This fish took my breath away and was now my number one target, despite both the Mug and Male being bigger. There were definitely more fish in front of Adam and down to the corner as it got hotter, so at 8pm that evening when Adam left, I dropped in behind him.

On the Saturday morning, Jamie came round with a guilty grin on his face. The spawny git had only caught the Male for the third time! What was it, his bloody pet? We did have some trouble when we went to return it and for the next couple of hours we took it in turns to hold it in the margin, as it kept rolling over. In the end, we took him round to the windward bank and propped him up facing the waves, with the meshed strip of my sack over his mouth. The extra oxygenated water pumping into him did the trick and as he became stronger, it was with much relief that we watched him swim off.

My mate, Hugh - or Savay as we called him - had my February fully-scaled that afternoon, off the Point, and in the middle of the night I had my second of the season, the aptly named Skid Mark common, due to a big bald patch. Guess the weight – 15lbs 12oz ; now I'd had the honour of catching the smallest mirror and the smallest common. A bit different to spawny bollocks, Mr Woods! After doing a few fish in those first days, it went a bit quiet and the second weekend finished that way with nothing getting caught. Normality had been restored.

In anticipation of June 16th, Brian and I had bought tickets for Patshull Church Pool, a beautifully set, old estate lake stocked mainly with commons but the biggest fish in there was a mirror called Billy. It was in the Wolverhampton area and a bit of a hike at over 80 miles, a good hour and 20 minutes drive, but with the chance of a 30-lb common we hoped it would be worth it.

One of the best-looking fish I'd seen, the Linear.

Our mate, Phil Calloway, who lived close to the lake had recommended it and helped us to get a ticket. We felt that our sweet, creamy birdfood might lead to constant unwanted attention from the quite large eel and bream population so, on Phil's recommendation, we were using Premier Aminos, with a fishy flavour and Black Pepper Oil, and we rolled them in large sizes, 18mm and 22mm. Looking back now, perhaps we should have stuck with what was working for us and not fallen into the trap of using similar type baits to everyone else. You live and learn, don't you?

We got to the lake mid-afternoon and the old Astra had made it okay, but I was in the process of getting a diesel motor to help with the fuel costs because my mileage would be increasing dramatically. I drove down the long, gravel track. There were golf courses on either side with huge, old oak trees in the grounds and as I crawled along the road bank, I caught my first glimpse of water through the trees and liked the look of the place. There were a few bivvies already set up and I secured a likely-looking swim, known as the New Swim, and then went for a mooch around.

The dam end bank was out of bounds to the syndicate, so that left three banks; the long meadow bank, the road bank and the boards bank which consisted of platforms out in the lake with a staged, wooden walkway joining them up. I'd need some curtain hooks to screw into the boards before I fished that bank.

Patshull Church Pool, a beautifully set, old estate lake.

The aptly named Skid Mark common.

Jon 'Shoes' Jones - I gelled with him straight away.

The meadow bank looked to be the most comfortable with its reed-lined margins and flat banks, and as the road bank was at the narrow end, this was all quite close-range stuff. The thing I noticed most was coloured water and the absence of even a strand of weed. I wasn't used to this; coming off the back of fishing weedy, feature-filled lakes like Frampton and Farmhouse, this silty lake would present a different set of problems to deal with.

The first hurdle was trying to understand the locals. It seemed that everyone had a thick, Black Country accent. We were all well and truly outnumbered by the Brummie contingent, but they were all nice guys and we were soon made welcome. The guy in the next swim, which if I remember rightly was called Welshmans, was Jon 'Shoes' Jones and I gelled with him straightaway. It was obvious from day one that he knew what he was talking about and being thirsty for knowledge, I grilled him on all aspects of fishing the Church Pool.

I opened my account just after midnight with the first slab of the season. Although the odd fish showed, I wasn't on them and with the lake full, there was no opportunity to move. A 30-pound common got caught off the road bank, and Brian had a small common out of the little bay to the side of the road point he was on. I woke up on the Sunday to find them spawning and so headed back Gloucester-bound, down the M5.

I had my new car for the following trip, a rather sexy (not!), black Nissan Bluebird. It was better on fuel than my petrol Astra and it would be cheaper to run, plus Japanese cars are very reliable I was told, that was until the clutch burned out on me when I was halfway to the lake. Great start!

I rang the garage, told them where I was, the guy said he'd be out with another car on a trailer for me, and he'd take mine back to fit a new clutch. They arrived an hour or so later with my old Astra on the trailer, so I swapped my gear into the red wagon and went on my way to Patshull. Darkness was not far away when I dropped on to the road bank, but I soon had a couple of rods sorted at close range. A northerly wind was blowing into me but despite looking good for a bite, only a tench was forthcoming in that department at 5am on the Saturday morning. The wind was dying off so I had a move up to the other end, in the Big Tree swim when that became vacant at about 4pm, but another blank was the order of the day.

I did quite like the place and the locals were good company when you could understand what they were saying, (only joking), but there was something missing and with no definite spots it was a bit of a lottery where to cast a rig. Unless there was a bubbling or showing fish, there was very little difference in casting on to one bit of silt as another.

I thought that bait might be the key, but the more you put in, the more bream, eels and tench you caught, from what I could tell.

I returned to Farmhouse to have a rethink and carried on my blank run of form there, before having another three weekends back 'up north'. I even managed to get in three of the better swims; Little Tree, End Board, and Top Point, but apart from eels from the Board swim, I was still no closer to my first Patshull carp. Once again, Farmhouse - and the Mug in particular - started to fill my thoughts.

August was red hot and with the shallowest part of the lake being the first bay, I plotted up in the fourth swim down the tree bank. I gave it until lunchtime on the Saturday before winding in and going for a stroll. It was so hot that it was an effort just to wander round with a catty and a little bag of mixers, just in case. I got up a little tree on the bottom bank because I could see a few just below the surface, and as I climbed higher to gain a clearer view, there below was the Mug along with three or four other carp a bit further out. I watched for a couple of minutes and when the Mug started nosing the surface I thought she looked prime for a mixer, so I got down from the tree and catapulted a couple of pouchloads out in her path. She swam straight under the first two but then she slurped down the third one, then the fourth and fifth. Bloody hell, she was having them! I fired out another couple of pouchloads to keep her interested and despite the searing heat, I ran full pelt back to my swim about 400 yards away. I was dying

It rolled over and I could see its heavily-scaled flanks.

The first hurdle was understanding the locals.

by the time I got back to grab a rod, but all I could think of was those big lips engulfing the dog biscuits.

I quickly cobbled together a controller set-up and with rod, net, a few bits and some water, I legged it back to the bottom bank. I put some more bait out on my return but on climbing the tree, I could see that the big girl had drifted further out and had grouped up with the other fish. I tried for another hour but she just wasn't interested any more. The heat was draining my energy supply so I went back to my swim cursing myself for not having the rod with me when I went looking.

When I got back on the Friday, I soon found out that the Mug had been out the previous evening at 31lbs 12oz, out from the entrance of the first bay, so once again, my chance had gone. An easterly was blowing into the gate corner and it was still hot so I fished the first swim down past the snag bush. I walked a bait down the margin and placed it on the gravel shelf under the bush, along with 20 whole and chopped cream boilies.

The Big Fully-Scaled had come off this area earlier in the season, and in these conditions it looked prime for it. I found two clearings in the weed out in the bay and relaxed after a tiring week of working in the heat. Pigs and heat don't make a pleasant working environment!

I saw and heard the odd fish but it wasn't until first light that the margin rod wrapped round. Whatever was on the other end didn't want to give itself up and as I worked it back up my margin, it rolled over and I could see its heavily-scaled flanks. I hoped it was the Big Fully which could be over 30 by now, but as I jostled it into the net, I could see that it wasn't long enough and recognised it as my friend from the winter, this time a bit lower in weight at 23lbs 4oz.

With this disturbance and the wind swinging to a westerly I upped sticks and fished down on the bottom bank. The fish were going garrity on some naturals and I counted over 20 shows in half an hour that evening. I couldn't get a bite, but it wasn't for want of trying.

The red-hot conditions returned and, once again, there was an easterly come Friday so I repeated my traps in the same places as a week ago. This time, the take came an hour earlier at 4am off a small spot 20 yards out. It was an absolute ripper of a take and stripped line off me before weeding me solid. I kept the pressure on as I tried to budge it, but after ten minutes the line couldn't take the strain and parted. I was sick to the stomach because the most likely culprit of such speed and power was the Big Male. He hadn't been out for some time so he was due out as well.

September arrived and I headed back to Patshull. I had a blank weekend in the rain, fishing into a northerly in the Arches swim on the road bank, and I returned on a Saturday for a one-nighter. The lake was fairly busy, but Wayne Dunn was just vacating Road Point and as I hadn't fished the swim before and the odd fish was in the area, I jumped in. I put a line of bait out at 45 yards where the silt was slightly firmer, and stuck a slow-sinking bottom bait at each end. That evening and the following morning the odd fish quietly rolled.

Brian had gone next door and at 8.30am I felt my chance had gone, so with tea in hand I wandered in to see him. No sooner had I got there than my buzzer screamed and I sprinted back to my rods. There was no weed to worry about and I was super-keen to bend into my first Brummie carp. It came in fairly easily and, Brian slipped the net underneath it with a massive sigh of relief. It was a common, of course, and with it beating the 20lb barrier by 8oz, I was happy to break my duck.

Through the rest of September I carried on, a bit keener and more confident, but that was my one and only Patshull carp and the place wasn't quite living up to expectations, so I wasn't going to renew my ticket and was on the lookout for a new water to fish alongside Farmhouse; but where? I needed somewhere with at least a 30 or two in it, and a decent back-up stock, a bit closer to home would be beneficial as well.

Linear Fisheries had been running their day-ticket waters for a while but the following spring I got to hear of a three-lake syndicate they were running, and as Oxford is a bit closer than Wolverhampton, I arranged to meet Roy Parsons and have a look one evening.

It seemed quite a secure site and in the middle of nowhere so it was certainly peaceful and with not too many anglers about, my first impressions were good as Roy showed me round. It was the first lake, known as Yeomans, that caught my eye. It was the smallest of the three, but had done a common and a mirror over the 30 mark and although it didn't hold as many carp as the heavily-stocked Unity lake, the average size was much bigger. It was rumoured to hold a few originals, and as Linear had only been running the lakes for a year, there was potential for big, uncaught fish. A bit of unknown is always an extra-exciting incentive!

I wrote out a cheque for Roy, and as there was no close season, I could start straight away but because Farmhouse was shutting for the month of May, I wanted to fish on there for the remainder of April so I carried on blanking along with everyone else, with just the odd big chub falling to my rods, up to a monster of 7lb 2oz!

So, once May was with us, I hit the A40 to Witney and then the back roads to Guys. There were a few already fishing but when I spoke to them, it seemed that most of them struggled big time. The big, long island at the car park end was the biggest feature of the lake and this seemed to attract a lot of attention. Anglers were already moaning about the weed, and after a few casts it was apparent that there was weed coming up, but it was nowhere near as plentiful as the dense forests I'd been used to on Farmhouse and Frampton. After the weed-free Patshull, I was glad to have a bit of the green stuff to fish to and if this put off the other anglers then all the better.

I fished my first night at the far end of the island but with nothing doing and all the pressure around the island, I went for a good investigation of the top end come lunchtime. The far end bank was only about 50 yards long and was reed-lined and with no one there, it looked inviting.

As I rounded the corner, I saw a fish waddling up the margin so I quickly scaled a small sapling and after a couple of minutes a small group of carp came within no more than 10 feet from the bank. My mind raced as I formulated a plan. By setting up on top of them, I could possibly spook them because this bank was quite open. Opposite, though, was a swim from where I could fish the reed bed. I could cast 50 yards over on to the bank and then walk round and drop the rig in the margin onto a small gravel patch under the small overhanging tree that I'd been sitting in. Sorted. I packed my gear and moved into the new swim, cast a rig over to the far bank and then ran round, stepped into the margin, and lowered my rig in, along with a good handful of Scopex Cream baits in whole and chopped form. Another rod was fished to the reeds and I was set up and on fish.

Only about an hour had passed when the reeds rod wrapped round, catching me out as it sped into the reed bed. As hard as I tried, it wouldn't budge from my current position, so as it was only about four feet deep, I was forced to strip off and wade out along the reeds. As I got closer and achieved a better angle, the reeds started knocking and I jostled the carp out. With the odd reed wrapped round the line I was now back in contact and soon had the fish under my feet and in the net. It was only a double-figure common, but it was a start and I didn't have long to wait as the far margin rod accounted for two more doubles, and I also had one fall off.

It was the first lake, Yeomans, that caught my eye.

I didn't have long to wait.

From what I could gather, the Big Common seemed to get caught at the car park end around the island. It was always busy and most caught bugger-all, but over the next few trips while fishing the open water, I had action every time, with a funny-mouthed, scaly 22-pounder the best of the bunch. It was a lot easier than Farmhouse but apart from the two 30s, the common around 33/34, and the short, fat linear at just over 30, the majority of stock seemed to be doubles, with 20s few and far between. These were the stocked fish and I did start to worry about the lack of originals that were in the lake.

Farmhouse opened again on June the 1st and I went back, hoping for my long awaited 30-pounder. I managed to nail the Big Common off the bottom bank after a couple of trips and although he put up a fierce battle, and had torn off at lightning speed, he only went 24lbs 8oz, so I was still waiting for one of those big girls.

I carried on through the summer doing most weekends but Farmhouse was very weedy and was dead for weeks at a time. I went back to Yeomans for another go and on a cooler, wet weekend I caught from a very tiny silt strip among the grassy weed. I hooked one fish that I couldn't do anything with. It ripped line off as it ran away from me and up to the right and when I eventually stopped it, and got it coming back, my stomach churned as it all went slack and I wound in the lead, minus the fish. I'd hooked something special and I dearly wanted revenge.

Despite not fishing many weekends, it appeared that I was top rod and I'd only had one blank out of about seven trips. Work commitments caused me to miss a couple of weekends at the end of August, and plodding on at Farmhouse, I was seriously questioning whether my time would be better spent elsewhere. It looked like I'd have to travel, so after hearing tales of Yateley from my brother Paul, who had done a few weekends on Farmhouse with me, I started to give the idea of returning to my roots some serious thought.

When I returned in October, a strong wind was tanking up the top end of Yeomans so I got back into the Tall Reeds swim, a couple up from the island and where I'd caught a few and had lost that runaway express train from the silty strip. On dusk, a couple of fish stuck their heads out in the waves, and I went to bed quite confident.

A scaly 22-pounder, the best of the bunch.

I managed to nail the Big Common.

Another double rattled off at breakfast time, and at lunchtime I repositioned my hookbaits and topped up with boilies. At about 4pm, the right-hand rod went into meltdown and, once again, I was connected to a fish with immense power. I could only guess that it was the same fish I'd lost, because it fought in exactly the same way, and this time I didn't want a repeat of our previous encounter.

The weed had all died back so it was just a question of tiring out the fish; that was until it decided to get into the reed bed up in the margin. With my boots on, I managed to stretch out far enough and as each kick had less oomph to it, I was slowly winning. A pale mirror rolled over and as I pushed the net out it finally gave up and was beaten. It wasn't the mythical beast that I'd hoped for, but at an ounce over 25lbs it was my heaviest fish since leaving Frampton.

Although I'd enjoyed my last two seasons, it only proved the point that you've got to be on the right waters to give yourself a fighting chance of the big 'uns. Time to step up a gear and push on from where I'd left off at Frampton.

It wasn't the mythical beast that I'd hoped for.

Chapter 6 - Back home to Yateley - The Match Lake

After a couple of seasons fishing away from Frampton, I was still waiting for that next 30-pounder. Although Farmhouse, Patshull and Yeomans had all contained 30s, they were thin on the ground and it was probably only the Mug in Farmhouse that was capable of giving me the new personal best I yearned for. I felt I needed to get myself on a water where the chance of better fish was much greater.

A good head of upper 20s and a few 30s was the sort of stock I was looking for, but where to go? There was certainly nowhere locally, so I was going to have to travel. A return to Yateley seemed to be the obvious choice because the ticket covered the whole complex in those days, so I always had the option to fish whichever lake I fancied.

Although the lure of a real whacker was a possibility if I chose to fish the Car Park, North or Pads lakes, I felt it would be wiser to start on the Match Lake and if successful, work my way up the Yateley ladder, one rung at a time. I did give the Pads Lake some thought, but Jumbo was down in weight at around 35lbs and there were fish to almost that weight in the Match, as well as a lot more back-up fish, whereas the Pads only had five carp in total. A real ballbreaker of a lake!

Yateley stayed open all year round, for the second time since the abolition of the enforced close season, and I could start my campaign in April, so on the first Friday of that month I undertook the 100-mile drive east, and an hour and three-quarters later, I arrived at the Match Lake car park.

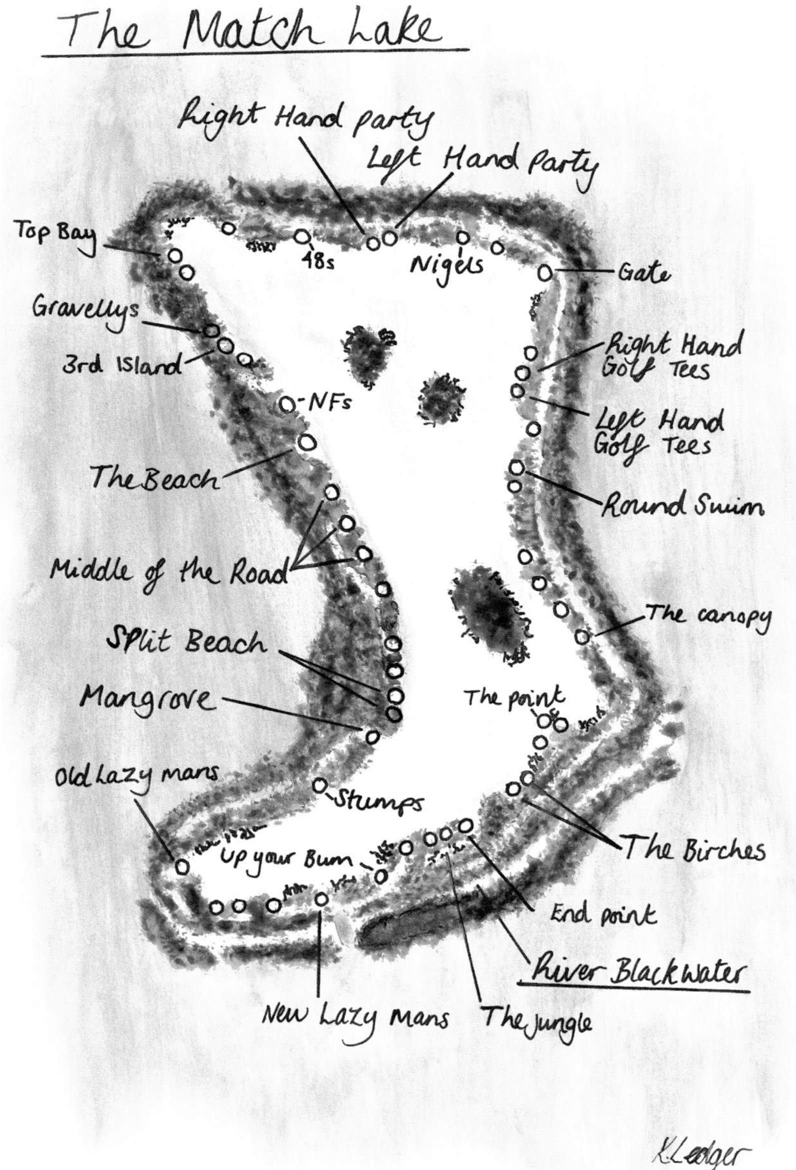

The Match Lake

Right Hand party

Left Hand Party

Top Bay

48s

Nigels

Gate

Gravellys

3rd Island

Right Hand Golf Tees

Left Hand Golf Tees

NFs

The Beach

Round Swim

Middle of the Road

Split Beach

The canopy

Mangrove

The point

Old Lazy mans

Stumps

The Birches

Up your Bum

End point

River Blackwater

New Lazy mans

The Jungle

K.Ledger

Eight years had passed since my last visit, when I'd fished the Nursery Lake for the first week of the season as I finished my GCSE exams. Not a lot had changed, apart from a new footbridge where we used to stash our bikes in the undergrowth, as me and my mate wandered the banks after school in the old days.

The lake had not changed at all, though, and as I stood gazing up the bottom bay, with the old familiar smell of the River Blackwater behind me wafting up my nostrils, I felt for the first time since I'd left Frampton that I was happy to be home and it was just like slipping on a pair of old, comfy slippers as I slowly crept round. The trees were in bud and everything was fresh and alive; it was good to be back.

My brother, Paul, as well as Lee, Odd and Woggy all fished the Match Lake so I'd be able to get up to date info, and I'd gone in with them on the same bait that they'd caught well on and so my Fish and Blood base mix was rolled up with Fresh Orange flavour. It became apparent that it wasn't just the Match Lake carp that loved their fruity fishmeals but it was the Match carp that I was concentrating on for now, and at least I knew my bait would work. That's always a nagging factor in the back of your mind when venturing on a new water.

There were a few bivvies dotted around, but with a light westerly breeze ruffling up the far end, I plumped for the left Party Swim. There was an island straight out to my right, and a channel between that and the Golf Tees island, as well as the open water in front, so I had a decent area with varying features to get to grips with, and so with the marker rod out, my long Yateley journey began.

The Match has a pretty uniformed bottom in terms of depth. The make-up of the lake bed varies in grades of silt, and smooth to rough gravel. I found two areas at 30 and 40 yards where the rough gravel went smooth before pulling into silt, so I cast both rods with Amnesia stiff rigs and bottom baits, and then took in the atmosphere of being back at the Mecca.

The only thing to trigger my buzzers that first weekend was a tench, but it did manage to get the heart thumping, if only briefly, such was the anticipation of that first Yateley carp. I had a good wander round on the Saturday, reacquainting myself with the swims, and all the anglers were friendly and chatty which made the whole Yateley experience pleasurable.

I couldn't wait to get back and as I crossed the bridge the following week, the wind hit me in the face as I wandered up to the out-of-bounds Jungle, an overgrown tiny bay with trees in the water, the carp's safe sanctuary. The wind was pushing into the mouth of the Jungle and I could see that the right-hand Mangrove swim opposite was free so I hurried round with my bucket. I found Woggy in the left-hand Mangrove, with a can of Stella in his hand as usual so I'd have some good company, as well as the chance of a fish.

Although the odd carp was coming out, they certainly weren't really having it so I kept baiting fairly light, to just 20 or 30 baits around each. I did have an occurrence that weekend on the rod fished three-quarters of the way across to the Jungle. It pulled up tight but on bending into it I hit thin air, with no connection whatsoever; a liner, most likely. I recast to the same spot and it soon pulled up again but this time I was treated to one of the Match Lake's slabs.

On the Saturday evening, I did get to see one of the biggies on the bank as Munchkin landed Scaley from the Split Beach and the sight of Scaley only added to my desire for a Yateley carp.

I returned the following week and after finding nothing after a look round, I dropped back into the Mangrove. On Saturday mornings a few of us visited the local café for breakfast. The afternoons were good on the Match, so it made sense to wind in at nine'ish, shoot up to the café, have brekkie, go to Tesco Express for fresh milk and supplies and be back to the lake with baits back on the spots by half-past eleven or so.

I decided on a move because the bottom bay was rammed out so I headed up to the NF swim on the Tri-Lakes bank. My efforts were rewarded with another bream in the middle of the night. Why is it, when you are fishing tight to an island, which is a tricky enough cast in daylight, that a poxy bream has to wait until after dark before playing a tune on your buzzers?

It was my birthday on the Thursday, and I hoped I could bag myself a late present when I returned on the Friday. After a rather unpleasant long drive in the rain on

the Friday afternoon, I arrived to find out that the bottom bay had done a couple of fish that day, so with a wet southerly picking up pace and driving into the bay, I set up camp in the Stumps swim almost opposite the bridge. I cast my marker over to the far side and drew it back in search of something significant to place my baits on. After a few casts it just seemed smooth all over; mmm!

Feeling the marker land, I could tell how soft or hard the lakebed was, so changing from dragging the lead, I lifted it in a jerky motion, feeling for the 'bump' as it hit anything firm. With a stiff marker rod and braid, I could decipher the hardness of the bottom. My new method soon found me a couple of hard spots among the softer bottom, and casting bottom baits tight to the float until I got a crackdown, hopefully I was on spots that had been grazed off. Just 30 baits catapulted tight to the float and my traps were set.

The rain turned to drizzle but the fresh breeze still pushed down the bay. The lake seemed a bit quieter for a Friday night so perhaps the rain had done a good job by keeping a few anglers away. I'd just climbed in the sleeping bag at about half-past ten when I heard a fish crash out but I was soon crouching by the rods as the ripples started to lap in. It wasn't far out and with my two rigs at only 25 and 35 yards, I was on fish for the first time. I made tea and sat at the front of the swim, hoping to see another one, but soon tiredness got the better of me and I succumbed to the draw of my comfy, warm sleeping bag.

At 1.40am, the right-hand rod pulled up and the clutch began ticking. I scrambled to the rod and it lurched over to a satisfying curve as solid resistance was felt. The whole time I was playing it, I prayed it wasn't one of the lake's many catfish because the fish was quite powerful and refused to give up easily. As it neared the margin, it kept swirling up before plunging back to the bottom and in the moonlight it looked quite pale. Eventually, it came close enough and as it hit the surface I scooped it up in the net.

I feared it was a catfish but as I peered into the net, the unmistakable shape of a carp lay there in the folds. Wicked; my first Yateley carp and a special moment. I weighed it by myself at 21lb 4oz and I could see that it was definitely a Match Lake original because of its tiny fins. I slipped it in the sack until daylight. I'd had my belated birthday present on my seventh night and it was time to celebrate with a hot cup of tea, but first I put on a new rig and cast back onto my nice, hard spot. Finding that spot could well have been key to the capture, and at least I had a method to find those little spots. I got the photos done when it was light enough, and the fish was identified as Ribs, named because the marks on its side looked like rib lines.

The sight of Scaley only added to my desire for a Yateley carp.

I certainly enjoyed my café breakfast that morning, and treated myself to mushrooms because I'd caught, the old Savay tradition of only having mushrooms when you'd been successful. I was keen to get back so I raced to the lake in double-quick time and with two good cracks of the leads, I topped up my spots with another 30 baits.

At 1pm, the same rod was away again. This time it definitely felt like a carp and when a big yellow belly rolled over I could see it was a bigger fish than Ribs. A nervous couple of minutes followed as it ploughed up and down in close, and soon after my second Match Lake carp was resting in the net. What's that old saying about buses?

The bottom lobe of its tail was missing so I knew it was one of the two Scissor fish, and at 27lb 12oz, it turned out to be Little Scissors. This was my biggest fish since Frampton so after sacking it in deep water, my feet hardly touched the floor as I almost floated up to the Copse Lake to get my brother to take the photos. It proved to be a bit lively on the mat, but I managed to hold her still long enough to get a few shots before proudly lowering her back into the cool margins. With a flick of her half tail she was gone, no doubt off to the sanctuary of the jungle to nurse her sore lip. I couldn't manage the hat-trick that night but I wasn't bothered, I was more than happy with my lot. The drive home was the best journey back by far.

I almost floated up to the Copse Lake.

It was definitely a Match Lake original!

My third mirror lay beaten in the net.

The next two of trips followed the pattern of a couple of tench and a brace of bream. The only carpy action ended in disaster. In the early hours, fishing tight to the island in the Party swim, I got cut off as the fish surged up the side of the island. It was probably a mussel on the underwater branches that had cut my 15lb main line.

The middle of May produced a mini-heatwave and there were a few fish cruising between the top two islands. The Party swim was already occupied so I dropped into the NF swim. The weather was hot and sticky, but a thunderstorm on the Friday evening helped to freshen things up a tad. As was now the norm, I had a bream and a tench but at 1.30am on the Saturday night I ran to the rods to find the left-hand one with a much more alarming bend in it as I was locked up under the bushes of the left-hand island. It was a really mild night and the silence was only broken by the hooked carp boiling up in a bid for its freedom. Soon, my third mirror lay beaten in the net and although not a monster it certainly looked a 20, which the scales soon confirmed at 21lb 2oz.

That morning I learned that Dropscale had finally been caught after proving elusive for quite some time and at 33lb 5oz had come out from the Party swim, so it was only a matter of yards from the areas I was fishing from the NF. It could quite easily have been me with Dropscale and the other guy with the 20, but I was happy to be catching and my confidence was increasing with every trip. The next day I learned that Thompsons had come out of the top bay at 34lbs, so all three big'uns were in the 32 to 34lb bracket and that gave me a good goal to chase.

Farmhouse reopened on June the 1st and I planned to do a couple of trips on there in search of the Mug, which was unfinished business, and all three of the Match lake big'uns were below my PB, so either the Mug or the Male would give me the chance to up my personal best of the Brown One at 34lb 8oz.

I had to work on the May bank holiday so it wasn't until Friday the 13th, after two unsuccessful trips to Farmhouse, that I returned to Yateley. Farmhouse still hadn't done a fish so with the Yateley bug biting and the knowledge that Scaley had come out to Rick at 33lb 4oz, up a pound or so, I was keen to get back after Thompsons and Dropscale, both of which could be getting close to mid-30.

I dropped in to the NF swim.

I was straight back into action with a solid 25lb 6oz mirror.

The weather was hot but a fresh south-westerly was pushing up the top end. The Copse Lake bank was full, as was the NF and Gravelly, so I fished in the third Middle of the Road swim for the first time. A good-sized weed bed was growing up and I placed two hookbaits with 60 baits around each one, tight to the weed on the hard spots, after the float had been jerked out of the weed to fall vertically onto smooth, clean gravel.

On Friday evening, I was straight back into the action with a solid 25lb 6oz mirror and plenty of bites followed over the next two days, but somehow four roach managed to get an 18mm boilie in their mouths, and with a bream and two 5lb stockies, it turned out to be a mixed bag of a weekend. The open water swims seemed to be the best bet in the daytime. Most of the night bites came from the islands as the fish moved out of the weedbeds on dusk.

My next bite came the following weekend, just after dark, from the NF swim, tight to the back of the Golf Tees island. It felt like a good fish and as it kept on trying to get down to the left, I waded out, up to my knees. It was almost beaten but then it made one last dash down the margin and the bloody hook fell out.

I fished in the Third Middle of the Road for the first time.

I was gutted to lose the fish and there was no way I could get my hookbait back under the bush on the island in the dark. I didn't want to risk sticking it in the trees, so I had to settle for casting it out to the end of the island. I wasn't a happy chappy and I climbed into the bag to sulk. I stayed in that mood all the way home the next morning.

I spent the next couple of trips in the Party swim, the first one sheltering from the persistent rain and with a westerly blowing straight in, it wasn't the most pleasant weekend's fishing. The following week was much drier, though, and on the first night, I heard a fish under the right-hand margin bushes; that muffled sound when you know they are right under the canopy, before ripples start to emerge.

After the café on the Saturday, I took extra time to get the rig in the tiny hole that enabled me to get right under the bush. As it soared in, I let the rod tip go forward with it so not to alter the angle as it travelled and it donked in - the perfect cast. It was time to sit back and hope the fish would revisit the spot that night.

Just on dark at about 10.15pm, that bait was picked up and the line went bowstring tight. I walked back and after much kicking and twisting from the hooked fish, I managed to get it out into the safety of open water. I soon had it in close but had a feeling that it wasn't that big and after it had taken a couple of dashes up the margin, I had a small mirror in the net. At 16lb 12oz, it was one of the lake's smallest originals but a carp's a carp and after losing that last one in the NF, I was just relieved to get one in the net. A couple of hours later, the other rod screamed off but this turned out to be my first catfish, or should I say kitten because it was only about 8lbs.

A spell of really hot weather was coming in and the fish were all just sitting about in the weedbeds so when I returned on the Friday, I spent the weekend in the shade of the left-hand Golf Tees swim. Despite carp being in the area, they showed no sign of feeding and with Odd next door it was more of a social session.

During my time on Farmhouse I'd met a group of lads who'd been fishing days on the famous Savay Lake. They now had syndicate tickets and I'd decided to try my luck this season, doing a few days and hoping to get a syndicate ticket one day. I bought my days-only permit and as it was the Looney Rota weekend and my mate Hugh was fishing, I made the long journey to Savay.

Wow! What a lake! It was a bright, sunny day as I mooched around and The Cottage Bay looked stunning. Mature trees encased the glistening water that held some of the oldest and most famous fish in the land. As I stood in the famous Point swim, I had flashbacks from all the stories I'd read; Hutchie in the all-time classic 'The Carp Strikes

Savay. Wow! What a lake.

Back', and Maylin's tales from 'Tiger Bay'. I wandered up to Alcatraz before turning back and making my way around the North Bay and up the very long canal bank. I still hadn't bumped into a soul, but as I got halfway down the canal bank I spotted a bivvy and as I went further down I found Hugh and a few others down at the far end.

Hugh suggested I drop in up to his right in the Roach swim, and suggested that the area to fish was toward a feature known as the 'peacock tree' at about 80 yards. I quickly got two baits on and dispatched them there, getting a nice drop, and when a fish showed on the back of this area, I certainly got excited. I'd wanted to use an instant, high-attract bait because I was fishing for just a bite on the short days, so my old faithful Dairy Cream with Scopex was the chosen bait. It's an instant flavour and as it's a pale yellow, I hoped I could tempt a Savay carp to dip down and pick up one or two.

The only downside to Savay is that you have to be out of the gate by 9pm, so the quick evening session flew by and I was loaded back on the barrow at 8.45pm. There were fish in the area, but I had a syndicate member moving in behind me, so there was no chance of dropping back in the following morning.

I left most of my gear with Hugh, legged it back to the car, nipped into the chippy in Harefield for some food, and then found the gate to Pit 4, for which Hugh had given me a key. I parked up at the top of the lane and tried to get my head down on the back seat, but it was bloody uncomfortable and really cold in the car, despite being mid-July, and I just couldn't get to sleep.

After what had seemed a never-ending night, I was back at the gate for 6am and with my gear already on the canal bank, I raced round and set up right at the far end in a swim called The Dustbin which is between the famous Birches, where Hutchie did so well, and the Sluices. Hutchy used to catch them on a north-westerly and with the wind in this direction I hoped for some action.

Temperatures were rising dramatically and a daytime bite looked unlikely. I wasn't looking forward to a second night in the car, so I headed off to Yateley mid-afternoon and had a much-needed, good night's kip, set-up in the First Middle of the Road swim. I gave it until lunchtime because fish could be seen rocking in the weedbed, but eventually, I had to admit defeat and go home to do the afternoon feed on the farm.

The following week, it being the Toad Rota on Savay, I went back to the Match Lake and found Woggy in the Third Island swim. I climbed the tree next door, in the Gravelly, and saw that the weed out in front was alive with carp so I quickly scuttled down, put a bucket in the Gravelly, and huffed and puffed as I raced back to the car to grab my gear. With so many fish about, I dispensed with the marker rod and after checking the weedbed and the whereabouts of the majority of the carp, I flicked both baits tight to the weedbeds and after a good drop followed by a donk, I put just 20 baits around each.

In the meantime, Woggy had a screamer, and as he is as deaf as a post, I had to shout to tell him he had a run as he stood behind me oblivious to the fact that his rod was

in meltdown. A 24-pounder was soon bundled into the net and I only had to wait until 6.15pm myself before my right-hand rod, which was 20 yards out, bent round at an alarming rate, before pinging out of the clip and hurtling off. With so much weed about, I had to play it a bit heavy at first but once it was in close I could ease off a bit and played it under the tip. It looked like a 20-pounder and as Woggy netted it, I peered in and recognised it as the Big Twin, the same fish I'd had in May from the NF. It was my first repeat capture, which was a bit disappointing, but with so many carp in the area and the rest of the weekend ahead I thought I'd get more chances. I think the disturbance of two fish getting hooked had put the others on edge, though, and as Saturday dawned cooler and windier, the carp drifted away from my weedbeds and no more chances came our way.

The Loonies were back on rota, so I decided to have another crack at Savay but so I'd only have to have one night in the car, I thought better of battling the Friday afternoon traffic and instead got up early Saturday and left home about 4.15am to get to the gate for 6am. The various speed cameras on the A40 kept me alert so I didn't nod off at the wheel, and the roads were nice and quiet, so I made good time despite me questioning my own sanity for driving this far, at an ungodly hour to do a day session. I certainly hoped the carp would reward my efforts.

I arrived at the gate about ten to six and I was first in the queue. At 6 o'clock, I was in and a quick look in the Cottage Bay revealed it to be empty. I didn't want to waste vital time travelling right round the lake and felt the Cottage would be a good shout if I could get some baits in quickly before the sun got too high and too hot. I plumped for the Middle Rat Hole swim but as I put baits on, I heard a fish go over to my left, so I legged it into the Boards swim next door, and seeing the frothy patch in the middle of some rings 40 yards out, I grabbed my rods and cast a bait straight on top of it, praying for a drop. I got one and a nice thud as the lead hit what felt like sand. The other rod was cast to the right of that and a bit further out. I grabbed the rest of the gear, both baits were out with 10 freebies 'pulted out round each and I was fishing by half-past six. With the odd bubble popping the surface, I sat back and got a much needed first brew of the day on the go.

There was a clear blue sky, it was set to be a glorious day and although I was knackered it was nice to sit quietly by such a beautiful lake. At 7.30am the silence was broken by the clutch whizzing, as the bait that I'd cast to the showing fish was picked up. Nervously, I played it in and managed to stop it from getting bogged down in the weed. With the other rod tip dropped out of the way, the fish boiled up under the tip and I could see a common scaling.

I legged it in to the Boards swim.

The carbon soon subdued my first Savay carp and as I guided it toward me I lifted the net around it and there, less than four months after my first Yateley carp, was a Savay common. It definitely wasn't Sally, queen of the valley, but perhaps her daughter! I secured it in the net, and ran off to get some assistance; although it was no monster, I wanted a photo of this moment.

I found a couple of syndicate members up in the shallows and one of them kindly came with me to take a photo. At 16lb 6oz, it wasn't the stamp of carp I was after but the other chap informed me that the small commons were harder to catch than the big mirrors. Mmm, I think I'd prefer to have caught an 'easier' mirror. The disturbance made by the common as it charged off put an end to any more action, plus it took me three casts to drop back on to the firm, clean spot because of the weed, so I was lucky earlier to have got a donk first cast. Some things are meant to happen, eh?

In the heat of the afternoon, I wound in and went off to find Hugh to inform him of my success before returning to get the rods out for the evening and that night I kipped on the bedchair next to the car, getting a much better sleep than on the back seat. I was so tired from my early start that I could have fallen asleep standing up! I was back in the Boards at six, but nothing showed so I headed off back to Gloucester at lunchtime.

The weather stayed hot so I returned to the Match and it was a joy to fish all night without the tiring packing up, and kipping in the car business in the August heatwave weather we were experiencing. I fished in the NF but it was a quiet weekend all round, and I just sat in the heat and told everyone about my Savay trips. Savay is such a historic venue that my mates were all ears and full of questions.

Mid-August is harvest time, and that meant I couldn't fish the weekend after because we'd be getting in several lorry loads of straw for the year ahead. This was one of the jobs I hated because I'd sweat my nuts off, and after throwing a few hundred bales my tendons in my wrists would usually start pinging like guitar strings. It wasn't nice, but a necessary evil of the job.

I watched the weather forecast over the following week and a south-westerly wind was predicted for the Saturday. It was still warm and dry so I fancied somewhere up at the top bay end.

I arrived at a busy lake but I was pleased to see the Forty Eights swim vacant and wasted no time securing it for myself. There was someone in the Gravelly opposite so I felt it best not to fish straight out but instead fished one left and one down to the right. I found two cracking hard spots; the right-hand one, a smooth spot just my side of a very bumpy bar, and the left- hand one was like pulling across glass, tight to the weedbed. I was woken by a screamer at dawn but something didn't feel right and soon a big, long slug, which weighed 22½lbs in the net, slithered off.

As predicted, the wind sprang up and when I returned from the café, I got the rigs bang on again and paid particular attention to catapulting my 60 baits accurately; they all landed in a tight area.

At half-past eleven that night, the left-hand line pulled out of the clip and I pounced on the rod, holding firm as the fish tried burying itself in the weedbed. Once away from the weed, its head must have been clean because it fought hard with powerful surges and it certainly felt like a good fish. I waded out a couple of steps and in the moonlight I saw it give up and wallow on the top.

As its back broke the surface, I could see it was a big 20, at least as it slid into the net. I flicked on a head torch and the mark on its side clearly identified it as the unfortunately named Zit fish. The Zit had gone 30 in the spring but since spawning it had dropped a couple of pounds or so and became my second fish at 27lb 12oz.

It definitely wasn't Sally, queen of the valley.

The weather stayed mild and a medium-to-strong south-westerly was blowing. I couldn't believe my luck when the Forty Eights was free on my return the following weekend. Knowing my spots, I soon had the rigs on the money and this time I'd upped the level of boilies to 75 per rod. I'd also glugged the freebies in the liquid DNA lactose that I had included in my bait and this gave them an instant, sweet aroma with extra pulling power.

Later that afternoon, as Lee turned up for his weekend on the Copse, the left-hand rod let rip again and I endured the hardest scrap I'd had from a Match Lake carp. A good 20 minutes passed before it finally gave up, and when Lee informed me I'd caught Dropscale I was ecstatic. Not only was it a long-awaited 30-pounder, but it looked solid and could be close to a PB. Weirdly, Dropscale was hooked firmly in the top lip, the stiffness of the Amnesia rig having kicked the hook round into the roof of its mouth as it tried to eject it, but fortunately for me, it had failed in its objective. I could see where the needle was settling but I let Lee read it out and at 34lb 9oz, the verdict was a personal best by an ounce, and the heaviest carp the Match Lake had produced that year. With photos done and Dropscale slipped back, I sat back to bask in my glory and, Yateley being Yateley, a constant stream of visitors came to offer congratulations that evening and the kettle stayed on non-stop.

At half past ten, the right-hand rod screamed off and took 20 yards of line straight off me, only for the hook to pull out. Still on a high, I wasn't too despondent and made sure to get it bang on the spot which it cracked down on even better than before. I topped up with a few more pouchloads of boilies and got my head down for the night.

My belly was telling me that it was café time so I checked the watch to find it was 9am. I decided to give it another ten minutes and was rewarded when the recast rod from the night before wrapped round. This time, the hook stayed put and Scale on the Shoulder at 25lb 14oz became my second carp of the session. I was certainly liking the Forty Eights swim.

Breakfast that morning tasted better than ever and the mushrooms went down a treat. I was keen to get straight back and I didn't have to wait too much longer. While listening to the footy that afternoon the left-hand rod made it two takes all, and a little 16lb 2oz mirror completed my hat-trick before the half-time whistle.

Lee informed me it was Dropscale. I was ecstatic!

131

Fish were showing behind my right-hand spot in the weedbed all evening and it was only a matter of time on current form before it went. I waited expectantly, with bated breath. It melted off at 9.45 that evening, the fish tearing straight into the weedbed as it stormed off. As I brought it back through the weed, once again the hook just fell out. I was peeved to have lost another one but that's fishing in heavy weed for you and you can't win them all.

Just a catfish had me up that night, but before breakfast I landed a little 12lb stockie common and then, moments later, the other rod tore off and this felt like a right whacker - until an underwater moggy swirled up entangled in line. It hadn't actually picked up the hook bait but was trailing, so the least I could do was relieve it of the rig and the yards of line. This was my good deed for the day, paying the lake back for a terrific session.

September was now upon us - 24lbs 5oz.

I was certainly liking the Forty Eights swim.

The wind was swinging round to a south-easterly and this signalled the end of the action so I headed home, a very happy chappy, only to find out when I switched on the car radio that the nation was in turmoil because Princess Diana had been killed in a car accident. They say you always remember where you were and what you were doing at historic moments like that, and I'd had the best weekend's fishing on the Match Lake!

September was now upon us and the wind was still pushing predominately from the south-west. I carried on fishing in the Forty Eights, taking a 24lb 5oz mirror and losing two the following trip. Both losses were hook pulls so I changed my hook pattern to a wider-gaped hook that I hoped would give a much better hook hold and stay in.

On the third weekend of the month there was an easterly wind so I plumped for the First Middle of the Road swim. The lake had gone dead apart from a 25-pounder out of the Gravelly, so I went for a mooch on the Saturday afternoon and after finding out that a couple of fish had been heard right up in the top bay, I upped sticks and moved to the very end swim.

An impressive beast. Bloody ugly though!

I cast into a hole in the bushes to land right up on the marginal shelf and I bagged a 19lb 12oz mirror at 1.45am that night. It was quite tight up in the end of the bay so it proved to be quite an exhilarating fight in the enclosed space, with snags and bushes to both sides. I liked the top bay and when conditions were prime for it, then I'd certainly be getting straight in there in the future.

My only battle on the last weekend of September was with a monster catfish. By much shaking of the net, I just managed to squeeze it in, all 31½lbs of it. It wasn't what I was after but it was an impressive beast all the same, with immense power. Bloody ugly though!

October is often a blowy month but there was not a breath of wind when I pulled back into the car park on Friday. I found a few fish mooching in the now dying weedbeds down to the right of the Forty Eights swim, and as I had so much confidence fishing my spots I dropped back in there. Starting with a stockie common that night, I only had to wait till the hot time on Saturday which was during half-time of the football, and I banked my thirteenth Yateley original mirror at 23lbs 12oz from the consistent right-hand spot. Another couple of stockie commons fell to my sticks that night, but at 10.10am the following morning, I lost yet another fish. I was starting to wonder if it was the stiffness of the hook link that was giving me inconsistent hook holds, as opposed to the wrong-shaped hook pattern.

That was the last action of the month. The next couple of trips proved fruitless and the last weekend of the month saw me take another trip to Savay. This time I tried my luck in the North Bay, and despite seeing one crash out I had an unproductive trip.

With the onset of November, the first frosts hit and with fog about as well conditions were far from ideal but on the Sunday morning Odd managed a nice 28lb 4oz mirror out of Nigel's, while I was next door in the Party.

The next week, I chose the top bay and was rewarded that first evening with an 18lb 2oz mirror over 40 baits, so they were still feeding despite the much colder conditions. The south-west wind really picked up from midnight and I was well confident of more action, and at 8.30am I was in again.

My thirteenth Yateley original mirror.

I managed to jostle carp and branch into the net.

I managed to get the fish away from the snag but something wasn't quite right and as I pulled harder the carp could be seen bobbing on the surface. Another line was heading up into the tree; someone must have pulled for a break after casting into the tree and my fish had picked up the trailing line. I was now in a stalemate situation so I shouted for help. A bloke who I'd never seen before turned up and on seeing my predicament, he ran round, climbed into the tree and managed to snap off the offending branch. I then played in the carp, branch and trailing line. Fortunately, I had no further problems because the fish was knackered by this stage, and I managed to jostle carp and branch into the net. At 22lb 6oz, this was my fifteenth fish and turned out to be the last one of the year.

I had a guest trip on Savay for which I had the luxury of being able to do the nights now the rotas had merged, and another couple of unsuccessful trips back on the Match. It was soon Christmas, but I'd had a good year and the decision to return to Yateley had been the right one. I had a new PB under my belt and it was time to take the next step up the Yateley ladder. Thoughts of the Copse Lake's historic old mirrors started to occupy my thoughts … and my dreams.

It was soon Christmas. Odd with the Roach for a present.

Chapter 7 - Copse Lake

After a good season on the Match, the natural progression was to move on to the Copse Lake. The Yateley way was to fish the Match and Copse, which served an apprenticeship, before 'going over the road' to fish the elite waters. The Pads and North lakes were usually the next step before the ultimate - the Car Park Lake.

The Pads Lake was in demise because Jumbo had dropped from being in the 40s down to about 36lbs. In fact, the Pads was drained that year and the fish were moved to the North Lake. Not that this had a beneficial effect on Jumbo, who soon died in his new home. Henry didn't even make the transition; when netted he was wasting away and was in such a bad state that he had to be put out of his misery. Scale on the Shoulder was enjoying her new home, though, and with no Snake left in the North, she was now the next back-up fish behind Bazil.

At this stage I wasn't sure if I wanted to fish the Car Park Lake or indeed if I was ready for it (is anyone?), but the North was a beautiful lake and had the most famous carp in the land swimming in it, so after the Copse this was to be my destination. After all Baz wouldn't be around forever!

Talking of beautiful lakes, there are not many better looking than the picturesque Copse Lake. It's shallow and riddled with features, so it would be a good grounding for the North Lake. I'd spent my childhood living in the outskirts of Yateley and I'd fished all the lakes at some point, apart from the Copse. Not all of them for carp, but I had fished for tench, pike, or just generally coarse fished.

The Copse Lake

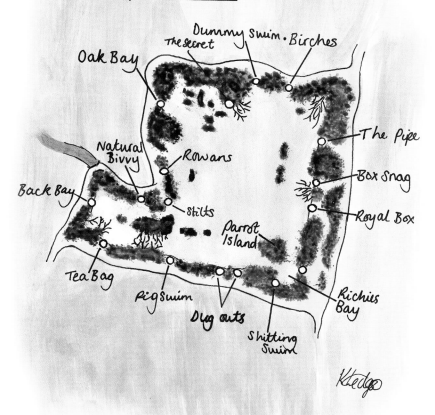

Oak Bay

The secret

Dummy Swim · Birches

The Pipe

Natural Bivvy

Rowans

Box Snag

Back Bay

Stilts

Royal Box

Parrot Island

Tea Bag

Pig Swim

Dug outs

Richies Bay

Shitting Swim

Ktedge

The last year before we moved away, when I was 15, I often used to walk the lakes after school and in particular the neighbouring Nursery Lake. Being a mega-keen youngster, I'd stop to talk to the Copse Lake anglers and one day I was chatting to this guy with long blonde hair when I said I'd heard that Ritchie McDonald was fishing the lake, only for the guy to inform me that he was Ritchie. Whoops! I'd only seen pictures of Ritchie when he'd had Bazil so I didn't recognize him after his image change. From that day on, I always stopped for a chat, and he always seemed to be there. His stories fascinated me and he was so free with tips and information that I'd often be late home for tea.

The icing on the cake was when I found him stalking in the Back Bay, not from the Natural Bivvy, or Umbrella swim as it used to be called, but under the canopy of an overhanging tree down to the right. With his waggler-fished Tropicano boilie in position, he sent me up the silver birch tree to relay the fish's whereabouts. The Parrot and another large mirror were circling the bay before heading under the bush to where Ritchie lay in wait.

I'll never forget getting down from the tree and wandering round and hearing him announce quietly that he had hooked one. He was calmness personified, while I ran about like a headless chicken to grab the net from the next swim. At this point, the carp decided it didn't like plodding about under the tip and headed out into the bay, so Ritchie took to the water and followed it out under the bushes. As he made his way through the shallow bay toward the end swim, I legged it round with the net and was just stripping off, but the mirror was coughing water, so I just needed to toss the net to the master, who scooped it up.

I was about to feast my eyes on a Copse Lake mirror for the first time, and not only that but I'd played a small part in helping one of England's finest anglers to land the fish. Mickey Gray came round from the Pig swim so I stood back and let the pros sort out the fish, which they told me was called Crinkle Tail, and if I remember correctly, it weighed 30lbs 10oz. I was in awe of the fish and didn't realise the blood, sweat and tears that would go into me trying to catch old Crinkle many years later.

That spring, things were a bit different to the last when the whole of the Yateley complex had stayed open. It had been great for the angler, but it wasn't the perfect situation for these old Yateley warriors. I'd enjoyed my time on the Match Lake and although the lake was always busy, and quite a lot of fish were caught, they probably didn't get a pasting like the old girls over the road. There was a perception of an 'easy 40' in the 'silly spring', so the Pads, North and Car Park were under relentless pressure and the likes of poor old Bazil seemed to be coming out on an almost weekly basis.

Fortunately for the long term health of the fish, Leisure Sport, who were running the lakes, imposed a close season throughout April and May, a two-month break for the carp, which in hindsight I feel was the best move and prolonged the lives of these great fish.

Things were to be a little different over on the east side of the road, too, because although night fishing was being stopped for the months of April and May, we could still day fish both the Match and Copse lakes. The previous season, I'd had the majority of my fish in the daytime, and I was in touch with the Copse Lake carps' feeding times and habits, so I felt I could still catch on both lakes, despite the limited rod hours over a weekend. However, I wanted to get my feet under the table, so to speak, with a few nights on the Copse before the night ban came in.

My fires were well and truly ignited for the tricky Copse mirrors when I saw Crinkle Tail on the bank again. My very good friend, Lee Picknell, caught her one very wet and windy Saturday night at the start of March from the Natural Bivvy swim in the Back Bay, so completing his hat-trick of Copse mirrors.

So the following Friday afternoon, (which just happened to be Friday the 13th and a full moon, to boot), I pulled up once again in the Match Lake car park. This time, though, instead of grabbing a bucket and racing round the Match, I loaded the barrow and headed off Copse-bound.

I had a quick scout around before deciding on the left-hand Dugout swim. This gave me a decent amount of open water and also the entrance to the channel that leads to the Back Bay, from which Lee had caught Crinkle Tail the previous weekend.

A few bits and pieces were going on in open water, it was beginning to feel as if a bit of spring was in the air and I cast out full of anticipation and optimism on the new water.

I'd given a lot of thought to rigs because these Copse Lake carp had seen the lot and although not quite as big as their cousins across the road, they were reputed to be just as cagey and ultra-rig-shy.

I felt I needed an edge rig-wise, and that the Withy Pool rig could perhaps give me that advantage. I could present a pop-up, but unlike the hinged stiff rig that had been the main catcher the last two or three years since Terry Hearn had done so well, I could fish the hookbait much closer to the deck, more like 1½-inches high rather than the 2½ to 3½ inches that the hinged rig was used at. The aggressive curve also meant that if I could prick the carp then the hook point was almost impossible to shake; the more they wriggled, the tighter the grip, so to speak because with the shrink tubing wrapped round the bottom lip, it was all over bar the photos. That was the plan, anyway, and the rig certainly performed outstandingly when I played about with it on my fingers and used my hand to resemble the mouth of a 30-pounder. The only way to truly test it, though, was to let the wily, old mirrors pick the bones out of it.

After a good season on the Match, on the Fish and Blood with Fresh Orange, I was sticking to that. My brother, Lee, and Jason had caught most of the Copse fish on it between them, so I knew that the mirrors liked it and knew what it was. That first night under the full moon on a new water was an exciting one and the following morning I was at the front of the swim with rod in hand. It wasn't the desired Copse carp that had fallen foul to my pop-up Withy rigs, though, but a tench and a bream. Despite those fish not being the wanted targets, I was suitably impressed with the hook holds and it was a job to unhook them, especially with chilly fingers on a crisp, March morning; the Nailer hooks were well and truly nailed.

It was the same on the Sunday morning and despite a bit of activity and bubbling going on, no one else had a bite, so I was confident that I could be on to something special. As the lake was going 'days only' on April the 1st I had managed to sweet-talk the old man into letting me have the Sunday afternoon off so that I could pack up Monday morning and then drive the 95 miles home to start work on the farm.

After fruitless Friday and Saturday nights in the Stilts I wound in and went in search of carp, along with Lee and Jason who were also on. There was nothing in view and just the Back Bay left to check out, so I climbed the very same silver birch tree that I had almost a decade ago for Ritchie Mac, and within a few seconds I saw a big, long, yellow-bellied mirror ghost into the bay before resting up in the overgrown bush from

Lee completed his hat-trick of Copse mirrors.

which Ritchie had hooked Crinkle Tail. After a few minutes, the mirror (which I was convinced was the Pretty One) glided over a shallow gravel hump on the edge of the bush down to the right and then meandered back up the channel and out of the bay.

The Stilts swim was in close proximity so I quickly moved and I was soon installed in the Natural Bivvy with my two Withy rigs flicked out; one down to the right on the gravel by the bush that the Pretty One had rested up on, and the other to the far bank snag where Lee and taken Crinkle Tail from three weeks previously. I was ready for her return.

I threw 20 baits round each, tuned into the Sunday footy match and enjoyed a pleasant relaxing afternoon in the early spring weather. That was fairly short-lived, though, because when I checked the spot from the birch tree, I could see evidence of fish rocking under the bush and the water starting to cloud up. The line bites soon started and I became a bundle of nerves as the fish grew more confident and came out from under the sanctuary of the bush. Surely, it had to happen, but this was the notorious Copse Lake and I'd often heard tales of fish feeding and then getting away with it and avoiding capture.

Suddenly, the buzzer screeched. I found myself attached to a bucking Copse Lake carp and on the shallow hump the water was being churned by a furious carp. I was soon out in the water and although a mirror could be seen, it was one of the smaller ones. At this moment, the unbelievable happened. The other rod locked up to the far bank snag and the line pinged out of the clip. With the line now bowstring tight,

I leaned back, grabbed the rod and with a rod in each hand, I yelled out for Jason and Lee. Jason was soon with me and with one rod between my legs, with the fish on, and the second one snagged in the far margin tree, I dragged the little mirror into the net wielded by Jason.

I got the chesties on and waded across to the halfway point in the bay before the water level dropped into the deep channel, and judging by the line angle it was obvious that the fish was down too deep to reach from the far margin just 10 yards away from where I stood. At this point, the Amnesia hooklink cut. I had other fish to sort out, so I weighed the mirror known as Stripes at 15lbs 8oz and had to settle for a score draw with the Copse Lake. I had a good idea it was the lingering Pretty One that had escaped. If only it had picked the bait up five minutes earlier, I could have been off to a dream start.

That was the end of the action, and no wonder what with all the disturbance, but the long drive home to work was a bearable one. I was gutted that I'd potentially lost one of the big ones, but I was off the mark, and rig and bait were working as intended. Two on at once in the Copse can't have been done many times before, if at all!

We were now into days only, between the hours of 6am to 9pm, and I'd generally get into a routine of turning up in the Match Lake car park about 3 o'clock, quickly get some rods out on the Match for the afternoon/evening, pack up at 9pm, then grab a takeaway and nip round to Odd's where I was staying the nights. We'd watch a bit of telly and then the pair of us would be up early doors and down to the lake to get started for 6am. A few of the regulars were doing this so barrow races at dawn soon started and everyone began to get there earlier and earlier, so by the end of May it was more like 4.45am when the first car went through the gate. It was all done in jest.

I was moving between the Match and the Copse, with my first success actually coming on the Copse, back in the Natural Bivvy on Saturday April 11th. Another of the small ones, a 14lbs 8oz common was taken from the bushes opposite. Just 20 baits with my popped-up Withy Pool rig did the business again.

Employing the same tactics on the Match also brought success the next trip. With an easterly blowing strongly down the lake, I got in the Mangrove and cast right across to the Jungle, one off the bush and one in the entrance behind the bar. Within an hour or so, at 5pm, after a decent fight, I stuck the net under one of the old originals I hadn't previously caught - Big Scale at 26lbs 8oz. Similar conditions were forecast for the next day; chilly and overcast with an easterly. I baited the entrance of the Jungle at packing up time and got back on the Saturday to an early start, but all to no avail.

Stripes at 15lb 8oz and I had to settle for a score draw with the Copse Lake.

The Sunday was set to be much brighter and the Copse fish seemingly only came alive when the sun was out, so I did the Sunday morning in the Oak Bay but although the odd fish drifted in and out of the bay, that's as good as it got.

The following Friday was my 24th birthday. I'd never fished on my birthday before, because it's in April and the old close season prevented me, so I really wanted to catch myself a present.

There was a south-westerly pushing up to the top bay and I felt that my best chance of getting one was in my favourite plot on the Match Lake, the Forty Eights. As I pushed the barrow up past the Beach swim, I could see through the bushes that my plot was empty and so, with a skip in my step, I moved up a gear and whizzed round. Having caught so many from this swim last year, it was easy getting the rods out and with a rare bit of sunshine after such a cold month, it really looked good and it was nice to be out angling. At 7.30pm the faithful right-hand rod bent round in the rests and a typical dogged fight from a Match original ensued. Again, another one I hadn't previously caught rolled into the net and on April 24th, on my 24th birthday, it weighed a welcome 24lbs.

My favourite plot on the Match Lake.

I stuck the net under one of the old originals I hadn't caught - Big Scale.

I wanted to get on with the Copse, but you know what it's like when you're catching. I was finding it hard to drag myself away from the Match. I topped up with bait and headed off to Odd's and the barrow had me veering back into the Forty Eights at dawn. The beauty of this swim was that it backed on to the Back Bay of the Copse so at least I could keep an eye on this area and if anything drifted in I could move on to it in a flash.

At lunchtime, the same rod as the previous day lurched into life and this time one of the old characters of the lake, the aptly named Hole in the Head, rolled in. Admittedly, it wasn't a pretty fish but it was in better health than it had been and the 25th had produced a 25lbs 3oz for me; a 26-pounder on the 26th then, perhaps?

Unfortunately, the pattern didn't continue, but the next weekend bites were followed with a stockie mirror, a 17½lb common, a couple of catfish of about 20lbs, and a monster moggy of 31lbs 12oz, which I thought was one really big carp until it slithered on the surface in the margins. This came right on last knockings, the rod had even been laid on the floor, with the buzzers already packed away.

The days were getting brighter and warmer. It was now May and time to start doing my homework on the Copse. I planned to do the Sunday morning back up there and so scattered a few baits along the bushes in the Back Bay on the Saturday night.

At 6am-ish (cough) I waded out from under the canopy of the Natural Bivvy swim, flicked my rigs tight to the far bushes, and with a dozen or so baits around them I sat back quietly to wait. Bright sunshine had been forecast and I hoped that a fish or two would drift in, and indeed, at least one must have done because the right-hand rod was picked up. The crafty bugger, headed skyward on the locked-up line and crashed in the bushes forcing me to pull into it sideways, and with the tip under water. The bush bounced, the fish thrashed, my hooklink parted and once again, I was left breathless and shocked by the speed of it all. Although I didn't believe it was one of the big fish, the Piglet had been skulking around, so I was well peeved. I packed up and took the long drive home.

The next weekend, I caught a 19lbs 11oz mirror out of the Match Lake on the Friday afternoon and intended to do the Saturday and Sunday morning on the Copse. I fancied the left-hand Dugout swim but failed to win the barrow races at dawn and found that my brother, Paul, had similar ideas and had beaten me to it. Most of the main swims were already taken, so I retreated to the Natural Bivvy and a couple of hours later was winding in as Paul had already landed the Slate Grey. This was another of the 30s I'd witnessed on the bank and it was throughout this month that I got to view them more and more in their natural habitat as well.

The one I wanted to catch the most was the easiest to find and it was the boldest of the four big ones. Its big, white lips, huge mouth in lockjaw position, a big black patch on its back that resembled a saddle, as well as that distinctive tail, made Crinkle easily recognisable. The yellow belly and sheer length of the Pretty One gave that one away, and the Slate Grey with its darker appearance and the lump on its side was easy to spot from the abundance of good climbing trees on the banks of the Copse Lake. The fourth big'un, Scaley, was much more secretive and along with the Leather would disappear for weeks at a time.

One area where these two would hang about was around the Parrot Island in the corner where the Nursery, Match and Copse lakes all border each other. This little swim, known as Ritchie's Bay (the same swim where I'd first met Ritchie Mac) was very under-fished but after doing the Saturday morning in the Box and then nipping down to the car park to get a batch of base mix from my brother, I noticed a few fish in and around the island.

Teamwork had landed the fish.

Everyone had to be off that evening at 5pm because of an open day on the Sunday, and as it was FA cup final day as well, the lake was empty, so I quickly grabbed my two rods and underarmed them once the fish had dispersed; one up to the island, and one on a gravel patch that separated a channel through to the Shitting swim.

With the bedchair back behind the brambles, I waited, hidden from view. It wasn't long before the right-hand alarm sung out, but a duck was the culprit. As I stood at the bottom of the bank to underarm it back, the other indicator cracked into the rod and from my precarious position, I leaned back to grab it. The line was bowstring tight. I was fishing a really tight clutch and with only about 25 feet of line out, the line cut into my hand as a big, angry carp erupted in the channel, making a huge wake. Before I could gain control, the 15lb line parted as it dropped behind the bar and I was left with a limp line hanging from the rod tip.

I now had no rods in, so I recast one and retackled the other, flicked them back out and collapsed on the bed, cursing the timing of these bloody Copse fish. It seemed that every time I was in a precarious position, they'd see me and pick up the bait! I couldn't blame my position at 4pm, though, when a fish returned and I was in again. Hitting and holding only resulted in me pulling out of it and I was starting to get the hump with the Copse Lake. I couldn't wait to catch my 30 and bugger off over to the North Lake.

It was hot the following Friday when I headed up to the Copse. I heard some shouting and found Rick Harrison in the Oak Bay. He'd hooked one on a floater, but because of light gear and the weed coming up, it was stuck fast in the weed bed. We soon formulated a plan. I wasn't a great swimmer, so Rick would swim out to the island margin where he should be able to wade across in the shallow water, while I would run round, with the net, to the line of islands from the Secret swim and get out to him from there.

The plan worked and on a short line we managed to bundle a big mirror and plenty of weed into the net; it appeared that the Pretty One had slipped up in the weed. We swapped over and I took the rod and net pole, while Rick swam the fish back in the rolled-up net. At 30lbs 6oz, she was long and lean and appeared to have had already spawned. Anyway, teamwork had landed the fish and a good friendship was cemented from that day on.

My next action continued on current form and another take in the Back Bay resulted in the smart so-and-so hitting the surface again, and because of the depth of water I was in, that resulted in it gaining line and smashing me up in the overhang suspended in the water. Night-fishing was just round the corner, so as the rig and bait was working on a regular basis, I felt that a move to the open water swims might change my luck.

We were able to fish the night of May 31st, so I got up extra early and had my barrow in the Royal Box by 5am. With a 'protected' area of dense weed beds out in front, as well as shallow gravel humps to my left, I was sure that my areas would be visited over the course of a couple of days. All the anglers threatening to fish on the Copse this year failed to materialise and only Odd, Paul, Jason Bowsher and I were there for opening night. We hoped that this was how it would continue because we were all on the same bait and so we wouldn't have too much outside competition.

May 31st was pleasant but quiet and after a café pit stop on June 1st, I returned in the sunshine to see fish turning up down to my left and in front of my brother, who was in Ritchie's Bay. I watched excitedly as Slate Grey waddled down the margin over my left-hand spot but the closest I could get to the fish was a shallow gravel hump surrounded by weed. It looked a perfect spot and my fear was that it would be too shallow, but a flick with the float revealed 18 inches on top and two feet down the sides; deep enough. I cast to the left-hand side of it and, one at a time, 'pulted 20 of the 18mm baits on top.

I made a brew and watched the spot come alive as the carp dined on the table of food I'd just served up to them. It was becoming clear to me that the sunny afternoons were prime time, and nervously, I waited for the rod to wrench round. After several heart-stopping liners, a hooked fish was left in no doubt as the shallow water on the hump erupted before dropping as a bulky fish vacated the area and then ploughed into the nearest weed bed, where it became stuck solid.

The bulk of a Copse Lake 30.

Paul had heard the take and the eruption and was soon at my side as I stripped off and took to the lake. I was careful to stick to the right-hand side where there was a shallower bar that I could wade out on. Several weeks later, with much giggling, I watched as Munchkin, who was blissfully unaware of this feature, filled his waders en route to a weeded fish. I did tell him to keep to the right, but I was a little bit too late! Sorry kid!

Anyway, back to the story; I was able to get within about 15 yards of the weed before the water dropped off. With strong line I gave it the butt and with reassuring words from Paul, who had followed me out with the net, the weed started to fizz and inch towards me. I wasn't sure that the fish was still attached, and it wasn't until it erupted almost between Paul's legs that it shook off enough weed to plough about under the tip, towing a big lump of weed around with it as it did so.

After a tense minute or two, the bulk of a Copse 30 lay in the net and I could see that my first big'un was the Slate Grey. We headed to dry land, weighed her at 32lbs 11oz and with photos done, returned her to the warm waters that I'd just shared with her. The ambition of a Copse 30 had been achieved, so should I call it a day and head North or stay and try to catch a few more?

On current form, if I could end the run of lost fish - and I hoped catching the Slate Grey meant I had turned that corner - I could bag a few more, because it appeared that my rig had the undoing of them. My dad was booked in to have a much-needed hernia operation, which would mean I'd soon have to work on the farm seven days a week. It was just too far to drive to do more than one overnighter a week (a 90-minute run on a good day) so it would make sense to continue on a water and fish for carp that I was wising up to, as opposed to starting afresh on the North.

Dad was to go under the knife at the end of July, so I had my weekends free until then, but I had to make the most of my time. Paul caught Scaley, and Jason had Slate Grey, and they both went over to the North, so at least the little Copse was a bit quieter at the weekends. I soon got among a few of the lake's smaller inhabitants; the '19' at 19lbs 8oz, and Stiff-As at 17lbs 4oz, followed by the lake's baby, a pretty, heavily-scaled mirror at 12lbs 4oz.

Stiff As at 17lb 4oz.

The lake's baby.

All were taken off my shallow hump in the Box, and I'd also lost two fish in the Back Bay, sandwiched between the mirrors. This area was turning into a right hot-spot.

My dad was due to have his operation, and I only had the Friday afternoon and night, so with my foot to the floor I hooned it to the lake in double-quick time. Sweat was beading my brow as I half-walked, half-ran the barrow all the way up the side of the Match Lake to my destination but I had a sudden feeling of relief and elation when I saw the empty Royal Box. I relaxed, parked the barrow up and surveying the beautiful, millpond flat surface, I scaled the tree.

The view from the ground might have been lifeless but from my vantage point it was a different story. My heart started racing as down to the left I saw the Pretty One and another good fish tearing up the bottom, and it was my hot-spot they were feeding on. There would be no need to go on the lookout around the pond today. I was down the tree in a flash and soon had a pop-up on a freshly-tied Withy Pool rig ready to go.

I went back up the tree. Both fish had eaten their fill for now of whatever they were feeding on, and I watched as they drifted out to the weedbed off the side of Parrot Island. The spot was glowing and visible from the bank, due to its brightness, so I cast my rig the short distance and as I pulled it back slightly as it touched the surface, I immediately felt it hit bottom in just two feet of water. Around 20 baits were fired straight on top and I whipped back up the tree to check their whereabouts. The fish were still chilling in the weed. I'd laid the trap without their knowledge, so it was game on and with only a night ahead of me, I hoped they were still hungry.

The buzzer confirmed this at 5pm as line disappeared off the spool. I pulled into it and headed out into the lake after it because it had immediately got bogged down in the weed behind the spot. Once again, I got to within ten yards or so and with the increased pressure of a short line, it came unplugged and erupted under my tip.

A bit of weed dropped down the line and over its head, I lifted the net and it came as no surprise that the long Pretty One lay inside. At 31lbs 14oz she was a bit leaner than normal, but very welcome indeed; she had made the long drive for a short session extremely beneficial.

I had a sudden feeling of relief and elation when I saw the empty Royal Box.

With so much disturbance I didn't expect much more to happen but I cast a rig back to the spot, topped it up with a few more baits and watched the sun set before getting my head down ready for the long drive home and work in the morning. I woke to a bright, crisp morning, with the sun beating down, so I put the kettle on for a brew, checked my watch and started to pack away. It was half-past seven, and as I needed to be out of the gate by 8am and it was a long walk, I decided to finish my tea and then wind in.

Suddenly, the tea went skyward as my spot erupted and the rod wrenched round. I played the fish from the bank and kept it from getting bogged down, and after a spirited fight a grey carp boiled under the tip before being engulfed in the mesh. A double-take revealed a rare visitor to the bank. The elusive Leather had made a mistake, but I quickly got him out, weighed him at 23lbs 4oz and I was impressed with the hook hold, which was well inside the mouth. The rig had made an excellent job of hooking this very finicky feeder so deeply. The drive home and work was much more bearable after that brace.

I carried on with an overnighter the following week and messed up a glorious chance. I'd dropped in the left-hand Dugout swim as there were carp in the

A rare visitor to the bank.

It came as no surprise that the Long Pretty One lay inside.

weedbeds over the back of the bar that extended past the row of islands between the channel and the Stilts. With a sideways flick, I got a bait on top of the bar and the carp were feeding confidently in shallow water, so I wasn't bothered about being in less than two feet of depth.

The bugbear of fishing so shallow is the accursed white water-chickens. Soon after getting my rig perfectly on the cleanest part of the bar, a swan sauntered along and despite me shooing and waving about, he dipped his head down and the indicator danced. This seemed to unsettle it and it buggered off. Right, do I recast it and struggle to get it back or leave it and hope the swan had just lifted the rig, and that the stiff Amnesia would re-present itself? I had a hard, cork-balled pop-up on, the bait would be fine, wouldn't it? I didn't want to disturb the area and the chance of a take perhaps any minute, so I left it and just flicked a few baits back around it. Big mistake.

When I opened my bleary eyes in the morning, I had to blink a few times to focus. A carp's tail was waving to me from my spot and I looked at the rod, expecting the tip to wrap round at any moment, then back at the tail, which I had a feeling belonged to the Piglet, and then back to the rod. After an agonising few minutes it had eaten all the baits and drifted back to its lair in the weedbeds behind.

Quickly, I whizzed the rig in and to my horror discovered only a loop of floss hanging from the rig ring. What a Noddy! I don't know if I was angrier with the swan, or with myself for not checking it, but the chance was gone and that morning the expletives of road rage were drowning out the tunes of the stereo on the trek back home.

With Slate Grey and the Pretty One ticked off the list, Crinkle Tail was the one left to catch, as well as Scaley, but Scaley had not been out since the first week when my brother had her. However, after Munchkin had lost the fish in the Pig swim on a cut-off with braided main line, she hadn't even been seen and on such a small, clear pond it was rare for someone not to have seen her. We all hoped she was just being moody and unsociable, and not that she was tethered up in the vast snags of the Pig swim!

The next week, I booted it Yateley-bound as soon as I'd got the afternoon feed done. It was more like lunch but the pigs weren't complaining. On arrival, to my good fortune, not only did I find an empty Copse Lake but also from the willow in the Secret, Crinkle Tail and the Piglet were waiting for me; two of the three I had left to catch. They kept browsing on a tiny gravel patch about 15 yards out and the Piglet was nuzzling Crinkle and looked a bit spawny, but Crinkle Tail looked like she was up for a bait.

With trembling fingers, I got a pop-up tied onto my rig and as the rod was ready to cast, I returned to the tree. I didn't want to lose a second once they'd moved a safe distance off the spot, so I'd climbed the tree in my waders. I waited until the opportunity arose and when they'd waddled off to the weed at the rear of Oak Bay, and I could make out a couple of backs, I half-climbed, half-slid out of the tree and then waded out so I could perform the cast, because the Secret only allowed an underarm cast due to overhead foliage.

The spot was visible with the Polaroids on, so I flicked the lead and once I was certain I was on it, I just teased the lead and when it instantly slid an inch I knew I was on the cleanest, smooth, sweet spot. With five baits thrown on top, I pulled the line tight to the bottom and when back on dry land put the rod on the rest. One rod was enough.

My stomach thought my throat had been cut, so I whacked the kettle on and devoured a pasty to satisfy my rumbling belly. Curiosity got the better of me when I saw a fish heading in, and I quickly walked out on the willow bough to see if the culprit was my target fish. The big, black patch on her flank and the white lips left

Usual scenario of taking a dip for a weeded fish.

me in no doubt as she swam straight over the top of the rig before doing a U-turn. I had started to walk back along the bough when she dipped down, and as the alarm below suddenly burst into life, I saw her power off.

I launched myself down to the ground and walked fully-clothed into the margins to get the tip up. With Crinkle powering into the weed, and as I was already soaked, I felt the best course of action was to walk out to the fish that was in knee-deep water. I backtracked to grab the net and chucking it in front came out of the deep trough, and just as I stepped up into the shallow water, the tip jumped back straight. I sunk to my knees and skipped in the lead. The hook had pulled and I'd have swapped any of the previous good hook holds for this one to have stayed in Crinkle. I stomped back to dry land and sat on the ground in a sodden mess. I could have cried and felt like driving home there and then.

I got some dry clothes on and as the swans had moved in I went for a wander to try to get some motivation back. I had been just a few steps away from scooping the fish that would have completed my Copse mission, but it was gone now and I'd just have to plod on. I didn't spot anything on my travels so on my return I checked from the tree again and there was a fish grubbing on the spot. It obviously wasn't Crinkle, but I got a rig back out and spent the evening playing it over in my mind, again and again.

Eventually, I drifted off to sleep under the stars and was awoken early with a consolation prize of the Plate at 24lbs 8oz. The Plate was an original Copse fish but had spent several years in the Nursery before being moved back to its rightful home.

A couple of weeks later, Odd had a successful week's holiday bagging the Pretty One, the Piglet and the friendly Plate. While I was away, another guy, who turned out to be a phenomenally successful angler on Yateley, had started to bait the Copse and was catching them systematically, one by one.

My next trip was a Friday night. Rick was in the Dugout, Odd in the Rowans, and the new guy, Little Jon, was in the Back Bay, so I dropped back into the Royal Box. Heavy rain moved in and as the Box swim is mostly dirt, the rain splashed muddy crap everywhere and I huddled in the back of the bivvy.

About midnight, I heard footsteps and was treated to a right sight. Wearing just a sodden T-shirt, boxers and wellies, there stood Odd with his head torch switched on, forcing me to squint.

In these conditions, I wasn't expecting a lot to happen but Odd informed me that Crinkle had just been landed by Little Jon in the Back Bay, the lucky chap. I grabbed my jacket, something Odd should have done, and went to help out. I was eager to check her mouth out and there on the very tip of her lip was a small tear. A few millimetres back, and it would have been me holding aloft all 34lbs 6oz of her, but it was Jon's moment, and we all lent a hand to get her back no worse for wear. I was off early that morning but with the luxury of all weekend on the next trip, when my dad had recovered, I'd start all over again.

I wasn't sure if Crinkle would get back on the feed so quickly, but if I could get a bait in front of her you never know your luck, so after finding Crinkle along with Slate Grey and the Leather in the inaccessible Pipe swim, I set up just around the corner in the Birches. The Friday night passed with only mosquito bites, but with the knowledge that I didn't have to pack up in the morning I enjoyed it nonetheless.

Several fish were seen cruising about in the day, and I watched them closely. They seemed to be using a definite route into and out of the swim, a narrow channel in the weed to my right, so after checking that nothing was about, I quickly plumbed it and found a smooth, broken ground spot in the entrance of the channel. I moved a rod on to this, along with my usual 20 free offerings, and hoped that staying a second night would prove fruitful.

I woke at half-past six and from the comfort of the sleeping bag I saw the odd bubble pop up as the mist rolled off the still, glassy surface. Then the silence was pierced as the right-hand rod peeled off and the carp, as was now the norm, dived straight into the weed. I got the waders on but the Birches was a deeper area so I was unable to get close. However, I gained a few feet as I tiptoed along the bar in front, water seeping down the back of my chesties, giving me a wet arse, and I had no option but to lean into it. The rod creaked, the spot became a fizz of bubbles, and the water blackened as the silt below was disturbed.

The fish popped out of the weed and wallowed in. I kept her coming and a big pair of shoulders broke the surface. I held my breath, hoping it was Crinkle Tail, but as she slid over the drawstring the unmistakable plated flanks of Scaley were obvious and as she sank into the mesh I yelled, "She's alive!" The lads were soon round and although she was down from my brother's capture, this time bang on 29lbs, we were all very glad to see her.

With three of the big four now under my belt, I was solely focused on Crinkle Tail and it now getting well into September. I knew that finding her would soon get harder once the colder conditions set in so I seriously considered a move to the North Lake. Bazil was still likely to have a capture in her, or maybe even two, and as my brother had already caught her, first fish out, there was a possible chance of my first-ever 40.

I decided that if I could carry on finding Crinkle, then I'd fish for her but otherwise I'd go over the North and start learning in preparation for the next year.

As I pushed the barrow on the big hike up to the Copse on the following Friday, I was reliant on finding Crinkle because setting up blind might only lead to a recapture at best. I dumped my gear in the Box and made my way round the pond, searching out all the nooks and crannies, playing monkey up all the trees, and as I stood high in the oak, surveying the Oak Bay, I could just make out a big shape among the weed.

I scurried back down from the tree and was running off to get my gear when Little Jon came down the path with the news that he had the Plate in the net. When the photos had been done, Jon returned the favour by asking if I wanted to know where Crinkle had been feeding that week. That was my sole reason for being there so I bit his hand off and we returned to the Oak where there was a lovely, glowing spot in the margin. The chunk in the bay meant that two plus two equalled four; at least, I hoped my maths was right!

I parked the barrow in the Oak swim and then went for another look. Those big, white lips could only belong to one fish. Despite Jon informing me that the Pretty One was hanging about with Crinkle and getting on the spot with her, there was no sign of her. Crinkle was all on her lonesome so I hoped my Copse mission was almost over, the finishing line in touching distance. Crinkle was out in the weed, in the middle of the bay, and I cracked on with setting the trap.

I lowered my rig on to the cleanest part of the depression to my right that they'd dug out by cleaning up the bait, and popped my usual 20 baits in and around it. The other rod was in the margin to the left. My lines were slack and I set up right back in the woods, I couldn't afford to mess up this chance.

Bite times had switched to the hours of darkness now we were well into autumn, and at 4.30am, my heart raced as I pounded the few yards to the rod like a barefoot Olympic sprinter. The nocturnal culprit didn't seem to have the weight of Crinkle Tail and as I felt into the net in the pitch blackness, I knew that my gut feeling was right. A much smaller fish lay at my feet, a little linear that weighed 14lbs 4oz, and after a quick brew to calm my fraught nerves I lowered the rig back into position.

Dawn broke with that October chill that forces you to wear a jacket, and I scaled the tree to see if Crinkle was evident in the bay. She sure was, and she'd moved literally just a few feet since the day before. Surely, it was only a matter of hours before she fed back on the spot.

She hung about all day and became more active as the afternoon wore on, so I was certain she was itching to get on the bait. Sleep was hard to find that night but in the autumnal chill, I snuggled down in the bag and eventually drifted off.

This time I had to wait until 5.30am, but as the same rod roared off, I knew instantly that I had a totally different animal attached as it plugged into the weed bed on the far side of the small bay. I yelled out to Rick who was in the Back Bay and he came to the rescue by wading out from the far side and as I held the rod as high as possible, Rick got hold of the line and followed it down to the fish. With no stretch in a short line, the carp became unplugged and now I had her moving and on the way in to my margin.

Rick legged it back just in time to slip the net under a big fish. It had to be Crinkle. I sank my hand into the net to feel that uniquely-shaped tail, but as I did that, the fish went into one and thrashed about, angry at her mistake. As she settled, we heaved her out and she lay on the mat with the moonlight glistening off her leathery flanks. I pinged on the head torch and my heart sank as my desperate desire for it to be Crinkle had morphed into the Pretty One.

As the sling was still wet from the previous night, we weighed her at 34lbs 2oz but despite her being in tip-top condition, I was so dejected because it was a recapture that I lowered the sling back into the Oak Bay and let her swim off without a photo.

I'd seen Bazil in the flesh a few weeks previously, when Stevie Pag' had banked her at 46lbs 2oz and that image was still fresh in my mind. I felt the recapture of the Pretty One was the lake telling me that was my lot, so with bigger fish to fry, it was now time to move on. In future, I'd be turning left off the Sandhurst road, instead of right. I'd make the move 'over the road' to fish with the big boys and head North, in search of the best-known carp in the land.

Bazil's image was still fresh in my mind.

Chapter 8 - King Bazil

My first trip to the North Lake was on the last weekend of October and I thought I had discovered gold as I peered down into the depths of the channel behind the Corral Island. After a few minutes of straining my eyes I could make out the width of the fish, and although initially I'd thought I was looking at carp, it soon became obvious that they were just big slabs of bream. I searched for a couple of hours in the pouring rain and then decided to fish the Bazil's Bush swim, mainly because the wind was pushing into the bay.

Bazil had already been caught from the other two bay swims; Steve had her from the Destiny swim, and my brother from the Mouth of the Bay, so if she was in the bay, I hoped that she'd feel more comfortable in the sanctuary of the snags of the Bush. It was the closest swim to the car park, too, so that was another bonus in the pouring rain.

I must admit, I didn't enjoy my first trip to the North Lake, mostly because of the persistent rain the whole time I was there, and as I was fishing at the bottom of the bay, I felt a bit claustrophobic staring across to the Bush.

The following weekend, I opted for the open water and set up in the End Works swim. I felt much happier here and soon found an abundance of features that I would be able to put to good use in the future. It was all quiet on the fishing front, but far from it elsewhere. The sky was constantly lit by fireworks, and every display seemed to be in competition to see who could make the most noise!

After a couple of guest trips to Savay, and a few weekends on the Match Lake, I went back on the North at the beginning of February. I was on the North Lake proper now, and would see it out until the end; Bazil or insanity, whichever came first. I tried to fish several swims in order to build up a picture of the lake in my head. There were fewer anglers and less weed in evidence, so if I could find spots now, I'd know where to look in the summer without having to thrash the water when fish might be about.

I did have an occurrence at the end of February. I was fishing the End Point swim at about 6pm on the Friday evening when the middle indicator pulled tight to the rod and after hooking a fish at 60 yards range, I thought it might be a tench. Suddenly, it started to kite fast to the left and just as I began to get excited, thinking it was a carp, the hook pulled.

I was using a straight bottom bait on a standard stiff rig of 20lb Amnesia, with a loop at the swivel end. I had hooked a lot of fish on the Match Lake with this rig, but had experienced quite a few hook pulls, so I decided I needed to come up with another rig, which had the benefits of the stiff rig, but with the flexibility at the hook end to give me a better hookhold. Chances were few and far between on the North Lake, and I couldn't afford to be losing fish through poor hookholds.

The days were getting longer as March arrived and Bernie Loftus caught the first fish since the end of October, an upper-double from the Christmas Tree swim. The lake was now starting to get busy and the Christmas Tree swim was permanently occupied until the end of the season on March 31st .

Scale-on-the-Shoulder made an appearance from the Corral on the penultimate weekend of the season. The ex-Pad Lake mirror, now second in command to Bazil, weighed in at 33lbs 15oz, to Mark Rosewell. Bazil made it through to the end of the season without capture, though, and with a two-month close season, I headed back over to the Match Lake to experiment with a few new rigs and put the new bait through its paces.

As far as I knew, all Bazil's recent captures had been on bottom baits. In addition, I remembered a conversation I'd had with Steve when he told me that he'd observed fish in the 30/40 swim shying off pop-ups, so I wanted to fish bottom baits, thus removing any doubts I might have about Bazil or his mates reacting adversely to my hookbait.

With this in mind, and Kryston bringing out their Snake-Bite hooklink material, which could incorporate stiff and supple parts in the same hooklink, I started to play about with the new material. The mechanics of the rig I wanted to achieve were such that when the fish picked up my bottom bait, the hook could turn unrestricted. However, directly behind it would be a three or four-inch stiff section, which would twist on ejection, thus sending the hook to the side of the mouth. With a wide-gaped hook, which could turn freely, the fish would be hooked in the scissors of the mouth.

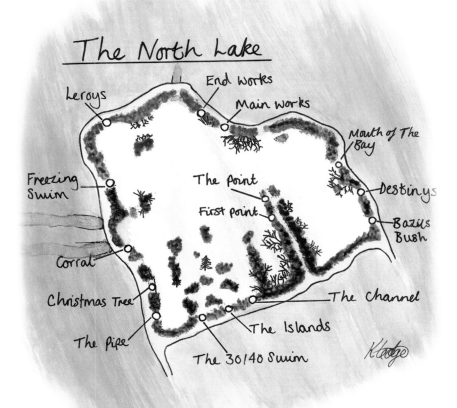

The North Lake

To achieve the turning of the stiff section, I needed a supple section behind it, and after a couple of experimental rigs that I played about with at home, I came up with one that I felt would do the job. It consisted of a size 4 or 5 ESP Raptor T-6 hook, knotless-knotted to 25lb coated Snake-Bite, with a hair long enough for the bait, and a small gap between bait and hook.

Leaving a quarter of an inch of the coating from the eye to form a bent hook effect, I peeled off 3mm of the coating to form a hinge for the hook to rotate. A four-inch stiff section was followed by a two-inch uncoated braid section. To increase the anti-tangle properties of the rig, I tied the hooklink to the swivel using a loop knot, leaving it coated to form a stiff loop, which would kick the rig out from the lead. Leadcore wire was tightly wound around the middle of the hooklink to keep it on the bottom. The only way to find out how well it would work was to get some takes, so I took the new rig to the Match Lake at the start of April.

I also had a new bait to try out, with help and advice from Gary Bayes at Nashbait (where we'd just got a deal, thanks to Pinky). Gary had made up a bait for us from our own recipe, to use on a few of the Yateley lakes. Our chosen mix was a fishmeal and so with the track record of Monster Pursuit mix, it was an easy choice, and Gary added a few extras to it. On the liquid side, we left the optimum levels in Gary's

A fish I wanted to catch - Fagburn.

The rig and bait had both scored well.

capable hands, and chose Banana Oil Palatant as the main sniff. We also had liquid Betaine and Regular Sense Appeal added, to boost the liquid attraction in the mix. Fruity fishmeals were a particular favourite of the Yateley mirrors. Bazil liked her boilies, and that was what I intended to feed to her; I ordered 30 kilos of the new banana bait in 20 millers.

The Match Lake reverted to 'days only' throughout the spring, and I took a roving approach. If no action occurred within a few hours, the barrow was loaded and off I would go in search of carp.

After no action on the Point on the first Saturday, I found a carp flashing its orange belly over a gravel spot right in the far end snags in the Top Bay. I quickly moved my gear in and with the new rigs and bait on, I cast one bait to the snags at the end of the bay and one to the far bank snag, just 25 yards away. That was at about 3pm, and at 6pm the far margin rod produced a fish which I had caught a couple of years before; the larger of the two Scale-on-the-Shoulders, at 25lbs. The fish was well hooked in the corner of the mouth, as I had hoped. The rig and bait had both scored well. Two hours later, and it was getting even better. After a good scrap in the edge, keeping it out of the marginal trees, I slipped the net under a fish which I had wanted to catch, Fagburn, at 27lbs exactly. Again, a good hookhold, and the bait was obviously pretty instant.

I continued to catch a few carp.

I continued to catch a few carp through the spring on the same bait and rig, and was happy to take them both on to the North Lake come June 1st. The draw for both the North and Car Park lakes was happening on May 31st, which was a bank holiday.

I arrived for the start a couple of hours before the draw, and judging by the number of cars and people already in the car park, it appeared that a few people would go home without getting a swim. After saying a few hellos, I headed straight up to the North Lake to have a scout around to see what I could find. I turned left as I got to the North, and had a look in the snags down by the islands, and the 30/40, but there was nothing to be seen. It was the same in the Pipe and Christmas Tree swims, but then I heard a fish just up the bank. I quickly legged it up to the Waiting Mans and saw the ripples coming out from under the Waiting Mans' island. It hadn't sounded like a big fish, but it gave me an option if I came out late in the draw. The Corral looked good and the weed was certainly coming up.

A look from up the Freezing swim tree revealed what I was looking for – carp, and quite a few of them, milling around in the weed. A big fish waddled out of the weed below me. Could it be? No, not Bazil, but Scale-on-the-Shoulder looking good and fat. There were at least another eight carp in the area, and I felt Bazil couldn't be too far away. No one else had spotted the fish, or me up the tree for that matter. A few people had actually walked straight past below me without even stopping! I decided the Freezing was my number one choice, with the End Works second, and the Corral third.

The Bay and the top end of the Works Bank looked devoid of fish, and I definitely felt that I needed to be on that northern side of the lake. Twenty tickets went in the bag for the North and, with only 18 swims available, two anglers were going to be disappointed and the Car Park draw was worse, with about a dozen more anglers than swims. Busy, busy!

The Christmas Tree went first, and then the Works Bank swims. Tensions were building and the expressions on people's faces told the story. Those who were out early in the draw were all smiles, while those who were waiting, including me, were starting to feel worried. A good draw was essential to start the season in the way you wanted it to continue, full of confidence.

The Corral was still vacant, so that's where I chose to go.

Eight names had been drawn and everyone seemed to be avoiding the Freezing and the Corral - fingers crossed. Draw number nine was Mark Rosewell, and as Mark had fished heavily in the Corral before, everyone was shouting out, "Corral, Corral." At this point, Mark bottled it and stammered, "Freezing swim," and everyone laughed and shouted abuse.

My first choices had gone and I felt a bit disappointed, but the next out of the bag was me and amazingly, the Corral was still vacant, so that's where I chose to go. There was an island to my left and another to my right, plenty of weedy, open water in front and more importantly, carp close by. I was well happy and relieved to get a good swim.

Most people were expecting Bazil to get caught within the first couple of days, probably to the first big munch she had, so I decided to put 150 of the 20mm Monster Pursuit boilies around each hookbait.

For my right-hand rod, I found a slight clearing on the bar out in line with the church tower, at 65 yards out, which had three feet of water on top and five feet down the sides. The middle rod was cast towards the Middle Works on a fairly large sandy area off the side of the Corral Island, and the left-hand rod down the silty channel next to the bushes on the inside.

I'd fished the Corral in the winter so I was able to find my desired spots without having to thrash the water to a foam; the homework was already paying off. The weed was bombing up and the rest of the swim was becoming choked with it, so with my lines clipped and marked with black permanent marker pen and the spots baited up, I went for a social to wait for the 9pm casting-out time.

The first baited rig went out on the stroke of 9, and as all three rods hit the clips and I felt the leads hit bottom, I was fishing and happy. The night was quiet, but once the sun started to rise I took two tench and a bream from the middle and right-hand rods. The first carp was caught that evening, a 19-pounder for Simon Giblin, out of the Pipe and a couple more were caught by the second day; I caught a couple of bream. There was still no sign of Bazil, but a carp did head-and-shoulder near my right-hand spot that day.

The weedy spot was becoming increasingly weedy and it was taking more casts each time to feel bottom, but when pulled back, only thin, scraggy weed was on the bar, so to help with presentation I changed the rig slightly. Instead of the hair, I tied a small loop, and tied a pop-up hookbait to the loop. Then I inserted lead wire into the pop-up until the hookbait just sank to the bottom with the weight of the hook - perfectly balanced.

I slipped the net under a short, chunky mirror. Yessss!

After a few casts, I felt the lead just touch bottom. If there was any light weed, the hookbait would be lying gently on top with the green material of the hooklink blending in beautifully. I topped up the spot with 80 baits and felt fairly confident because I was sure there was a fish or two about.

This was my last night. I had to pack up early the next morning to go to work on the Thursday and Friday, but I'd be back at the weekend. Bernie Loftus moved into the Waiting Mans next door and we sat up that evening, chatting about the old Frampton days and drinking tea. I always enjoyed Bernie's company and he's fished hard for Bazil in recent years so he had a wealth of knowledge. Some people prattle on as though they know everything and are usually just full of shit, but results speak for themselves and Mr Loftus had the pedigree, so I listened intently, trying to pick up the odd snippet of information that might benefit me in my own pursuit of Bazil. It turned out to be a nice evening after the rain of the night before and conditions looked ideal.

I awoke at 5.30am to a screaming buzzer and found a family of swans at the end of the rods. I wasn't impressed, not until I noticed the right-hand rod bending round to the right, and the swans surging off to the left. The exact same thing had happened when I caught my first 30 at Frampton. Could history be repeating itself with perhaps my first 40? I pulled into my first North Lake carp of the season and it soon hit the surface about 50 yards out. I directed the fish between the weedbeds and soon had it in the edge, and after a nervous minute or two, I slipped the net under a short, chunky mirror. Yessss!

On slow-sinking balanced hookbaits, I took a 16lb 4oz common.

The fish was lying quietly in the net so I woke the comatose Bernie, grabbed the scales and sling and once the mirror was on the mat, I slipped the size 4 Raptor out of its bottom lip. Bernie seemed to think it was the bigger of the Pad Lake stockies and at 21lbs 4oz, I was happy. I packed up to drive home for work, well satisfied that the bait and tactics were working.

Mark Rosewell couldn't resist moving into the now vacant Corral and, on the Saturday took Scale-on-the-Shoulder again, this time at 35lbs-plus; they mustn't keep meeting like this! The odd carp was coming out every couple of days and on June 16th I had a phone call telling me that Danny Morris had not only taken Scale-on-the-Shoulder, but the following morning he'd also landed Bazil at 44lb 9oz from the End Works.

He'd lost a good fish out of the Bush the first weekend, and Danny felt his chance had gone, but now he'd been rewarded big time for persevering on the North Lake, despite having planned to be on Richmond Park Lake that glorious June morning. Good decision.

I turned up on the Friday lunchtime to find the lake fairly busy. Surprisingly, on the last weekend in June, the Main Works was vacant so I moved in and set about finding the spots I had discovered in March. Clear spots were found, but the weed was getting thicker by the day and a lot of it was already on the surface. I put 80 freebies around each, on slow-sinking balanced hookbaits, and I took a 16lbs 4oz common on the Saturday morning, and the Pad Lake 26 at 24lbs 2oz on the Sunday morning. I stayed and did the Sunday night but the run of action didn't continue. Still, it had been a productive session.

The following week, there were a lot of carp deaths reported in the Colne Valley so both the North and Car Park lakes were shut down for a fortnight as a precautionary measure. Two days after it reopened, Simon Giblin continued his impressive run of fish, taking Bazil at 43lbs 5oz from the Corral. Well done, mate!

I fished the End Works that weekend and since it was scorching hot, a number of carp were sitting on the weed between me and Odd in the Freezing. Odd had just come over from the Copse Lake and as we were on the same bait, we had twice as much going in. Odd took a little mirror that weekend, so I hoped that the extra bait would benefit us both.

The Pad Lake 26.

I had my first sight of Bazil in the water that day. Solely interested in sunbathing, she sat peacefully just in the weed, on her own away from the main group. Scale-on-the-Shoulder was also present and the pair of them dwarfed the other carp, which were more active by far; very impressive indeed.

I struggled for the rest of July, and most of August. I was trying to fish in Bazil's swim, but to no avail. Odd was having better luck and had a couple of commons and the Two-Tone Pit 10 fish at 24½ lbs from the Channel, so I knew the carp were still having the bait.

Come the middle of August and, although Bazil had been regularly seen, she hadn't been out for nearly five weeks. Bazil generally came out half a dozen times in those days, from June to late autumn and had in recent years shut up shop completely in the winter. Although six times may appear to be a lot of captures, you must appreciate that Bazil only has to blink and she is immediately surrounded by capable anglers using good baits and rigs. The fish has seen immense pressure over the last 20 years since going 40lbs.

The Macmillan cancer charity weekend was organised for the following weekend and, with Bazil due, I paid my £25 along with a few other regulars, and fished in the End Works. Saturday morning signalled a stuttery take and after the initial excitement I knew something was amiss. A three-foot fish surfaced but this one had teeth! It wasn't even hooked in the mouth but the leadcore had somehow become wrapped up in the jaws of a 21lb snapper.

At 7am on Sunday, though, it was definitely a carp that I was connected to, albeit briefly, before disaster struck and I was holding a lifeless rod. A lost fish is always hard to stomach but a possible Bazil loss was unbearable. Was it Baz? I had to tell myself that it wasn't.

My mind was put to rest when Bazil made her third appearance of the year to Craig Dunne on August 17th, on a Wednesday for the third time – not much use when you can only angle on a weekend. The Main Works was the scene of Craig's success.

A long-standing friend, Lee Picknell, had his fortunes change dramatically. He'd had a completely blank year on the North Lake the previous year, but from mid-July Lee had lost a series of fish; a 17lb mirror, the Pretty One at 26lb-plus, but just 36 hours after Craig, he had Bazil, at the same weight of 44lbs 12oz, from under the canopy of the island from the First Point - a right result and evidence that you should never give up.

A right result for Lee and evidence that you should never give up!

Bazil had been caught twice in quick succession so I didn't hold out much hope that she would be out again in a hurry, but you never know. Scale-on-the-Shoulder, however, hadn't been out since mid-June, so that was the one due.

I did a night on the End Point Swim, but moved on the Saturday after finding the Big Common and a couple of other 20s down in front of the End Works. Nothing was caught, but I did find a nice feature 20 yards out and tucked round to the left of the swim; I noted the spot for future reference. I now had several options in this swim and it was fast becoming a favourite of mine. On each of the Yateley lakes there had been one swim in which I could do no wrong, and if I could get the swim in the right conditions, then more times than not I'd catch. On the Match Lake it had been the Forty Eights, and on the Copse it was the Royal Box. Would the End Works be 'my' plot on the North? Only time would tell.

The next weekend was the August bank holiday, and with three nights available I went back in the End Works. I fished the back of the Corral Island and took my first carp for two months, an 18lbs 2oz common. On the Sunday night, I had a repeat capture of the Pad Lake 26 at 23lbs 4oz off the new spot to the left. I'd found it the week before at the back of a two-foot deep bar. It was clear and firm in three feet of water and tight to the weed that dropped off into deeper water. After long, hot days, it was a perfect night spot.

September started the same way as August had finished – red hot. After working on the Saturday, sweating my nuts off moving hundreds of bales of straw, I made the long drive to Yateley in the early evening. I arrived with about an hour and a bit of daylight remaining, and hurriedly pushed the barrow up to the North and around to the Corral.

Before I left home I'd phoned Odd, who'd had the week off in the End Works. Knowing that Bazil and Scale-on-the-Shoulder had been sunbathing between Mad Martyn in the Freezing and Odd in the End Works, I anticipated that they would mooch out into open water come the coolness of dusk.

This was the first time I had been able to get back into the popular Corral since opening week and I had yet to see anyone fishing the long spot towards the church, from where I had taken my 21lbs 4oz mirror. With balanced baits tied on, I chucked the marker rod out toward the church to see if it was still free of weed and fishable. There was weed on the surface, in front and beyond the mark, but I found a thin strip of silt just to the left of the original spot I had caught from in June and after a handful of casts, I felt the lead land softly on silt. I was happy with that so, with sweat dripping off me, I fired out 80 of the 20mm baits.

The other two rods were simpler. I cast the middle rod tight to the back of the weedbed to the right of the Corral Island, and the left rod just short of the island.

My first carp for two months!

I felt that I had all routes covered if the fish should head out my way, so with my house up and bed ready, I phoned Odd to chat over his week's events.

He'd had one small mirror and lost a good fish early in the week, but was confident after seeing the two big'uns that afternoon. After a bit of friendly banter, he told me that he reckoned he was going to catch Bazil that night, so I said if he was having Bazil, then I was having Scale-on-the-Shoulder. I told him I would see him in the morning for the photos, we said our goodnights, and as the temperature dropped refreshingly, I chilled out with a cup of tea and watched the lake for a while before hitting the sack.

Soon after 5am, a couple of bleeps got me up and after unhooking a snotty bream, I recast to the edge of the weedbed and slipped back into the bag. I was just dozing off when the right-hand buzzer bleeped and I heard a click. Thinking, 'damned bream', I got out of the bag. It registered that I had heard a click, and then the penny dropped; the indicator still hadn't moved but the line was tight and now out of the clip. I looked to where the line was entering the water, saw it inching to the right and struck into the fish as a big boil became visible in the half-light.

I gained line and kept it moving in order to prevent it weeding me solid, but there was a huge patch of algae on a weedbed between me and the fish, so I just had to grit my teeth and heave. Luckily, the fish stayed just below the surface and the patch of floating algae drifted in with the carp, but now, just 10 yards out, I had the problem of netting the fish, which was behind the scum.

I slipped into the water and with one hand holding the rod high I started to break up the scum with my other hand. Gradually, it broke free and the carp waddled out a bit further, but I'd experienced similar problems on the Copse Lake the year before so I knew what to do. With the rod pointing out behind me, I let the fish drift across in front of me. I knew the length of the leadcore I was using so I could make out where the fish was and gently, I lifted the net around it.

As I pulled lumps of weed out of the net, I could make out a sizeable carp. I scrambled back on to dry land, bit off the line and heaved out my prize on to the waiting mat. The size and shape of the carp was unmistakeable as I lifted it out; Scale-on-the-Shoulder was mine and boy, did she look fat!

I slipped the hook out of the corner of her mouth, covered her with a wet sling and then grabbed my mobile to ring Odd. When he answered, I asked if he had kept his side of the bargain.

With her retained safely, I sorted out the camera for Odd's arrival.

"What are you on about?" he asked, half asleep.
"Well, have you got Bazil? 'Cos I've got Scale-on-the-Shoulder and she's bloody massive!" I laughed.

I slid the bulk of Scale into the sling, hoisted her on the Reubens and by using the landing net pole, with the scales hanging from the spreader block, and the handle in against a root, I was able to hold the scales nice and steady. The needle flew round to just short of 39lbs and settled on 38lb 14oz, Scale-on-the-Shoulder's biggest weight by far and a new personal best for me.

I slipped back into the water to make sure that she was retained safely, and then sorted out the camera ready for Odd's arrival. It was getting light and as I put the kettle on, I heard someone coming down the path. It was Derek Rance, down early to get on the Car Park Lake when the weekenders left. When he saw my wet sling and mat and the grin on my face, Derek's eyes lit up and he motioned (Derek is deaf and dumb) "Bazil?"
"No, Scale-on-the-Shoulder," I indicated by patting my shoulder.
"How big?"
"38lb 14oz," I mouthed.
"Noooooooo?" said Derek, shaking his head.

I wrote the weight in the mud to confirm it for him and he promptly shook my hand before going round the lake to tell the others. Odd and Lee, who were fishing on the Car Park Lake, soon arrived with cameras.

"How big then?" they asked.
Derek had told them 38lbs 14oz but they thought he might have misunderstood. Surely she couldn't be that heavy? I lifted her back onto the mat and left them in no doubt that she was that big. Summoning up all my strength, I held her up as the EOSs got to work, and as she waddled away, I turned with arms raised and cried, "Come on Bazil!"

I'd now had three in a week, and six North Lake carp in total, and I felt close to catching Bazil. I was buzzing. I went home on the Monday morning with no more action, but very confident.

"I've got Scale-on-Shoulder and she's bloody massive!"

Amazingly, the following week I managed to get back in the Corral which had been vacated that morning. We had a barbecue planned for the Saturday and usually, when a barbie was due to happen, Bazil would make an appearance prematurely, and it would be cancelled because everyone would pull off the North. However, come Saturday afternoon and with no sign of Bazil, a group of us enjoyed a good feed and a couple of beers.

I felt there was a good chance that Bazil would be out in the next week or so since we were coming up to the middle of the month, which was the period when Bazil had been coming out this year, every four weeks or so. In addition, September had always been a good Bazil month in the past.

Bazil had now been caught from the End Works, Corral, Main Works and First Point; all Bazil swims. Although Bazil had been caught from virtually every swim on the lake in the past, I always felt much more confident fishing in the main Bazil swims than, for example, the Christmas Tree or the Islands.

Now, one area which Bazil had always liked in the past and from which she hadn't been caught this year, was the Bay. Hardly anyone was fishing the Bay and I thought Bazil might be lying low in there because she hadn't been seen for a couple of weeks. Knowing that I couldn't get to the lake until Saturday lunchtime when the lake would be busy, I felt there was a good chance that the Bay would be free, so I asked Odd, who lives locally, to put a couple of kilos of boilies into the far margin opposite the Bush and Destiny swims.

When I arrived on the Saturday, the Bay swims were indeed free but as I had a good look in Bazil's Bush, not even a roach was to be seen and as the water was crystal clear, it didn't give me much confidence. The rest of the lake was busy, as expected, and when I found Odd in the Christmas Tree he told me he hadn't had the chance to bait up. I told him not to worry; the Bay looked dead, and at least I hadn't wasted the bait. The Freezing swim was the only alternative and although no fish were evident in the clear water, and there was a strong south-westerly hammering into this corner and that end of the Works Bank, it looked a far better bet than the Bush. In addition, I was close to the End Works, which I felt would be the best area to move to on the Sunday.

The wind was getting stronger and after putting the rods out and the house up, I sat down with a cup of tea to listen to the rest of the football. Just as I was making the tea, Spike, who was in the Middle Works – a swim which was usually only fished when the water was busy – had a one-noter which weeded him up shortly afterwards. I saw Spike put the rod on the rests, so I rang him to see what was occurring. He said it had gone solid, but judging by the way the fish had torn off, he guessed it was only a common so he had put the rod back on the rests to see if it would swim free on its own. That's not something I have the confidence to do, but Spike had done it before with great success.

Nearly an hour passed, during which he had pulled into it a couple of times, and then the fish tore out of the weed giving Spike another screamer. Ten minutes later I was watching the whole thing through binoculars as, with the help of Mad Martyn, a ton of weed and the fish went into the net. As I saw bits of weed flying out I had a funny feeling what was coming next.

The 'Bazil' shout went up, so I wound in my newly-cast rods, grabbed my mat and camera, and legged it round to the Works Bank. Spike's three-year wait was over and after weighing the fish at 46lb 2oz, he was well happy.

A crowd soon formed and with someone acting as goalie either side of the great fish, she was held up for the cameras. Her big, black back and gold scales were shining and she was certainly a stunning carp. She was as good as gold for the pictures (well, she knows the craic by now), before being lovingly returned to her home.

Well done, Spike, but how long would I have to wait for my chance? Could that have been her last capture of the year? I felt – well, hoped, really – that there was one more chance in October, if the first frosts held off.

Since I'd caught Scale-on-the-Shoulder, there didn't seem to be much point in staying on, so a quick pack-up was followed by a social night on the Car Park before driving home on Sunday to rethink my plans.

Apart from a North/Car Park ticket, I also had a Harefield permit. I'd only done a couple of trips the previous season because I was into fishing the Copse, and I'd only done one trip this year. I'll be honest and tell you that the size of the venue put me off, because a lot of it was extreme-range fishing so I was never quite taken by the place. However, with Bazil coming out and me being on rota, it seemed a good opportunity to have another go, but all to no avail and with that fresh image of Bazil etched in my memory I pushed the barrow back up to the North at top speed on Friday the 1st October.

I found that Rick was already installed in the Main Works

Spike's three-year wait was over.

A strong westerly was blowing on to the works bank and I knew this was where I needed to be. I spoke to Dan in the Channel swim. He'd just had a blank week in the Main Works and, despite the same conditions he hadn't seen anything on the works bank, but this didn't deter me and I headed round there.

I found that Rick was already installed in the Main Works, so I asked if the End was free and was relieved to be told that it was. Rick also informed me that the Corral was shut due to the old dead tree supposedly being cut down that weekend. That was a bit of a bonus, because I could now fish my left-hand rod long, and so I wouldn't be disturbed by anyone in the Corral.

Odd turned up later and, not knowing where he fancied, I said I didn't mind if he went in the Middle Works because I was fishing my left-hand rod long. I showed him the close-range spot which was really in front of the Middle Works and told him to get a bait on that. We set about getting the rods out before dusk and then the talk turned to the winter. We all agreed that the works bank would be the place to be for the winter, and vowed to keep bait going in all the time.

I was having a nightmare getting the left-hand rod as I wanted it when I was recasting on the Saturday afternoon. The middle rod was to the back of the Corral Island, and the right-hand rod was on the back of a gravel hump, just before the bushes which hang off to the right of the Little End Works Island - not too much hassle there – unlike the left-hand spot.

There was a side breeze on the lake, so I was able to get the float to come up in a narrow strip of silt, about three-feet wide between weed at about 70 yards out. However, with floating braid on the marker rod and all the algae moving about on the surface, I ended up dragging the whole lot in two or three times. I already had the spot marked on my line and clipped up, so I had to abandon the float. Using a piece of weed near the channel as a visual aid, I repeatedly cast until the line hit the clip and then I waited until I felt the lead land on soft silt. Finally, after a couple of hours of trying to get the rods out, I had all three baits on the money. I was glad that I'd persevered.

I awoke on the Sunday morning at 8.30am, fearing another blank. Suddenly, there were a few bleeps on my left-hand rod and as I looked down to the sticks, I saw the left-hand tip curved right round before catapulting back, and the clutch started spinning as it came out of the clip. I was down in a flash and after getting it halfway in, it weeded me up. I shouted to Odd and Rick, and after putting on chest waders I waded round the corner to see if a different line angle would shift it - nothing.

I waded back into the swim but a few yards out was as far as I could go. As I bent right into it, I felt it moving slowly. Inch by inch, the rod crept back before coming right in and as I waded back to dry land, Odd slipped the whole lot into the net. It wasn't a monster, but a nice mirror in stunning autumn colours and at 19lbs 12oz, it was one of the Tels. All the hassle of getting that hookbait onto the spot had paid off, and I hadn't blanked after all.

I chucked it back out and put the kettle on. It was a really nice morning; the sun was out, the sky was blue, and there was very little wind. It was a pity it was nearly time to pack up. I took down the bivvy and stood it with the overwrap in the bushes, in the sun, to dry off the dew.

A good mirror was soon recognised.

I packed all the tackle into my carryall and I was nearly done when the right-hand rod, which was locked up down to the little island on the right, bent round to test curve. The fish was brought toward me before suddenly flat-rodding, and then Odd arrived on the scene.

"Don't let it have any more line!" he said.

"I'm trying not to," I replied.

Luckily, the fish hit the weed just to the right of the bushes and with my composure regained I pulled it out of there and back to the waiting net. A good-sized mirror was soon recognised as the Two-Tone Pit 10 fish and at 25lb 15oz it was at its best weight for the year. Unfortunately, there was a nasty sore on its belly by its pelvic fin so, after the photos, we applied Klinik liberally to the wound.

I'd taken two fish from different parts of the swim so it was obvious that I was on them. The first frost was forecast for the Monday night and I felt this was a golden opportunity not to be missed, so I phoned home to check all was well and to say that I would be stopping the night and going to work on the Monday morning. I had the bivvy back up and my gear sorted, and then I headed round to Odd's to get a bit more bait out of his freezer, and go to the shops for supplies.

On my return, I found I had the lake to myself and with two fish under my belt that morning I was well up for it. It was flat calm and I was able to get the marker in position to the left-hand spot, out in line with the Waiting Man's Island. After a couple of casts to the right of the float, and feeling the lead hang up on the weed, the next cast went to the left of the float.

It landed on the clip a yard to the left and I felt the lead fall cleanly through four and a half feet of water, then it thumped on the bottom. I was hoping to feel it land on silt as before, but it felt more like a patch of sand, which was even better. No way was I moving that cast. Quickly, I tightened up the marker out to the right of the swim in order not to get the lines caught up, and then fired 80 of the 20mm boilies along the clear channel next to the float.

The rod to the back of the Corral Island was more troublesome but eventually I got it to bump down. The right-hand rod was easy, that went on to the back of the hump from where I had taken the two-tone mirror. Once the rods were all sorted, I sat back to enjoy having the lake to myself.

That afternoon we had a torrential rainstorm and there was almost a full-blown river running under the groundsheet and down the steps into the lake. Well, if

Turning to the lake I gave it the big'un. "BAZILLLL!"

that didn't wake Bazil up, nothing would! There was a freshness in the air after the storm and as darkness descended it certainly looked good.

At 4.45am I steamed down the steps because the left-hand rod was off to a real flyer. As I bent into it, I felt the satisfying lunge of a hooked carp but I was well aware of the amount of weed between me and the fish, and I knew I needed to keep it moving at all costs so I played it harder than I usually would. I kept it coming all the way and when I saw the weed on the line surface about 10 yards out, I pulled up my jogging trousers and slipped into the water.

The weed was up to the spreader block as I gently lifted the net and a big tail slipped over the drawstring. In the moonlight, I could make out a very wide back and I knew it was one of the big two, I also knew one quick way to check; Scale-on-the-Shoulder only had one pelvic fin. I slipped my hand down the side of the whacker which was lying quietly in the net. Yes, I could feel one pelvic fin down that side. Now down the other side for the moment of truth. Nervously I felt down and, oh yes! Yes! Yes! Two pelvic fins!

Excitement was building up inside me and, with my heart racing, I was 99.9% certain of what I had as I folded the arms down, bit through the line and heaved her up on to the mat. Shakily, I laid my conquest on the mat and I could see that unmistakeable line of scales through the mesh. Turning to the lake I gave it the big'un. "BAZILLLL!"

I'd done it! The hook was well in the bottom corner of her huge mouth and I gently slipped it out, covered her over with the retaining flap of the mat and Velcro'd it down. With shaking fingers, I zeroed the scales, wet the sling and carefully slipped her into it. Then I hoisted her up onto the scales with the help of the landing net pole and weighed her; 46lb 4oz was her best weight for some time.

I made sure she was lying safely in the cool, deep margin and then got on the mobile to Odd. My watch read 4.55am and after quite a few rings, Odd answered blearily. "I've got her mate," I blurted out over the phone.

Unfortunately, Odd told me that he was working away that week and had to set off in 20 minutes, so he wouldn't have time to come down to take the photographs, so I checked that Bazil was lying happily in the sack, wound in the other two rods and legged it down to the Car Park in search of photographers.

I was sure Lee was on for an overnighter but I didn't know what swim he'd pitched up in. I ran down the works bank, squelching in the mud and on hearing someone snoring in the Dugout, I stuck my head in, only to find Jim Shelley dead to the world. I ran back round and down the main bank, sure that I'd find anglers but, unbelievably I found every swim unoccupied. Eventually, I found a bivvy in the Islands and whoever it was they were going to have to be woken up. It turned out to be Ev. I told him that I'd got Bazil and then asked him excitedly if he knew whether Lee was on. Ev was

sure Lee was in the Beach so I continued legging it round the lake and woke up Lee with the good news.

"Didn't you hear the shout?" I asked him.

"I thought I heard something," Lee said, "but I didn't know what it was, or if I'd dreamed it."

As Lee was on a work night, he started to pack up straight away and I left him to get on with it. I said I'd meet him back at the End Works and on finding out that Mark Rosewell was in the Christmas Tree, I returned via Mark's swim. I woke him and told him of my success. Mark said that he hadn't heard my Bazil shout either, but asked if I'd heard him shouting, because he'd experienced a nightmare and thought he'd woken himself up.

"No, your nightmare was someone else catching Bazil!" I laughed.

With Mark in tandem, we arrived back at my swim at the onset of dawn and when the kettle was steaming, Lee arrived right on cue. As soon as our tea was supped, we got the great fish on the mat. Bazil knew the score and behaved herself very well, apart from a couple of little kicks, and while Lee manned the cameras, Mark goalied and kept her nice and wet. As I held her aloft, I realised that I'd joined an elite group of Bazil captors: McDonald, Maylin, Hearn, Sharp and Pagulatos, to name but a few.

I waded back into the margins of the North, lifted her for the last few return shots, and then lovingly lowered her back into her home. She sat on the bottom for a minute which was worrying, so I waded out and gently lifted her from the silty lake bed. Her tail waggled strongly, and as she regained her strength, I released her and proudly watched her glide out into the depths. Job done!

I'd had a perfect year on the North, top-rodding with nine carp, including both big'uns and I'd thoroughly enjoyed my time on the lake, with nice surroundings, a good bunch of lads and no hassle. I was overjoyed with catching Bazil, but there was a tinge of sadness as I pushed the barrow down the works bank for the final time. I knew that my time on the North was over, but as the path turned, there in front of me was my next mission; the Car Park Lake - the ultimate challenge.

I released her and proudly watched her glide out into the depths.

Chapter 9 - The ultimate challenge begins - The Car Park Lake

After capturing Bazil the king of Yateley, it was obviously time to move off the North and as my ticket was valid for the Car Park as well, the queen of Yateley in the shape of Heather the Leather was the next ultimate prize, although when I started, the target was just to catch any of the prized Car Park residents of which there were nine, every one of them a special carp.

Although Heather had always been the largest one, Arfur had overtaken her at the start of the season, albeit with spawn, but Arfur was the first Yateley carp to break the 50lb barrier, after not getting caught for a season or two. I soon learned what a tricky customer old 'fatso' was going to be. Heather was close behind with the much sought-after Single Scale at mid-40. Single had the reputation of being a bruiser. Big, wide-set shoulders meant Single was a bit of an animal. Big Orange and Chunky were now both regular 40s, which bought the tally to five with the Dustbin not far off the magic mark as well. The remaining three mirrors were all 30s; Baby Orange at mid-30, and the other two, Pearly Tail and Ugloe, at low-30s - an impressive list in a water of around eight acres.

I'd only done one night on the Car Park when Spike caught Bazil, but a few friends were fishing the lake that summer so I had an idea of how hard the lake was, although I had no plans to stay on the lake indefinitely. I just wanted to catch one and I'd be happy to walk away, or so I thought at the time.

The first frost of the year descended on Monday night, just 24 hours after the capture of Bazil, so I'd caught her just in time. The North Lake was much shallower than the

Car Park, on average, so I hoped the extra depth wouldn't put the Car Park whackers off the feed yet, and as my confidence was high, maybe I could fluke one out quickly.

The Car Park was always busy, and many of the anglers who fished there had a lot of time on their hands, certainly more than me, anyway. Arriving on a Friday afternoon isn't the best on any lake and it soon became clear that I'd be slotting in to any available swim I could, for the time being anyway, but with Bazil and Scale-on-the-Shoulder under my belt, this season I could afford to tread carefully and as long as I could get a swim, I'd be learning for when an opportunity came my way.

My first trip was memorable, to say the least. I'd set up in Waiting Mans, so named because it was next to Trumptons and basically, people used to fish it just waiting for Trumptons to become vacant. After returning from a Bazil celebratory café breakfast (double mushrooms) and doing a circuit of the lake, I was standing in the margin in my chesties having a plumb around with the marker to see what features I could find for the third rod, when I looked over to the Islands opposite and saw Steve Pag' up to his knackers in water playing a fish.

I tried shouting across to gain him some assistance, but Derek, who's deaf, was in Dessies and Pinky was fast asleep in the Curly, so I got no answer. I shouted out to Lee and Dave that Steve was in and told them that I was going round to lend a hand. If you've ever wondered why athletes don't wear waders then let me tell you there's a bloody good reason. I was fit to drop by the time I'd puffed and panted round to Steve's swim.

Steve had hooked the fish under the trees down the right-hand margin, but it was now out in the open water and it looked like plain sailing until it steamed back toward the snags. Steve thought it might be the Dustbin because he'd seen a big, ghostly-grey, leathery fish minutes earlier on his spot.

Steve was using braid and the carp started dragging him deeper down the shelf as he hung on, desperate for it not to reach the snags. I still had the chesties on, so I was able to steam in and grab the back of his shirt because he was up to his chest already and in danger of being dragged off the shelf into much deeper water.

Fortunately, Steve's soft blank absorbed the angry lunges and he was able to regain his composure and step back into shallower water to lead the fish back under the rod tip. As the big, grey carp surfaced, I stretched the net out and under the monster and encased her in the safety of the mesh. After a quick check we could see that it wasn't the Dustbin, but the true nude leather of the lake - Heather.

This was the second time I'd seen her and both times Steve had been the lucky captor, although I think even Steve would admit that he'd got lucky the first time. He was only fishing the Car Park because Bazil had been caught but this time he'd put in a lot of time and effort, particularly on the set of snags down the Island swim margin

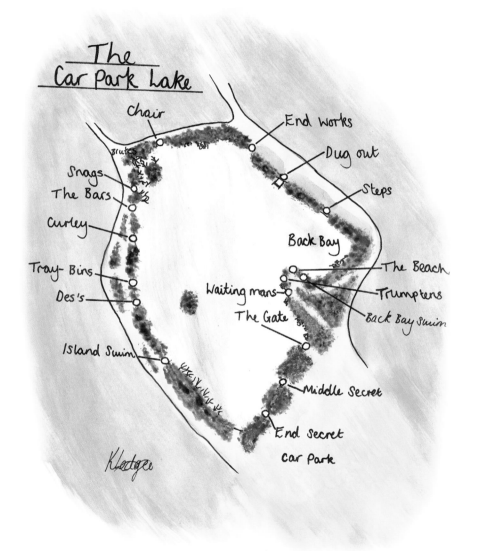

where he'd hooked her. Soon, everyone on the lake was present, and Heather had set a new lake and Surrey record at 51lbs 4oz; a true monster and the biggest carp I'd ever seen.

I was well pleased for Steve and was glad to have been involved in netting her for him but it soon became obvious that one or two individuals had the hump because Steve had doubled up on Heather. The ugly side of carp fishing reared its head as the aforementioned stropped off back to their swim, instead of hanging about for a celebratory cuppa or two. What an impressive fish! I fell in love with the big leather carp that day.

October fished well on the Car Park, with first Arfur coming out to Dave Mallin from the Snags swim, and then Heather coming out again one Friday night from the Curly. Darren Emberson turned up to cast out, just on dark, after a pair of chest waders had 'kept' the swim for him that afternoon. Darren's rigs had only been a matter of a few yards from mine. I was set up on Trumptons which also controls the 'Bermuda Triangle' in the middle of the lake, but Heather preferred Darren's hook bait to mine that night, and it soon became clear that Heather 'liked' certain people and not others!

I continued through the winter months, on and off, and was fortunate to witness the eccentric Lewis Read catch the Dustbin one Sunday morning out of the Beach swim. I was packing up from another fruitless weekend's fishing in the Chair when I heard the commotion from Trumptons and hurried round to see Lewis hold aloft the enigmatic Dustbin at 38lbs.

I finally had a bite at the end of March, just before the lake shut for two months and, sad as it might seem, I was well chuffed to land a tench! The Car Park Lake didn't give up any of its fish easily and at the end of a long winter it felt like an achievement just to catch a tinca. I'd learned a few spots and now as a regular, I was accepted into the Car Park fold so fingers crossed for the summer when I could seriously start to try to catch one of the majestic Car Park Lake creatures.

At long last, the close season drew to an end and a load of hopeful carp anglers congregated in the car park for the draw for swims. The North Lake draw took place first, and after that was completed with a full North Lake, the Bazil hunters dispersed and the Car Park Lake anglers all popped their tickets into a rather splendid carrier bag. Head honcho, Raymondo, gave it a shake and the first name was drawn. Little Jon chose the Back Bay, which was a bit of a surprise, but little did we know what Jon had been up to all close season and it turned out to be an excellent decision.

Fourth out of the bag was me, and seeing that the Islands was still free, I plumped for there and I was well happy with that. Not only did I have a good amount of open water but also the snaggy margin to the right, from where Steve Pag had caught Heather. I baited under the tree with 3mm pellets and a few big ones because I was going to use a large pellet as a hookbait.

I'd found a clear area about 40 yards out so I baited it with boilies, among the weed beds, left the rigs hanging in the butt rings and went for a social around the lake. The witching hour was 9pm, so wearing chest waders, I waded down the margin and lowered my pellet onto the baited patch of little pellets that I'd put in earlier. I had two backleads attached so I hoped everything was pinned down and then with a donk on the boilie rod, I was fishing and my Car Park quest could now begin.

At 7am, while sitting on my bedchair, the snag rod signalled action as the bobbin hit the top. As I scooted toward it, the tip bent right round before pinging back straight just as I got to the rod. I was already in the process of grabbing it and soon had the lead swinging into my hand to check the rig. Whether it was a pick up and the culprit had managed to shake the hook out as it came up in the water I'll never know, but it certainly made my heart race for a short while. I soon learned there was no lake quite like the Car Park for getting the adrenalin pumping through your veins!

On the afternoon of the 17th the silence was broken with an 'Arfur!' shout and I could see a net held off the Trumpton boards so presumed it was Bally who was in

I heard the commotion from Trumptons.

Trumptons. I wound in and legged it round only to find Little Jon was the conqueror of the stumpy-finned beast. LJ had stalked her from the end bank in the bay; top angling, and at 47lbs she looked pukka and in perfect condition.

In typical Yateley fashion it was like the paparazzi swarming into Trumptons, but once the photos had been taken, I got chatting to Jon about my occurrence the day before and L J said it may well have been Chunky because he'd had it feeding there all week in the run up to the start. That was just what I needed to know –a chance of a 40 gone begging! There's nothing like the sight of a big carp on the bank for refreshing enthusiasm, and I returned extra keen and paid careful attention to getting the rigs in spot on.

That week the carp had a spawn and on my return I found Little Jon was weaving his magic, now in the Island swim. The right-hand margin rod tripped up the magnificent Chunky and a spawned-out Arfur, now down to 39lbs.

It transpired that L J had been baiting his spots for the previous two months and could almost hand feed them with trout pellets. Jon was fishing full time and as there was a 7-day limit on the lake, Jon was fishing 6 days a week with just one day off, and he held the Islands for weeks at a time, knocking out the lake's prizes one by one, with only the rare capture by anyone else.

I've never seen anyone dominate a lake like Jon did that year and fishing the open water spots was almost a waste of time. Their magic beans were in the margins and it soon became clear that there was little point in fishing anywhere else.

My first opportunity came in September when I moved into the Island on the Saturday morning. I'd done this a few times. I'd set up on a Friday evening somewhere, moved in behind Jon on the Saturday, and then handed it back to him on Sunday morning. This suited Jon, and at the time I thought it was giving me a brief chance, but that was miniscule because, unbeknown to me, Jon was filling in the 'safe' area deeper in the snags with enough pellet to stop them from venturing up the margin. Selfish angling, yes, but to succeed on the Car Park it sometimes requires you to look after number one; be it keeping a sighting under your hat, sneaking a bit of bait onto a spot in the middle of the night, or sometimes, putting out the odd 'blind'.

I used to have a bit of fun with Simon 'Trawlerman' Davey as far as the blinds went. Trawler was a switched on angler and would notice what people were up to, so when I saw him after doing a circuit of the lake, he'd always ask me what I'd seen.

Little Jon was the conqueror of the stumpy-finned beast.

Quite often it was nothing, but when I replied, "nowt mate," he'd always think I was blagging and say, "Come on mate, what you seen?" I soon learned that I could have a bit of fun and if I had seen anything on my travels it was easy to lure him away.

I'd know he was watching so if I saw a fish, the trick was not to hang about too long in that area and lure him away by hanging about in a totally different place, getting up and down a tree or two, and then on my way back when Si asked the usual, "What you seen?" question, a bit of body language like a grin, or looking away as I said, "Not much mate," would have him throwing obscenities at me as I walked away laughing. The hanging about in the wrong area would soon have him investigating the barren swims, giving me a chance to move on to the fish, and when he came round to tell me that he hadn't seen anything up at the other end, I'd say, "I did say I hadn't seen much, didn't I?" Off he'd stomp, muttering more abuse and leaving me giggling.

Although this was a running joke between us, Trawler, being the capable angler that he is, had the last laugh because during his time on the Car Park he went on to catch the massive Heather, not once, but twice. What was it I said earlier about her liking particular people?

Anyway, back to the Islands; after moving into the swim on my return from the café, I got one rod placed under the bough of the overhanging tree in the margin, and

one out in open water. I had a look in the trees that afternoon and I thought I made out a shape drifting past at the bottom of the shelf. The light wasn't great and waves were lapping in so I was unsure, but it was encouraging.

I'd planned to fish most of the Sunday on the strength of this and at Sunday lunchtime, when I could make out a white dot moving about down at the bottom of the shelf, I decided to do the Sunday night. Now, let me explai;: that year the Dustbin had a white mark about the size of a 10p piece on his right flank and I was sure it was him mooching about on the shelf leading up to the bait.

I told Little John my sighting and he looked decidedly nervous that someone else might nick one off his spot, but as I was doing another night he'd have to wait for the Islands.

Now for anyone reading this thinking I'm fishing on the back of Jon's hard work then yes, I was, but LJ had done such a job on these fish that if you didn't fish pellet in the margins then you might as well stay at home. The Car Park carp were totally preoccupied! Little Jon was full time so could do what he'd done but as a weekender desperate for just one fish, then I had to get in an area where they'd feed.

Anyway, I was sure the Dustbin was about, hopefully not alone, and I had until 6.30am the following morning. I put about six handfuls of pellet on the spot, which was enough to get a bite but not too much if just one fish came up onto the spot. I went to bed that evening full of expectation and fell asleep dreaming of an eventful night.

In the early hours, that event happened; not quite what I'd been dreaming of but exhilarating all the same. Odd woke me up, grinning from ear to ear, with the news that Bazil was safely in his net.

So, an earlier than expected wind-in was called for and although I was disappointed at having to pull the bait in prematurely, seeing my good mate hold aloft the stunning, as always, Bazil, as I clicked the shutter on the camera, certainly made up for it. Well chuffed, Odd had successfully ended his North Lake campaign but now there would be another angler on the Car Park - more pressure!

The rest of September and early October went by with Little Jon, the Pied Piper, still playing his tune, bracing one week with the Baby Orange and Heather at over 47lbs. With LJ now having caught all the originals (some a couple of times) except Single Scale and the Big Orange, Jon's tally was more than the rest of the syndicate put together.

It soon became clear that there was little point in fishing anywhere but the margins.

It was now over a full year since my capture of Bazil and I was desperate for a fish, any fish, to end my drought. On Friday, October the 20th, I wandered round to find the lake quite busy but the Chair swim was empty so I had a good look down both margins, the Brute's corner and the margin that backed on to Bazil's bay in the North Lake. As I crept though the undergrowth, I spotted something of interest; not a carp, but a gravel patch that was glowing golden. It hadn't been like that before so I could only surmise that it had been cleaned off by being fed on. That was good enough for me, so I left my bucket to claim the Chair swim and returned to the car park to load the barrow.

As I walked past the Islands, Jon asked me where I was going, I told him I'd be in the Chair and he informed me that the Pineapple had been up in that margin during the week. The Pineapple was good enough for me, despite having a funny mouth and being the smallest mirror in the lake, so I decided that I'd better try to catch that one.

I got on with sorting the rods out because the evenings were drawing in early now so light levels faded quickly, and with margin traps you really need to see what you're doing. The Brutes margin rod required the marker, not to locate the spot but because getting the line over as a direct cast was impossible. By walking round to Brutes, though, I could underarm cast the marker in front of the right-hand gap in the Chair swim. Then I'd prop up the rod, set the clutch slack, and return to the Chair.

Using just a lead and a big hook, I could then cast over the braid, hook it up and pull it close enough to grab. Then, with the braid in hand, it was just a case of pulling in the float, tying my rod's main line to the swivel, and winding the whole lot back from Brutes, holding the main line, ready to tie on the leadcore. It sounds simple, but mistakes were made early on. The more I did this sort of thing, though, the more lessons were learned.

Brutes was deep and tree-covered with loads of twigs littered in the channel and I soon learned that if I wound the marker back with the lead attached, it would pick up debris, dead leaves and twigs that would foul the line. It was best to cut off the lead, tie direct to the main line and then wind it in across the surface, keeping it nice and straight so that it didn't foul on any sunken branches.

Another trick I found useful was to return to the swim and tighten the clutch right up once the line was across and secured to a tree branch. This way a backlead could be attached and slid down on a tight line as far as needed, which would help to pull out the leadcore in a straight line as it sank down when I lowered the lead on to the spot. A slack line would leave the leadcore in a pile, and there could be a chance of it looping round a root or branch when I tightened up at the rod end. Everything needed to be laid out straight to enhance the line lay so that a carp entering the area wouldn't be suspicious.

The Pied Piper was still playing his tune.

The Chair swim.

The left-hand margin spot was much easier. There were no snags in the way so I could place the bait by hand before walking back up the shallow margin, sinking the line as I went, before placing the rod on the rest.

This week I'd changed my hookbaits to try to mimic the pellets that the carp were so preoccupied with. Previously, like most people, I was using a cut-down boilie, but this week I just felt that I had to go one step further.

A pellet would have been ideal, but it was not feasible for a 4mm pellet to stay on the hair. The oil was washing out of the pellets, and they obviously went lighter in colour so I felt a small fragment of cork would be ideal, and to give it some smell and for personal confidence I glued a pellet to either side of the cork. This way, I had pellets on the hair but if they did break down, although the glue would slow that process, I still had a hookbait in the form of the cork. With a tiny shot pinched on the hair to sink it and placed in a very small PVA bag with 30 or 40 pellets, the whole lot would shoot in, and the large strong hook would fall to the floor of the mouth and catch hold. That was the plan, but I'd learned that the Car Park Lake has a habit of chewing up plans and spitting them out.

I'd fished some difficult lakes in my time and after coming off the back of catching 20 fish from the Copse and North lakes which are not exactly runs waters, over the previous two seasons, I was seriously questioning if I'd bitten off more than I could chew in taking on these Car Park Einstein carp.

Anyway, I baited with a decent-sized patch of pellet just beyond the rig and added a further three patches of only a handful to mimic my PVA bagful patch, with a good foot or so separating each one. My thinking was, if they sucked up the hookbait patch they'd have to move at least a foot to the next pile, giving the 4oz lead and seven-inch hooklink enough room to bury the hook.

I went to bed that evening dreaming of the Pineapple. That's what this lake had done to me! It should have been Heather or Arfur, but I was so desperate to catch, that a snub-nosed 17-pounder had become my target. Despite having two backleads on, I still had a few little liners on the left-hand margin rod in the night, and on checking the spot at 9am I could see that all the bait had gone, except for a few pellets around my rig!

With no snags in the way I could place my bait by hand.

The majestic-looking Chunky.

I'd been done up like a kipper but it had given me the kick up the arse for revenge and so after a quick café breakfast, I was back and eager to lay the perfect trap.

With my little bag of pellets tied around the hookbait and an AAA shot halfway down the braided hooklink, I waded under the bough to survey the scene. I felt the best place for the rig was where the biggest patch of bait had been the previous night and hoped that they'd revisit and mop up my hookbait.

The water was clear and the light levels much better than the previous evening so I was able to examine the lakebed much better and on the edge of where I'd wanted to lower my rig was a concrete block wedged in the bottom, with a raised edge of about an inch.

I knew the Car Park mirrors liked to flank the bottom when feeding and I wondered if this was what had given me the liners the night before as they picked up the leadcore with their fins. I lowered my rig about six inches from the corner of the block, and still holding the leadcore until the bag started to melt and sunk to the bottom, I then bounced the lead back to the block. This partially straightened out the braided hooklink and with the lead in position, I could lay the leadcore tight down the edge of the raised block which would not allow them to get their fins under it, hiding it from their attention.

Just as I was about to let go of the leadcore, I noticed that it was caught up on a thin root that stuck out from the bottom. I tweaked it to the side and it fell in underneath and flush to the bottom. Phew! That could have seriously jeopardised my chances!

I clipped on a small backlead a few feet back, another one at the bottom of the shelf and my trap was as perfect as I could set. Now I just had to wait and see if last night's culprit returned for seconds. Before the light faded too much I checked the spot and it was all intact so it looked like the pellet thief was sneaking in under cover of darkness.

The breeze died off after dark and the moon was bright, but with some cloud cover it was a mild night for the end of October. The first frosts were likely not too far away, though, and I needed to catch before the winter set in, even if was only the Pineapple.

The adrenalin was pumping.

At 4.20am the carefully-positioned trap was set off and all hell broke loose as my set-up twisted with the ferocity of the take. I leapt on the rod as the reel jammed up against the alarm and hung on as if my life depended on it, as it lunged on the end. Fortunately, the size 5 T6 hook held firm and as soon as I turned its head, the carp let me lead it straight back up the margin. It bobbed up at the end of the platform, forcing me to backwind a couple of turns so it wasn't on too short a line. I chucked the net in and the fish plodded out a few yards and wallowed just below the surface, sending ripples across the millpond surface.

The tip nodded as the hooked fish moved its head and I coaxed it back gently toward the net. I held my breath and felt an overwhelming sense of joy and relief as I lifted the net arms around it and pulled the net into the end of the platform.

Assuming it was the Pineapple, I grabbed my head torch, kneeled on the end of the board, and flicked it on to see not a fully-scaled double but a sparsely-scaled 40-pounder lying beaten in the folds of my net. My heart was racing as I rolled it on to its side and saw that the majestic-looking Chunky was my extremely hard-earned and overdue reward.

It was a year and 18 days since I'd captured Bazil and I'd saved up a lot of lung power so with all my frustration released, I bellowed, "CHUNKY!" out across the lake, scattering dozens of birds that were roosting out on the bar and sending the geese into a bout of indignant honking.

I staked the net at the end of the board and ran round to get Spike who was in the Snags. Not only had I got off the mark, but also with one of the real gems of the Car Park, and almost certainly my second 40-pounder.

Spike gave me a hand to unhook and weigh Chunky at 42lb 6oz, and he was in perfect condition. We laid him quietly in the margin and waited until daylight when I legged it round to inform everyone of my success. Mad Martyn was in the Gate and he said he knew something had happened when he'd woken up in the night and thought he was still dreaming because loads of birds were squawking and all flying toward him!

Once the crew were all assembled, we lifted Chunky on to the mat and carried him the short distance to the works bank so we'd have some decent light for the photos and with 'goalkeepers' either side, I lifted Chunky up and extremely proudly held him out to the clicking cameras assembled in front of me.

Adrenalin was pumping so I managed to hold him despite aching muscles, then slipped into the margins of the End Works and after a few returners had been taken I lowered him back among the tiny lilies and watched the long-awaited, and most hard-earned, capture of my life waddle back to its rock-hard home.

I'd finally caught my Car Park mirror but now I'd caught one, maybe, just maybe, I could catch another one! The lake had cast its spell on me, and little did I know that it would be many years before I could break that spell. The Car Park Lake and its inhabitants would possess my mind.

I lowered him back among the tiny lilies.

Chapter 10 - Car Park - The second step

After the success of capturing Chunky, I was confident of setting traps in the edge and I continued fishing the margin swims for the next few weeks. The cold weather was moving in and that meant the fish had most likely pushed out into deeper water and the sanctuary of a weed bed and although I persevered throughout the colder months, only tench and the occasional big bream had the bobbins moving.

Little Jon had caught all the mirrors except for Single Scale and the Big Orange, which even Jon labelled impossible to catch, and as Bazil was now attracting his attention, it looked as if next summer would see LJ out of the way. As is often the case, though, when you get rid of one top angler, another one comes along and (my soon to become) very good mate, Fudgey, was going to be fully focused on the Car Park after his September capture of Bazil.

Fudge is a very capable margin angler and between him, me, and one or two others, we could keep the trouties going in on a regular basis. Steve was fairly local so most evenings saw him down at the pond trickling a few of the magic beans in on the margin spots. I lived nearly 100 miles away so that luxury was not a goer for me but with no real spring water to fish I was heading to Yateley at the weekend and doing a few hours day fishing on the Match Lake and either kipping at Odd's or going over to the Split Lake, which is right next to the Car Park, and doing nights on there. Either way, it gave me the opportunity of baiting the Car Park and watching the fish at close quarters, trying to learn about the feeding habits of my quarry.

One particular look-see comes to mind; it was a Saturday evening, only a week before the draw, and I was doing my last circuit before going back to the Split Lake to chuck a couple of rods out before dark. As I made my way past the Chair swim, I crept down the path through the brambles, down to the spot where I'd caught Chunky, and leaning against the trunk of the overhanging tree, I peered down to the spot I'd baited a couple of hours previously. I saw the flank of a mirror as it ghosted off the spot so I pulled myself up the trunk a bit to gain an extra couple of feet in height and, as I lay on the trunk, the unmistakable Arfur circled in and went straight down on the pellet. She was literally six feet below me and was shovelling the bait down like one of my greedy pigs at home.

As I drooled over the size of the fat girl, I watched with interest how she fed. She wasn't the most agile. Being fat, wide and with tiny fins meant that she couldn't turn very quickly, so she'd go down on the bait, hoover up a line of pellet and then, as she reached the end of the patch, she'd waddle up off the spot, waggling her stumpy tail, and circle in as tight an arc as possible, before dropping back down on the bait to shovel in some more. She was so big, clumsy and - on this evidence - greedy, that she looked an easy fish to hook, but how wrong can you be? I'd say that Arfur was the wiliest of the lot.

The Chair was now my number one choice for the start but I knew how much Fudgey liked that swim, so I'd have to come out before him in the draw. Anyway, I watched Arfur have her fill until the light faded and then I loaded the spot with more magic beans and went to put out a couple of rods for the night. I was awoken a couple of hours later when one of the Split's giant slugs tore off with my rig, forcing a bit of a tussle what with all the lake's snags and islands.

The draw was the following weekend, on the bank holiday Monday, so I went down on the Sunday and fished the Split on the Car Park bank, up behind the Snags swim so that if the Car Park fish were active at night I'd know their whereabouts. It was fairly quiet that night after I'd got rid of an excited Fudgey but he was back at first light, calling out the famous Yateley catchphrase, 'kettle on boyeee!' One of Yateley's characters, Big Tony, had made this a popular phrase on the banks of the Car Park. With steaming mugs in hand, we sat in the Bars swim or the Snags and looked out for any signs of carp as the mist wisped up off the surface.

As the morning dragged on, more and more guys turned up, all keen for another campaign. With L J out the way, maybe there were a few more captures to go round the syndicate, as Jon had finished the season with, I think it was, 11 out of the 20 mirror captures, including seven different ones. Total domination!

My first choice was the Chair, with my next preferred swim being completely at the other end of the lake - the Gate. I'd had Single feeding on more than one occasion just off the bank down the margin toward the Gate snag. It wasn't fishable from the swim and would have to be stalked, but it was hard, clean gravel and was close enough simply to lower a bait on, straight off the rod tip. It would be nice to get the Islands, but I knew that would go immediately, so unless I was lucky enough to come out first, it was unlikely I'd get in there. The Chair and Gate however were realistic swims to get as long as I didn't come out too far down the line.

All the tickets were put into the hat, or should I say Tesco carrier bag, and the anxious wait for my name to be called out began. Predictably, the Islands and Back Bay soon went, as well as the more popular open water swims that were known about by new members; the Curly, Trumptons and Dugout.

As we got down to about tenth out, neither of my swims had been taken so I lived in hope, but whose name should come out next but Fudgester, and despite umming and ahhing, he took the Chair. My name came out next and I whispered, 'git!' as I passed him and called out 'Gate', took my ticket and returned to the crowd. Opening day was still a few days away, so I put in a bucket of pellet on the stalking spot and headed home to prepare for a full-on assault of the Car Park Lake.

I arrived back about 5pm on the 31st of May and backed the car up into my swim. No barrow necessary in the Gate! There was a northerly blowing and it was pumping straight into me but despite the chilly wind, my mood was red-hot as a carp nutted out, literally 15 yards from my swim. Result! I sat and watched for a few minutes and then another one popped out; they were probably both commons, but definitely carp and a great sign. I'd planned to fish the bar just out in front at 20 yards, bait the margin spot and have a rod ready if anything should get on it. With carp in the vicinity, I quickly set up, ushering any visitors to the back of the swim.

We could keep the magic beans going in on a regular basis.

I was confident of presenting a trap in the edge.

The barbecue was going full swing in the car park, so I left my baited rods leaning against the bivvy and with the swim quiet, enjoyed the barbie and a beer before the short walk back across the car park to flick out my small bags of pellet for the 9pm kick-off.

As usual, when all the leads and lines were out, everything went quiet and although I spotted the odd fish, no Single Scale, or any fish for that matter - barring the odd tench - visited my baited edge spot. Fudge managed the Long Common off the left-hand Chair spot but nothing else came out from the edge.

I was now back to weekends, so it was a return to the Friday afternoon bucket run and with only a handful of swims vacant, and others turning up at around the same time, it was a case of claiming a swim and then if I could find a fish, dropping something in that swim and running back to free up the earlier choice.

The Car Park fish were always fairly easy to find in the day but there was little guarantee that they'd be there at night or the next morning. Despite a few more getting caught out in the lake after their annihilation in the margins last year, and more bait going out in the pond with the likes of Chilly and Shelley loading the middle of the lake, I was predominately still fishing the margins. I was confident of presenting a trap in the edge and was able to hide everything humanly possible, even going to the trouble of prodding the line into the bottom.

The summer passed me by and with the nights cooling down through September the carp seemed to be visiting more the high-oil pellet larders that were in the margins. With Si Croft having caught Bazil, and with more competition for the margin spots, what with Simon having time on his hands, the whole process of getting to fish a glowing spot got harder.

Simon first paid attention to the Islands but soon got bored with that area and baited the margin between the Gate snag and Waiting Mans. The Big Orange, Pearly Tail and some commons were usually in the Gate snag and as Simon was holding the Gate swim, he could protect this area and by baiting spots up the margin, he was slowly luring them further up toward Waiting Mans and into a clearing in the trees where he could safely stalk them. Si is like a heron, he's so tall and lanky and he was standing behind a thin tree, watching for hours as his targets grew more confident and fed further up the shelf.

One day in September the 'uncatchable' Big Orange sucked up his hookbait and wading straight in, he played her out under the tip; a class piece of angling. With the

The 'uncatchable' Big Orange.

- -

Big Orange hooked, he vacated the area but Pearly was still feeding in the Gate margin. She was now more wary, though, and Si was finding it hard to get her up to the spot.

At the beginning of October, Simon had to leave on the Saturday and I said I'd have the Gate off him, but because of my much more limited time, I was going to fish it from the swim and cast across into the small hole, get hold of the line, tie on my leadcore, and place the bait by hand.

As it was much closer to her home - the snag - I hoped she'd feed more confidently but with the snag only about 15 feet away and the likelihood that a hooked fish would kite for this sanctuary, I planned to use braid for my main line, giving me instant indication and, with no stretch, more chance of stopping anything reaching the branches. The plan was formulated; now it was time to put it into operation.

As I moved my gear in, I was winding up Si saying that I'd have her out of the hole as it was too spicy for him. Fudgey joined in the wind-up and I could tell Si was a little bit worried. Yes, I was fishing off Si's hard work and in an ideal world I would have let Si get on with it, and I'm sure he'd have eventually caught Pearly, but as a weekender only and having waited nearly a year for a good opportunity, this was my chance. With so few captures it had to be every man for himself and Si understood this as much as any angler. He said his farewells and through gritted teeth wished me luck. Laughing, I told him I'd let him know how big she was.

I'd fished the spot before and casting into the bush above the hole meant that by going round to the far margin with a long telescopic pole with a buzzer bar attached, I could hook up the line. I had an old, adjustable one that had the screws underneath and this was ideal for hooking up the line. Once the line was in my hand, I could cut off the little lead and pull the trailing line through the leaves. On this occasion, however, I had access to a mate's bait boat and this made the process much quicker.

With the line towed under the canopy of the trees and the boat on the bank I slid a backlead out to the drop-off and with my leadcore leader and baited rig tied on I lowered the rig into a likely-looking spot.

- -

Pearly Tail and the commons were still in the area.

I lowered the rig on to a likely-looking spot.

As the little PVA bag melted, I dinked the lead away to semi-tighten the braided hooklink and letting the leadcore fall away from me, I double-checked that everything looked right. I fed a big patch of pellet a couple of feet to the snag side, hoping a good safe feed would encourage Pearly to venture further. I put a handful higher up the shelf and one the other side of the rig, making sure that no pellet went over the leadcore. I returned to my plot and gently tensioned up the line before popping on the hanger and locking up the rod in the rest, with a tight clutch. I cast the second rod out on the bar to the left.

At about 4.30pm, I had a few bleeps on the margin rod and hovered over it watching the line as it entered the water and assumed it was a liner, what with the braid showing instant indication. Shortly after, Fudgie called in for a tea and with the kettle on, I got him to sit on the rods while I quickly checked my spot. I ran round and crept in the small gap but the light was fading fast and I was unable to make out the baited spot so I just had to sit on it until the morning.

That night I heard a couple of rolls off the tree line and was hopeful of a bite, but I sat on my hands until midday, before checking the spot. With much better light I could see the bottom clearly and apart from a few pellets around the rig, I'd been totally cleaned out. She'd done me and that's what the bleeps I'd had the previous afternoon must have been about.

I could stay another night as I didn't need to be home until the morning. After the recent foot and mouth epidemic, and the fact that there was no money in farming despite the hard slog all year round, I'd decided that at 28 years old, if I didn't get out now, then it would be too late to do anything else. I told my dad that I didn't want to do it any more and we decided to wind it all up. I secured a job at Hinders Fishing Tackle shop so I would be working doing something that I knew about and loved, and I'd have more time to fish and be on more money; all good!

The animals would not all be gone until the November, so I was doing a Tuesday and Thursday at the shop during September and October because I could manage to feed and clean what pigs we had in an hour or two. So, with this in mind, I didn't need to get away until the Monday morning.

I lifted out the rig and put a new bait on. I'd moved on from a cut down bit of cork to a sliver of brown foam with pellets glued on, and with a tiny PVA bag attached, I did as I'd done with the Chunky capture and lowered the rig on the spot that had received the big patch of bait the night before. I'd put the pile of bait a couple of feet to the side furthest from the snag, and I hoped that the reverse baited trap would

fool her this time. Everything went sweetly and with the wind still ruffling into the tree line and the weather being dry but warm it looked good for it.

Fudge had packed up from his weekend's fishing and sat at the top of the steps with me having a brew when the right-hand rod hooped round against its locked-up post and as I flew down the step, I'll always remember hearing Fudge shout out, "That's a carp!" That made me move fast and with the rod in full fighting curve, I plunged the tip under water as I walked out into the lake, frantically trying to get a couple of reel turns on the fish as it bucked and twisted, kiting for the main snag in the corner. If it reached the snag I was done for but with no stretch in the braid it gave me vital inches and my 2¼ test curve Pursuits held firm.

With one big heave, I turned her over and as she came toward me I was able to ease right off so not to put too much pressure on the hookhold. Fudge was in the waders now and with praise and encouragement helped me settle down a bit. It was all a bit touch and go - talk about a mega adrenalin rush!

Now I was able to give a bit of line, she chugged out in front before plugging herself in the weed. The braid was a massive bonus and holding the rod high, I literally lifted the fish back out from the weed and led her into my margin. I kept the tip high as every nod and shake of the head banged the tip down. It was a fraught fight but I was winning and as Steve stretched out, I drew her in with a lump of weed over her head and into the net screaming out a big, "YEEESSSSS!"

Fudge checked the net and confirmed what we pretty much already knew. "Pearly!" was yelled at the top of my voice and then Steve held her in the net while I grabbed the phone and made a few calls. I had to let Si know; not to rub it in but it felt only right to let him know first, and thank him for keeping the swim warm for me and, looking at how plump Pearly looked, for feeding her as well.

Si knew what I was gong to say as soon as he answered the phone, and it was good to hear his genuine congratulations. Si wouldn't have fished my spot and although the fight was hairy I'd landed her safely and not once did she hit any branches as she sped under the tree line so I'd made a good decision, that's for sure.

A few mates hurtled into the car park and the mats were waiting for her, so we hoisted her out. Pearly's liking for pellet meant that she was in tip-top condition and at her biggest-ever weight - a plump 36lb 9oz. Everyone lent a hand and all I had to do was hold her up for the camera. These moments take so long to happen but go by in a blur and as I stood in the Gate margins doing the returner, it dawned on me that I'd caught two of the lake's nine mirrors. I had more time on my hands now, so maybe I could catch another one quite quickly and then I'd be a third of the way through them.

Coming on to the Car Park to catch just one, had changed to catching as many as possible, with Heather the Leather the ultimate target. The lake had its claws dug into me now and had no intention of letting go.

Pearly's liking for pellet meant she was in tip-top condition.

Everyone lent a hand.

Chapter 11 - Car Park -
Year of the video

The responsibility of the farm was now over and I felt that a great weight had been lifted from my shoulders. My new work pattern was four days on and four days off, so my fishing time was greatly increased and I could do three or four nights in every eight-day period. To be successful consistently on the Car Park Lake demanded this sort of time, so after 12 years of being a weekender only, I could now compete on a more level playing field with the other anglers.

On the other side of the coin, though, it soon became apparent that due to the extra time, more was expected from me which only added pressure, most of which took the form of banter and the odd dig, but stupidly, I put pressure on myself because lack of time was now not a reason for not catching.

The Dustbin was the prime candidate for a winter capture and as it was one I ideally wanted, I was going to plod on doing two or three nights each trip, throughout the cold period. The central area of the lake, and in particular the Curly Wurly, had the best form for a winter bite and especially for producing the Dustbin, so this would be my base camp for the winter unless, of course, I saw or heard something elsewhere.

The first weekend of December, I fished in the Gate as one of the full-timers was in the Curly and on waking up on the Sunday morning to dense fog, I decided to pack away and join a few of the lads who were heading up to the Sandown Carp Show. Conditions looked awful and I'd soon be back anyway, so we had a bit of a giggle at the show and bumped into a few old faces. That evening, after getting dropped back at the Car Park, I jumped into my misted-up car and with the heaters on full blast, I headed back to Gloucestershire.

On the Tuesday morning, I had a text telling me that the Big Orange had come out of the Curly, so my reasoning that the swim was the place to be for the winter was confirmed. A few days later, and in much better conditions, dry and mild with the odd bit of sunshine, I found the lake empty and soon had all my gear barrowed round to the Curly. I was just getting the rods ready when Little Jon strolled round. He said he'd bumped into the guy who'd had the Big O, and he wasn't happy because I was in the Curly. I told LJ I was after a winter Car Park fish and the best chance of that was from the Curly, and as the swim was empty when I arrived I'd jumped in it. Competition was fierce, even in December!

A marker float hurtled into my water from Trumptons, and a 'polite' Car Park battle cry of "Oi!" echoed across the lake. He got the message and was soon on his toes. With him gone it was a nice quiet lake again, but unfortunately that's how it stayed – quiet, for most of the winter, in fact! Apart from the regular visitors of an evening, Fudgey, Odd, Lee, Fat Al and one or two of the others, which meant my kettle was on almost continuously, only the odd tench broke the monotonous, long, dark nights.

Come February and, once again, a few more anglers started to venture back on a more regular basis and it was difficult to get into the Curly, such was it popularity. Everyone was expecting it to do another bite.

One Friday night I will always remember was when I was set up in the Bars swim. The dark nights meant that Lewis would turn up late, about 9pm or so, after he'd been home and had his dinner. Anyone who knows Lew will tell you that he's pretty relentless with the piss-taking and doesn't let up with his weird sense of humour, so as I was making us a tea, I thought I'd take his mind off ripping me and put the focus back on himself. As the first wisps of steam came off the kettle, I poured a dribble into the cold cups and with a little swill I 'accidentally' deposited the water on the instep of his trainer. I'd counted to three when he suddenly shot up off the bed chair, hopping on one foot and doing his impression of an Irish jig as he pulled his trainer off. Meanwhile, I rolled on the bedchair doubled up in hysterics. "That'll teach you for taking the piss," I spluttered, as I fell about laughing. He always kept his distance when ripping me after the hot foot incident.

My winter carp was not forthcoming and I looked forward to June the 1st with high hopes, now I had a good amount of fishing time at my disposal. I didn't fish a great deal in the spring; just did a few trips to Manor at Linear Fisheries in Oxford after the big mirror known as Cut Tail. I only managed stockies but I remember one day when Terry Hearn gave a masterclass on floater fishing, taking half a dozen fish to high-20s, all off the top. Despite my only action being with the net and camera, it was a memorable day as I watched one of the best pick off fish after fish, systematically. Cut Tail remained elusive for the pair of us and when some knobhead turned up to my left and cast down to his right straight over my lines, totally oblivious to his actions, I decided that day-ticket lakes weren't my cup of tea, and I waited for the Car Park to re-open.

Opening night soon came round and the pattern of me coming out further down in the draw continued. I'd managed to get a swim, though, and some lads didn't even get that, so I had to be grateful for seeing the season in on the lake. The Middle Secret on the car park bank was generally the weedier end, and as long as it didn't get too hot there should be a few about and it was Heather's preferred end, so I hoped I'd get a chance.

I went down the particle route so I had a big bucket of maples and a few 'special' nuts, these being the excellent Brazils. The Car Park fish liked a nut and so using a Brazil offered them something a bit different to the more common tigers. Both my spots were within 30 yards and I could just about reach with the catapult as the maples fired out brilliantly, being perfectly round and dense. The little Pocket Rocket was employed for a bit of hemp and Partiblend, as well as a few broken Brazils.

At 9pm that first night, the lake looked like a re-enactment of the Spanish Armada as all the bait boats chugged out. I had two clipped-up casts, bosh, bosh, on my spots and with lines sunk I was sorted. So many boats were going out at once that a couple of the lads were having an absolute nightmare because they were picking up each other's signals and the boats were going off in all directions. Don't you just love technology? I didn't giggle … much!

I put myself at a disadvantage by not using a bait boat, but it just didn't feel like proper angling so I always cast out my rigs. I had used a boat the year before to put in particle but when Steve Allcott turned up one day I felt embarrassed to be using a boat, albeit just for the bait, and vowed to fish the 'old school' way from then on; the spod would be my plan of attack.

This year, 2002, was to become known as the year of the video. My good mate, Odd, was hoping to get as many captures as possible on film and as he lived and worked locally, he could get down to the pond pronto, as soon as a fish was landed. If Odd could get all the Car Park residents on film it would be a special piece of carp angling footage. It was now up to us anglers to catch them. Lewis was the first to score, on the first afternoon, up at the far end in the End Works when he had Ugloe wobbling into his net at a 'fit to explode' top weight of 37lbs.

At about 6pm on the Thursday, the shout of the season went up as Rick landed his first Car Park carp, and what a way to start! Arfur was lying in his net as I legged it round to Dessies, but where was Odd? I soon found out. Odd was doing the Kentucky run, so after ringing him to find out that he was waiting for the food, we let Arfur reside in the mesh until his return.

Arfur looked like she'd also been on the KFC. She was well plump and pulled the scales past the 50lb mark, settling on 51lbs. Rick was suitably made up and grinning from ear to ear as he held her up for the cameras and camcorder. What a start for Rick - and a great opener for the video!

The fish never really got close to me and the Dessies spot was as near as they came. After I left, Rick continued his starring role in the video as he then knocked out the highly desirable Dustbin at 41lbs 7oz. Rick's season was already made, with a 50 and a 40. He had always been a consistent angler and although I had outfished him on the Copse and North lakes, he was making the Car Park look straightforward, and I was envious of such a brace.

Dessies was the swim to be in. After a fraught boat battle, Turking Stick landed the Baby Orange later that week after moving in behind Rick, and Mad Martyn also caught Chunky out of the Snags. So that was five of the mirrors out in the first week, over half of them, and as Odd had captured them all on film, bar Ugloe, the video had the best of starts.

With all the captures coming to nuts, I continued with a tiger on one rod and a Brazil on the other, but I'd dropped using the maples because I found that they went black very quickly, so hemp, partiblend and the nuts formed my spod mix.

Arfur looked like she'd been on the KFC.

The remainder of June was tough going and the fish were well back in the groove of being rock hard to trip up. Doing four nights at a time enabled me to clock up the rod hours but with no bites forthcoming, I was starting to get a bit frustrated. Everyone was winding me up, I had pressure from the lads at work as well as the boys on the pond and I was biting better than the carp!

At the start of July, having clocked up about 16 nights already, I arrived about 7pm after finishing work, and with bucket in hand, went hurriedly in search of a plot. I stopped at the Islands and after a chat with Steve Pag', it was revealed that the fish were active in the big weedbed in front of Trumptons. Both Waiting Mans and Trumptons were free but it appeared that Chilly had given up trying to find any clear areas and had set up in the Dugout instead. With Dessies and the Curly both taken I'd have to find something in Trumptons if I wanted to be on the fish. I did a quick U-turn, moved the car up behind the Gate swim, quickly loaded the barrow and headed off Trumptons-bound, whizzing it round the short distance.

My plan was to fish one on a spot I knew of in Waiting Mans, but to cast to it, if possible, from Trumptons, leaving me to fish the other rod straight out to the pylon area, hopefully getting two bites of the cherry.

Marker rod in hand, I went into Waiting Mans and after a couple of casts found the clear area, popped the float up and then walked back into the Trumptons boards and eyed it up from there. The trees to the right of the swim made it an awkward cast, but the thing that bothered me most was the lump of surface weed directly in line, immediately before the spot. The line lay would be awful and with the line at such a steep angle I'd be sussed in double-quick time. I wound the float in. That spot wasn't a goer from Trumptons.

For the next hour and a half I stood on that board thrashing the water to a foam in the vain hope of finding a clear hole. Sweat was pouring from my brow and, thoroughly hacked off, I threw the rod in the rushes and stormed round the lake to cool off and calm down.

I went back round to see Steve and Rick and they offered me a beer. Normally, I wouldn't until the rods were sorted but I was so wound up that I gratefully cracked one open and then, swigging it down, headed up to see Odd in the Curly. After a good whingeing session to all of them, I had to decide what to do because the light would soon be gone. I could move round to the Bars which had a few clear spots, but the fish were not in that vicinity so it seemed pointless.

Still pondering my next move, I called in to see Chilly as I made my way back to Trumptons. He was on the phone to Lynn but after a couple of minutes said his goodbyes and I had a quick chat with the old fella - only joking, mate. He told me what he'd seen earlier and it appeared that the back of Dessies area was the place to be. I had about 15 minutes before it would be dark so I decided to get one rod on the Waiting Mans spot, but fish it from Waiting Mans. This way, the line would fall down the side of the floating stuff as opposed to over it and at least I'd have a rig in the right area of the lake!

The raft of weed was still just visible in the fast fading light so I could use this as my marker and as long as I went just left and a few feet past it, I should land on the spot. Quickly, I partly drilled out a Brazil and with a cork insert, tied it onto the ring on a D-rigged Big T with a mono hooklink and hoped a tangle wouldn't be an issue.

On the first couple of casts the lead caught the weed on the way down so I whizzed it back in and recast, but then it went too far and landed in the weed at the back of the spot. I needed to land about five feet past the floating stuff but in the semi-dark it was getting hard to judge. I skipped the lead in again and when checking the bait, I noticed that the floss had cut the soft nut. Cursing my luck, I ran back to Trumptons, where all my gear was, and with a new hookbait back on, legged it back to Waiting Mans. I took a deep breath, used the Force, and let the lead sail out smoothly, feathering it down behind the ever-so-slightly visible weed. It looked good and went in with a smooth, clean drop; I was so relieved to feel it hit bottom as it hit the lake bed with a tip-vibrating crack. I let out a 'hallelujah!' shout, which was followed by clapping from the far bank. Now happy that I had a rig on the water, I thought I'd better put some bait around it.

With the Pocket Rocket chucked out and clipped to what I could gauge was the right range, I sent half a dozen spodfuls of particle out into the dark before pushing a couple of banksticks in, and with the bobbin on a slackish line I began to move the bedchair and all my gear the few yards from where it was strewn in Trumptons.

I chucked the Evo over the top of the bedchair, pushed in a couple of pegs, sparked up the stove and for the first time since arriving some four hours before, I began to wind down and with a tea in hand I could relax at last. Who said this fishing lark was to ease stress? It looked a bit odd, sitting behind just one rod, but one on a presentable rock-hard spot was better than two stuck in the weed.

As soon as my head hit the pillow I was out like a light and my evening's exertions had certainly taken it out of me. At 8am, I woke with a jolt as my one rod went into meltdown and I bent into it while the culprit ripped line off me and tore away. I managed to stop it and gain a few yards back before it slammed the rod down again and headed left behind a big weed bed. The density of the weed slowed it up and I got a few turns back on it before it ground to a halt and went solid.

Now wide awake, I yelled out for the boat. This was stored directly behind my bivvy but I needed help and within a minute, Rick, Steve, Monki and Odd were at my side with lifejackets. Odd was holding the video camera, Rick and Steve got the boat into the water and with our life jackets on, I got into the front of the boat and Rick jumped into the back with the net and rowed me out to my weeded fish.

I'd never had to go out for a fish before so I was a bit unsure of how to play it, but as Rick inched us closer to where the line met the water, I pulled gingerly from above. The rod hooped over but nothing was moving and I wasn't sure whether the fish was still on or not so I laid the rod out to the side, grabbed the line, and with my sphincter muscles twitching, teased the line up by hand, ready to let go should the fish go into one.

As I led across the front of the boat, Rick kept it steady and stopped me from panicking too much. Gently, I started to pull off the weed and as the line picked up, I could see the end of my leadcore; I was a four-foot leader away from hidden treasure. I was just picking up the rod again to see if I could move it when it dawned on me that with the fish being so close, if indeed it was still on, I'd be better off hand-lining it into the net.

I grabbed the net, pushed it deep under the weed and with the end of the leadcore between my fingers, lifted it vertically. The stretch in the mono was now removed and I was holding the leadcore. The fish nodded its head and I shouted excitedly to Rick, "It's still on!" I lifted the net around where the fish should be, still totally engulfed in weed, and as the drawstring came under it, the water exploded. For a second, I thought it had bolted off and then it exploded again on top of the net. With the weight of the weed, the arms of the net just twisted over as I lifted it and I've never been so grateful to see a hand come over my shoulder as Rick grabbed the arm of the net and between us, we managed to imprison the fish within.

I bellowed "YES!" and got a round of applause from the gathering crowd in my swim. Everyone was keen to know what I'd caught so I ripped out the weed to reveal the unmistakeable bulk of Single Scale.

A fist-punching "SINGLEEEE!" scream was captured on video, and I felt a sudden rush of happiness and relief as the pressure was instantly released. Rick slowly rowed us in as I cradled Single at the back of the boat, taking care that he faced the right way and holding him away from the edge of the boat. As we drifted into Trumptons, Chilly came up the path, beaming.
"Lovely clear spot in Waiting Mans," I chuckled.
"Good job I moved out then, boy," Chilly went on.
He had caught Single the previous year and he knew how I felt.

As the boys held the beast in the net, I dug out the necessary scales, sling and camera and then for the next couple of minutes just wandered about grinning as the lads got on with unhooking and weighing him. Steve and Rick made a comment because my hookbait was still attached, so with a wink and a grin they passed me the rig with the cut-down Brazil still intact. He was well hooked in the bottom lip so at long last I had an open water rig I could have faith in: nine inches of Maxima, knotless-knotted on a size 7 Big T which, with the bait balanced, would sit directly above the hook when mounted on a small D on the shank. Simple, but tangle-free, and it would disappear over a clear lake bed, and the bait covered all sight of the hook, which I also felt was crucial.

Keen to see what he'd weigh, I stood behind as the boys hoisted him up with a bankstick through the handle of the scales. The needle settled at 44lb 9oz - that'll do me! The light was very poor on Trumptons so we carried him out to the edge of the car park, and with every man and his dog there now - well, Steve's two dogs actually - we placed Single onto a collection of mats and then I tried to lift him up.

What an awkward fish to hold! He hadn't fought much, so Single was still full of energy and he bashed me up on the bank, much to the amusement of Lewis who was yelping, "Beat him Single! Beat him!"

When the fish had calmed down, it was a case of just balancing him on my hands because his sheer width meant that I couldn't get my fingers round to his pec. With chief goalkeeper Monki on hand, we got him upright and the cameras whizzed and clicked. It was nice to be the centre of attention at last and as Single was one of the chief A-listers, I was on a huge high. What a turnaround in less than 12 hours.

Thankfully, I had perservered and got that one rod bang on. The other lads reckoned it was the can of beer that had done it so now it looked like the beers were on me. We carried him back on the mats to return him in the Middle Secret, and Monki took his duties seriously; he waded out to give me a hand for returners because it was likely Single would be lively and sensing freedom as I picked him up. Fortunately, he behaved and with a few returners done, despite the light levels being poor in the Secret, I lowered him into the water and let him power off.

The video camera was still rolling when Monki, in his wisdom, decided it would be a good idea to wrestle me in, but as we jostled I told him I couldn't swim. Lewis was screeching to me to push Monki in, so he let me swing him round and with a little push he leapt out into the Secret's depths. The onlookers were howling with laughter and Lewis, being louder than loud, was heard over everyone else. I just remember him screaming, "What's he like?" As we both trudged out of the margins, I shook Monki by the hand and it topped off a brilliant morning. Big thanks to all the lads who helped on that day. It was one of my most memorable captures of all time.

It was nice to be the centre of attention.

One of my most memorable captures of all time.

Single: One of the chief A-listers.

I had one of the elite in the bag so to speak, so I could relax a lot more. I was in a better frame of mind and more confident now I had a method for the margins and the open water spots. I knew what I was looking for in regard to the spots.

The weed bed had shifted during the Single battle so I struggled to find the exact spot I took him from, but the rock hard 'crack' I'd got when the lead had hit bottom was etched in my memory and I was sure this was a significant factor in the capture. My previous edge captures, when I could see where the bait had been eaten and where it had been left, suggested strongly that there was definitely a hot spot within a spot, and from that day on I always paid special attention to find that extra hard crackdown point within the area I'd located with the marker float.

The special captures that I witnessed that summer both involved Steve Pagulatos. Steve and I had become good allies and between us, by hanging from trees and pooling the information, we could usually locate most of the fish so we both had an idea of the whereabouts of our targets. We had already caught different fish so we could get on the fish we were after without stepping on each other's toes.

Going back to just a week or so before my capture of Single, I'd walked round the pond and found Steve dropping a boatful of mixers out in front of the Snags water. The Big Orange and Arfur were in the area, so I left Steve to it and carried on round in search of the others. On my next lap round I found a small gathering in the Chair swim. Monki and Chilly were giving a commentary from the top of the silver birch and it appeared that Arfur was slurping down the mixers while Steve was trying to get his hookbait into position.

Although it was helpful to know where Arfur was coming from, my observations of carp reaction to the human voice made me sure that Arfur was aware of our presence and was suitably shying away from coming any closer. Sure enough, it wasn't until everyone had dispersed and left Steve to it that Arfur regained her confidence and came in close enough so that Steve was able to dispense with the controller float and his freelined mixer was engulfed by those huge, unmistakeable white lips.

When I heard the shout for the boat I knew instantly where it had came from. I ran up to the Chair and found Steve standing there with the rod bent double; Arfur had plugged herself into the weed out by the bars. The sound of bumping and clattering of the boat being moved on Trumptons meant that help was not far away and with the odd couple, Chilly and Shelley, rowing toward us, all Steve could do was wait. Jim got out of the boat, Steve jumped in and they were soon back out the 25 yards to where Arfur was weeded, and with overhead pressure up she popped. After a bit of to-ing and fro-ing and thrashing of water, Steve slipped the net under her as Chilly kept control of the boat.

She hadn't yet spawned and it looked like Steve had just caught his second 50; one off the top was something very special. As everyone got everything ready I held her in the net alongside the platform and Odd was there with the video camera. A hefty heave lifted her out and the scales confirmed that I hadn't lost all my strength since my days of manual labour. Not only was she a bit bigger than Rick's opening week capture, but she had also just pipped Steve's personal best of Heather by two ounces. Arfur weighed in at a lake and county record of 51lbs 6oz. The sun was shining so a few beers and a barbie were the order of the day, and the works bank saw a good old Yateley social as all and sundry called in on hearing the good news.

The weed was now reaching forest proportions and the carp were spending most of their time just sunbathing. Despite there being up to 12 anglers on every night throughout July, the only other capture that month, apart from mine on the 10th, was Simon Scott taking Pearly Tail on a floater out of Trumptons. These big fish have to eat, but somehow they continue to get away with it.

August was well and truly Steve's month. First, he bagged Single Scale, stalked out of the edge in the Back Bay, before going on to catch a further two 40s. The weed was so dense that the boat was being called into action a lot, and after returning to my swim in the Back Bay where I knew Heather had been visiting when Steve had caught Single, I was a bit despondent after chatting to Chilly because I found out that Heather was frequenting his areas up in the End Works.

I was soon jerked out of my despondency by a cry for the boat. It sounded like Steve but it couldn't be, surely? He'd only left me some ten or 15 minutes previously. I ran across to Waiting Mans and there, opposite, standing out in the water with rod in hand, was Steve. I ran to the car, grabbed my life jacket and as I slipped that on and dragged the boat into Waiting Mans, Chilly was by my side and with an oar apiece we were paddling over like an Olympic pairing, or maybe more like the Chuckle Brothers.

Chilly got out of the boat, Steve got in with rod and net and I eased us out to the weedbed that the line was pointing into. I asked Steve if he knew what it was he'd hooked and he said he was sure it was Dusty, as that was the one he'd had feeding.

The next few minutes saw the pair of us hanging over the side and pulling up lumps of weed. Each time we got close and more pressure was applied, a huge eruption of bubbles would hit the surface and she'd lurch from the cleared weed, straight under another. We were getting nowhere fast, but we now had a routine; Steve would keep the pressure on and I'd pick the weed off, keeping a more direct pull on the fish.

As we got nearer and could see the controller, another line of bubbles started fizzing up and there below in mid-water, a big, grey shape with an unmistakeable white saddle down its back shot out from its lair. I looked back at Steve and said, "Is that what I think it is?" and with an agreeing nod from Steve, we both burst out laughing. Heather the Leather had swum the full length of the lake to follow Steve and slurp down his floater. Talk about the Pied Piper, she was like his bloody pet! Once again, I was to be the bridesmaid but not the bride and now, more relaxed because we knew what was on the end, we had a right giggle trying to weave her out of the weedbeds and into the net.

Chilly had picked up on what the outcome was going to be and with a resigned groan, he shouted, "Is that the bloody leather?"
"Sure is!" I shouted back.

I watched in awe as she twisted and turned, right beneath our feet, while sending up streams of bubbles. Steve had already caught her twice so he was quite relaxed and when she boiled up close to the boat Steve just laughed, "Go for it!" I did, and leaned out and managed to scoop her straight up. I shook the man's hand and rowed us back to dry land and the growing crowd of onlookers.

It was Heather's first visit to the bank that year and Odd was soon on his way. The Leather played the starring role, only Ugloe and the Big Orange were proving shy in front of the video camera, and for the record Heather weighed 48lbs 14oz so it was a sure-fire bet that she'd be an autumn 50. Catching her then, though, was far from certain.

Steve's run of form was red-hot and his position for top rod looked good when only the next week he went on to land the one he thought he'd hooked a few days previously; the Dustbin. Three 40s in a matter of days proved how special the Car Park Lake could be to some people, sometimes.

Autumn was around the corner and I was once again getting itchy feet. I couldn't settle unless I could find fish, so I was spending a lot of my days searching for them. At the start of September my days off coincided with the weekend and after spotting a pale

fish, possibly one of the Oranges, off the bars in front of the Chair, I set up stall in there on the Friday morning.

The lake was filling up fast for the weekend, so a move would be unlikely until Sunday, but with a view of the whole lake, at least if something showed I might be able to get on it for my last night, if the lake emptied out as expected on the Sunday.

Sunday morning gave me the motivation to step it up a gear. I heard a buzzer going off in the Bars, which incidentally hadn't done a mirror capture for about three or four years, and I was chuffed to hear my good mate, Odd, shouting "Chunky!" across the lake.

It was Odd's first mirror from the lake and after he'd been filming everyone else from behind the camera, it was nice to see him cradling a carp and having his moment of glory. I noticed what was coming out of Chunky's arse; hemp and hemp alone, so knowing Steve had caught a couple of his on sweetcorn, I decided to use straight hemp with just a few golden grains sprinkled in and a little single grain of fake pop-up corn as a hookbait. Perhaps they'd be less suspicious of that than the nuts. Now all I had to do was hunt out a fish to feed it to, so as I had one night left and the majority of anglers were going back to pack up, I grabbed a bucket and went in search of a carp.

Call it fate, or luck, but as I walked up to Trumptons I was just coming to the boat when, by the sound of the splash, an obvious mirror boomed out. I legged it to Waiting Mans and the frothy patch in the middle of the rings clearly showed the exact whereabouts of the culprit's skyward exit. It was only about 15 yards out, just behind the left-hand trees, and I mentally logged the precise spot. If I could find a clear area as close as possible, I might have just found its dinner table. Lewis, who was packing up in Trumptons, came rushing in to the swim and I pointed to the spot.
"You moving then?" Lew enquired.
I simply pointed at the bucket dropped behind me.

With renewed enthusiasm I sprinted back to the Chair, packed up in double-quick time and was soon in my new swim. First things first; I had to check out the spot the fish had shown on, as I knew the other rod could go out to where I'd had Single from. It was a little bit round the corner so I tossed the float over the outgrowing bushes to my left and feathered it down behind them with an outstretched rod and I felt it land in weed. That wasn't what I wanted but when I tweaked it back, it fell free and thudded to the bottom; wicked. I made a couple more casts exploring the spot and then felt I'd hit the jackpot. If I got it just right it would crack down hard, much like the Single spot and was exactly below where the fish had boshed out earlier.

Steve's third 40 in a matter of days.

With a dinner plate-sized hard spot in the middle of an unhooking mat-sized clearing, it was crucial to be accurate but at close range this wasn't a problem and I was soon confident that I was on the money. With 10 small spods of hemp and corn dropped on top, the trap was laid and with the other bait on my Single spot I was really confident, for the first time in a little while. My brother dropped in next door in Trumptons and regular callers throughout the afternoon and evening kept us entertained.

About half an hour before daybreak I was dragged from slumber by the shrill sound of my Neville and with the close-in rod's tip pulled down and bent round it was obvious my jumping friend had returned for an early morning snack.

There were plenty of weedbeds still in the vicinity so I shot forward and with the rod in full battle curve I subdued her powerful dash for freedom by hand pressure to the purring clutch. Paul heard the screaming take and he was soon standing alongside, waders on and net in hand, as he crept into the misty, dark margins. Line was slowly gained and having hooked her just a little way out, she was soon in close. I waded in to the cool water so I didn't get caught out should she dive for freedom in the marginal bushes. I kept her on a short leash and with some weed gathering over her head, led her in over the sunken net.

In the first throes of daybreak, my fourth Car Park mirror coughed air and was engulfed in the net. As we both peered into the mesh, a big set of pectoral fins and

sloping head gave away her identity and I was immediately brought back from heaven with a jolt as a repeat capture of Pearly Tail was evident. Odd was called and was soon with us. We weighed her at 34lbs 10oz and in the half-light I once again held her aloft for the cameras. I was happy to have caught, but a repeat had definitely taken the shine off it, and compared to the first time I'd caught her, 11 months previously, it was a bit of an anti-climax.

Having now caught two mirrors this season from two different open water spots gave me a lot more confidence and I was back at first light on Friday with a fresh spring in my step. There was a bit of movement out in front of the Bars, so I dropped my bucket in there and once all the gear was in the swim I set about finding a clean, cracking spot.

I had to go a bit further left and away from the weed to find the spot, but on the back of a bumpy bit of gravel it just smoothed off and the lead banged down, prompting a resounding vibration from the rod blank; just what I was looking for. Just 10 Pocket Rocket loads of hemp and corn, which was the lucky number, was deposited round my single piece of corn to which I hooked a piece of PVA tape with four golden grains on it. This not only gave me extra confidence that I had some natural corn in close proximity to the hookbait, but also a tiny bit of extra weight and resistance in flight, which would prevent the rig from tangling.

I saw the odd bubble over the area so I had a gut feeling that something was investigating, and at about 7am on Sunday morning it rattled off again, almost instantly weeding me. The weed was not at full strength so I managed to get the whole lot moving from the bank and soon had fish and weedbed drifting toward me. Some of the fronds broke away and I could feel the fish swinging around behind the ball of weed; it was definitely still on.

I had help to bundle the whole lot in the net and then the fun began as I ripped out the green stuff to discover the jewel that lay beneath. The shoulders were exposed and the criss-cross pattern of golden common carp scales caught the first glimpse of sunlight as it peeped over the skyline above Trumptons; my first common from the lake, or should I say 'chevin' as we referred to the commons. There was a little wart on the side of its gill plate as reference for identification,and we recorded a weight of 22lb 8oz, and clicked off a few slides before slipping her back. Suddenly, I was on three fish but despite nearly catching Steve up in numbers, his three 40s and a 50 were a bit more impressive!

No more takes were forthcoming but I did notice a bit going on out off the end of the second bar and with the winds moving the drifting scummy weed rafts that had been sitting over the area, I felt that area would be worthy of investigation on my return in a few days.

A big pair of pecs and sloping head gave away her identity.

With little else to go on and no other captures occuring I did indeed drop into the End Works when I returned. From the top of a tree, I could make out one or two shapes drifting between the bars and that snotty-like scummy weed was drifting back to the main weed so there was only a small raft of it preventing a clean channel to the area that I hoped was clear. Back on hard ground in the swim, I dug out the marker rod and whooshing it out landed it into the scum and immediately pulled back smoothly. I managed to get the floating raft to break up and drag toward me, opening up a gap to a small hole, where I'd seen the fish show the week before from the Bars.

The raft of scum had been dragged into my margin out of harm's way, so I sent the marker out, this time to the back of the hole, and I had to chuckle when it slammed down hard. I was literally at the far corner, at the near end of the middle bar, so was fishing in about four feet of water and I could keep my line just in the same depth, so the line lay to the spot should be good.

A cast further to the right and the line would lie over the pronounced end of the bar, lifting it off the bottom. If I could continue my run of good form, then this was the spot and I fished the other rod well out of the way so not to ruin my chances to the end of the bar spot.

Clearing a channel in the scum opened up a path.

The criss-cross pattern of golden common scales caught the first glimpse of sunlight, revealing my first 'chevin'.

I surged into top rod position.

Within the next two days, I'd surged into top rod position as my plastic corn was snaffled by another two commons. Despite having the last four fish, the problem was they were steadily getting smaller, with these two at 21lbs 12oz and 17lbs 12oz; the little one was nicknamed Kevin the Chevin. If I'd had five mirrors to date I could have been done on the lake perhaps, but with Single the only new mirror, there were still lots left on the wish list. Steve, on the other hand, was almost done when at the end of October he braced Ugloe, and Single for the second time, rightfully taking back his position as top rod. Things were slowing right up and my brother, Paul, caught the only fish in November; Ugloe proving to be the only one up for a munch one cold, foggy Saturday morning in the Back Bay.

With the Dustbin still to play for I plodded on through the cold months, doing a few nights a month but much like the previous winter, apart from the tench switching on at the start of February not a single carp was caught until the middle of March. The Curly was the swim to be in, despite the bitter easterly blowing straight into it, but Jonny Mac was a sealed unit and braved the elements. After losing a fish, he was rewarded with Ugloe(once again)pulling his string and in the wintry sunshine it was a sight for sore eyes.

The lake was now almost rammed out to the end of the season. The fish were keeping their heads down and it wasn't until the last few days that a young Matty Halliday and I found all nine bobbing about in front of the Secret swims. Matty went in the End Secret, and I jumped in the Middle Secret, but with only one night of my trip left I unfortunately ran out of time. The next morning, though, Matt was smiling in front of the lens with the Baby Orange at 36lbs-plus.

Odd's video was just missing the Big Orange from the tape, and Benny Hamilton duly obliged the next morning by banging the Big O out from right up the other end in the Chair swim at 44lb 2oz. The year of the video was over and overall, for me, it had been a good one, despite some lean periods, and I now felt I was starting to get to grips with the place. The problem was that each year seemed to pan out differently and we all started with a blank sheet again. I hoped that I could carry on from my prolific autumn spell, but for the time being I was off to pastures new for the spring and with all the flowers blooming I was off to Oxford in the hope of picking myself the Petals of Christchurch.

They were getting smaller. Kevin the Chevin.

Chapter 12 - Petals' Pond

I share a birthday on April 24th with my mate, Simon Croft, so we arranged a social fishing trip to Linch Hill's Christchurch Lake in Oxford. With an impressive head of low 30s and 20s it was a good option for the spring but the jewel in the crown was Petals; a uniquely-shaped fish with huge shoulders and clusters of scales in a petal shape, hence her name. This fish was in the 45-47lb class, so it could even push Bazil for a new PB.

There was loads of work on at the shop so I did a few extra days in early April and waited for my trip with Si. He was travelling down on the Sunday but as I didn't finish work until Monday, I would meet up with him on the Monday evening and as our birthday wasn't until the Tuesday we could have a catch-up then.

On Sunday afternoon, I had a call from Si. He told me that he'd arrived at lunchtime, found some fish showing on the reed-lined end bank, cast out a couple of bags of pellets and had already banked a 31lb common; a right result and an early birthday present for Si.

Obviously, I couldn't wait to get down there and after getting through work on Monday, I was whizzing down the A420 to Linch Hill, and then winding down the country lanes in search of the site. I'd looked round there once a couple of years previously so I had an idea of where I was going and was soon pulling into a space in the car park. There were a lot of cars there but with three lakes on the complex, I didn't know how many were on Christchurch. I gave Si a bell and he said it was busy

It was only a matter of time - Danny with Petals.

with only a couple of swims empty - great. Anyway, with plenty of fish in the lake, I could slot in and hope that a few fish would move through.

The first swim inside the gate was the Pipe and this was by far the most prolific area on the lake. When this was switched on, the extra oxygen and water movement would get the fish going and it was permanently occupied but I kept walking and it appeared that this whole bank was taken. I found my mate, Danny Stroud, at the far end. He'd been bagging up of late and it was only a matter of time before Petals fell to his rods. He suggested I go all the way round to the far side where the second-last swim was free. I think it was known as the Plate swim, because there was a plate stuck in the bushes behind it.

I'd been hoping to plot up near Si but he hadn't seen any fish in front of him since the wind had dropped, and he already had a 30 under his belt so I carried on round and dropped in the Plate. It's a small world; to my left in the first swim was an old North Lake buddy, Paul Harris, and to my right was Hampshire Chris, a friend of my mate, Hampshire Graham, with whom I was fishing the Car Park.

The light was fading fast so I had a quick lead about and with the fresh new weed growth shooting up I found a clean, silty, firm strip at about 35 yards. So, tying up a PVA stick with some oily mix and a few grains of corn in it, I balanced off my fake buoyant corn hookbait with a small split shot and threaded on the stick.

The cast landed just beyond the float and I felt it down for a nice thud. The other rod was fished in closer over a bit of bait, so I left it at that and with the bivvy chucked over the bed, I sat with Paul drinking tea until late.

No buzzers were heard that night but at 8am as I swung my legs out of bed, the PVA stick rod melted off and all eyes were in my direction as I bent into my first Christchurch carp. The lake was as clear as tap water, so when the fish came out of the depths I could see the scaly beast despite it being about four feet below the flat calm surface. Si had heard the take, wound in and come down to assist. The fish stayed in the higher reaches and it was a very visual fight. As the sun's rays pierced the depths, sparkles of bronze and gold flashed like sovereigns, twisting and dropping through the water column.

An early birthday present for Si.

The pressure soon told on the fish and Si looked back over his shoulder.
"Happy birthday, mate," he said. "You've got a 30-pounder there."
Si was right and a cracking-looking 32lb mirror was a very welcome 30th birthday present. The fish had a slightly twisted mouth on one side and a few years later I found out that my birthday carp was one known as the Hamster, which grew on to be the biggest in the lake. It hit 47lbs before passing on. A few people left or moved and Si managed to get within a couple of swims of me so, with a 30 apiece in the bag, we had a good birthday social before both heading off the next day.

Petals was a fairly regular visitor to the bank at that time of year and I felt it was worth a few more trips. It's not as if I had anywhere else to fish until June, and although it was well busy, with a PB mirror and common possible, I'd have to endure the crowds.

Over the next three weeks, I did a couple of nights a week and although the odd fish was coming out I received only liners. I noticed a few of the syndicate boys fishing all their rods on the one spot, one tight either side of the float and spodding their bits and pieces tight on top; some were even fishing three rods on the same spot. Fishing places such as Yateley, I was paranoid with line lay, so fishing two lines either side was a completely foreign exercise for me. I could see the logic of concentrating the bait on one spot and that multiple catches were possible, because if one ripped off you still had a rig on the spot without having to chuck a lead back on it.

Toward the end of May, and what was going to be my last trip, I arrived to find the lake a bit quieter for a change. The weather was still quite hot with a light breeze ruffling the surface pushing up the far end. I was pleasantly surprised to find the Point swim vacant so I dropped my bucket and scaled the thin tree on the right-hand side. I could see a big head of fish just below the surface and ran back up the bank to fetch my barrow.

Once all my gear was in the swim, I set about rigging up a couple of rods and with 'fresh' fake corn on the long hairs, still dripping in sweetener, and PVA sticks threaded on, I scaled the tree to see the lie of the land. The breeze had increased in strength, the fish had drifted right into the corner, several 30-plus commons and mirrors mingled on the marginal shelf and there among them was a huge, waddling hulk, with massive shoulders.

Petals was unmistakeable and my heartbeat suddenly went up a gear. Plans raced through my head; what was the best course of action? Was she stalkable? Could I lower a bait onto the shelf and walk it back without the fish spooking, or should I sit tight and watch, locate her preferred spot and once she drifted off get the rig in? Dilemma, or what? I made the decision to wait. I had three nights ahead of me and I didn't want to risk spooking her by clumsily rushing in and ruining my chance.

In the next hour, a bank of cloud pushed in and the wind became quite strong, causing waves to lap into the reeds on the end bank, exactly the conditions in which Si had caught at that end of the lake. I got a bait lowered onto a gravel spot, and some pellet sprinkled on it, and found a lovely little silty spot among the bottom weed about 25 yards out. It was just big enough for two rods and as all the other areas were weedy, I fished two tightly together with fake corn hookbaits in oily stick mix which landed firmly on the silt pocket.

The Christchuch carp have unusually small mouths so bits and pieces seemed the way forward. I spodded about ten Rocketfuls of mixed pellet, chilli hemp and half a tin of corn right on top and then noticed someone setting up on the end bank in the gap in the reeds and flicking their baits out just off the reed beds on either side. Shortly afterwards, I heard a call for help from the end swim so I ran round and there was Petals, lying beaten on the top. All I had to do was scoop her up in the net. My decision to wait had turned out to be the wrong one.

What a fish, and at 47lbs it blitzed the lad's personal best! I was kicking myself. This was my last trip before the Car Park reopened and my dream of catching Petals was over. I trudged back to my swim after taking the photos but I managed to console myself as over the next three mornings I caught a total of eight carp, a mixture of commons and mirrors, between 18 and 24lbs and the highlight was one of the big commons at 31lbs 15oz - a new personal best common. All eight runs came off the silt strip that I'd fished the two rods on, and eight carp was just the tonic I needed to face another assault on the Car Park. Despite the disappointment of missing out on Petals, with a 30lb mirror, and a 30lb common under my belt, I could take on the challenge with confidence; probably the single most important key to tackling those alien fish and keeping your sanity.

The highlight - one of the big commons.

Chapter 13 - Seeing the light

Three of the nine originals had seen the inside of my net, and it was time to start focusing on one particular fish, the largest leather carp in the land – Heather. Now, although Heather would get all over the eight acres of water of the Car Park, she certainly had her favourite areas. She was a bit of a sun-worshipper and would spend all day in one of her weedy saunas topping up the tan on her nude leathery back, a thick, white scum building up on her dorsal line as the sun baked the dry skin.

When Heather was 'parked up', she'd often be there all day and only when dusk descended would the water rock as she shuffled about before a kick of her paddle had her drifting off to where, I didn't know, but I was confident that the car park end was the place she'd go.

With this in mind, I was concentrating on the Islands and Waiting Mans, if at all possible. I had caught from two spots in Waiting Mans so I was confident of where I was putting the bait, and the rod hours were clocking up as June was ticking on, so confidence was never more important. The lake was as busy as it had ever been, and with the likes of Terry Hearn and Jon McAllister on the water, the competition was fierce.

The densest weed was between Trumptons and Waiting Mans and fish were always there during the day. It was for this reason that the area was so tempting, but getting good line lay to the spots was nigh-on impossible and in hindsight, perhaps I should have ignored the temptation.

Daz soon started to catch them one by one.

I wasn't the only one who was sucked in by the sight of whackers hanging in the weed. Terry was also lured to the area and most weeks throughout June saw Tel in Trumptons and me in Waiting Mans, but although I had raked narrow channels to my spots with a homemade castable weed rake, liners were the only bites I could muster. The opposite bank was noticeably less weedy and with a fairly uninterrupted route to the back of the Trumptons weedbed, line lay from Dessies was excellent in comparison to our bank.

Darren Mills was full-time and able to get in there regularly. He soon started to get among the fish and I could only watch with envy as sheets of bubbles hit the surface over his spot, and Daz soon started catching them one by one.

Tel was struggling, like me, but after catching a small common from the spot on the edge of the Dugout water, he moved to the Dugout itself, and with a different line angle the fizzing continued until 10am on the Friday morning, when the Neville shrilled. Judging by the force of the fish, it was obvious that one of the big ones was attached.

The fish had tangled Tel's other line, so with the help of Hampshire Graham, he was forced to take the boat out, but I was unable to see clearly what was going on from my position in the Islands, so I wound in, grabbed the camera and legged it round to the Dugout.

With a close-up view of events we fell about laughing as Little and Large swung about in the boat trying to disentangle the lines, Graham almost taking out Tel with the oar a couple of times. The offending line was bitten off and pulled into the boat, and Tel was back in contact with the carp as it tore from weedbed to weedbed.

Tel only had Arfur and Chunky left to catch from his previous stint a decade before, so it was probably best for all concerned for Tel to have Arfur on because that would be Tel done, the red card given, and one very good full-timer would be off the lake. The Car Park being the Car Park, though, gave us all a kick in the nuts as with the net slipped under the beast, Tel punched the air and shouted out, 'Heather!' to the assembled audience.

Tel was suitably chuffed with the leather at 48lb 2oz.

As much as it was always nice to see her on the bank, it was another repeat capture and although Tel was suitably chuffed with the leather at 48lb 2oz, it would have been better all round if it had been Arfur.

Surprisingly, I was the only one who had brought a decent camera round so with just mine and Tel's cameras getting the trophy shots, for once I didn't have to jostle for a good position. Heather looked immaculate and I wondered how long it would be before she made another mistake.

I had two nights of my trip left so I returned to the Islands to get the rods sorted, hoping Arfur might soon be out. There was the odd fish visiting the weedbed to my right and from the Island tree I could make out that they were travelling over my baited area of hemp, corn and tigers so I was sure the oil off the hemp would have signalled the presence of the small patch of goodness. My balanced tiger hookbait was positioned on the near edge of the spod mix.

All was quiet throughout the evening but in the night, one boomed out to my right, sending the coots into a raucous squawking and as I crouched by the rods, ripples washed in, lapping the railway sleeper at the front of the swim.

I returned to bed until 6.30am when I had the most ferocious run a carp could give. As I picked up the rod it was almost wrenched from my grasp, despite the clutch whizzing into a blur. I heard footsteps behind me and saw Jon Mcallister from the corner of my eye. The fish had stripped about 30 yards of line off me before she started to slow and then my world was turned upside down as the line fell slack. I turned to Jon for an explanation.
"There's nothing you could have done, mate," he said, simply.

The sulking Baby Orange in the Gate snag.

I thought the hook had pulled out but as I wound it in, I realised that there was nothing attached and on inspection, I could see that my line had been cut clean. I was using 15lb Maxima because it disappeared well in the clear water, but the abrasive resistance was lacking and as the stop was still on the line that had stopped the flying back lead, I could work out that I'd been cut about 18 inches above the lead core. If only I'd had a longer leadcore leader on. My spot was a glassy, rock-hard spot right behind a crunchy, rough bit of gravel so I could only assume that my line had caught against a sharp bit of rock, damaged the line and the immense power that the carp had inflicted on it had forced it to part.

The take, the fight, even the spot I'd hooked it from all suggested the culprit was Heather but she'd only been out two mornings before, so surely not? She had been out twice in two days before a couple of years ago, but no, I couldn't think like that. It would only do my head in.

Half an hour later, a couple of fish were evidently turning up, so I scaled the tree and could make out that one was Arfur, looking perfectly happy. So, it definitely wasn't her, not that old fatso could swim that fast with her physique and stumpy fins. The other fish might have been the Baby Orange but it headed out into the Secrets water so I couldn't tell for sure.

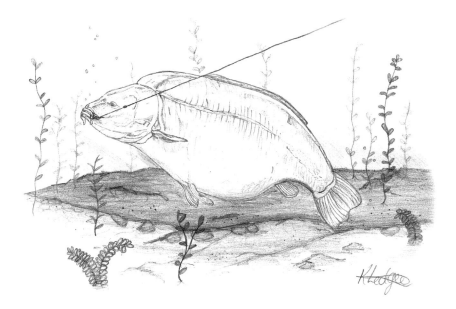

About 9am, Hampshire lost a fish from Waiting Mans. He had a rod out in the Gate water and with his hooklink parting at the hook knot, only the hook was lost, whereas I'd lost everything including the leadcore leader. Naturally, I was devastated that I'd lost a Car Park mirror, and I was also concerned that the fish could be trailing the leader.

I packed up and after loading the car, stopped off at Trumptons to see the lads. They all knew what had happened and some gave sympathetic comments, whereas the evil buggers took the mick and revelled in my despair. I'm sure they were only trying to snap me out of my gloom, eh Lewis? Graham checked the Gate snag that afternoon and sulking in the back was the Baby Orange. There was no sign of anything hanging from its mouth so it looked likely that it was this fish that Graham had lost.

July passed fairly uneventfully and despite being close to fish throughout, I never was convinced they were feeding on my spots. Darren, however, was slaying them in Dessies and was getting a take or two a week. Good line lay and the consistency of baiting on the exact same spot, keeping the feeding area small and tight, being the key.

On August the 1st I got a text telling me that Darren had caught Chunky and Jon McAllister had landed Heather. She was down a bit in weight at just over 46lbs, but more concerning was a tear on the inside of her mouth; not from Jon's hookhold, but from a loss, and with no other losses on the lake since mine, it looked certain that it was indeed Heather that I'd lost, and the tear had been sustained by getting rid of my size 7.

The wind-ups started all over again and the realisation of losing the chance of my dream fish gnawed away at my mind. I was biting big-style, feeling quite depressed and all I could do was sit and watch Darren ticking off the lake's mirrors, one by one.

I was feeling really low and I was tired all the time, so I visited my doctor who prescribed Prozac to boost my energy levels. At the time, this seemed to be a good idea. If I could just be a bit more pepped-up perhaps I would regain my confidence. All I needed to regain some swagger was a fish on the bank and I'd be back in the game. The doctor did say there was a possibility of side effects but assured me that most people were fine with them. I started the course and with a six-nighter planned starting after work the next day, I hoped a bit more energy would bring a change of fortune.

It was early September, the nights were drawing in fast, and it was all a rush to get the rods out. I set up in the Dugout and by the time I was all sorted, it was pitch black and I was hungry and exhausted. Benny Hamilton was next door in the End Works, so I wandered up to him with a sarnie and had a tea with him. I felt a bit rough so I didn't even bother with the bivvy and just crashed out under the stars for the night.

I woke about 7am and felt really rough. As I raised my head off the pillow a sick feeling overwhelmed me and I was running to the bushes to throw up. I collapsed back on the bed chair, in a sweat, hoping the sickness would pass. After a couple of hours I realised I couldn't stay. I felt really emotional as well as feeling sick to the stomach and there was no way I was taking any more Prozac if this was how they made me feel. I walked up to Ben and instantly, he could see I wasn't right so he helped me pack away my gear and gave me some words of wisdom. Cheers, mate.

Once the gear was back in the car, I made the long journey home, where I spent the next few days in bed. Those few days gave me time to think and reflect and I realised I'd been pushing myself far too hard both physically and mentally. I was living and breathing the Car Park Lake.

I returned in mid-September with a fresh head knowing that I needed to relax and enjoy it more, and then surely the fish would follow. Two days previously, on the Friday, Ben had landed Heather from the Islands, and at 47lbs 8oz she was on her way back up. This time I was pleased for Ben, as he'd been the one to help me see where I was going wrong. I went in the Bars because fish had shown in this area and it was quite easy to get the rods out. I was fishing in a short period of time, but without getting stressed, and I sat back and chilled.

Darren was slaying them in Dessies.

I was pleased for Ben.

Although I'd planned to stay in the Bars and relax, gently getting back in the groove, old habits were hard to change and after a stroll round in the sun on Monday morning, there was no way I could ignore what I found out in the main weedbed in front of the Islands. Heather, Arfur and both Oranges, meant that four of my six targets were present and as I'd always been happy and confident fishing the Islands, I moved my gear down. I only had 48 hours left and hoped they wouldn't move too far. I found that my Heather spot was still very clean, so with a tiger nut balanced with cork, over 10 small spods of hemp, corn and tigers I was more than happy with that trap.

Although the odd fish stayed in the area, they didn't stay in numbers. Perhaps, as Heather had been caught from the area, she'd pulled the others away once an angler's presence had been detected.

Odd was next door in Dessies and I really enjoyed the session. As I was packing up, Odd sat on my bucket waiting to move in behind me, and at 11am he spotted a few bubbles. I looked up excitedly.
"That's right on me," I said, and decided to give it another half hour.
Everything was on the barrow, and I sat down on a bucket next to Odd, my eyes staring at the spot. At ten past, another small cluster of bubbles peppered the surface but the indicator failed to move. A few more minutes past and just as I joked, "It was probably only a tench," the indicator slammed into the rod and as I was standing right next to it, I was able to pull into it instantly.

Odd was wondering what the hell I was doing. He thought that I'd kicked the rod, not realising I actually had a take. As the fish came toward me, I was still unsure what was on until it pulled down hard to the left and I assured Odd that it was a carp. He skipped the other rod in, out of the way, and waded out with the net. I also got into the water because whatever I was attached to was doing its best to get under the bushes to the left.

As it turned and rolled over it looked really orange, and Odd turned to me remarking that he thought it was one of the Oranges. I hadn't caught either of them so I played it gingerly, under the tip, and as she came up again Odd expertly scooped it up. I strode forward to see which one, and as the mirror rolled over I couldn't believe it; the wind was completely knocked out of my sails as there lay Pearly Tail again, my third capture of her!

My tiger nut was balanced with cork.

I'd been on a high, believing I'd achieved the capture of another new one, only to see Pearly again. The lake was as unforgiving as always, but after recent events I had to laugh, and at least it showed I could still catch them, even though it was the same one all the bloody time. At 36lbs 12oz, Pearly was at her best weight and looked very good in the morning sunshine.

I returned on Saturday with renewed enthusiasm and confidence and with only the Chair as a viable option for the night. After seeing one pale mirror, which I thought was the Baby Orange, and a couple of commons present, I set up with a view to moving into the Islands after Fudge in the morning.

I put one bait on the end of the bar that the fish had been mingling over and one down the left-hand margin on the spot I'd caught Chunky from. I chose to fish a cut-down boilie over pellet on this rod and at 9.30pm a tench was being unhooked after tripping the trap.

I waded it back down and an hour later, the rod hooped round big style. This was no tench and I hung on for dear life as it tried to gain line in its bid to reach the snags further down the margin. Just as I turned its head, the hook popped out. Naturally, I was gutted, but at last I was angling well and had the old buzz back! I'd spent 11 months with only one lost fish to show for it and now in my last four hours of angling I'd hooked two!

October has always been one of my favourite months and on current form I hoped it would be kind to me once more. I had six nights ahead of me, starting from the Sunday, and after setting up in the Beach, I immediately moved to the Islands as from Fudge's swim, the Steps, I'd seen a big fish nut out in Islands water.

As the mirror rolled over I couldn't believe it; Pearly Tail again, my third capture.

Just before dark a real big'un jumped out in Dessies and Darren moved round from Trumptons to Desmonds. The carp were active and the next couple of days saw the odd fish show between the Gate and Waiting Mans and when Odd moved out of the Gate after catching the Pineapple, I went for a look in Waiting Mans with the marker rod. My spot, that I'd caught Single from, felt prime so propping the marker rod in the tree I returned to get the rest of my gear.

A really warm north-westerly had sprung up and was blowing into the Gate corner. It all looked good and Darren had the same idea as me and moved to Trumptons. Jamie Clossick missed out and as he came for a look while we were setting up, he left saying, "They'll be on this wind." Darren and I certainly hoped he was right.

The wind strengthened and I felt that the small spods would get blown off track, so instead of ten small spodfuls, I introduced six large spods tight on top of the hookbait and after getting a really hard crackdown I was well confident. For once everything went smoothly and I was all done by 2pm.

Monki turned up about 3pm for tea and while we waited for the kettle to boil, I filled him in on recent events. About 3.30pm, the elusive little common jumped out right over my right-hand line and my buzzer started bleeping, which made me think that he must have bumped the line as he dived back in. The bobbin kept twitching up and down so I nonchalantly bent into it. I wasn't expecting the rod to hoop over and I just managed to knock off the anti-reverse as the fish woke up and as he realised he wasn't getting off now, he tore away like a steam train toward the End Secret.

The fish ignored the fact that it had a dead weedbed in its path and ploughed straight through it, taking a good 40 yards of line off me. I now had the fish on a long line and as it changed direction, panic set in as it headed for the Gate snag down to my left. The only way I could win this battle was to gain line and in double-quick time. I waded in up to my waist, pumped and winched as fast as I could and thankfully, the weight of weed on the line slowed the fish and with just enough line back on the reel I'd made it by the skin of my teeth.

Now I had to get it up my snaggy margin, and the weed over the fish's head allowed me to guide it all the way along, like a dog on a lead. Darren manned the net on the edge of the trees as a big ball of weed appeared, and he scooped it all up. As I dug the weed out there was a big, scummy mirror's back and the deep orange flanks meant it could only be one. I bellowed out "BIG ORANGE!" across to the watching audience in the Curly.

The Big O was in her best condition for years.

Odd and Rick came down to do the pictures and the Big O was in her best condition for years; at 45lbs, the weight reflected her good health. Pizza and beer that evening topped off a brilliant day and Jamie had been right, they were on that wind!

With a couple of nights still to go, I hoped there were more fish in the area and on the last evening one did crash out about 30 yards over a new spot I'd found. Needless to say the close-in rod was moved out on to this spot for the last night but my luck had been used up and that was my lot for the week. I plugged on over the next few weeks but winter was drawing in and sightings became rarer and rarer. I didn't do as much time throughout the winter period and just fished when conditions looked favourable.

There was a bitterly cold easterly blowing on the first weekend of February, and an ECHO do was on. I chose the social option and left the rods at home, travelling up on the Saturday to Odd's where I was to crash after the ECHO bash before driving home on Sunday.

As I got to Odd's front door, he informed me that Gary Allaway had just caught the Baby Orange out of the Islands. This was the first capture of the winter and as it was so bitterly cold outside I was a bit surprised. However, that night while some of us took the warm option, listening to Simon Scott's Wraysbury conquests and having a beer and a laugh, the guys who were sitting it out back on the cold pond were rewarded as the fish woke up.

Darren had his second capture of Pearly that year at a massive 37lbs 7oz in the early hours and then the icing on the cake came when Lewis finally caught one of the big ones - and what a way to do it! Just after first light, he struck into the Leather and after a good tussle Heather was landed at 47lbs 12oz. Our phones went into meltdown and Odd and I were soon pulling into the car park and marching round to Waiting Mans. Lew was suitably dumbstruck and elated; he'd got his just rewards and we gave him a big pat on the back.

Finding out that Conningbrook's Two-Tone had been out on the Saturday also, to John Pack at a British record weight, meant that something was definitely in the air that weekend. Little did we know, at the time, that John would be heading our way from Kent to add to the already intense pressure on the pond.

The big, scummy mirror's back and the deep orange flanks meant it could only be one.

Darrell Peck turned up after all the fuss and dropped into the Curly. He went on to catch Ugloe on the Tuesday, so in less than 72 hours the lake had given up four of its nine jewels. This just confirmed what a mental lake the CP is. When conditions look spot on nothing happens, and then it does four fish at the start of February and its piggin' freezing arctic conditions.

Motivation was fully restored. It was time to get back in the groove and for four trips on the bounce I fished the Curly. I knew my spots and consistency meant that regular baiting of my boilies on the same areas could be an advantage if and when the carp should switch on again.

The weather warmed up as March progressed and the lake was once again busy 24/7. Getting in the popular Curly again was unlikely and when Nick Jones caught Dusty out of Waiting Mans, I wondered whether I'd got it all wrong.

When I got back on the Tuesday evening after work, I had one final throw of the dice. It was March the 24th and it was already dark so there was no rush to set up. I could wander around and hoped that I'd choose wisely. It was the last week and I already knew that all the main plots had been sewn up, but as I walked in the Curly to get Matty to make a brew, I knew something was up because there was gear strewn around the swim.

Matt was a bit coy at first but as I quizzed him more, he came clean and admitted he was packing up so he could take the night off, meaning that he could return the following morning and do the remaining week. Dodgy little full-timer!

"Right, I'm in here then," I said and plonked my bucket down firmly, dashing his plans to get back in the Curly in the early hours. He reckoned he was not trying to get back in there but I knew his little plan had backfired. The Car Park could be a ruthless lake but to catch, you had to look after number one.

I left Matty to pack up and went to get a tea off Darren and tell him of my stroke of luck to get the Curly for a few days, and we chuckled at the wheels falling off Matty's plans. I pushed all the gear up to the Curly and Matty departed for the night. I got the bivvy up and took my time to get the rigs perfect and baits tied on. Having fished the swim so much recently, I knew where to cast my two rigs and with a full moon illuminating the lake from high above Trumptons, I hoped I could get them spot on.

I lined up to where the reeds on Trumptons would be, swung the lead back and sent it soaring toward its destination. Judging the distance, I feathered it down and felt it

"Right, I'm in here then."

fall through the six and a half feet of water onto the gravel hump. Crack! I felt the tip vibrate and I couldn't have got it better in broad daylight. There was no need to clip-up and re-chuck with that rod. As I catapulted 15 or so boilies, one at a time, I could just make out the odd one, so I knew my distance was good. The back lead was on and the line slackened; that was one down, one to go.

The left-hand rod was to be fished at the back of the second bar so I cast just past it and pulled until I felt the first taps of gravel, then pulled off five feet of line and put it in the clip. My recast put me in the silt behind the bar and once again I 'pulted out a few baits in the zone. By this time, it was gone 11pm so I had a quick cup of tea and was ready for bed.

I woke just before 8 o'clock to a mild, still morning, having had no interruptions from the alarms during the night. A couple of bleeps on the right-hand rod had me scanning the surface for signs of bird life but nothing surfaced, and then the bobbin slowly rose to the top and twitched up and down. I pulled on my boots and headed to the rods expecting a tench to be the culprit.

I was overjoyed to see a big, yellow flank roll over.

The rod hooped over but as the fish was now coming toward me and to the left, I wasn't sure what I was attached to and flicked the anti-reverse off just in case. Keeping the tip high so it swam over the other backleaded line I was still unsure what I was connected to because the bream go 15lbs and often feel weighty as you pull them through the depths.

The fish ducked under the overhanging bushes so I turned it, led it out and as it rose in the water the long length of leadcore came into view. I held my breath hoping it wasn't a bream, and for once I was overjoyed to see a big, yellow flank roll over before diving deeply back down.

Now I knew it was a carp, I went into super-focused mode and with the net in I crouched on the edge of the platform as the big mirror came to the surface and although my initial suspicions were of it being Chunky again, I could see the charismatic Ugloe as it gulped air. The net enveloped her and I let out an 'Ugloe!' call across the lake.

Soon after hearing the shout, the lads started to turn up and saw me holding a net at the end of the platform. A few of them were expecting it to be Matty, unaware of our 'under the cover of darkness' manoeuvres. Matty wandered in and everyone ripped him, but he took it well.

As we hoisted her out, the sun poked its head through the clouds and with some decent light I managed to get some good pictures. What a way to start a session and I was able to sit back and enjoy the next few days with my fifth mirror under my belt.

With four to go, I would have to be a bit more selective, and if I could catch Heather, that would be enough for me and I could call it a day. The rules changed from seven days down to 48 hours on, and 48 off, to help to reduce the pressure, and the next season would bring its own set of problems, but after having five carp takes in both the last two sessions, I felt that for the first time I had the measure of these Car Park fish. How wrong you can be!

The charismatic Ugloe.

Chapter 14 - Frimley jewels

Frimley Pit 3 was a water that I'd been hearing about. It had been a 'days only' venue (except for the bailiffs) but this had changed and a Gold Card could buy you access to the nights. I had more time available to fish since I'd stopped working on the farm and because Frimley was open in the spring, and the Car Park was shut for two months, I needed somewhere else to fish; Pit 3 looked to be the answer.

The only problem with the Gold Card was that it came with a golden price and that first year, I had to stump up a grand. The Goldie did give me access to all RMC waters, though, so I could fish the Car Park on this ticket. The only other place I looked at in 2003 was the Road Lake at Longfield, a small water with a good head of 30s that had just returned to the RMC angling portfolio. I only visited the Road Lake once that first season, and more of that later, but the reason for upgrading to the Gold Card was the big commons.

I took my first look at Pit 3 in February. Odd took me over so that I'd know where to find it and where to park. As there was no car park, it was a bit of a lottery finding a space up at the Hatches, a residential road that is just over from the railway. February is a good time to look round a lake because there is no foliage on the trees, and if you like what you see in the winter, it's only going to get better once it all greens up.

We had a stroll round and I was quite impressed with the place. At about 15 acres or so, it was a nice size but quite manageable and being quite a long lake, nowhere was out of range. I liked the make-up of the lake because if it was busy in the spring, the number of bays and the long, exposed bar broke it all up into different areas, which would eliminate the casting into your water by other anglers, hopefully!

I liked what I saw and as my personal best common was the Christchurch one at 31lbs 15oz, a PB was a very achievable target for the spring. After all my time spent on the Car Park, I hoped I could get among a few fish and have confidence soaring for the big push come June the 1st, when Heather would fill my thoughts once again. The capture of Ugloe at the end ensured that I was on a high for my Frimley campaign and I was hoping to get off to a good start.

Easter fell on the first weekend of April, and I knew the lake would be busy. The bailiffs and Gold Carders were only allowed a maximum of 48 hours, and I hoped most would be going on the Sunday so I planned to arrive at dawn, find the fish and hoped to slot in when someone pulled off, and before a day-only angler could beat me to it.

I lived almost two hours away, and I didn't fancy driving that far in the early morning, so I drove down to Yateley and as Fudge and a couple of other mates were fishing on Mill Lane, I spent the evening there, before crashing out on a bedchair behind Fudge's plot. I was up and away at first light; a 15-minute drive and I was slotting into a parking space at the Hatches.

I loaded the barrow and I was off down the road, over the railway track and into the lake. There was a chap in the Wooded Point, so I left the gear safely there and went for a circuit around the lake. The sun broke from above the trees, which were starting to bud with fresh green life, and as the mist drifted gently off the lake's surface, I realised why I love this carp fishing lark so much, and when I heard that familiar 'buh-dosh' sound, it had me scampering for its exact whereabouts. It had come from the other side of the bar as I stood looking across from the Noddy swims.

I could see movement opposite through the evaporating mist, so I knew the Double Boards swim was occupied. I ventured round in that direction and as I peered through the woods as I rounded Daisy Bay, a couple of familiar faces came into view. Nigel Sharp and Damien Clarke were bivvied up and by the look of Damo's swim, it seemed that he'd had a successful night.

I'd turned up at the right time as Damien not only had a carp in the net, but two in fact; a stunning 24lb scaly mirror, and a scale-perfect 29-pounder. Taking up my services as goalie, Nige snapped away as Damo held the beauties aloft, the spring sunshine glinting off their wet, golden scales.

My appetite for a Frimley stunner was well and truly whetted, and I quizzed the boys on the carp's whereabouts. The common had been caught from Daisy Bay and a lot had shown there in the night, so I chose to set up round on the Deep Point, where I could get a rig into the mouth of the bay and also fish the end of the exposed bar.

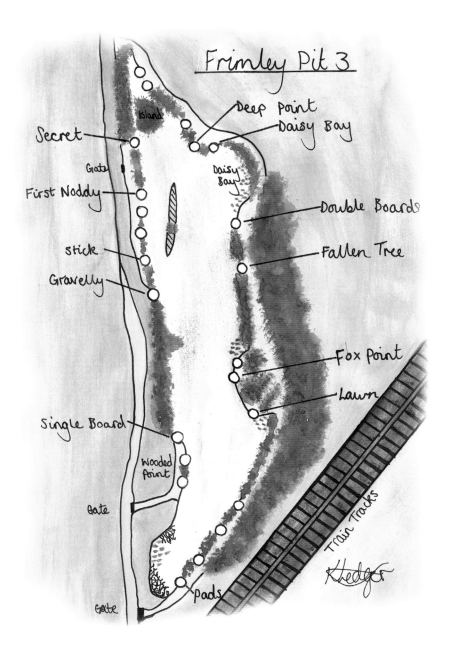

Frimley Pit 3

This swim also boasted the best view on the lake. I could see the majority of Pit 3 from here so if the nomadic Frimley carp should move, I could see where they were.

Getting the lowdown from Damien that his fish had both fallen to maize hookbaits and bags of pellets, I chose to fish two rods on plastic sweetcorn and PVA sticks of oily stick mix, and one rod on a boilie with a scattering. I would fish one of the corn baits on a bed of bait and one as a roving rod. There were only about eight trips available before the Car Park reopened so I needed to learn fast. It's always nice to get into action straight away on a new water, and action is what I got that first night. The trouble was that both culprits were snotty bream.

My plan for getting up with the lark was dashed; because of my early start the previous day and the bream disturbance through the night, the dawn chorus was played out and they'd had time for a lot of verses, by the time I dragged my arse out of the sleeping bag.

With a couple of sweet teas inside me I started to come back to the land of the living and soon started to see fish show at the opposite end of the bar. One after

I liked what I saw.

the other they showed, but despite me having everything crossed they refused to head my way.

A quick move was in order before someone else beat me to it and although the Stick swim was occupied, which was where the bulk of the shows were, the Gravelly next door appeared to be free. I raced round to secure this swim with a bucket, hurriedly packed down and with everything on the barrow, whizzed round to my new plot.

As is often the case in this game, the activity had ceased by the time I got round to set up and with the disturbance of me and the guy in the Stick swim getting rigs and bait in, the carp were nowhere to be seen that evening. I'd found some nice areas but it quickly became apparent that these Frimley carp wouldn't tolerate leads and spods constantly being chucked over the top of them.

On the next trip, I arrived on the Sunday afternoon to find that the Frimley carp were well and truly turned on by the strong wind and rain. Low pressure was sitting over us and it was lashing it down as I headed into the Wooded Point to find my old mucker Lewis Read, doing a day session.

Lewis was huddled under his brolly, babbling on about how fish were everywhere and showing but they seemed to be on the move down the lake, and as I looked in that direction, a real big'un nutted out down in front of the Gravelly. 'I'll have some of that,' I thought and wishing Lewis luck, I rushed round to the Gravelly.

It was properly tipping down so I quickly threw the bivvy up and huddled under it, got three PVA sticks ready and onto the rods, leaving them in the bucket, and waited for the fish to show me where they were. There was a 'bosh!' as a big common flopped out. A dunk in the fish oil and out went the stick into the rings. While I sank the line, out came another fish, so I grabbed the second rod and chucked to that one. Another five minutes later and I had all three rods on showing fish. Time to sort the bivvy out and get the kettle on.

Lewis rang me to say that he was on the move as they'd stopped showing in front of him and no sooner had I put the phone back in my pocket than the first rod I put out rattled off. I'd been told these commons fought well and this one was certainly up for a ruck and took me out into the lake. There were no snags or weed so I let it go, allowing the line to tick off the clutch while I called Lewis back before he disappeared round to the other side of the lake. After a quick, 'get your arse round here mate, I've got one on', I was back playing the fish two-handed.

Lewis arrived on cue and recognised it as Quasimodo.

It came in quickly and continued to bore up and down at the base of the marginal shelf, but eventually the leadcore popped out of the water before plunging back down. The pressure was telling, though, and the next time a huge pair of shoulders broke the surface she succumbed to the waiting net. With Lewis imminent, I got her out and weighed her at 31lbs. A proper character, this one, with its freakish big hump, which had mismatched common scales. Lewis arrived on cue and recognised it as Quasimodo. A cracking start to my Frimley campaign.

I put the rig back out to the 60-yard mark that I'd taken Quasi from, but as the rain eased, the carp had switched off and that mental frantic spell of activity had ceased. In fact, that was it for the next two days, but I'd got off the mark and I'd learned that getting a rig quickly on to fish was a very worthwhile method.

My ultimate target was Charlie's Mate and she had a reputation of being a bit of a loner, so with the luxury of three rods I decided to fish 'traps' on two of them and a big bed of bait on the other one. I hoped that would give me the chance of catching a few along the way.

Despite being told that beds of bait wasn't the way at the moment, the carp seemed to disagree. The following week produced commons of 27lbs 4oz, 25lbs, 22lbs, and a 30lbs 9oz, all over about four kilos of pellet, hemp and corn, spodded out tight at the bottom of the shelf of the bar in the Double Boards swim. I liked this swim for obvious reasons, and with Charlie's Mate usually getting caught in the bar area, I was increasing my chances of her by fishing the right areas.

With the May bank holiday came the news that the lake was busy and the big girl had been out at 41lbs. She'd been caught from the first Noddy swim, which is opposite the Double Boards, so my thinking was on the right track. I did the first night in the Single Board but was not feeling it and so on Monday moved down into the Double Boards when it was vacated.

Lee was doing the day and moved straight in the Single Board behind me. As I pushed my barrow down the lake, the wind sprang up and was straight into my face, pushing up from where I'd just come from.

The fourth fish over four kilos of bait.

Despite being told that big beds of bait wasn't the way, this 27lb 4oz common disagreed.

I hadn't even made it to the Double Boards when the texts started. 'You sure you made the right move' was soon was followed by, 'Just seen one.' Lee was having a right giggle at my expense. With the luxury of a night ahead of me, I was sure they would visit me in the hours of darkness for the feast I was about to lay out by the bar for them. As fish continued to show up at the other end, I noticed Lee latched into one and soon the text came through, '29 common. Quack!'

I'd made the move now so sticking to the plan I loaded the spot in front of the big tree on the bar and it felt even cleaner than the previous week, so I was sure this spot would produce once the pressure of the weekend was over. During the evening I caught a 16-pounder, so at least I had a limited amount of ammo to fire back at Lee.

I heard a couple of fish bosh out through the night but only bream dragged me out of the bag. In the early hours, the gentle patter of rain started and by dawn it was much heavier. The only thing guaranteed was a wet pack-up but with this pressure drop, and heavy rain, I hoped it would stir the carp into feeding much as it had done when I'd caught Quasi.

A bleep jolted me from my daydream and with waterproofs pulled on, I braved the elements to wind in what soon became apparent as another snotty. I imagined there was little bait left so finding the pole elastic mark, I clipped the line behind the spool and wound in, threaded on the largest of my remaining pre-tied PVA sticks, glugged it with oil and launched it toward the centre of the tree on the exposed bar. I feathered it down onto the clip, the lead swung down with a nice thud, the oil flat spotting the rippled surface directly above - pukka.

I huddled back under the bivvy, fired up the stove and warmed my wet hands before popping the kettle on. As I sipped my hot tea, I noticed another flat spot hit the surface over the recast rod and checked the time - it was 9am. Another hour and I'd have to start packing away because I was meeting Odd and Rick at Linear Fisheries for a bit of a social.

As I finished my tea, the same rod was away and as I dived out into the pouring rain, the clutch picked up pace as she headed up the bar. Once I'd got her swinging away from the bar she came in quite easily before speeding up as she headed into Daisy Bay.

The bait was doing the business with another five the next week, up to 31lb 8oz.

I managed to buck the trend.

I really had to hang on and let the rod subdue her attempts at getting into the pads in the bay. With her now beaten, a very long common slipped over the draw cord and an almost certain PB common was mine.

My legs started shaking when I could see the full length of it clearly, but unfortunately, its belly wasn't as impressive. With the help of a day angler who was fishing next door in the Fallen Tree, I hoisted the fish out onto the mat and removed the size 8 hook from her bottom lip. She recorded a weight of 34lbs and I noticed when I rolled her over, that she had a barbule missing which revealed the name of my capture – One Barb.

The drive to Oxford was a much more enjoyable one than I'd envisaged with a load of wet smelly gear, and I couldn't get away from the commons as I winkled out one at 21lbs from Hardwick Smith's lake.

The commons kept coming from Frimley and the bed of bait was doing the business with another five the next week, up to 31½lbs. Having spent all that time grinding out the odd fish at Yateley, I was certainly enjoying this run of action and I hoped that a mirror or one of the huge commons would soon come my way if I could keep racking them up.

A missing barbule revealed the name of my capture - One Barb.

On the penultimate trip in May, I managed to buck the trend and on this, and my final trip, I had five mirrors, accompanied by eight commons, including the biggest of the Frimley mirrors – Gums. Once again he fell to a single grain of fake corn over the bed of bait just before pack-up time and at 33lbs 13oz, he was my second biggest Frimley carp, to date.

On that last trip in May, the fish were close to spawning and pulling the rods in close to the bottom of the marginal shelf after experiencing several liners and spotting a few bubblers I was treated to two in the net at once, a 27lb gorgeous, fully-scaled and a 27lbs 8oz common, a very welcome Frimley farewell, for now. I'd be back, but once again Heather would be my focus and the fun and games would start all over again.

Two in the net at once.

Chapter 15 - Long road to a brace

My focus was on Heather and Arfur now and I'd decided to concentrate my efforts on finding one, or both, of these and setting up accordingly. Because of the relentless pressure of past years, the length of stay this year was to be reduced to 48 hours, and then you wouldn't be allowed to return for a minimum of 48 hours. I was still working a shift of four days on, followed by four off, so this rule forced me to fish some of the other lakes on my Gold Card, and as the Road Lake, Horton and Frimley are all within half an hour of Yateley, a bit of 'touring' was in order. I hoped I could keep fresh by fishing other venues and if either the Road Lake or Horton was busy, or not fishing, I could always nip down the road and try the other one.

The Car Park was still my number one water but it was typically fishing rock hard, so I headed up the M3 to the Road Lake after my 48-hour blank. I'd fished the Road Lake once the previous season and as it was small and gin clear, I hoped that finding them would be a doddle, and if I could get them feeding the rest should fall into place. However, the Road Lake was already earning a reputation for being decidedly tricky, so respect was due to its scaly inhabitants.

On my visit last season, I'd found a 30-plus with scattered linear scaling in a set of snags next to the No. 1 swim and, once again, I found fish along this snaggy bank. With the June sunshine beating down, the carp had taken cover in the shade of the snags, including the lake's largest prize, the Dink. So I set up in the No. 1 swim and with the aid of my marker rod I managed to winch a line under the bushes and using a baiting pole, lower my rig onto a sandy patch.

While doing this, I could hear voices coming round the road bank so I stashed the marker rod in the bush and ran back to my gear. A group of local teenagers were wandering round with a spinning rod and as all my gear was in the swim, I was a bit uneasy with only Tony Parker on the lake down in the Bars swim.

Obviously, they didn't have permits, but there was little point in challenging them and I told them there were no pike in this lake, and they'd be better off trying somewhere else. Sod's law, they'd hooked one before, so I had to admit there was one or two, so they'd been very lucky.

Come on guys, take the bait, I thought to myself, when one of them started shouting about down the bank. He'd cast into a snag and, fortunately for me, the snag was stronger than his line and he'd lost his spinner. Result!

They drifted off and left me to the peace of low-flying aircraft and nearby road noise. The Wraysbury area is notorious for this sort of trouble and I was on edge for a bit, but once satisfied they'd gone and with my marker rod retrieved from the adjacent marginal bushes, a few handfuls of pellet and tiger nuts were introduced in small patches on the shelf to get any feeding carp moving from spot to spot. I'd tipped the hookbait nut with a PVA nugget-sized bag of pellets, too. With the other rod fishing the gravel hump off the end of the snags I sat back confidently, and as the sun dipped behind the trees and set, and darkness descended, the sound of the planes finally began to diminish.

I was fishing under the stars so at daybreak the dazzling rays of the sun penetrated through the tall trees and woke me from my slumber; another bright day was on the cards. The Road Lake is predominately a daytime lake for bites, and particularly in the snags, so I wasn't too disappointed that the night had remained quiet - at least the teenagers hadn't returned.

A buzzer screeching out had me off my bedchair, but it wasn't mine and I looked down the lake to see Tony bent into a fish. A while later, he turned up in need of me for camera duty as the Dink was lying beaten in his net. The Dink had been in my set of snags at dusk, but the Road was such a small pond that fish could turn up anywhere and the Dink had certainly vacated my area to go and feed.

With the honours done and the Dink returned, this time down in weight at 37lbs, I went back to my swim. I had my baited rig sitting safely in a bucket, so I quickly repositioned the hookbait and with the other rod back in one cast, awaited the carps' arrival.

- -

The Dink had certainly vacated my area to go and feed.

Steve Pagulatos turned up at lunchtime for some floater fishing and he sat on the rods while I stuck my head through the bushes to view my spot. Nervously, I watched four carp browsing the bait, so with my heart racing I whipped back to the rod, expectant of immediate action.

I was still sitting on my hands when Steve returned after a lap, and with the kettle on, I checked the spot again. The sight that greeted me was tails up, wafting, as the mirrors gorged on the pellets and nuts. It was just a matter of time, but time was ticking away and still the rod tip failed to nod, let alone wrap round. I was starting to worry that something was wrong and by early evening and still no take, I donned the waders and after first checking the area for fish, examined the spot.

I traced my line down with the baiting pole, scooped up the lead and there on the end was something dangling. Guessing it to be a leaf, I swung the lead up to my hand and lifted it out. There, completely encasing my hook and hookbait, was a bloody great swan mussel! Unbelievable! Of all the baits down there, it had to clamp onto my hookbait. I had a feeling this place wasn't going to be plain sailing. Round one to the Road Lake!

I did a few more short sessions on the Road, but it was Heather that occupied my mind and along with going to Horton a few times, as well, I couldn't get my head into anywhere else. Horton was just too deep and choddy and was not my cup of tea at all. Trawlerman had given me some tips on the place and felt I'd like it, but I think he was just trying to get me out of the way on the Car Park.

There were a few snakes in the Wraysbury area.

I started doing the odd night on the Match Lake and if I did 24 on the CP I could walk over the road with just the barrow, do a night on the Match and be back at first light for 48 hours. That way, I'd get three out of my four nights on the Car Park, not that it was doing me any good. My odd night on the Match, however, was quite productive, with Heart Tail at 27lbs, but with no one about I had to slip that one back. A few stockies also helped to keep up the confidence levels.

One of these trips was quite memorable, but not for me catching. In late September, after driving to Horton and not feeling it, I went to Yateley and did my night off in the Beach swim on the Match Lake. My phone rang in the early hours, and an excited Fudgie babbled that he had the Baby Orange in the net. There was only an hour until daylight, so I packed away and pushed the barrow back over the road and into the Gate swim where Fudgie and Monki were guarding the net.

As the light grew brighter, more turned up. I was crouching by the water's edge guarding the net when the fish turned and, despite the half-light, I could tell Fudgie's prize wasn't what he thought it was. I motioned Hampshire Graham over and pulled the mesh so that the fish rolled over slightly.
"That's the Big O isn't it?" I said.
"Sure is," he laughed.
We decided to keep Fudgie in blissful ignorance as he hadn't caught either of the Oranges and with everyone collected behind, mats at the ready, Fudge came down the steps for his prize.
"You do realise you've caught the Big Orange, you numpty!" I chuckled, "and it's well over 40lbs!"
"Is it?" said Fudge.
"So much for you and Monki knowing your fish," I said.
"It was dark," was his feeble reply.
Fudge's smile grew bigger as the Big O rocked the scales round to 43lbs 7oz. His little campaign in the Gate had paid off handsomely.

The 48-hour rule made it nigh on impossible to get anything going. I wasn't local so I couldn't keep bait going in during my time off. One or two came out in late autumn and fireworks certainly occurred over the bonfire weekend in the Curly.

Trawlerman banked Heather for the second time(bloody fish!).

Firstly, Trawlerman banked Heather for the second time (bloody fish!) at a high of 52lbs 8oz on the Saturday night and with his 48 hours up, he pulled off, and Fudge was in there like a rat up a drainpipe. From the shorter spot, he also went on to double up in the early hours with Arfur at 51lbs. Both big'uns and both repeat captures, the Car Park was being cruel to the ones that desired these two colossal, ancient creatures.

With my two main targets getting nailed so late, it was unlikely they'd be out for some time and to be honest, I was all fished out. It had been a tough, tiring couple of seasons, and fishing the Car Park Lake in particular had consumed my life. I didn't want my passion to make me ill again and so I consciously took a break.

I was now of an age when I knew the winters were too gruelling, so I threw myself into going to the gym. I was getting fitter and stronger, which not only improved my health, but I'd be in better shape to fish hard again, physically and mentally. I returned in March with a much clearer head. My overall confidence in myself had improved, and with my new highlighted hairstyle and more muscular physique the lads now referred to me as Mini Mart, a smaller version of Mad Martyn.

The last couple of weeks were well busy despite the winter having not produced a fish. The first fish that graced the bank was a common, shortly followed by Chunky out of the Bars, both taken by Gary Allaway. This end of the pond was suddenly getting the attention, but it was the car park end that I fancied; both Heather and the Dustbin were liable to do a bite in this area.

With the 48-hour rule, it was a bit of a chess game when to turn up and pull off, to get a desired swim, and with this in mind I turned up the evening before I wanted to start. Utilising my Gold Card, I could set up behind on the Split and move into my chosen plot first thing to get the last full 48 hours.

I trudged round the pond in the pouring rain and found Matty set up in the Islands and as Matt was pulling off in the early hours, this was a potential winner. I also knew Darren was going from the Bars in the morning. We huddled under Matty's brolly with him and Mad Martyn, but we all piled out when we heard a fish turn over.

Fireworks certainly occured over the bonfire weekend in the Curly.

With the heavy rain it wasn't possible to pinpoint its whereabouts exactly, but it was definitely out between the Gate and Waiting Mans, not far from the Islands water but definitely further over. This put the thought of the Bars out of the equation. If I could get a good plot down this end I'd stand a chance. The Islands or Waiting Mans then, and with the latter being vacant I could have started straight away, but I wanted to fish the last full 48 hours and as it was do or die time, I needed to cast out in daylight to be spot on.

I left my rods with Matty and just set up the bivvy on the Split Lake, behind the Snags swim, and after a couple of teas with Darren, went back and snuggled down in the bag with my alarm set for 4am.

About half-past one, I was woken by the sound of footsteps. I sat up and then a couple of heads popped round the bivvy door. The fun and games had started as Gary Lewis, Trawler and Darren Emberson were mooching about for swims. It was suggested that if we decided between us where we were going, there would be no 'racing at dawn' games. I told them I was going in the Islands, Darren wanted the Curly, I think Trawler was in Dessies and Gary was going to go in the Bars but I could tell he wanted the Islands. We agreed to wait till 4am before putting gear in the swims. All very gentlemanly, or so I thought.

I went back to sleep and woke to Emberson telling me that Gary had gone in the Islands. It was five past four, and my alarm had failed to work. I ran down to the Islands and Gary shook his head saying it was past the agreed time. Five bloody minutes! I could have argued that I already had my rods in that swim, which I'd left with Matty, but I couldn't be arsed to argue with the underhanded tactics and leaving him to it, I grabbing my rods and stormed off round to Waiting Mans.

The rain had cleared and with spring in the air, the lake's birdlife started to wake, the friendly robin singing its lungs out. I chucked the wet bivvy and bedchair on the barrow and whizzed round to my plot for the last chance to save my season blank. Not only was I knackered but I was also pissed off with the night's antics. Darren, to his credit, had offered me the Curly because I was there before him, but that fish I'd heard was in Waiting Mans water, so perhaps Gary had done me a favour. I chucked the bivvy up, cast out two singles and got my head down. I would cast out properly and bait up once I'd sorted my head out and been up the shops. Ben Hamilton was dropping into Trumptons next to me once Nick Helleur had packed up, so at least I'd be in good company for the last couple of days of a funny old season.

If there was anyone else I wanted to catch her it, it would be Lee.

Waiting Mans was by far my most successful swim on the lake; I knew the spots and with so much weed still present, particularly down to the left in front of the Gate, this was a good job and I soon had a lead cracking down on the Steven's spot at about 40 yards, followed by 30 freebies.

The left-hand spot, despite being closer at about 25 yards, was tricky but it was there. I got a marker on it but it seemed the 'crack' spot was tiny and I wasn't best pleased when shortly after getting it cock on, a red-eyed tinca swam off with my little red pop-up. He did however act as a weed rake and dragged in a clump of weed that was interfering with my line lay. It looked like the tench were well and truly turned on because Ben, next door, was having a job to keep a rod in the water. Luckily, after my one, they left me alone, which was a good job as I didn't have a lot of my shellfish squid red baits with me. I glugged my freebies with a bloodworm concentrate to get some smell into the water as I was sure the carp were coming out of their wintry slumber. Monki dropped into the Beach and we sat up late, reminiscing over past captures and wondering if these last 36 hours would produce.

The penultimate night was quiet but dawn broke not just with the robin singing but also the shrill cry of a 'Heather' shout. We couldn't make out who'd put up the shout until I could hear Lee in the Gate on the phone remarking that he'd only just gone and landed Heather the Leather! I legged it round the short distance and there was a beaming Lee. As much as I desired to catch Heather myself, if there was anyone else I wanted to catch her, it would be Lee and I was made up for him - the first time anyway; the second time was naughty, and the third time was plain bloody greedy!

Despite her being so big in November it was unlikely she'd held such a big weight through the colder months and so it proved as the finest leather to swim in English waters recorded a weight of 48lbs 14oz.

I asked Lee where he'd hooked her and was surprised to find out that is was under the trees, a spot she'd never come from before. I'd had a few liners on my left-hand rod, so it made me wonder how close I'd been to her as there was a good chance she'd passed through my swim on her way to the snag. With every Heather capture, I'd question whether I'd ever catch her myself and I'd get a bit despondent, but fortunately, Ben was beside me this time and being a good friend he saw I was down and gee'd me up a bit. With one final throw of the dice I made sure my rigs were spot on. Their positions needed to be bang on, and only a rod-trembling crackdown would suffice.

The longer rod went down perfectly on the third or fourth cast, but the left-hand spot was proving more troublesome. Call it perseverance or stubbornness but I'd get it right if it took me all day. On about the tenth cast and seemingly landing in the same place again, the lead found its destination and I instantly knew it was 'the one' as the rod tip vibrated, such was the hardness of the spot.

With a half-ounce backlead clipped on and teased out halfway, I slackened right off and with 30 freshly glugged 15-millers 'pulted tight behind the float, I'd done as much as I could. I was now in the hands of the carp, or should that be 'fins of the

A lot of envious eyes fell upon her famous clean flanks.

carp'. We'd all got our rods done at the same time and after the excitement of Lee's capture I, for one, was knackered so we decided an afternoon siesta was in order.

In the warmth of the bag, I soon fell into that cosy state of mind and dozed off. I must have been dozing for an hour or so when I was jolted into consciousness as the left-hand bobbin cracked into the blank and as the tip bent round, I swung my legs out into my boots. As I took the few steps to my rods, it pinged out of the clip and the clutch purred. I bent into it and was left in no doubt what species it was as it stripped about 15 yards of line off me, ploughing into a weedbed. In a panic, I called out to Ben, and with him by my side I gained my composure.

With steady pressure, the dead weedbed started fizzing up and slowly moving in my direction. I just had to keep it moving, and pray that it stayed on. Ben assured me it would be on and with the whole weedbed getting close now, Ben moved the other line out of the way and crouched in front of me, sinking the net. Monki was still dead to the world as the leadcore surfaced and Ben asked how long my leader was, so that he'd know where the hidden fish lay. I had four feet of leadcore, so Ben pushed the net down deep and up around the weed. It was one of those moments when the world stops in your head. I held my breath until the arms broke the surface and with them the unmistakeable, stumpy, rounded tail that could only belong to one fish - the Dustbin - came out of the water, still on the wrong side of the draw cord. Feeling its freedom was in danger the Dustbin started to thrash and with my adrenalin racing I didn't even feel the ice-cold water as I plunged my boot in over its limit, grabbed the drawstring, shook the tail in and screamed, "DUSTBINNNNNN!" across the Blackwater Valley.

Relief, happiness and excitement overwhelmed me and I ran over to Monki's bivvy, where he was still comatose, slapped his cheeks and screamed, "Dustbin!" in his face before running back to Ben as he pulled the weed out of the net. The boys all arrived and as there was still plenty of light to get good photos done, we carried him round to the car park and weighed him. Dusty became my fifth 40, at 40lb 12oz, and spared a blank season in style. A lot of envious eyes fell upon her famous clean flanks and with still about 16 hours to go, I was now revved up for another one. So with Dusty put back in the Gate margin, I returned to my plot to get the rod back out.

With a new hook section knotted and blobbed back onto the boom section I found my remaining pop-ups were just not buoyant enough, so with the Dustbin hookbait still tied onto the ring, I slipped the rig ring over the new hook point and with a rubber stop pushed round the gape to opposite the barb, proceeded to find my spot again. Again, it took another 10 or so casts, but I got that crack in the end and with the last of my red bait gone, I topped up with Scopex Squid boilies glugged in the red bloodworm concentrate. Again, 30 baits fell into the ripple of the previous one and with well-wishers popping in all evening, copious amounts of tea was made and consumed.

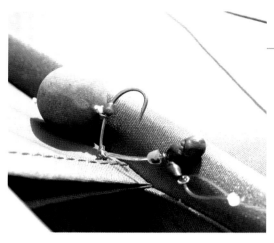

We all had to be off the lake at 8am so at about 11pm we all turned in for the final night. Sleep was hard to get as my mind raced with the events of the day, but tiredness eventually overcame my hyped-up emotions. That was until 3.15am when the same rod's hanger once again kissed the blank. I dived onto the rod and was unsure what I was attached to as the fish kited left. I gingerly held the rod out at arm's length to keep the line out of the bushes to my left margin and anxiously coaxed it up the margin. Suddenly, I realised that it was on a very short line, so I back wound a couple of times, just as a big carp rolled over just off my other rod tip. A big deep flank was evident in the moonlight and I shouted for assistance.

This time, Monki was first to respond and he grabbed the net as Ben held the other rod out of the way, and I steered the big mirror back toward the net. The depth of the fish and the ponderous fight led me to believe Arfur was approaching the net and as Monki lifted the net arms around it, I dropped the rod and grabbed the torch. Willing it to be Arfur, I shone the beam on the carp's bulk to see the more handsome beast that is Chunky puffing his gills.

I'm not keen on repeats but 12 hours before I'd been staring a blank season in the face and now I was staring at my second 40-pounder. A brace of 40s, and a Car Park brace, to boot! Chunky weighed a couple of pounds heavier at 42lbs 12oz to record my best-ever day's fishing. I quite liked the old Car Park Lake again!

I quite liked the old Car Park Lake again!

Chapter 16 - Scattering the seeds of love

It must have been the shock of catching, as shortly after the brace I was extremely sick for a few days and apart from trips to the bathroom, I lay dying in my bed. The Angling Times were on the phone wanting my brace story and keeping it brief I managed to relay events to Rich Wilby in between chucking up!

Eventually, I started to feel better and as my strength returned, I began to look ahead to my second campaign on Frimley, and Charlie's Mate in particular. This fish was the goal, so I decided I would have to resist the temptation of multiple captures from the Double Boards and concentrate more on the opposite bank. The Gravelly down to the Noddy seemed to have done the lion's share of the big girl's past captures, so to increase my chances of singling out my target would mean the deeper water in the Gravelly in cooler weather, and the Stick or Noddy swims closer to the shallower bar would be the best bets once the spring temperatures ascended.

It soon became apparent that the fish were showing less than the previous year, no surprise as they'd taken a right hammering. I'd had 30-odd fish myself, and they'd learned that showing themselves usually led to a lead landing on top of 'em.

Most of the anglers were using just singles and bags and with no fish sightings to pinpoint actual feeding spots, I ignored advice that no one was catching over bait and although not as much as last spring, I was fishing my hookbaits on the outskirts of a baited patch of 6 to 8 spodfuls. If Charlie's Mate was sending her smaller, greedier comrades in first then a hookbait just off the patch might fool her into making a mistake.

I soon started to catch, but the big girl, and the entire A-team eluded me and the best I could do was a stunning 26lb mirror. In fact, out of the dozen carp I caught, a third were mirrors, all beautiful, sequin-scaled specimens, but as hard as I willed that giant common to trip my traps, come June it still hadn't happened.

With the monster that overwhelmed my life, otherwise known as the Car Park, this year I'd made the decision that as much as I dearly still wanted to catch Heather and get the hell out of the place, if it was meant to happen then it would, and stressing, and physically and mentally draining me wouldn't help the end result. I'd seen many anglers sucked in, chewed up, and spat out, to know the danger signs. Many a good angler never wet a line after the CP had destroyed them.

I was of an age when I felt I needed a lady in my life, and not just the thought of a wet slimy fish in my head, and I'd changed my work pattern from four-on, four-off to five days work and three days off. With the odd Saturday night out clubbing with my mate, Steve, from work, I hoped that my rod action would improve!

The CP and Road Lake were on 48-hour limits, so it meant I was generally only doing two nights in an eight-day cycle; not half as much time as a year or two back, but if I could keep a fresh head I'd be in a much better position to spot opportunities, rather than grinding out the time stuck in a rut.

June and early July didn't present any real opportunities and with the CP rammed most of the time, it was time to reacquaint myself back at the Road Lake. After the swan mussel incident, I felt the place owed me one and with this in mind and a bit of holiday tagged on to my time off, I planned a night back after my 48 hours on the Car Park.

The heat of the July sunshine meant I'd just spent 48 hours watching Heather sunbathing in the thick weedbed out off Trumptons, and with a night out in Swindon planned for Saturday, I headed up the M3 for a 24-hour session at Longfield. Maybe it was the fact that it was a Friday lunchtime, or because the sun was out, but the motorway was horrendous. The 25-minute trip took about an hour and a half and if the next junction hadn't been the M25, that I needed to get on to, I'd have got off the M3 and stomped back home.

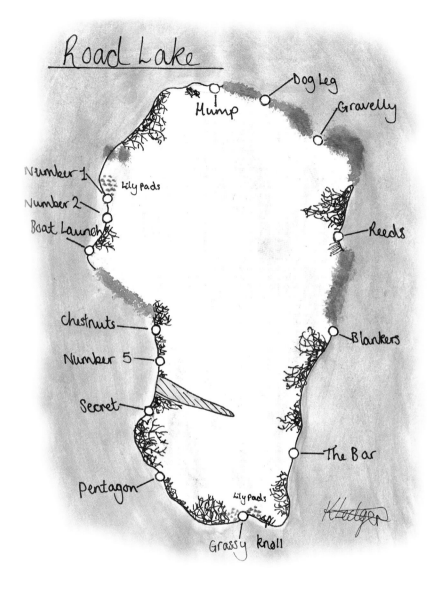

Road Lake

I watched with breath held, as below were most of the A-team pack.

Gasping for a drink, I pulled off the M25 and a minute later was unlocking the big black gate on the Longfield site. There were only two cars in the car park so it looked like sitting in the traffic hadn't cost me too much. I grabbed a guzzle of water from the water butt and carrying it down to the lake, I could see the two anglers set up opposite in the Gravelly and the Reeds.

I dropped my bottle in the No1 swim and went round to view the snags and as I peered from behind a tree trunk, I could see several of the big'uns in under the trees. Happy with this, I nipped round to see Frogger who was setting up in the Gravelly. Frogger only had Three Scales and the Scattered Linear left to catch and as the former was in the Gravelly snag, he was naturally excited and confident.

I nipped in to see Tony, in the Reeds, and after a quick circuit of the pond, put all my gear in the No. 1 and went for another butcher's in the snag. Creeping in low, I slipped into the fork of the tree and lying against the bough, watched with breath held as below in the crystal water were most of the A-team pack. Barring Clover and Three Scales, the remaining four jostled and brushed against each other below. The Dink, Orange Spot and both Linears were all within the snag, just a few feet from where I'd be casting my rig on to the sandy hump on the edge of the branches. As all of them, barring the Scattered Linear, had been out I knew I had four, 35lb-plus carp to angle for. The day was definitely taking a turn for the better.

I slid back down to the ground, tiptoed down the path and with a spring in my step, raced back to get the rods ready. With a balanced barrel hookbait on a simple, gold-brown coated hooklength and a sandy coated in-line lead with five feet of leadcore, I hoped my set-up would blend in. The trickiest task was getting the rig in without

disturbing the fish so I'd crumbed up a few baits and sprinkled them below the tree. The scent from the shellfish boilies would not only get the carp's taste buds watering, but also would pull them temporarily deep into the snag, giving me enough time to cast a bait in without spooking them.

The crumbed bait was leaking off attractors and immediately, the carps' pecs twitched and the greedy Dink was soon hoovering up the crumb. As the others came to investigate, I shot off to get the rig in. In order to judge the distance perfectly, I chucked the marker float long and wound it back to the post that marks the far end of the tree.

I jumped the lead back until it landed on the hard bottom of the smooth sandy gravel, slid it back a yard and let the float up; then I nipped back round to see where, in relation to the float, I needed to cast my rig. I had half a dozen PVA parcels of pellet, stick mix and whole and broken boilie in my pockets, and I gently lobbed these into position around the float and one or two in the edge of the snags to lure them out.

With this done and the fish still grubbing, blissfully unaware of my presence, I legged it back and with a PVA stick already attached I made the 30-yard cast. It landed just past the float and I held the tip high, let it swing in and the lead thundered down a treat. The float was quickly wound in and a perfect trap was laid. I'd done my part, now it was down to the fish.

A check of the watch revealed that it was 5pm, so knowing the carp would leave the snags for the weedy depths of the main lake before nightfall, I realistically had about four hours to get a take or I'd have to wait until morning and hope that they returned for the day.

Every now and then my heart raced as ripples pushed out from the edge of the snags, and I visualised the beasts barging each other to get to the parcels of bait on the edge of the snag. The odd bubble would ping up outside the branches and I sat on the edge of my chair willing them to sample my hookbait.

As I parted the mesh I saw the instantly recognisable and most elusive Road Lake resident. The Scattered Linear.

PVA parcels were lobbed into position from the tree.

As the light began to fade, about half-past eight, I was starting to fear that I'd been done again when the Neville bleeped and the line cracked out of the clip. I was on the rod and bent into it as the tip started to bend round.

I held the rod low and hung on as a powerful, heavy fish bucked like a bronco trying to find sanctuary. I needed to gain line so with the rod almost in the bush to the right, I leaned out and winched some line back onto the spool. The carbon creaked under my hand but was subduing her attempts toward freedom. With her head turned I was able to gain more line and as the line cut out into open water, I could breathe again and raise the rod tip. She momentarily got stuck in the weed but heavy pressure got her back on the move and I guided her in close. Now only 10 yards out, and with a small set of pads in my margin, I eased off to let her ghost around the back of them, and got the net chucked in.

In the clear margins I could see it was a big fish, but which one? With a last bid for freedom she shot off down the right-hand margin and as there were no snags to worry about, I let her chug down a few yards before turning her back. From my elevated position and with the water level down, I could make her out tight to the bank so I allowed her to drift past and simply lifted the net around her. I'd got my Road Lake carp, and as I parted the mesh I saw the instantly recognisable and most elusive Road Lake resident - the Scattered Linear - lying beaten.

I shouted out to Frogger and Tony and to their credit, they both wound in and legged it round to help. I heaved her out and was taken aback by her beauty. The visible white marks in the water appeared to be just red blemishes on the edge of the large golden scales. The light was fading fast, but we weighed her at 35lb 7oz, which was no surprise as she still looked plump and as I held her aloft, Frogger did the honours.

We watched her waddle away, and Frogger remarked,"With that one in the bag, you've got the chance of catching all of the A-team. That was the hard one, already notched up." I didn't know about that but I was off the mark and with Clover the one I wanted along with the linears, I'd be happy to walk away if I could follow up with them.

I just managed to get a rig back into position before dark but unsurprisingly, with the Scattered rucking in front of his mates, the snag was uninhabited come daybreak and throughout the day. I certainly enjoyed my night out in town that night, and more success continued!

The Car Park had always fished relatively well in August so not wanting to miss out I split my time between the CP and the Road. I felt that my best bet for singling out Heather was the boilie approach and the red Shellfish Squid baits that I'd caught the Scattered on, as well as the March brace, was being introduced by kilos. I was concentrating predominately on the Islands and would pepper the spot with a kilo or two of 20 millers on a regular basis.

Despite being told Robin Red baits had blown on the Road Lake, I kept faith and at the end of August the carp struck back as I lost a fish out from the Reeds. After a period of bubbling, the bobbin smacked the top and the fish ploughed into the weed roots. I climbed to the top of the bank and the extra height and pressure eventually won; among eruptions of bubbles the weed dislodged and I was gaining. As I descended the steps, the fish shook its head and somehow the weed fell off and it tore down to the left. Just then, the hook pulled and I despondently swung the lead into my hand, wondering what might have been.

On September 10th my life changed for ever when I met the girl of my dreams and fell in love from the off. (She says it was lust at first sight, on my side.) Lynn was my girl now and Heather was demoted. Not only did I have a beautiful girlfriend to distract me but with three children as part of the bargain, my life was turned upside down and although Lynn had no problem with the 'other woman', she had ways of luring me home early, leaving Fudgy, Dazzler and the other Heather hunters to slog it out.

With the Dustbin in the bag, I'd planned not to fish the winter on the Car Park and therefore occupied my time with other activities! On the weekend of Lynn's birthday in March, I took the plunge on one knee and despite Lynn laughing, thinking I was joking, she agreed to be my wife and as an engaged man I did a couple of trips on the Car Park before the end.

Not wanting to go into details, I was now out of work for the first time in my life as I'd walked out of my job at Hinders at the end of January. Those who know me will know why, but I will leave it at that. I had the feelers out for work but certainly in the angling industry there was nothing about, though that was soon to change.

With my relative success I'd been doing quite a few articles, predominately in Carpworld, which brought interest from sponsors and with a new set of rods as well as a load of end tackle and clothing from ESP, a return to Frimley to christen the said new rods was in order for the spring.

The wedding was planned for the following summer, so this would be the last full year on the Gold Card. The escalating price, now £1500, was unrealistic, so it would be pastures new for the future. However, I had this spring and then another year to try to catch one or more of my remaining targets – Charlie's Mate, Heather and Clover.

The carp struck back as I lost a fish from the Reeds.

Chapter 17 - Rolling in Clover

My first trip in April coincided with some much welcome sunnier weather and with the fresh smell of tree buds and the sound of the birds chirping, I pushed my barrow once again down the Frimley path towards the Gravelly. The water temperatures were still numbing our fingers, and I felt that the deeper, silty troughs out in the open water could be where a big 40lb common might be sampling a bit of grub.

Squinting into the bright sun, I soon found my mark out in the open water with the float, and then a big splash had me refocusing up the right-hand margin. The open water rod could wait, and my rig soon had a glugged-up PVA stick threaded onto it and the 30-yard cast off the tree line landed firmly with a donk, bang on the money.

I tied up another rig and stick for the open water spot, but I was soon interrupted and with stick mix flying everywhere, I grabbed the rod as the tip bent round at an alarming angle. As with most of the Frimley commons, this one tore about but with no other lines out yet, I could let it have its head and enjoy the first carp of the year.

The common looked every inch a 30 but the cold winter had probably made it use up its fat reserves and the needle stopped short at 28lbs 12oz. This was a great start and the opportunist method of casting to a fish showing had worked in double-quick time.

After spodding out a bed of hemp, pellet and small boilies, I was constantly hooking and unhooking bream for most of the night so perhaps it was time for a change of tactic.

After Rob Maylin's success on the maggots last season, I could have jumped on that bandwagon, but we'd had a cold winter and spawning wasn't too far away so boilies had to be a food source the carp wouldn't ignore to boost their weights. At least with boilies, and most areas of Frimley being within catapult range, I could dispense with the spod rod and the disturbance that the spod caused. I'd learned, in my time, that they were very wary of fishing spodded areas.

The following week, I put the boilie plan into action and armed with a few kilos of Scopex Squid and Withy Pool rigs, I set up in the Double Boards. I was starting to doubt if Charlie's Mate would come out of the Boards as it seemed to come out more from the other bank, but as she'd just been out of Daisy Bay at the weekend along with Charlie, I was fishing for bites this trip. I 'pulted a few kilos of boilies over the top of the bar from the Stick swim with the large pouched Boiliepult, which was making short work of the job. With three concentrations of boilies, I returned to my plot, cast my pop-ups over onto the baited areas and it wasn't long before I was plucking the hook out of the bottom lip of a shorter, deeper 28lb 8oz common.

I was now catching steadily on my trips and notching up six or seven fish each time, but couldn't get among any of the 30s; a 29lbs 1oz mirror being the best. Charlie's Mate kept coming out on the weekend, twice from the Gravelly swim, but with so many carp in Pit 3 it was never going to be easy to select the big girl.

I'd got myself a new job in May and was back in the fishing trade, working at Premier Angling in Chippenham. I had a 'five days on, three days off', work pattern so I could do two nights in an eight-day spell, and still get a bit of time with Lynn and the kids.

At the end of May, I was off to Frimley straight after work and finding a day angler in the Double Boards, I had to wait until he packed up. The light was fading and I wouldn't have time to run round and bait up from the far bank, so getting the rigs cast out while I could still see, I then put a few baits across with the throwing stick. The baits were still partially frozen so getting the range and the accuracy wasn't easy. I did manage to winkle out a 25lbs 8oz in the morning, but I felt I'd missed out by not getting a boilie feast spread along the drop-off from the far bar. At lunchtime I rectified this situation and deposited three kilos of 15 and 20mm boilies in the usual three spots.

As the first mozzies came out biting, so did the carp, and I soon notched up commons of 28lbs 10oz, 27lbs 12oz and 24lbs 4oz and then just as the pre-dawn chorus started up I lost a further fish. There was no time to get depressed as the longer range rod ripped off and a heavy weight slammed the rod down hard. This fish had no intention of giving up and I started to get excited that at long last I'd hooked one of the elite pack. As the darkness evaporated, I stepped up to the reed-lined margin and in the first throes of daylight, scooped up the bulk that coughed the dawn air. A big set of shoulders and a belly to match lay beaten in the net and I was sure I'd secured myself another personal best common.

I gave Steve Mogford a ring and being a star, he came straight down to the lake to sort out the photos for me. At 36lbs 14oz, it was indeed a new PB but I wasn't too sure which fish it was. I got all the rods back out after Steve had gone and having been up all night, I tried to get some kip but the fish were having none of it. A 19-pounder slipped up at 7.30am, and even with the gear all packed away and the rods lay on the boards, I still had not one, but two more! A 23 and a 21, completing an eight-carp catch and as the Car Park and Road Lake were back open the following week, that was probably my lot for now on Frimley.

On my way home, I stopped off at Yateley Angling Centre and bumped into Nigel Sharp. I excitedly informed him of my captures but was unsure which fish the 36 was, so nipping out to the car I showed Nige the digital pictures on the camera and he instantly informed me it was Shoulders, the fish he'd targeted for a long time. Not a common visitor to the bank but undoubtedly a common carp of impressive beauty.

I didn't come out for the draw on the Car Park for the third time in a row, so I decided to go back to Frimley. While getting set up on the evening of May 31st in the Boards, I got a phone call from Gareth, letting me know Nick 'Turking Stick' was only doing the night and was off at 6am. Now with Nick being in Waiting Mans, my lucky swim and a good area of the lake for Heather, I set the alarm for 4.30am and before I knew it, with bleary eyes, got packed down and got to the Car Park for 5.30am. I put a bucket in Waiting Mans and went and scrounged some tea from Gareth.

As per usual, opening day proved to be an anti-climax but the following evening with me back at home, I got the call that Rick Harrison had just landed Arfur at 50-plus.

The second time Rick had caught Arfur at over the magical weight.

This was the second time he'd caught Arfur at over the magical weight, this time out of the End Secret, a swim where I'd come close to Arfur myself in the past as she'd power roll over the shallow hump.

Heather would most likely trip up later in the year and, this being my last season on the Gold Card, I'd decided to fish the Road Lake for the next few trips, and then return for a Heather mission in August/September time. I was unsure whether this was the right thing to do but hoped that I could capitalise on both lakes. That was the plan, anyway!

The plan hit the first hiccup when on June 16th I got a text telling me that my good mate and fellow Heather hunter, Fudge, had completed his mission in some style. Fishing the Islands (there's a surprise, eh mate?) the glorious leather was flourishing in my absence as Fudge had smashed the complex record at 54lb 8oz. I was chuffed for Steve, knowing how super-keen he was for that fish, so with Heather out, it was time to crack on with the Road Lake and hopefully get Clover before Heather came out again.

My first chance came at the end of June. It was a hot and sticky summer day and I found several good fish holed up in the Number One snags. The Road Lake was mainly a daytime water, so I needed to be on them throughout daylight and if no one set up in Number 2, I could swing the baits out into the deeper, weedy open water for the hours of darkness.

However, I didn't have to wait that long. My dry lines were still taking on water and slowly pulling the bobbins closer to the rod, and because I was fishing locked up to the snag, I only had a small drop on the bobbin. Stupidly, I hadn't slackened them off after they'd crept up tight and because of the insensitivity of my Neville alarms, it was only the line snapping out of the clip that brought my attention to the rod. By the time I looked up, the tip was bent round and the alarm still hadn't bleeped.

I pounced on the rod and endeavoured to steer the fish away from the snag, but I could feel the line grating before everything went solid. There was a guy in the Launch so I shouted to him and, armed with a net, I stripped down to my boxers and ran round to just short of the snag and waded in up to my chest. With the guy holding the rod high, I managed to get hold of the line and following it down the tree-lined margin, I waded along and soon had the leadcore in my hand.

The glorious leather was flourishing in my absence as Fudge had smashed the complex record.

The bottom had stirred up a bit so I blindly ran my hand down the leadcore and then gingerly down the hooklink. This was the moment of truth! If there was a big rubbery lip at the end I was ready with the net. The wish for a set of lips, though, turned out to be a slimy branch and the hook was embedded in the wood. I pulled it out, chucked the rig clear of the tree and despondently climbed ashore. It wasn't the start I wanted, but bites breed confidence, and when fishing lakes like the Road Lake, with long spells between the action, you have to maintain confidence.

I had a week away with Lynn and the kids and the summer seemed to be passing me by, so sticking to the plan, I returned to the Car Park in August. Bait-wise, things were set to change; despite being happy with the Nash bait that I'd been using, I had an offer from Richworth which I couldn't refuse and after explaining the situation to Gary Bayes, he gave me his blessing to move on. I respect Gary hugely in the bait department, so thanking him greatly for all the bait I'd had and his understanding in the matter, I hoped my new bait would bring a change of luck and that new beginnings would mean fruitful results.

I decided to use the Ultraplex bait. I felt that the smell and taste of the bait was right for the Car Park and Road Lake, and the texture was nice - a firm skin but a soft, pasty make-up. I soon started to pile in the new bait as I felt boilies was the answer to selecting Heather.

I'd started to fall into the trap of only fishing Heather swims, concentrating mainly in the Islands and Curly and when the great Leather slipped up at the end of September it was from the opposite bank, in the Dugout, so I'd got that wrong. Lee Petty landed Heather, his first fish from the lake! Time was running out fast so I decided to return to the Road Lake for a couple of trips and then after Heather had recovered, come back for a final push.

The first week of October had always been good to me and I'd caught a few of my big fish in that period so on Sunday, October 1st, I headed back to the Road Lake and after not finding anything, plotted up in the No. 2 swim. This swim had accounted for Clover a couple of times recently, so with the deeper water and dense weed beds plentiful, I felt this was the best bet. Knowing these carp loved their hemp I spodded out a bit and with half a kilo of boilie on each spot and hoped this would tempt them into a munch-up.

I can't remember why, but I could only do the night and come back on the Wednesday for another night. I must have had something on with Lynn but my memory eludes me. I hoped that during a 48-hour break away from the lake, the carp would have got on to my baited spots and that I could return on Wednesday and drop straight back in.

On October 4th, the seventh anniversary since I'd caught Bazil, I pulled into the Road Lake car park to find just one car present. As I peered through the trees, sure enough, I could see a bivvy in No. 2. Typical! One angler on and he just had to be in my baited swim. I popped in to see Slippery John, and he told me that nothing had been out in my absence so I took a slow walk round to see if I could find anything.

For a change, the No. 1 snags were devoid of fish, as appeared to be the case out in front of the Gravelly and Reeds. As I made my way down to the Bar swim, the wind seemed to strengthen, pushing down to the end I was walking to and as I stood at the top of the bank, I spotted a couple of bubbles, shortly followed by a small plume of fizz in the alcove of the weedbed which was flattening the water from the gentle breeze.

It looked very carpy but I guessed the spot where the bubbles were peppering the surface was most likely weedy, due to its proximity to the surface weed. It was worth a closer look so I headed to the car park to grab the marker rod. I did spot one bubbler in the Launch but with the wind pushing down to the Bar and it having good form of Clover and the Big Linear, I decided to investigate the spot first. I set up the marker rod and the bubbling ceased, so I cast to the back of the spot, clipping the back edge. The lead sank uninterrupted, and I was pleasantly surprised to feel it thud bottom. Game on! Time to get the barrow!

I spotted a couple of bubbles, shortly followed by a small plume of fizz in the alcove of the weedbed.

I even managed a four-foot drag back; a nice firm silty pull gave me plenty of room to get a rig on to it. The weed in front of the spot was within a couple of feet of the surface so I quickly tied up a long eight-foot length of fine leadcore and with my corkballed pop-up weighted down with a shot just to sink it, I threaded on a PVA stick. I needed the leadcore to drape down the wall of weed this side of the spot so I wanted the hookbait as far to the back of the area as possible and then instantly slackening off. I hoped that the long, supple length of leadcore and heavy fluorocarbon line would disguise my trap. I also needed to try to get it in first cast, in case the bubble blower was still in and around the spot.

First cast, and it appeared to land spot-on but I felt it brush weed on its descent so I whizzed it in and tried again. Same again, and it wasn't until the fourth cast that it sailed down uninterrupted, thudding down on the spot. I let the tip drop instantly and with the bail arm opened, let it all sink down.

After four casts I felt I'd messed up my chance of a quick bite so I got out the Pocket Rocket and deposited five spodfuls of hemp, a few small bloodworm pellets and 20 broken and ten whole 14mm Ultraplex. The trap was set and time now to let it settle. With the other rod underarmed to a small gravel spot to my left, I was soon all done and had the kettle on by half-past three.

I was starting to wonder if I'd scared the fish off when, while talking to Lynn on the phone, a carp nutted out in line, but about 15 yards past the middle of the bay rod. "Getting closer then, babe," Lynn commented, and as I put the phone down a big proper

I hoped the long, supple length of leadcore and heavy fluorocarbon line would disguise my traps.

fizz came up right on top of the bait. It was time to sit on my hands. Instead, I lay on my bedchair, my eyes glued to the spot. Whack!

The indicator slammed up to the rod and I pounced, and as I held the rod high, I could feel a heavy fish lunge on the end. As the fish began to come up in the water, I kept the rod high and watched in awe as a big, yellow carp waddled out over the hole and over the candyfloss weed, straight for the fallen tree up to my right. I now had the rod low and outstretched and I frantically winched line onto the spool, turning her just in time and she was now right at my feet. In a panic, I chucked the net in, and at the same moment, she was in. Wham! Bam! Thank you, ma'am!

From right above the fish, I peered in and it looked very Clover-shaped but didn't look big enough. However, as I lay down and reached in to check its tail, it drifted round and the full size of it hit me. There was the top lobe damage to her tail; I'd snared the queen of the lake, and just three hours earlier, I'd still been on the motorway. I shouted out to Slippery John that I'd got Clover and within five minutes he was round to assist.

Excitedly, I phoned Lynn to tell her I'd got the big'un, and then with John's help weighed her at her top weight of 42lb 12oz. Having not had a 40 for a while, she sure felt heavy but with the adrenalin coursing through my veins, I held her up proudly as John snapped away. As I lowered her back into the margin, she looked so wide and full and it was easy now to see why she'd recorded her top weight. John legged it back to his swim, leaving me with my thoughts and admiring my pictures on the camera. I put a rig back out and hoped for a second chance but I'd caught the one I wanted most out of the lake, so it was time to return to go after the one I wanted most in the world, a bit quicker than anticipated.

Do you ever get the impression that some things aren't meant to happen? With my imminent return to the Car Park, Heather came out again. Gary Lewis snared her out of the Snags swim, the first time to my knowledge that she'd ever come from there. Arfur was a more likely culprit now to slip up and I plodded on throughout November, but as soon as the weather took a decline, that was my lot.

I was a bit older and wiser now, and with the choice between snuggling up with Lynn on a cold night or shivering in a bivvy, there was only one winner. I did a couple of trips in January, on Frimley, when I managed to catch a little mirror from the Gravelly, had a social with Benny in the Stick swim, and caught a long 26-pounder out of the Noddy on a Tutti, but that was my entire winter fishing. We were making wedding plans and preparations, though, so I certainly didn't have time to miss fishing the winter on the Car Park.

I returned for the last couple of trips in March, but it was more in hope than expectation of getting a farewell chance of Heather. A week before the end, Matty Halliday ended that tiny glimmer of hope as he also finished his Car Park campaign in the style that I so dearly wished for; Heather weighing in at over 50lbs again. Not only was this Matty's and my last season on the Car Park but also Fudgey, Darren Miles, and one or two others were all going. The end of an era! Despite moving from Waiting Mans to the Islands in pouring rain for the last night, as I was sure I saw a shape move deep down in the Islands margin, I wound in for the last time biteless.

The wedding was planned for July 28th and we were buying our own house so my priorities had shifted and the obsessive Car Park Lake and extortionate Gold Card were now a thing of the past. I had one last spring on Pit 3 at Frimley and then it was on to new waters and fresh challenges.

Driving home after that last trip, I made it on auto-pilot. Although there were times when I hated the place, most of the time it was magical. The huge fish were always the focus but the nature of the lake and the people you fish with are what makes it special and in the years I'd fished there I had been privileged to fish with some top anglers who were also top guys, and it was the mates I'd made that I'd miss the most.

Fish on!

I'd snared the queen of the lake.

As I cruised down the motorway, a smirk appeared on my face as I recounted countless memorable funny moments. They often involved Lewis or Mad Martyn, and I remember vividly Lew hyperventilating after his capture of Pearly, the third time for that matter. It was an effort to hold the camera still as he tried to breathe normally. The time when Lew did his best to put me off as I was spodding in Waiting Mans, to Lewis standing in front of me gyrating and singing to the tune of 'Go Johnny, Go Johnny'! Fortunately, every spod landed perfectly, much to his disgust. There's a first time for everything - the accurate spodding I mean.

Mad Martyn was also a good source of humour and often had my jaw and belly aching with his quick and unrelenting wit. Darren and I were in agony with laughter as he ripped poor old Yommie one cold winter's night; Yommie's accent and lack of teeth being the subject of our stomach cramps.

Another time which also involved the Yomster was Martyn running into the Curly screaming "I've got one, I've got one, Yommie!" before legging it back to the Bars. As Yommie came puffing and panting into the swim, asking, "What you got Martyn?" Mart's dry reply was, "An egg and bacon sarnie, Yommie!" Priceless!

The hyperventilating Lew! Good times!

324

A long 26-pounder out the Noddy in January.

Talking of priceless situations, I can remember this one as if it were yesterday. Numpty Mark sat on the woodchip in my swim, Waiting Mans, in 34-degree heat, while Dazzler and I chatted about Darren's lost fish earlier that morning. We stared in amazement as Numpty - who we thought might have had one too many smokes - made a full-scale castle out of used tea bags, complete with moat, I might add, only for it to get demolished as we shouted at him, telling him to run to Trumptons because his rod was in meltdown. Numpty was in a world of his own, as usual. In the blazing sun, at 10.30am, the Big Orange lolloped into my net. I say 'my net' as his was so floppy and full of holes I couldn't bring myself to use it. Needless to say, the castle was rebuilt after the Big O was back in the sauna of the Car Park's margins.

Good times, and that's how it should be. It was time to move on, and besides I could always go back.

Chapter 18 - Final
Frimley flurry

April is always a nice time to be out carp fishing and with spring in the air and the sun finally having some heat to it, I'd now put the Car Park Lake in the past and was hoping to catch a few fish at long last.

Frimley had been relatively kind to me, but despite having the big mirror, Gums, in my first stint and Shoulders the year before, I hadn't got to the 40lb barrier. Hopefully, it was only a matter of time and sticking with the boilies, this time the new KG1 bait, I'd get my opportunity before the end of May.

I knew Chilly and Moggy had been horsing in the boilies through the cold months so this type of food source could be preferential to the humble maggot which had dominated last season. Chilly had caught his dream fish the previous month, so that was the paratrooper out the way and one fewer in competition for the big girl. The warmth of the sun's rays was heating up the shallower water quickly and the exposed bar was drawing the carp like a magnet, so I set up stall in the ever-consistent Double Boards swim.

The first night was as dead as a dodo, but in the early hours of the second night, a bit of cloud had moved in and I could hear the odd bosher out long, toward the bar. Soon after, the activity transferred to the rods and the long rod bleeped into life. Frimley fish rarely give up easily and this was no exception, but it was a bit more ponderous than usual so it came as little surprise to find a mirror sulking at the bottom of the net.

Chilly caught his dream fish.

Not just any mirror, though, but the oldest original in the lake, Daisy the carp, at a healthy 27lb 8oz, proving there was life in the old dog. I mean the fish, not me!

The first fish on a new bait is always special and I hoped that the oldest fish in the lake was in cahoots with the biggest. With Charlie's Mate in mind, I tried the deeper Gravelly swim on my next trip. She had come out from this area twice the previous spring and I felt she might be sitting back away from the bulk of the fish, her being a bit of a loner.

Clear skies meant that the nights were still fresh but with two rods out in deep water, I kept one bait in shallow water up the right-hand margin, in anticipation of the fish getting on it as the sun beat some heat into the area come morning. Just setting a single carp trap of a maize/chopped-down boilie snowman, with a small oily PVA stick, I hoped the subtle trap would prompt a pick-up.

As the sun climbed, so did the bobbin and my right-hand margin trap had been sprung. Big Jason was doing the day in the Stick swim and by the time he'd stepped the few yards to my swim, the carp had travelled back in front of me and was now off under the overhanging branches of the left-hand margin. After a few minutes of boiling down deep, steadily she started to tire and twisting and turning came higher in the water.

First impression was of a low-20, and the higher it came the bigger it got, but it wasn't until I lifted it on to the bank I realised it was a right chunk. It must have been over three feet in length and its perfect common armour shone like gold sovereigns in the ever-increasing sunshine. At 35lbs 2oz, it proved to be my second largest common and was a well-appreciated start to the morning.

The fishing on the lake was very patchy so it wasn't a huge surprise that it was my only encounter of the trip. There was a mini-heatwave for the time of the year, and the carp were beginning to shoal up as sex was obviously starting to occupy their minds and a succession of small males were all that came out the next week.

The oldest original in the lake - Daisy.

It must have been over three feet in length.

The only big female was a 32lbs 4oz common that I nailed out of the Double Boards on my very next outing, along with a succession of smaller males that tipped the scales to weights of 22lbs, 15lbs, 25lbs 3oz, 17lbs 8oz, 18lbs 4oz, 19lbs 8oz and 21lbs 4oz, as well as one fish dropped that felt of a similar stamp.

This proved to be my last big hit and throughout the month of May I just managed one carp per trip, the best being a black, old scaly mirror off Deep Point on my last visit. Once again I'd finished without my ultimate target, Charlie's Mate, but the reality was that a Gold Card was no longer affordable. Some you win, some you lose.

With two new tickets acquired it was time for a change of targets and new beginnings.

The only big female was a 32lb 4oz common.

Chapter 19 - New beginnings

Time was at a premium with a house move and the wedding on the 28th of July, so I needed venues that would give me a reasonable chance of getting amongst them. I'd looked around Fox Pool on the Longfield site back in March on my last trip to the Road Lake and with a reasonably good head of carp that were starting to knock on the 40s door, I'd taken the ticket when the application came through the letter box.

Fox Pool is not a large venue at about five acres, but quite deep and with gin clear water I was excited by the opportunity of close, visual fishing that the forthcoming season should bring. The snaggy margins looked prime, and floods of memories of the Copse Lake were prominent in my mind as I'd crept the historic banks back in March.

Although the clear depths were no longer home to the old A team of Jack, Shoulders, and the Parrot, a new gang of big'uns was in residence. Having failed in my attempts at a 40lb common from Frimley, it looked like Fox could hold not just one but two that would break the barrier in the not-too-distant future. With three or four upper-30 mirrors finding home in the snag-infested pool, one of which went by the name of Bazil, there was plenty to have a go at.

The other water was one I'd had my eye on for a while and that was Pingewood Lagoon. Bang on the side of the M4, it was on the way to Fox Pool so it was in the right direction and should it be busy, I could carry on to Fox and vice versa, because it would be on the way home. The main attraction of Pinge, however, was a very large, crusty old mirror with a bumpy head by the name of the Brute. Little did I know, but this beast would make me work my nuts off in pursuit of the dream. Like Fox, Pinge held a good head of 30s and with second-in-command, Big Pecs, a bullish animal of a fish pushing 40, the Brute wasn't the only desirable target.

The Fox ticket started on June the 1st, and the next day I made the familiar trek up the M4, glancing at Pingewood as I headed eastbound, before getting off at Datchet, past Wraysbury One, and arriving at the big locked gates in just over an hour. Once I was the other side of the big black gate, away from civilisation, the fish hunter instinct could take over temporarily from the thoughts and stresses of the outside world.

Things were piling up in my life. Not only was I moving into our own house on July the 13th, Friday the 13th - probably not the best date they could have picked, but the wedding was on the 28th, too. Lynn and I were doing everything ourselves to help keep the costs down and now I knew I was going to be a real daddy, as Lynn had given me the wonderful and exciting news that she was expecting. The trials and tribulations of trying to catch a fish didn't seem quite so crucial anymore.

I had a couple of days on a new venue to chill out. I hoped I'd get to view my quarry at close quarters, and if my luck was in maybe even nick one out. I'd certainly be giving it a go and as the Fox car park was less busy than the Road Lake one, I hoped the opportunity to get on fish would arise, at least.

The Pool was now in full summer leaf and a totally different sight from the barren lake that I'd seen back in March. It was much more enclosed and intimate and I immediately felt at home as I crept along the heavily matured, overgrown banks, peering through gaps down into the steep-sloping, golden gravel margins, my eyes searching out any sign of my prey.

As I rounded the Ruins Point and peered down into the snag-infested Goose Pool, I could see those dark outlines that get a carp angler's heart thumping, and eager for a better look I tiptoed like a thief in the night up to the water's edge, gently parted the foliage and peered through the window that I'd created.

I could make out at least six fish, but two commons of gigantic proportions had my full attention. Spawning obviously hadn't taken place in their two-month lay-off, and both of these fish looked to be over 40. One was a big, wide, silvery fish with a gut of beer belly proportions, which I discovered to be the Patch Common, and the other a pristine chestnut coloured fish of classic shape and build - the Twin Common.

I set about getting a bait as close to the dead snag as possible.

Either of them could cap a season and the sight of them at my feet had me dreaming of cradling them in my arms before a big, fat, pale mirror ghosted in from down the right-hand margin, snapping me into action to form a plan of how I could tempt them out of their jungle environment and into somewhere that I could present a bait.

Fox has some funny rules so I was unsure how to tackle the area. The closest swim was 'day only', according to the map, and with time getting on, the only viable option looked to be the next swim up, where a sideways cast could get me to an old, dead snag that I hoped the carp would use as they entered or exited the tiny Goose Pool area. I collected the gear from the car and set about getting a bait as close to the dead snag as possible.

It was plain that the pool was going to be heavily weeded this season, and with depths of 10 to 13 feet, the open water spots would be hard to extract the carp from easily as there was no boat present on the pond. The snaggy margins looked to be the key to not only finding the big fish but also, setting up tight to the rods and being on full alert would be the best tactic for extracting the lake's jewels from its depths.

Monki turned up after a couple of fruitless days at Horton and decided to drop in next to me for a social, keen to fish a few waters on his newly-purchased Gold Card. I showed Monki the two commons in residence deep in the inaccessible Goose snags, and he backed up my guesstimation that they were just over 40.

Apart from the odd liner, our first night on the new water was deathly quiet so we wound in mid-morning and went for a stroll. While chatting with a bailiff in Concrete Corner, I was informed that the 'day only 'rule was not in force any more, so I quickly moved up into Goose for my second night, with Monki moving up into Teds, which I'd vacated. At least now I could fish one in the near margin as well as putting one across to the dead tree. Although this spot was clean and silty, there was a drawback. It was 13 feet deep and with the fish in the upper layers enjoying the June sunshine, the depth of the spot meant it wasn't a great ambush point.

With the odd bait flicked in under the bushes between my swim and their lair, my confidence in the bait was raised as the big, fat, ungainly Lumpy continuously troughed any free offerings I trickled in. His shape, along with the way he ate with gusto, reminded me a lot of Arfur from the Car Park, but I hoped this one wouldn't be as tricky to catch. I soon learned that despite him liking bait he was indeed a tough cookie to crack.

I spent a lot of my time crouched, watching my quarry, trying to learn their habits and characters, even managing to photograph them as they quite happily lazed in their 'safe' sanctuary.

The second trip pretty much followed the same pattern as the first as the draw of those big carp on full view in Goose Pool drew me like a magnet. Once again, they'd spend all day in the corner before 'playing' on the trunk that was like a telegraph pole stuck in the bottom, with the tip of it protruding from the water. Every now and again, the log would bob sending ripples across the surface and on closer examination I could see the carp flanking against the smooth bough, rubbing their sides when they powered over it, before they buggered off out into the main lake as darkness set in. It was a fascinating sight.

My Pingewood ticket started on the 16th and with only a night at my disposal I found myself standing on the noisy banks of the second new venue I was tackling this season. The monotonous drone of the busy M4 was running just 50 or so yards from the bank, and there was a fully-operational gravel workings plant at the other end, so only a deaf man could describe it as quiet, but although not as picturesque and intimate as Fox Pool, it had something about it. Several hours later, I was beginning to question what that something was, as my attempts to find a clear spot in my chosen swim were proving somewhat troublesome to say the least.

There was a tanking south-westerly pushing into the bottom of the Cottage Bank and I'd set up stall in the first swim on that bank, Tom's. A friendly guy, called Andy, had told me of a close-in spot from which the Brute had been caught before, and after scaling the top of the tree and surviving getting nearly blown out of it, I'd sort of located the area from the bank with the aid of a marker rod.

The spot was far from clean and with repeated casting I'd got it as good as possible and while sorting this rod out I'd spotted three or four shows about 70 yards out, and although this was more in front of the Nettles where Paul was, if they continued their path on the wind, I felt that I might have a chance of intercepting them.

There was a large, visible weedbed between us so I set about casting two chodernosters on to the thinnest area of weed on my side of the weedbed. With four feet of 4lb mono and my choddy running on a couple of feet of leadcore, I could keep the hookbaits visible, sitting on top of the weed, by using small leads and slackish lines as soon as the rig landed. A couple of exploratory casts on to the desired area revealed just the odd sprig of weed coming in on the retrieve, so I'd be fishing my rigs presentably.

I'd scattered 100, or so, freebies over the whole area and I was done in. Maybe it was the relentless headwind, or the noise and fumes of the neighbouring motorway, but I had a stinking headache so a cup of tea, something to eat and a couple of hours kip seemed the best course of action. As I woke from my afternoon siesta, the traffic started to relent, so did my headache and by darkness the wind had blown itself out and the gentle lapping of water against the front board gave a more soothing effect to the place. For the first time, I could take in the atmosphere of the lake and enjoy the summer night.

I lay back on the bedchair and started to drift off, but moments later I was racing to the rods. My chodernoster pop-up had been picked up and the culprit was emptying my spool and heading for the middle. As I hung on, the fish continued to take line and having the knowledge that the Brute had fallen as first fish to a few people over the years, I even thought it could be the big girl; it certainly felt a good fish. Could I be that lucky?

The lead had been lost, the line having parted on the take, most likely and I managed to keep the fish coming toward me and not getting stuck for any length of time in the numerous weedbeds. As the carp neared the bank, I slipped into the margins, to make netting easier and avoid the other lines, and I held my breath in the moonlight as a carp wallowed over the drawstring.

I peered inside the net and although it wasn't a monster, it was a good-looking fish and once it was on the bank, I was admiring a stunning little mature linear. Pinge had a reputation of containing some very pretty fish and this 23lb 4oz woodcarving was a perfect start. I was off and running, first night on.

The memory of this baby linear would keep me going over the next couple of months as my free time was completely occupied. The house move and all the wedding preparations, complicated by the biggest floods experienced in my lifetime, made July a mental month but on the afternoon of the 28th my beautiful fiancée became Mrs Claridge and with my unborn baby nestling in her womb, all thoughts of fishing were forgotten, for a few days anyway.

Most of my Yateley buddies travelled across to Gloucestershire for the wedding and we had a fantastic day. On the Sunday, Mrs C and I headed off to Cornwall for our week's honeymoon - just in time for morning sickness to kick in. Bloody good timing, that was! After a relaxing week away, though, it was soon time to pick up the kids (and dog) from their grandparents and settle back into a 'normal' routine.

At the end of August it was time to get back fishing and although I was struggling to get the motivation to sort all the gear out, Lynn told me to get back into it and with 24 hours at my disposal I returned to Pinge.

What greeted me as I pulled up to the gate resembled more a freshly mown paddock than a lake. Whichever direction I looked there was weed stretching across the surface. Never had I seen a lake so overtaken by the green stuff and despite finding full time Paul fishing a small hole 10 feet from the bank, it did nothing to inspire me.

Back in the car, I headed to Fox Pool. There was only one car in the car park and at least I could see some water; with little competition I might be able to find and get on some fish. It was just the motivation I needed.

Trying to resist the temptation of the deep Goose Pool, I donned my Polaroids and headed in the other direction and as the angler present was in the main Noddy swim, I had all the corners to consider. Common Corner was the first area that I looked in and as I eased myself across the trunk of the overhanging tree, the old instincts clicked straight into gear as a big, long mirror ghosted past me, heading for the corner. From a more lofty position, I could see several carp enjoying the lazy, late summer afternoon, and disappearing under bushes and milling about under the scum deep in the corner.

I put my bucket in Common Corner, confirming my base for the night and after a short trip to the car, I soon had gear strewn all over my swim as I eagerly got baits and rigs ready. The scummy corner looked good but I was unsure if it was clear, so I tied on a Withy Pool rig, mounted a pop-up and flicked the 2oz lead over the protruding branches and feathered it round the overhang. With my finger on the spool, I felt a clean descent and the lead thudded moderately down. I was in about seven feet of water and this shallower depth and firmer bottom felt a far better bet than the much deeper Goose spot.

On the afternoon of the 28th July my beautiful fiancée became Mrs Claridge.

As carp drifted backwards and forwards, I periodically fired out 30 baits while getting the other rod ready. The far side of the snags was hanging over, and in much shallower water because the gravel shelf was at a far more gradual gradient. I cast tight to the bushes hoping that was getting me on the shallower gravelly shelf; fingers crossed.

With a bare lead attached, I sent it the 30 or so yards across to the trees. It landed short and hit weed so I stripped another few feet off and put the line in the clip. This time the lead cleared the weed, landed within inches of the bushes, swung down and thudded - beautiful.

With only a yard pull-back before the resistance of the weed was felt, I'd need to be accurate, but with the line already in the clip, I wound on four feet to compensate for my leadcore leader and with a PVA stick masking the hook should it clip the trees, I sent the prepared rig to its destination. The lead shot in under the trees and with a good thump down, I slackened straight off to allow the leadcore to settle.

I fired a handful of PVA bags of pellet and boilie mix tight to the bushes, and 'pulted over another 80 baits in the hope of tempting a few to feed. With only the night and morning ahead of me I didn't want to go overboard.

The carp activity had subsided since my arrival and although I'd got both traps set with minimal disturbance, I'm sure the carp were all too aware of my presence. There was so much weed across the corner that my right-hand line was literally strung just under the surface and as dusk crept in, the fish crept out, knocking my line as they swam into open waters. Mmmm, perhaps as in the Goose, the carp spent only the days in the snags, and to maximise my time in future perhaps I'd have to fish the corners in the day and the open water swims throughout the hours of darkness.

After a bit of a lay-off, and the anxiety of moving and getting married, I was just glad to be back on the bank and it would soon be morning, when I was sure the carp would return. My traps were already set and it was time to chill and wait for their arrival.

There was no likelihood of rain, so I set my bed next to the locked-up rods and kipped under the stars, at one with nature, you might say. After a couple of hours, though, nature was doing my head in as the relentless buzzing and biting mozzies sucked my blood like famished vampires. The temperature cooled, the mozzies dispersed and I drifted into a deep sleep only to wake to an already rising sun that forced me to squint as I focused my eyes on the far bank snags. A few bleeps to the far trees rod got my interest and as there were no visible carp cruising across the corner, it meant that the collision with the line must be at the rig end.

At half-past ten the indicator danced again but much more aggressively and when the rod creaked in the butt rest, I instantly went into battle mode. I walked back, with the carbon creaking from the lunges of a twisting fish, and soon had him turned and away from the danger of the branches. Part one of the battle had been won by me; part two was to get the fish through the dense weed.

The fish hit the wall of weed and by giving it the butt, I gained a few inches before stalemate. Solid! I tried the usual pull from different angles and even stood on top of my chair to gain a bit of extra height, but it wasn't giving. A few bubbles peppered the surface, the pressure was telling and eventually, the whole lot began to inch closer. I hadn't felt anything since it hit the weed so I netted the lot, lay on my stomach, and reached into the depths of the net. That sinking feeling took over as I realised that the only bulk in my net was weed, and the fish had slipped the hook.

It's never nice to lose a fish, but the first bite on a new venue is special and to come away empty handed was even harder to take. Revenge was top of my agenda so I took out the marker rod, tied on the cast-able weed rake that I'd made from my Yateley days, and dragged a channel. If I was to get a bite from this spot again, a less weedy path to draw it in was the key and as it was nearly September, the weed should be dying back soon. I put out a good dose of baits on both spots and headed off home.

I hoped that the mountain of weed I'd left in Common Corner would put off any anglers in my absence. This swim certainly had potential and I could be the one to make the most of that.

On my return, the carp were in residence in the Common snags, and with similar bright conditions I hurriedly got two rigs in as I'd done the week before. I'd put my buzzer bar on the landing net handle and used it to push the floating weed to the sides and suddenly, the swim looked more fishable.

Going on the evidence of the previous week, I planned to fish the open water Royal Box swim through the night and move back to the corner at breakfast time but on this evening the carp seemed in no hurry to disperse and when Tony Parker turned up and headed round to the Box my indecision was taken out of my hands. Stay put for the night it was then. I hoped fate was playing its part. At least I wouldn't have to disturb the swim in the morning and with the odd liner breaking the silence through the small hours of the night, at least one or two were still in the area.

I dragged myself out of the bag at first light and scanned the flat-calm surface for signs but it looked like the fish were having a lie in, even if I wasn't. Nothing was

The fish had a small head and was thick-set, resembling a small beer barrel.

showing so I got back into the comfort of the bag where I stayed until 8.45am when, this time, the left-hand rod arched round, the snag bar preventing the rod coming off the rest.

I was on it in a flash and kept the tip under water to keep the line out of the bush. I held on strongly as the bucking bronco kicked, but the strong tackle won the day and I led him out from under the bush like a dog on a lead. With a really deep margin under my feet, the fish stayed down right under the tip but soon the pressure brought him up, and my first carp as a married man kissed the spreader block.

A good fish lay beaten, so I staked the net in place, legged it up the bank to get some help, and raced back excitedly to examine my first Fox Pool carp. The scales read 31lbs 6oz and I was pleasantly surprised because I'd thought initially that it was an upper-20. The fish had a small head but was thick-set, resembling a small beer barrel. It was almost black and was identified as the Dark Mirror so I'd got off to a flying start and the loss of the previous week was now a distant memory.

I had one more blank at Fox and then stopped off at Pinge on the way home because I'd heard that they were cutting the weed with some contraption on the back of a boat. Much of the lake hadn't been touched but an area in front of the Paki swim looked interesting. There was a good 50 yards of clear water in front and because of the minimal pressure that the fish had been under, I felt it was worth a session if the area was free.

The Paki was indeed vacant on my return a week later, and by casting tight to the visible weed I winkled out a 19lb common on the second night. As I recast this rod at first light, a strange sight came up in front of me. I held the rod aloft and for a second I thought I was seeing a coot, but my eyes focused on a bloody great carp's head shuffling a good 10 feet along the surface before dropping back down. It was a sight more likely at a zoo with a performing dolphin than a carp in a wild lake. Shuffling was not uncommon on Pingewood, I soon learned, and the Brute and Silt Pit were the two biggest performers. This was bizarre carp activity that I've never witnessed on any other carp venue.

I cast a bait to the shuffler, which was closer than the spot where I'd taken the common because the ever-increasing wind was shifting the mass of floating weed continuously towards me, and willed the indicator into life.

It was my stepson Bobby's birthday the next day and we were taking him to the fair that evening so I couldn't get a much-needed extra night and with motionless bobbins

at 2pm, I packed away and filled in the spot with 2½ kilos of KG1. We had a good time at the fair and I tried not to sulk too much. I was sure that shuffler was a massive fish, most probably the Brute.

My grand plan backfired as soon as I next pulled into the Cottage car park when all I could see was a sea of weed. I wandered up the bank with the wind in my face; the expanse of weed, from against the bank to over 100 yards out, had rendered the whole area unfishable. To add insult to injury, I found out that the guy who had been next to me the week before had jumped straight into my baited swim and in the depth of the night had got a fish into the margin. While trying to get the weed away from it, he had felt the fish and was convinced it was the Brute as it thrashed about, throwing the hook. He should have netted the whole lot, the bloody noddy!

I was going to write Pingewood off until the spring and just fish Fox Pool until the weather changed, and as my daughter was due in March, I'd limit myself to the odd day session at a local park lake in the winter. We were now well into October and the nights were getting longer. I set up in the Royal Box. A fish had nutted out as I walked into the swim and Martin Ford was due to arrive later to take pictures for a Carpworld article, so I could have a social without fishing locked up to snags.

The night proved fruitless despite the odd show and after I'd posed for the photos, I decided a move was my best bet and as I sneaked along the snags that back on to Common Corner, a couple of big, dark shapes ghosted over the gravel. A return to Common Corner was in order and soon I had baits on my two productive spots. Both rigs were in position and I wanted to check that I hadn't spooked my quarry so I peered through the bushes and saw that there were still carp gliding over the sandy bottom, big, white clay marks on their heads and flanks. I was sure they were feeding in the area because they'd rubbed themselves over the clay bottom. The food signals emitting from my bait would surely tempt them to investigate.

Investigate they did, and in the depth of night I crouched in the darkness hanging on to my close-in rod, the only light being the piercing red from the latching LED of the buzzer. As that switched off, I managed to gain a reel turn before the clutch clicked a couple of notches and the carp tried to reach the sanctuary of the snags in the corner. My determination and strength won the day and the carp, knowing it was beaten, was soon on my side of the overhanging tree and coughing air among a lump of weed. I scooped the whole lot up. With the fish safely in the confines of the net, I grabbed my head torch and struggled to heave the whole lot out without falling in; precariously, I got the fish out and onto the mat.

It was a more rounded fish and at 33lbs 4oz was a very welcome wake-up call.

It was a more rounded fish than the Dark Mirror but at 33lbs 4oz, a very welcome wake-up call and as there was no one on the pond, I took a few self-takes and slipped her back. I'd had a productive move, and the Common Corner was becoming a bit of a favourite for me!

With the onset of November, the leaves were dropping fast and I knew my limited fishing time was drawing to a close, doing nights anyway. I wandered round the pool but the poor light levels made the water look inky black and I couldn't see any fish. My usual close-in spot in Common Corner looked free of leaves so I hoped it was fish activity that was wafting the leaves from the sandy bottom. It was the only thing I had to go on so, once again, the two rigs were flicked on the usual spots. The water temperature was dropping so I limited the amount of baits, just 20, 14-millers plopped around the far side of each hookbait.

My gorgeous little Isabelle.

A bit of a gutty character.

The following morning dawned crisp and fresh but my body overheated with a heart-in-the-mouth, close-range battle and my first Fox common was nailed. A bit of a gutty character and keeping my average up she tipped the scales at 32lbs 8oz; a trio of 30s so far. Perhaps I could have made that four because as dusk descended the other rod woke up but after snagging me in the far bushes, the fish came adrift and my last chance of an early Christmas present was gone.

The weather was getting colder so I hung up the rods and knocked it on the head. Lynn was getting bigger by the day and the prospect of becoming a daddy was becoming more real, all the time. I did the odd day at the Park Lake, just to keep my sanity more than for any other reason, but my unborn daughter's heart was a bit erratic so I stayed home on my days off after that.

On March 10th, at 9.30am, my life changed dramatically, and for the better I might add, as my gorgeous little Isabelle was born (well, not so little at 9lb ½ oz.). The birth hadn't been plain sailing. The hospital rocked in gale force winds, and I have never been so frightened. I was tired and emotionally drained from the whole experience, but it all worked out in the end and the next day I was bringing my two girls home.

Settling into fatherhood wasn't easy and the lack of sleep made it hard to function, but as the season ended at the end of March, Lynn let me go fishing for the last night and although I spotted a couple of fish, the uninterrupted sleep was something I wasn't complaining about.

I just had Pingewood to focus on through the spring and I hoped to get among a carp or two early doors, but not coping with the lack of sleep very well I was struggling to get motivated. April was proving to be cold and miserable every time I managed to get out for the odd night.

Even rarer was a two-nighter, and it wasn't until the start of May, when I found some fish in Motorway Bay, that I started to get the old tingles back in my blood, and after baiting under the trees, I did the following morning in the flooded Pallets swim. As I waited and watched from the top of a tree, a big common came waddling into the bay, soon followed by a few more scaly companions. Although, typically, today they didn't want to venture over to the baited far tree line, the juices were flowing and at last I felt like I was angling again.

I was now working Wednesday to Sunday every week so my permanent days off were Monday and Tuesday. I arrived the following Sunday evening for a two-nighter and found the lake quite busy. The Cottage end was stitched up as the wind was pushing into this bank, but with the forecast of a changing wind, I set up in the Lawn swim for the very first time. The Lawn controlled a good amount of the central area of the lake and had very good form of producing the Brute; the capture of her a couple of weeks before, at 44lbs, had come from here. My brother had also caught her from this swim so I knew one definite spot to cast to. I fished a pop-up on the firm bottom of the second tree at 70 yards and fished the other two with chodernosters over thin weed.

Before long, I started to get liners and these came sporadically all through the night. I was obviously fishing too far and when I saw a big'un push out at 45 yards to the right, I knew I needed to explore areas at this range.

The wind had swung round in the night to a north-easterly and the temperature had taken a turn for the worse so before recasting I took a brisk stroll round to see Andy who was down in the Plateau. While chatting and having a brew, I noticed a lot of weed blowing into Andy's margin. When I commented on it, Andy said it had been blowing in all morning, and when I looked at the direction it was coming from, my brain started ticking.

Did all those liners mean that fish were ripping up the bottom, causing the weed to float to the surface and blow in on the fresh wind? I needed to find the spot and with the sighting earlier, that area was the first port of call to explore.

I cast the marker float to the spot, felt it down and just made out it hitting bottom. As I dragged it in, there was definitely weed growth present but it felt sparse, so being careful on the retrieve I swung the ball of weed that clung to the marker lead to hand. Bingo! Not only was it the smelly, lush onion weed that carp love at this time of year but it was infested with little black snails, too. It was plain to see why the carp had been active ripping up the weed in search of the succulent molluscs.

At last I felt like I was angling again.

I felt a particle approach might be the best course of action and seeing that Andy had some Brazil nuts on him, I'd had the foresight to ponce a few before I returned to my swim. With the inner drilled out and plugged with cork I was able to fish the Brazil popped up on a chodernoster.

With a light touchdown I was fishing on the short, fresh onion weed and should I get a take, the light link could snap, losing the lead and meaning a direct contact to the fish. After a few spodfuls of hemp, chopped tigers and chopped Brazils were trickled over the feeding zone, that rod was in position A and finding two other likely spots I went to bed confident that evening.

At midnight, I was awoken to a screaming commotion. The buzzer was howling but the culprit was a Canada goose which had swum through the line at the rod tip and was now trying to get up the bank. Seething, I grabbed the rod trying to keep the lines out of the bushes and luckily, as the bird flapped about it freed itself. I checked over the two lines it had picked up and there was no sign of damage so I found my elastic markers on the line, popped them behind the clip, and then wound in the middle and right-hand rods that had been moved.

They were both on chodernosters so it wasn't too much of an ordeal to get them back but I did notice that the middle rod, where the fish had shown, bumped down clean this time. Perhaps the weed had been cleaned even more since I'd cast out. The tips were sunk underwater to avoid another suicide goose attack, and I climbed back into bed.

The next thing I knew, the middle rod was in meltdown and the clutch was whizzing. Fortunately, there was no flapping of wings in accompaniment this time and I bent into the fish as it picked up even more speed. Taking the opportunity to step into the chest-waders I applied finger pressure to the spool in a bid to slow it down. Just when I thought the fish was joining the motorway it slowed as it hit a bit of weed. I soon had it coming my way and was able to get some much needed line back on the reel.

Through the blank, I could feel the carp shaking its head angrily and adrenalin was certainly racing through my veins. The other two lines had been sunk out of harm's way so I stepped into the margins with the net and the fish surfaced no more than 20 yards out. The lead had long gone so the fish stayed in the upper layers and as it was now on a short line the pressure was starting to tell. As daylight started to break, I guided the unseen beast into the net and eagerly checked the contents of my net. It was one of the big mirrors but with a normal-shaped head so it wasn't the Brute.

The first of the Pinge A-listers for me.

The choddy was right in the middle of its bottom lip and I popped the hook out before registering a weight of 34lbs. As I peeled the sling back open I recognised the fish as the Silt Pit fish. A few years back, Ev had landed her at over 40, so she'd slipped back a bit, but it was the first of the Pinge A-listers for me and I was now firmly back in the groove.

A return to Fox at the start of June saw an influx of new, keen anglers and as Pinge was becoming much less crowded due to a lot of other lakes now being open, I decided to leave Fox alone until September when the banks would be quieter and the carp, hopefully, on the feed. I stuck with the Brazils on one rod over the particle, and constantly caught well throughout June and July, taking five commons up to 23lbs 5oz on the nuts as well as the boilies.

At the start of August, a move away from the Avago bank over to Motorway Point kept the run of 'chevins' going as on the first night I landed a 19lbs 15oz. I longed for a mirror, though, and just two hours later the middle rod went into meltdown leaving me in no doubt that a long-awaited mirror was putting as big a distance as possible between us. Foolishly, I faffed about stepping into my chesties, as my finger got hot from the friction of the fast-rotating spool. The runaway steam-train bulldozed through a weedbed and that horrible feeling came over me, of the whole lot going solid.

There was nearly 100 yards of line out, but the pressure of the rod was having no effect on coaxing the powerhouse from its jungle lair. I walked back with a tightened clutch, the carbon creaked and I just prayed for some movement; if I could get it to kick its way out I'd be back in business and with 18lb line, surely the pressure would get it on the move. After about ten minutes of pressure even the high breaking strain line couldn't handle the load and I almost fell backwards as the main line gave way, leaving me gobsmacked and with a limp line hanging from the rod tip. Occasionally, you get caught out on the size of the fish until it ends up in the net, but by its speed and power I was positive it was a mirror and with them all being special prizes, any lost was heartbreaking.

How long would I have to wait for my next bite? Well, until about 11am, to be precise, and disastrously this went the same way as the last; this one diving straight into the weed on the take. It could have been a common or a mirror but it was a fish I couldn't afford to lose.

Cursing myself for using the new, untested line, I soon had the old faithful 15lb GR60 on for my return and with a rare three-nighter ahead of me, I arrived Monday morning keen for revenge on the Pinge carp. I'd kept my fish losses to myself and left a mountain of weed in front of Motorway Point, so I hoped the swim had stayed vacant in my absence.

As I pulled up to the gate, I could see Paul set up in the Lawn (nothing new there eh, mate?) but as I looked beyond, I couldn't see any rods on the Point. With fingers crossed I pulled the car up behind Paul and wandered across. I could now that see the Point was indeed empty and my mood instantly perked up. I was keen to rectify the events of the previous week.

As we stood chatting, right on cue, a huge head rose out in front of the Point before sliding back down. We were both looking at the spot and as we turned to each other, I remarked, "That'll do me."
"I should think so! You know what that was, don't you?" Paul replied. "that was the Brute, mate!"
I'd been pretty certain just by the sheer size that it was her, but a second opinion had me heading round the gravel track like Colin McCrae, keen to get baits out.

I threw all the gear on the barrow and then gave the cars on the motorway beside me a run for their money and arrived on Motorway Point puffing and panting. I knew the spots already from the previous week and as the Brute had shown in that general area, I quickly put the rods together and cast out three hookbaits. The left-hand weedy one was on a chodernoster so it would be presentable, but the other two were fished with my pop-up, 90-degree, fluorocarbon rig. After having my last three Car Park mirrors on this rig I knew it could fool the trickiest of carp and the Pinge mirrors were certainly tough cookies to crack.

There were no signs throughout the afternoon so I made sure to get them all perfect that evening and baited each area differently. The right-hand rod, which was on a firm silty channel that seemed cleaner than the week before, was treated to eighty 18-millers, the middle rod was given a double dose of boilie, and the choddy with the Brazil nut had half a dozen spods of hemp and nuts rained over the top. I'd given the Brute a choice of starter, mains and dessert, and I didn't care which course he dined on, as long as he licked his plate clean, hookbait included!

The previous week's two takes had come during the night and I tossed and turned restlessly in the bag, expectant of action and keen not to let any takers put too much distance between us. I awoke around 6am and was just toying with the prospect of dragging myself up when I was abruptly given a kick up the arse as the middle rod's line pinged out of the clip and started to click off the tightened-down clutch.
.

I scrambled to the rod, keen not to let the fish have its head in the weed. There was a wall of weed between me and the fish so I needed to bully it over, and if I could achieve that and get it in the deep clear channel in front of me there should be no more dramas. Fingers crossed!

The loosely-fitted tail rubber ensured that the lead had been ejected on the take, the desired effect, and as the fish was rocking just below the surface, I kept the pressure on and walked back. This not only kept the pressure steady but also put me on higher ground, keeping as much line as possible out of the water and away from the weed. Once the carp was over the high weed, I breathed a sigh of relief and eased off as she dropped down and headed up to my left.

Passing the rod under the left-hand line, I let her plod up the margin as I stepped into my waders and went out a few steps, with the net chucked in front. I kept up a direct pull, with the rod tip high, able to subdue any sudden lunges. The fish certainly felt heavy and on the evidence of the sighting yesterday, was this my chance of the Brute? I willed it to be and kept telling myself to concentrate and not stuff this up.

As the end of the leadcore slid out of the water I saw a big mirror roll over, showing off a creamy belly and making me even more tense. I was praying it was indeed my target, as it stripped more line off me not keen to meet my acquaintance just yet. Slowly, I gained line on her again and each time she came back easier, the rod zapping her energy reserves. As she rose in the water she had one last boil and the top lobe of her tail broke the surface; surely it was the Brute at last.

Once again, I brought her up off the bottom and this time, beaten, I imprisoned her in my net and faced the moment of truth as I lifted the net arms up to peer in for that unmistakable head. What looked back at me was a beast, for sure, but with a normal sloping head. It was clear that the Brute had evaded me again, at least for the time being.

I rolled down the net and with her fins against her body it was obvious it was a big 30. I struggled to the mat that was on level grass up behind the bivvy, keen to examine the hookhold, and the curved hook was buried right in the middle of the bottom lip. I cast my eye over the big, slate-backed mirror, rolled her over and judging by the evidence of the raised lump on her flank, I knew it was the rarely-caught Broken Rib that had been fooled by my rig.

Having not been out for a couple of years, she could be close to 40 and I watched eagerly as I hoisted her up on the scales. At 37lb 3oz I wasn't complaining; I had my biggest Pinge fish to date in the bag. I got Paul round to take the photos, and brimming with confidence I looked forward to another two nights' fishing.

I lowered Broken Rib back into the clear margins, and by her sheer bulk it was easy to see why I'd thought I had the Brute on - or was it just wishful thinking? I repositioned all the rods and had an iffy bite on the second night. It was on the chodernoster and the hook fell out within a few seconds. I wasn't even 100% sure it was a carp, but one of the small commons seemed the most likely culprit.

On the third evening, I had the lake to myself and as the drizzle increased so did my confidence as between 7pm and 7.30pm I saw the Brute shuffle out three times. I was in a quandary. What should I do? She hadn't shown in the exact same spot and was in between two of my baits. Should I cast at her, or should I sit tight and hope she'd find the carefully laid traps?

I was concerned that she was slightly longer than where I was fishing but certain the area would be weedy so because of this I chose to leave the swim undisturbed and hope that her high activity would mean that she'd come across the bait in the night. My heart was pumping so hard that I felt a bit sick, and the atmosphere that evening was electric due to the anticipation. When the bite came at dawn, it was an anti-climax to say the least, as old red-eye splashed about under the tips.

A week later, she tripped up opposite the Point in the Slipway, but not to my rods. In the high 47s, she would be a personal best, but with her now nursing a sore lip I decided my time would be better spent up at Fox Pool, and come back for the Brute in October.

With the onset of September, the nights started drawing in noticeably and so time would be limited when I arrived on Sunday evenings. I'd had all my Fox bites out of Common Corner the previous year, so this swim would be the easiest to get two rods out quickly but it was a popular swim so it was likely to be occupied, unless angling pressure had decreased significantly since my last visit.

I had my biggest Pinge fish to date in the bag.

As I rounded the Road Lake car park, there were three motors parked outside Fox, so I was going to be lucky to get a good corner swim. I was sure that the snaggy corners were the places to catch the big fish from, all my captures so far having been 30s. I put my bait bag over my shoulder and my Polaroids on, unlocked the personal gate and headed down in the direction of Common Corner. There was a bivvy in No. 1 - that was a bonus - and a few strides later, I was pleasantly surprised to see two more bivvies through the bushes in the direction of the Noddy swims.

A quick chat with the occupants revealed that only the odd small one was coming out, and that the open water swims were doing the bites. This suited me just fine; all eyes were on the middle, leaving me to investigate and bait the edges.

In the early evening light, I was struggling to see under the snags and so I was unable to make out any fish. I dropped the bag in the swim and ran off to check out Concrete Corner quickly. It was the deepest corner and the forecast was for hot weather so I didn't waste too much time and as there were no obvious signs, once again I ran up to Goose. It was always a good bet to find carp in the safety of the fallen trees in Goose, but tempting them in to feed was a different story altogether. This was my reason for not jumping straight in the swim when I saw three fish, including possibly Bazil lying right in the corner.

Shit! What to do? I was really unsure, so with only an hour of light remaining, I sprinted back to Common for another look. I really needed to choose correctly because I'd only given myself four two-night sessions before returning for the Brute and time was precious.

There was still nothing in Common, but I was sure they'd turn up in the morning once the sun got high in the sky. 'Aaargh!' I checked in Goose again; one fish had already vacated the pool and the others look agitated as though they were ready to move out. 'That does it,' I muttered to myself as I ran to the car to load up, and sticking to my gut instinct, I went straight ahead and not right, ending up in Common Corner. I put two rigs on the old spots and trickled my bait in as the first bats swooped over the pond, dining on insects. I hoped the carp were as ravenous.

If the carp were to turn up then I expected their arrival at about 10 in the morning but with still no signs of life except a little one throwing itself out in Concrete, I was now thinking I'd got it all wrong come midday. It was time for some serious carp hunting, so with rods wound in and Polaroids on, I headed round to Goose, after checking the snags and fully expecting to find them all in there, and my gamble of the previous night a complete balls-up.

However, the crystal water of Goose was fishless as well, and the margin along the Ruins was barren so I guessed they all had to be holed up in the weedbeds out in the pond. It was time for a brew and re-evaluation. I put the kettle on, wandered back down to my corner and on parting the branches I saw four big fish gliding along the gravel shelf. Bastards! They had to wait until I'd wound in before turning up, didn't they!

I had no more concerns about my swim choice; now all I had to worry about was getting the rigs back in without spooking them. At least with the lines clipped up I could get both rigs in first cast, barring a Claridge cock-up.

I put fresh baits on, consumed a sweet tea to settle my nerves, and checked the spot for fish. They were deeper in the corner so I flicked out 20 or so 14-millers followed by my pop-up with a lighter 2oz lead attached - a good donk and I was happy that one had gone to plan.

I didn't know if anything was on the opposite margin bushes, so once again, I baited first; at least that way a boilie landing on their heads might only push them deeper into the bushes whereas a lead might have them flying off looking for the exit door. Water splashed the leaves as the lead landed tight. I'd done all I could and now it was 'sit and wait' time.

I waited all afternoon, which drifted into evening, and when I awoke at dawn only to the sound of the birds, intermittently drowned out by a jumbo jet overhead, I was starting to worry that my return to Fox was kicking off with a blank.

The fish were arriving late so I rung Lynn to say I'd leave it until lunchtime before winding in and, fingers crossed, they'd turn up in time. My old buddy, Wadey, turned up as I was packing down and after a quick chat he went off in search of carp himself, leaving me to load the barrow and stand behind just a pair of rods. I was keen to get home to spend some precious time with my baby girl and missus, so I checked the watch and it was 12.25pm. I wanted to be home by 2pm; I'd give it five more minutes and then wind in.

'Bleep...bleep...click...' and I was on the rod in a flash. The rod hooped over, I took a step back, and then another, determined that the fish wouldn't make the snaggy branches through the stretch in the line. The pressure was telling and I gained a vital few turns on the reel handle. With the lead discharged the fish started coming up in the water and I could make out a big shape moving over the candyfloss weed a few feet below the surface and away from the snaggy margin. Easing off, I guided him through the clear channels and into the depths of my margin. He stuffed his head in some weed but he was under my feet and the pressure lifted him up, tail pointing upward, as the lump of weed rose in the water column. I literally wedged the net under him and scooped the lot up.

It was all over in three minutes and with a minute to spare before half past. It was obviously a 30, but as I staked the net in the margin so I could go to grab Wadey, it looked a bit familiar for my liking.

With Wadey in tow I got back to my swim and lifted the carp out onto the mat, revealing what I'd thought it was - a repeat capture of the Dark Mirror. Although a bit bigger this time, at 33lbs 10oz, the fact that I'd caught it the season before took the shine off it a little. Anyway, I was off the mark on the first trip and deposited a kilo or so of boilies off the Goose Pool snag before I left, hoping that would give me another option on my return in a week's time.

I had the week off but I didn't turn up until the Tuesday, and with the Common empty and fish in the vicinity, I couldn't resist. I gave Goose a trickling of bait, and hoped the deep spot off the snag would be fed on and cleaned off a bit.

Once again Common did me a take, but with the fish finding sanctuary in the snag it ended with only half a hooklink. The snagged fish preyed on my mind and I was thinking of a change of scenery, so before leaving on the Thursday I gave the Goose spot all my remaining boilies. The planes helped to muffle the sound of raining boilies. The engines roared overhead, keeping the baiting between me and the carp and not attracting any attention from other anglers.

I had no work on the Sunday so I was able to get down mid-afternoon and with only two anglers on, I crept excitedly round to Goose. From the tree on the high bank, I could see three or four big grey shapes ghosting through the sunken tree branches

and as they weren't stuck deep in the corner, they looked more likely to be tempted out on to my spot on the edge of the dead tree. I hoped that the free food they'd had would make them keen to investigate.

I spoke to Tony Parker in the car park as he was leaving and he felt that I was also in with a good chance because most of the big'uns had been in the Goose all weekend and the angler who'd been in there hadn't used much bait, so with fewer lines in the pond they might venture out. On the evidence I'd seen, they already looked more relaxed and I was buzzing with optimism as I headed back round with the gear.

Due to the amount of liners I'd been getting, I'd loaded up my spare spools with 16lb fluorocarbon for this trip and with the much deeper water, I felt by slackening off I could get as much line on the bottom and not cutting across the bay, so any patrolling fish could swim through happily.

Although previously having used heavy leads, I continued with the smaller 2oz weights as not only was there less splash but much greater control on the cast. It was an awkward sideways cast to drop it on the left-hand side of the dead tree, so the angle had to be just right and good control was necessary to land spot-on.

With the rig ready to go, I crept up the bank and I could make out three good-sized carp lying deep in the corner, pecs waving as they lay suspended, giving the odd flick of the tail and showing off big, plated mirror scales as the flank flexed, leaving a little boil on the surface as they happily jostled against each other in their underwater haven.

I dragged myself away. As pleasurable as it was to view them at close quarters, the objective was to hook them, so it was back to trap-laying. I put in a quick handful of boilies, one by one, just in case a straggler was on the spot, and now for the rig. As I crouched by the water's edge, I laid the rod out to the right, looked back to the spot and half flicked, half lobbed toward it.

From the moment I released the line, I knew it was the one. You just know when the weight of the cast and trajectory of the flight of the lead is dead true, and trapping the line at the last second, the lead dinked in just shy of a protruding dead twig. I knew that the depth was 12 feet-plus, and I let the tip follow through the cast so the lead would not pull back toward me, and as the rod met the horizontal, a lovely thud vibrated back down the line; better than expected and certainly firmer than the last time I'd put a lead there. It looked like the fish had fed on the spot, so someone must have been sneaking some bait in on the sly!

It looked a bit familiar for my liking.

I immediately slackened the line, noting precisely how much I'd peeled off, and marked it accordingly for future recasting. It was now mid-September and there were at least three big carp close by so I felt a bit more bait than normal was called for and put the best part of a kilo of 14- and 18-millers over a bedchair-sized area along the edge of the snag.

So that I'd have only one line crossing the bay, I put the other rod out to my right in open water, and hoped this might entice a night/early morning bite. A kilo of boilie was 'pulted on top of that hookbait also, and then it was time for a well-earned brew. Darkness fell over the pond, so I grabbed myself something to eat and nearly choked on my sandwich as I bolted down the bank when a good splash set the coots squawking. As the lapping ripples gave away the fish's exact whereabouts as the centre of Goose, I knew the carp were getting restless and would shortly be on the forage.

Excitedly, I phoned the wife to let her know that I was all sorted and I was 'on 'em'. As my wife always says, "You're not just there to see them; you're there to catch them!" She wished me luck and we said our goodbyes. The light of the stove was blocked out behind a bucket and water butt, so I bent down to light it, only to be interrupted by the blue LED from the snag rod lighting up the swim as the indicator wedged up against the alarm. As my hand hovered over the rod in case it was a liner, the click of the line clip coincided with me bending into it. Fortunately, the angle and the now bowstring tight line made the carp kite away from the snag and tighter into Goose Pool. I piled on the pressure and gained some vital yards of line. The fish was now in front of me and I willingly backwound as it bore away from me - danger over, or so I thought.

As I tried to gain line, I realised that all was solid. It could only be bogged down in weed but as I gently applied more pressure it didn't want to budge. Knowing it was literally only 10 yards or so out, I stood right by the water's edge and leaning out tried heaving from above.

I put a lot of pressure through the rod and it was almost trembling under my hands. I was unsure if there was any movement and as the clouds parted I could make out the tip ever so slightly creeping up against the backdrop of the low full moon. Yes, it was definitely inching up and then in a split second it came unplugged and, once again, I had a plodding carp moving freely. I consciously kept it high in the water and away from the thick weed roots and soon it was swirling, and tail-slapping on the surface, and I brought it up to the spreader block before lifting the draw cord and engulfing it.

The torch flicked on to reveal a short, fat, rounded mirror and securing the net, I nipped round to the Perch and grabbed Wadey. Fortunately, he had a visitor so leaving him to guard the rods, Wadey came and helped out. As I lay the fat mirror on the mat, I couldn't believe it when I recognised the fish. It was only the Number One fish again. So not only had my first fish this year been the Dark Mirror, the same as my first blood last season, but my second victim was a repeat of last year's second capture. Were there only two bloody mirrors in the lake, or what? Anyway, at 32lbs it was a great way to start the session and if I could catch a third fish, I just prayed it wouldn't be the common that I had as Number 3 from last year!

I daren't try to cast too close to the snag in the darkness or I'd end up hooking the branches, so casting it out short, I gave the missus the good news and set my alarm for first light to get it spot-on. Time for tea now.

In the early hours, I struck a liner on the recast rod, so there were still fish about. I didn't want any more disturbance, so I propped the rod up against the bivvy and got back into bed, awaiting my early morning wake-up call.

The impetus of catching the 32 made it easy for me to drag myself out of bed, and with a fresh pop-up on and checked, I cast the rig out from the next swim, found my elastic mark on the line and clipped up, returning to get it back on position A.

The trajectory was good but it looked like it was heading a little to the left. Distance-wise it landed spot-on but was at least a foot further left and landed a bit softer than the previous night. Leads always sound louder at dawn so I felt that was close enough, and topped up with another half kilo of boilie.

At half-past ten, I was regretting not getting it back on the firm spot because for the past 90 minutes I had watched frustratingly as fizz after fizz erupted over the bait, with only the odd, heart-thumping bleep.

By 11 o'clock, the Jacuzzi was well and truly over so I skipped the lead in as I knew something wasn't right. The bait must have all been eaten so it had to be the presentation of the rig. The rig looked fine so I could only assume that the stiff fluorocarbon boom section was stuck up as the lead had plugged in the softer silt. Although literally only inches different, it just went to show how crucial bait placement could be from catching to not catching.

I had to get it back on the firmer ground so the boom would lie out flat and the first three recasts all landed soft. I let the fourth cast go a fraction too far as the lower trajectory meant that the clip failed to stop it in time and the rig fell over an outstretched twig. Grimacing, I tweaked the tip back and luckily, or so I thought, the lead fell free and it sailed to the lakebed with a resounding thud. 'I'll leave that,' I said to myself as I didn't want to create any more disturbances. I topped up with more bait and soon watched the greedy leviathans return and fizz up the area again. Surely the tip would wrap round, but apart from a couple of bleeps, once again the bubbling subsided as all the bait was scoffed and still a take was not forthcoming.

At 4pm, I skipped the rig back in and could instantly see why my hook had failed to snare a bottom lip as the hook was caught around the hooklink. The rig must have tangled when it clipped the tree! Aaargh! Another wasted chance and I should have had at least one if not two bites today.

It was do or die time. The rig had to be 100% perfect, and I'd achieve this if it took me 100 casts. The majority of the bubbling was a little shorter of the tree than I'd been trying to get it. So on only the second cast I held the tip back a bit and let the lead sink down so it arced back a couple of feet. This helped to 'lay' the rig out and a good donk was felt so I knew it was spot on. I got the remaining kilo of boilie out and just leaving a handful to the other rod, and a handful in case I caught, I sprayed the rest just short of the visible branches of the dead tree.

There were no liners that night, and I hoped I hadn't blown my chance, and when at 9am the bubbles failed to materialise, my enthusiasm started to wane. It was a bright, sunny glorious late September morning; all it needed was a big carp on the mat!

I slowly started to pack down, constantly looking at the spot, on bubble watch. Once the bivvy was in the quiver and all my bits and pieces packed away, I plonked my arse on the edge of the bed and checked the time. It was 10 'o' clock and as I looked back out, a single bubble popped, or so I thought. Was it?

Yes! A tiny stream fizzed up right on top of the hookbait and then the rod was rocking in the rests. Keen not to make any more mistakes, I was on it in an instant. It was kiting left just like the last one and I took the opportunity to gain some line.

I had watched frustratingly as fizz after fizz erupted over the bait.

As it swung in front of me I soon lost what I'd gained as it slammed the tip down forcing me to backwind hurriedly. With the steam train high in the water, I could afford to give it ground as it was well above the savage weed roots. The fish continued right and I was leaning out as it headed into the margin. As I worked it slowly back, a big line of mirror scales glimmering like gold sovereigns twisted and turned below me.

As she rolled over on her side flashing a big creamy belly I knew it was one of the elite fish and with a deep breath I leaned back with the 12-footer and she was mine. Exhaling at last, I lay on my belly and hung over the edge, trying to identify the beauty angrily puffing its gills just inches from my face. She was Bazil shape, and looked Bazil size (upper 30) but didn't seem to have enough scales on the wrist of the tail.

I was all alone on the pool and I needed a photographer because, although I could do a decent self-take, a fish of such size and beauty deserved a good shot, and another pair of hands is always best when they are on the bank.

I phoned Sharpy as he was up the road on Horton. Nige had his sticks out so was reluctant to wind in but was sure Rick Golder was on the Road Lake, so I skipped the other rod in and found Rick round in the Hump. Slippery John was also there and offered to do the photos as he was going to do a 48-hour on Fox because his 48 hours on the Road was almost up.

As we got back to Goose, John also felt it was 38-plus as he'd only just photographed Clover the previous day at over 40. I heaved her up and she certainly felt closer to 40 than 35 and I had to double-take when the scales stopped at 34lbs 8oz. Not Bazil, but Pimple Scale was my sixth 30-plus on the trot from Fox. The corner snaggy swims certainly came up trumps with the big ones.

That run of good averages slipped on my next and last trip when I landed a 20lbs 8oz common from the aptly named, in this case, Common Corner after moving from a now inactive Goose Pool. I'd had four carp from four trips so I was full of confidence and keen to settle scores with the Brute in October, but that didn't exactly pan out as I wished.

The lake was not overly busy but had enough anglers on to occupy the three swims that I wanted, and I felt the Brute would come from, namely: The Lawn, Slipway and Motorway Point. Three anglers with the same idea was enough to scupper my plan and after feeling increasingly rough on the first trip back, I headed home for the missus to rub something on my chest. I offered to return the favour but she wasn't up for it; funny that with me coughing and extruding snot constantly!

Not Bazil, but Pimple Scale was my sixth 30-plus on the trot from Fox.

Colder conditions were coming in more prematurely than I'd hoped and the prime swims were constantly stitched so I knocked it on the head at the end of the month and got myself a ticket for the local park lake. With no weed and a bit of history for producing in a mild winter I started baiting the Humpties but on the way home from work one evening after dark, I started sticking out bait and then it dawned on me that the water level was significantly lower than it had been two days previously. As I investigated further, I realised the lake was a good three feet down and as I was baiting the shallower end, at about five feet, I gave that up as a bad idea because the water was only going to be inches deep - another plan scuppered. It turned out that the lake was being drained low enough to perform maintenance work on the dam wall. They could have told me that when I bought the ticket!

A return to Fox coincided with me landing another small common but this one was hooked fair and square in the pelvic fin, the first carp I'd ever foul-hooked. Its mouth was so small and twisted that it was probably unable to get my pop-up in its gob. It had been sucking up the maggots I'd dribbled in and bumped into the pop-up, the hook spinning and grabbing its fin!

Back at the park lake, I fished a night in the Secret. Although the water was creeping back up, it was still only three-feet deep in the Secret, but with a couple of milder, bright days I felt the shallower water might just warm up enough for them to investigate. If they did they weren't interested in my hookbaits.

The rest of winter consisted of snow and ice, so I took a much needed break and got some jobs done at home as well as spending some quality time with my baby girl and the missus. Lynn had fallen pregnant again, so you can gather it was quality time with her as well!

2009 was going to be another momentous year. The baby was due at the end of October so I'd timed that one spot-on - one plan that did come off with pinpoint timing!

20lb 8oz from the aptly named Common Corner.

Chapter 20 - Fox hunting and Pinge pearlers

Spring was in the air as I returned to Fox in mid-March with three trips planned, the final one falling on the last two days of the season. The Pool was shutting on the 31st March for a two-month break allowing the occupants a couple of months rest and recuperation.

The light levels were still poor for finding carp, so with the sun hitting the shallowest margin of Common Corner for the greatest part of the morning I plotted up and got two rigs on the tried and tested spots. There was no foliage on the overhanging bush to the left and the branches didn't bend down so much, so it was an easier task to cast over and behind it and keep the line from catching the twigs with the outstretched rod.

As when I'd foul-hooked the common on my last trip, I kept trickling in a few handfuls of maggots to liven up the spot and hopefully induce some feeding and, on the Monday afternoon, this seemed to have the desired effect as the occasional bubble pinged to the surface and the odd little liner indicated fish presence. At this point, my good mate, Ben, popped in before setting up on the Road Lake and I confidently predicted a take was imminent. This time I got it right and ten minutes later the tip nodded and the indicator danced to the top.

I leaned into it and with the tip underwater, I dragged the offender out from under the bush. It came in a little too easily and when the tip started juddering, I knew it wasn't a carp. I led it into Ben who grabbed the leadcore and popped the hook out of an ancient, big, black tench.

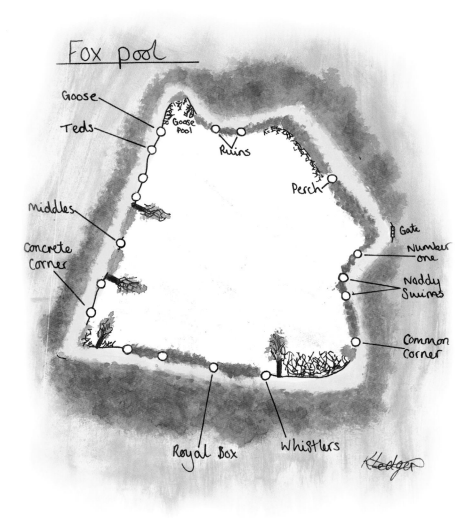

Fox pool

Goose
Teds
Goose Pool
Ruins
Perch
Middles
Gate
Number one
Concrete Corner
Naddy Swims
Common Corner
Royal Box
Whistlers

KHodger

At least something was feeding but not wishing to catch tench and spook any carp, I left the maggots in the bucket and baited solely with boilies.

There was no more fish activity of any kind and so the following week I felt I'd have a go in the opposite corner in Goose, but by the Monday afternoon I got bored and with itchy feet I packed down and moved back to Common Corner. I hadn't seen anything but something was telling me it was the place to be and as the drizzle started to fall, I pushed the barrow round to my new plot.

The rain was getting steadily worse, but I quickly tied on fresh pop-ups and got both rods out hassle free. The wind had suddenly sprung up from nowhere and was hooning into my corner and as the heavens opened I chucked up the bivvy, stashed all the gear and huddled beneath it until the storm passed by.

As the wind blew in clearer skies, I crawled out from under my cover and catapulted 40 or so 14-millers on top of each hookbait and then settled down for the night. The bitter wind was still causing waves on the sheltered little pond so I snuggled down deep in my sleeping bag and awaited daylight.

A call of nature woke me up at 6am. It was just light when I jumped out of the bag to relieve myself and I was just giving him a shake when the ever-faithful left-hand rod cranked round alarmingly, the snag bar preventing it being ripped off the rest. I dived on it and hung on as the power nearly dragged me off my feet. Rather than giving line, I took a step forward and as the rod subdued the heavy weight I took that step back and after a bit of toing and froing my weight advantage took charge. She came out from under the canopy of the bush and then it was plain sailing under the tip. I knew it was a good one but it wasn't until I rolled her over in the net that I realised I'd landed one of my prime targets; with huge apple-slice, golden scales the full splendour of the Winter Mirror pouted in the net.

Knowing that Ben was on the Road Lake, I grabbed my key and my feet hardly touched the ground as I floated round to his swim. Ben and Kodak were the only ones on, so I was in good company for a photographer. Kodak accompanied me to do the honours, and what an honour it was!

Such a handsome, scaly beast, and the chestnuts, oranges and golds stood out even more prominently at this time of year. At 38lbs 1oz, its bulk matched its beauty and proved that my gut instinct to move had been a good call. Despite the bitterly cold wind, I was shrouded in a warm glow and had a big silly grin on my face. I was out of the starting blocks and in pole position to run a good race.

The last two days definitely warmed up a bit and predictably, I got back in Common Corner and was overflowing with confidence. The Pool had the last laugh, though. All its inhabitants failed to trip up and had made it for their holidays. With no other distractions, it was back to Pingewood to restart the cat and mouse game in pursuit of the Brute.

Its bulk matched its beauty.

The Brute had got steadily bigger so the pressure on the lake was increasing and this season saw several new anglers. One, in particular, who was on unstoppable big fish success was Kev Wilson.

Kev was doing Sunday to Thursday every week so he'd always beat me down and outstay me by at least double the time. There was competition for the big girl, certainly, but I had a bit of experience of the place on my side so I hoped I could still beat Kev, and everyone else, to my cherished prize.

Zigs were accounting for the first few fish captures and on the first full moon in April, Lee Barter landed the Brute on a bit of black foam. Anyway, there was still Pecs to play for. That was until I was about to leave home on Monday the 20th April and a call from Paul Norman revealed that he'd just put the net under the freak that is Big Pecs, black foam scoring again. The car was all loaded and it was a lovely day so I got on the M4 and in 45 minutes I was unlocking the gate. Paul said he'd hang on for me to do the photos but as I pulled the car up behind the Lawn swim, I could see him just slipping it back.

Kev who'd been doing his time in the Lawn (he'd obviously been doing his homework) was now ensconced in the Slipway as he'd caught a couple of little ones at range on the zigs. In fact the eight fish that had been out so far this year had all fallen to zigs and we were still waiting for the first bite off the bottom.

I only had one night at my disposal and a great track record in the Lawn so I wasn't going to pass up the opportunity of getting in there. With a pop-up on my 90-degree rig cast onto 'the spot' on the right-hand side of the first tree, I baited with 60 or so 18-millers. They had to be ready for some proper food; foam wasn't going to fill them up, certainly not bits with hooks in.

For the curiosity-induced chance, I fished a single 'yellow one' ten yards to the right of the baited patch. The Brute was known for liking a bright one so I hoped the old Pineapple Hawaiian would do the trick. The left-hand rod I fished as a zig suspended two feet below the surface. I hadn't come to terms with the method thus far and I must admit I fished it more in hope than with any form of conviction.

I had a great track record in the Lawn.

As the midges came alive that evening, the traffic slowly died down and I drifted off into the land of Nod. At 1am, I was up and unhooking a dreaded snotty and typically, the point wasn't as needle-sharp as I'd have liked. Resisting the temptation to jump straight back into bed, I connected a new rig and with the pop-up tested, tried casting back to the clip. I say 'tried' but the fluorocarbon main line was having one of those days, or should I say nights! Every time it went dead true, the line would slap the butt and drop agonisingly short and the times it sailed out it would land too far left in the sticky silkweed, and each time I'd have to pick this off as it stuck to the rig like shit to a blanket. On about the tenth cast and losing the will to live, only my stubbornness kept me redoing it, I was rewarded for my determination with a nice thud. Thank God for that! I slackened off, indicator on, buzzer turned up and back in the bag.

Six hours later, the recast had been picked up again but with the clutch spinning there was little chance of a bream brace. As the rod bucked in my hands and the clutch gathered pace I was in little doubt it was a Pinge mirror. At about 85 yards, it turned right and as more line came out of the water it was obvious she was heading skywards. As I stopped her out in front of the Avago, the flat-calm surface rocked and as I let her go again an impressive wake of water shifted for Kelvin, who was watching in the Plateau, to witness. As I felt her rise again I was ready for it and once

more she created a mini-tsunami. As I looked round, I saw Kev coming with cup in hand, unaware that I was doing battle.

I had already stepped into the chesties and gaining line fast as I moved into the margin. She came out in front of us and Kev lifted the right-hand rod as I manoeuvred myself and the fish under it. We both thought it was a good one but it wasn't until she kissed the spreader block and I peered in that a very rare visitor was evident. On her right flank was not the hoped-for one big scale but a broken line of pearly button-sized scales. The Pearly Linear had made her first mistake in two years and a boilie had finally done a capture. Compared to the Winter Mirror, this one looked equally big and although she failed to reach the 40lb barrier that some were anticipating, she weighed a very healthy 38lb 2oz. A crowd gathered as we carried her out into the sunshine and everyone was in awe as the cameras clicked and whirled.

The capture of Pearly made it 3rd, 4th and 5th biggest in the pond falling to my rods, and I felt even closer to numbers 1 and 2, but being close isn't always good enough. Thick Wrist had also been out that morning and these two captures signalled the start of the carp actually eating bait. The Brute often came out in May, and with the full moon due at the end of the first week of the month, surely she'd trip up soon to a bed of bait.

Most anglers like bank holidays because the Monday gives them an extra day, but when a Monday is your day off they become a pain in the arse because most anglers don't leave until Monday, instead of on the Sunday, so that meant I either fished a rammed out lake on the Sunday or left it until Monday, only giving me 24 hours. A few of the guys were having weeks off at a time, so I was getting increasingly frustrated at my opportunities of getting on 'em.

My frustration increased with the text telling me that Bez had caught the Brute, long out of the Willows on the full moon, the second one running. Bez had done a two-week stretch, and I couldn't compete with that, nor would I have wanted to, to be honest; three nights is as long as I can manage these days and that happens only once or twice a year. Bez had been getting among them having had Thick Wrist and Big Pecs in the last month, so he'd deserved the big'un - at least that was another competent angler out the way!

My next opportunity came toward the end of the month and I'd chosen the left-hand Container swim. There were fish up at the workings end and several anglers were covering them, so the Container was a good ambush point should they drift further down the lake and I felt it was an area that the Brute could do a capture from.

Not the one big scale but a broken line of pearly button-sized scales.

The feeling was cemented when my mate, Gareth, and I were having a tea while I sorted out the rods. Not 25 yards out, a huge set of black shoulders and a back rose like a submarine before dropping back to the depths. We were both catching flies as the sheer size had us jaw dropping. We were of the same opinion; it was huge and could only be one fish – the Brute. My eyes were glued to the lake's still surface on such a breathless evening and I hoped for a repeat performance, but all was still and it was time to get the rods in.

I already had one rig out, not a million miles from the show and as it looked like it was just swimming through, as opposed to feeding on the spot, I looked for a clean area because the exact spot of the sighting was a bit weedy. This might have been a mistake and perhaps a choddy on the spot could have brought a result. I was to regret this just eight days later.

A week later, after a fruitless two days in the Container, I headed back up the M4 not too sure where I'd end up. Fox was back open and it was an opportunity to nick out a possible naïve fish at the start, but it was a full moon and as the Brute had fallen on the last two it seemed too good an opportunity to miss. My plan, therefore, was to stop at Pinge, and if I could find a plot I was happy to be in and that would give me the chance of the big girl, then I'd fish. If the lake was sewn up, then I'd be back in the motor and up to Fox.

On pulling up at the gate, it didn't look great as Richie was already installed in the Lawn, and the Slipway had a bivvy pitched up in it as well. Two good areas already out of the picture. After closing the gate I went to find out the latest from Richie and see what swims were left. On current conditions the only swim vacant that I felt had the potential to produce the Brute was the Motorway Point. It hadn't produced the big girl for two or three years but certainly had form in the past and because it gave me the best access to the middle of the lake, where I felt they would be resting up after the pressure of the weekend, I felt it was worth looking at more closely.

As I drove round to the Motorway car park, I popped into see Kev, who was setting up in the left-hand Container, the swim in which the Brute had shown the previous week. I clocked his marker float, which was only a few feet from where the fish had shown, but I kept my mouth shut because Kev was serious competition in the hunt for the Brute.

With our usual parting of, "I'd wish you luck, but I'd only be lying," catchphrase, I nipped round to the Motorway Point and as I stood in the swim I did get a good feeling that I'd chosen correctly. The Container, the Lawn and Slipway had gone, so this was my best bet, and dropping my bait bag in the Point, I trotted off for the rest of my gear.

Having fished and caught from the swim previously, I knew where to put my baits – if the weed hadn't swallowed the spots. One spot I'd hoped to fish was an area where I'd seen the Brute showing the previous August at about 85-90 yards. The marker float sailed out there with the 20lb braid and as the lead splashed down, I tweaked it off some weed and felt it fall through the water and land with a satisfying thud. Result! After managing to pull it back about five feet over nice, clean silt, the spot was exactly what I was looking for. With a bit of tweaking and the rod held high, I managed to get the float up. Now I had to position the rig tight to the back of the float, and with fluorocarbon main line, I hoped things would go well.

It didn't let me down and on the first cast it flew in a perfect line and trajectory, and I feathered it down just behind the float. The lead landed with a nice dull thud – silt, perfect – and things were looking good for once. I kept my finger on the spool from where I'd trapped the line on the cast and marked it with pole elastic so I could find the desired distance should I need to recast.

Using the throwing stick, I managed to get a few baits on the money before the dreaded flying rats turned up, but with my far bank marker noted and knowing I was at full distance with the stick, I wound in and would put out more bait on dusk to avoid the gulls' attention. Why is it that they leave the baits that fall short, but without fail, they'll nick every bait that's spot on? It's just another frustrating aspect of modern-day carp fishing.

The other rods were fished at 65 and 45 yards, respectively; all three had my 90-degree bead rig. I managed to bait up the two shorter rods with pouchfuls of 18mms, between the seagull raids, and by the time the bivvy was up and all the gear sorted, dusk was falling but I was able to get some more bait on the long spot unmolested by the gulls in the failing light.

There was a full moon so the night was quite bright and it was already starting to get light at 4am when I had a bite. The long rod's buzzer bleeped a few times and from my position on the bedchair I could see the indicator wedged up against the alarm.

I scurried to the rod and pulled into the fish. There was definitely something on, but it was not pulling back; a tench perhaps. I kept the pressure on, gained line and about 40 yards out it started to kite left. Fortunately, I was still gaining line so it would swing clear of the buoy. I thought that perhaps it was a common until the rod bucked down hard and forced me to backwind as it headed up toward the top bay. A mirror, methinks! With the waders on I was able to get out up to waist depth and keep the rod up to prevent the fish burying in the weed in close, because it was deep in front of me. Was this my chance? A full moon, a now obviously big heavy fish, and as I got a glimpse of it, a big, dark grey mirror was definitely attached.

You know how it is; you're desperate to get the fish in the net but you have to keep telling yourself to take it easy, there's plenty of time, all the while praying it's the one you want, and willing it not to fall off. This is why I go big-carp fishing; for that feeling when your chest tightens in anticipation, for that often long, hard challenge bearing fruit, and the overwhelming relief and joy of the drawstring coming up behind the fish, and then the shout of success as you gaze at your hard-earned prize.

All this was racing through my mind as I stood alone with the mist coming up off the water in the half-light. After ten minutes of 'up and down the edge' she managed to pick up my left-hand line as she headed back in front of the swim. With the bail arm on that rod flicked open, I had to wade out and stretch for my now beaten prize as the other line stretching out in the lake was hindering me from getting her any closer. I eased off as the drawstring came up behind the tail and she sank down into the net. It was the moment of truth. Was the Brute mine? A look at the shape of the head revealed that my pursuit was not over. (Oh, God!)

I had convinced myself throughout the fight that I was playing the Brute, it took me a few seconds to realise which fish it was, but as the big mirror rolled over, that familiar line of pearly scales was evident - the Pearly Linear, again!

The lines were tangled and I tried to get the hook out but this only made her thrash about, so I left her in the net and rushed to the bivvy to grab some scissors. As I raced back, I saw the net sinking and as I splashed through the margin the draw cord fell over her face and she waddled out. Shit! I grabbed the rod and to my relief found she was still on, and having already been beaten once and with two lines restricting her I dragged her back into the net for a second time. Phew! Relieved at correcting such a numpty-level mistake, I cut my line and feeling around the line that headed out into the lake, I was able to get Pearly out unrestricted.

Now, this fish had proved to be the most elusive big carp in the lake, having not been caught for two whole years, but in the space of six weeks I'd caught it twice on the same rig and bait, so it obviously had a liking for me. I'd caught the Car Park Lake's Pearly three times, too. Maybe I should start fishing some more lakes with a Pearly in!

It was a frustrating recapture but it's hard to be too disappointed with a magnificent carp such as this. It was early June and the fish hadn't spawned so I thought she might be close to 40lbs, but the scales revealed only a four-ounce increase and she weighed in at 38lb 6oz. After a couple of self-take shots, I let her swim away and with a fresh rig and bait on and my line out to the elastic mark and clipped up, I recast and rebaited before the gulls descended.

Between 5.30am and 9.30am I witnessed the most shows and fizzing over and around my areas in all my time on the lake, but the bobbins remained motionless. As the activity fizzled out, my bed was calling and after snuggling down in the bag I was disturbed by a shout. I peered through the bushes and could see Kev Wilson holding a net in the water in the Container swim.

Fearing the worst, I picked up the phone and Kev confirmed my suspicions that he had outwitted the Brute, so after winding in, I legged it round to assist. Understandably, Kev was on cloud nine and so I guarded the net and admired the beast within. This was the first time I'd ever been on the lake when she'd been out so I was seeing her in the flesh for the first time. I only wished it was me that had banked her, but it was Kevin's day and as always it was an honour to see such a massive old character on the bank.

As I watched the needle on the scales spin round, it looked like they weren't going to stop. At 6oz under 50lbs it was a huge weight and I was even more envious as Kev got to grips with her while Ginge and I clicked away on the cameras. Despite having a great chance of more fish if I stayed, now that the Brute had been out, I felt my second night's fishing would be served better at Fox Pool, so I quickly packed up and headed up the M4.

The lake was fairly busy and some of the best spots were taken, so I plumped for Common Corner. Previously, I'd have been in there like a shot, but this close season the big overhanging tree to the left had been cut out and with that cover gone the swim was open.

I didn't agree with the decision to have that bush taken out because there are far worse snags in the lake and I'd landed all five carp that I'd hooked from behind the overhang - four of them being good 30s – and never even had one carp bump a branch. I felt the

best spot on the lake had been killed. Anyway the tree was gone and it was a case of getting on and finding new spots. I fished my usual two spots in the swim but the fish were not evident in any numbers now the bush and coverage had gone. Good old bailiffs; the best spot on the lake ruined!

The traditional June 16th start on a local park lake was looming and I'd been baiting with quite a few kilos of KG-1. With at least two trips planned at the start I was quite excited by the new challenge and if it fished like the previous start, I'd get off the mark quickly. I'd concentrated my baiting to one good area of the lake, which gave me the option of a few swims to fish from should it be busy.

I waited for the magical midnight moment.

It was an honour to see such a massive old character on the bank.

After work on the 15th, I raced to the lake and found my first choice of swim was free – as was most of the bank. The opposite side, which had produced the lion's share of the carp at the start of the previous season, was taking all the pressure. With the rods clipped up and baiting completed, I waited in drizzly conditions for the magical midnight moment.

It came and went and when the morning dawned the lake was devoid of fish activity. I had to pack up by lunchtime because my wife was having a scan that afternoon, and after seeing my baby on the monitor with a full set of tackle, I returned to the lake with the great news; I had a son on the way. I fished the same swim but it remained very quiet, as was my next session.

A few fish were caught the next week but when I heard that the Resident had been caught at under 40lb, I felt I'd leave it alone until the autumn and concentrate on trying to outwit my target fish in Fox Pool for the summer.

On the last Monday in June, I arrived back at the Pool in scorching heat and there were plenty of fish on show. The guy fishing the in-form Ruins swim had said the Goose Pool had earlier been vacated and that Lumpy had done the angler fishing there several times.

I'd locked horns with this carp in previous seasons and although it's quite a greedy fish, he rarely tripped up. Being such a deep-bodied, big-mouthed fish he reminded me a lot of my old foe, Arfur, who had turned me over a time or two! Common Corner was now not the same so, in my opinion, Goose Pool was the best area of the lake. I looked through the trees from the high bank, and could see that not only was Lumpy still present but also half the lake's population, including most of the big ones. I quickly secured the swim before returning to the high bank to observe their patrol paths.

They were definitely coming in under the trees where I was standing, and now the old rubbing log was floating on the surface and not stuck up off the bottom blocking the way, a carefully flicked sideward cast could put a bait on this marginal shelf. The major drawback to the plan was getting a rig in without spooking all the fish in the process.

All the gear was now in the swim so I got both rods fully ready so when the opportunity came along to get the rigs in, I'd be able to move swiftly and make the cast. A few fish started to disperse early afternoon and after quietly flicking in bits of broken bait followed by 14mm and then 18mm baits onto the spots, I'd pushed them away without completely spooking them out of the area.

By using light leads, I managed to flick them the 20 yards, or so, to the far margin without too much disturbance, and with the rods locked up against the snag bars on single sticks, I waited.

About 5pm, I struck what turned out to be liner on the left-hand rod and, cursing myself, I now had to get the rod back in again without disturbance. I needed to do it first time and because it was a side cast, my timing and trajectory had to be perfect to get it in line with the hole in the overhang, and to make the distance.

It fell a fraction short of the desired distance but as it cracked down hard it was obviously on a cleaned off area, more at the bottom of the shelf than on the slope. In hindsight, this was probably the best place to position the rig as this is where all the baits would roll down the marginal shelf, collecting at the bottom. As I was using fluorocarbon line, this would be less obtrusive as it could hug the bottom rather than lifting up if I'd cast higher up the shelf. The snags in close proximity meant that a semi-taut line was necessary. This could have been the explanation for the liner from the previous cast that was further into the hole and thus higher up the shelf.

At 8pm, the same rod wrapped round and with the snag bar preventing the locked-up rod from being dragged in, I was on it in a flash and all too quickly had to winch line on to the reel to stop the fish from reaching the sanctuary of the sunken trees in the far corner as it kited in that direction.

The lead had popped off on the take, a big pale fish rose up in the water and with my Polaroids on I could see it swing just in front of the branch that stuck out of the water. A bit close for comfort! Pumping it down my margin, I prevented it getting back down deep as it was trying to waddle into the dense weedbeds below it. As I rolled it over 10 yards down the bank I could tell that it was the unique pale shape of Lumpy lolloping under the surface. She wasn't built for speed or agility so I guided her in and over the outstretched net. It was all over in a minute or so; fast but furious!

I gave it the 'Lumpy!' shout and the guy in the Perch swim looked up and was soon on his way. While Lumpy lay quietly in the net, I staked it down firmly with a bank stick and got all the weighing gear ready. By the time I was ready to lift her out, I had assistance and between us we hoisted her on to the mat. The size 6 hook was buried firmly in the bottom lip.

Not the most stunning creature in the lake, but Lumpy was a proper character, just the sort of old, cagey mirror carp I like to catch, and at 36lb 2oz this tricky old customer was a good weight. After a few trophy shots, I lowered her back into the margins and watched her ungainly shape waddle down into the depths and away into the darkness.

I quickly got a bait back into position as night was drawing in, and topped the spot up with a good few handfuls of boilies. At this point, I was full of confidence in my rig, bait and the areas I was targeting, and felt sure that as long as I could find the big'uns and get the swim necessary, I would be able to pick off my targets one by one.

I'd like to say the summer panned out this way, but perhaps I was over-confident in my approach. Each trip, I was finding at least one or two of the big'uns but they continued to frustrate me either by disappearing or by simply not getting their heads down.

I did manage a couple of chances off the top on the floaters, and had one snub-nosed 30-pounder taking clumsily, but each time that distinct nose nuzzled my hookbait, it would shy off leaving me with shaking hands and a thumping heart.

As with most floater sessions, the seagulls spoilt the party and their constant diving on the baits put the fish on edge leaving them to drift away disinterested. The lake was fishing poorly and it was not only me who was struggling. Just the odd 20-pounder was getting caught from out in the pond, so I decided my time would be better spent back at Pinge.

In my time on Fox, the Brute had suddenly become a bit of a slag and throughout July and August was coming out on a regular basis, each time with fewer days between captures. I hoped there was nothing wrong with her and as much as I'd rather catch her when she hadn't been out for a while, beggars can't be choosers and it was too good an opportunity to miss to draw a line under the place.

Just the sort of old, cagey mirror carp I liked to catch.

Fox wasn't playing ball, so that Sunday I turned off the M4 much earlier than normal and was soon on an empty Pingewood – a very rare sight. The Brute had been making her mistakes from the Container down to the Canopy swim and as it was relatively flat calm I fancied the Lawn. I surveyed the water and left my bucket in the swim, made a circuit round the lake, but saw nothing conclusive so I set up in the Lawn. Crofty rang to tell me that he was on his way, and asked me to put a water bottle in the Slipway for him; we could have a good catch-up as we hadn't fished together for some time

The usual spots were nice and clean, firm silt right against a seam of a slightly rougher, fine gravel area. The Brute, as well as the other big'uns, were silt feeders, their black mouths being a giveaway to this fact, so I always looked for the cleaner, firm areas of silt when plumbing.

"Kettle on boyeee!" was heard across the drone of the motorway and I turned round to see Si 'Legs' Croft unlocking the gate. My rods were out and the kettle on, so I gave him a hand with his gear to the Slipway. Si had been 'working' the top end with the magic beans and the Slipway was simply a base camp to fish the rods for the night. With his spots loaded with pellet, we chatted the evening away and speculated when the Brute would make its next mistake. There was just the two of us on, so it was me or Si to catch her if she should trip up in the night. As I wandered back to the Lawn late that evening, it was just that thought that occupied my mind as I snuggled down in the bag, and as I drifted off, I just hoped it was me.

The sun poked its head out and with a clear blue sky it looked like it was going to be a cracking day. Brute time was between 9 and 11am so I left it late before recasting. Si was off to check his spots and with a big grin on his face, and even bigger strides than normal, he was soon fetching a rod and net. Despite him being tight-lipped it was obvious he had fish on his spots.

I was just about to sort the rods when my eldest daughter rang with news that they had just found my wife's cat dead, and as Lynn was obviously upset because the cat was older than the kids and they'd been through a lot together, I said I'd pack up and come straight home.

With half the gear packed away, Lynn rang to say it was fine to stay but some things are more important and I wasn't going to sit on the bank knowing she was upset at home. She needed a cuddle and the cat needed burying, so I loaded the car and went to find Legs to let him know I was off. I found him in Croptail Corner and with a rod in, he had fish feeding. Wishing him luck, I headed home.

With the cat buried and Lynn consoled, I texted Si to see if he'd been lucky and when the text came back, 'Got the Brute in the net', I rang him to see if it was a wind-up. He was unable to hide the excitement in his voice and it was obvious he was not telling porkies, and I only wished I could have been there to share in his success.

The Brute had indeed been stalked out, and Si had done it on his 9-footer. It seemed that the big girl was healthy and full of beans as it had taken Si 45 minutes to get her in the net after an epic battle as he stood up to his waist in the lake.

With September nearly upon us and usually doing a Brute capture, I hoped I could finally get a Pinge bite this month. My little Benjamin was due at the start of November and I needed to fish close to home in October so a return to the park lake was the plan.

September fished shit and apart from Pecs coming out of the Ladder, the whole month only produced one or two other small ones. With me back on it seemed the big girl had regained her dignity!

On October the 1st, Si rang me to say that he'd got down early and with a rod poled up to the Motorway margin had just doubled up on 'you know who' from the Pallets. Not only that, but she'd broken the '50' barrier at 51lbs 4oz. Wow!

Luckily the Stones was free.

The text came back, 'Got the Brute in the net'.

On hearing that news, I had all my part bags of boilies as well as a few more kilos defrosted in two big buckets. It was Thursday so I was going to put a 10kg hit of bait into the park lake after dark that evening. I waded out from the Stones and with a baiting scoop horsed the whole lot out on to a hard area, spreading it over a 10-yard radius. With empty buckets, I headed back home and would be back Sunday afternoon hoping the park's residents, and one resident in particular, would have munched on the feast of bait.

Luckily, the Stones was free on Sunday and after finding the Reserve fish at 40lbs and another big 30 had been out of swim 5, the angler boating his baits over to my side, I wondered if it had been over the bait. If that were the case, surely they'd eaten it and would be on the lookout for more.

As dusk fell, I waded up the reeds and distributed three kilos around the marker float and cast one on the hard stuff, one on the silty drop-off on the edge of the bait, and a chod another 30 yards out over a small scattering. This way I had it covered if they moved up or down the lake on my side and if they wanted a big feed or just a snack. The first night was quiet and I wondered if my plan of a big hit of bait had been wise but on the second night conditions changed. The wind had been pushing from left to right down to the shallows but after midnight it dropped and sprang up to a very strong south-westerly, hacking up to my left toward the Dam.

My son, Benjamin.

Whether this change in the wind was the signal for the fish to become active, I'm not sure, but something was definitely moving the indicator against the alarm and I soon found myself facing the buffeting wind and pulled into something. There was a weight on the end but it was doing nothing and I slowly pumped it in. Halfway, in I heard a clatter as the back-lead caught in the tip, so I had to put the rod down, slip on my head torch, and remove the offending obstruction from the line.

Eventually, I was able to wind down to discover that I was still in contact with the fish, and so with the other tips sunk I led what I thought had to be a bream over the lines and up to a gap in the reeds. I flicked the head torch on to make unhooking it easier, and to my amazement a ghostly pale carp lay on the surface, being washed closer by the waves.

I hurriedly threw the net in and scooped it up. Good job I had the torch, otherwise I'd have just grabbed the lead core to drag in the presumed bream. The mirror, although not big, was my first park carp but it was memorable only for the lack of fight it put up. I got it out and immediately it tensed up, going banana-shaped as it stiffened up, just like old 'Stiff-as' in the Copse Lake many years ago. I slipped her in the sling and at 20lb 6oz, she was much more welcome than a snotty old bream.

The fish was certainly a weird shape; its tail looked like it been stuck on at the wrong angle. It wasn't looking happy so I set up the camera and with a couple of self-takes snapped off I got her back among the waves just as the rain started. Diving back in the bivvy, I rebaited the rig and got it back on the hard spot. When positioning the rig the night before, I'd got the float up over a really glassy, hard patch of the rockier hump, and paying close attention to getting a nice donk tight to the float had resulted in a bite. Were the harder spots among the acres of silt the ones to look for? It was certainly food for thought for the future. The rain was unrelenting so I packed up wet but satisfied and was already planning another hit of bait in two day's time.

With six kilos put out again, I fished the Stones once more on Sunday but as the weather was already cooling I couldn't repeat the success of the previous trip.

Lynn's due date was nearing and my last night involved a move to the deeper bowl end. About 20 youngsters occupied the Bus Stop, and throughout the evening, I was treated to the boys and girls having a sing-off with a rendition of Oasis' 'Wonderwall'. The drink obviously flowed. I sat tight in the Dugout willing them to bugger off and as the drizzle fell, they eventually dispersed, leaving me to just the sounds of an owl hooting in the trees above. After the hooting and howling of rowdy teenagers, the nocturnal call of the owl was music to my ears. The lights of the hospital were in the far distance and I wondered if this would be my last night's angling before that became my destination.

This turned out to be the case. In the early hours of October 29th , Lynn's waters broke and after a relatively short labour, by Isabelle's standards, Ben was born naturally in theatre, after frightening the life out of us as his heart rate dropped. Once again 'bite time' was 9.30am and my heart stopped jumping out of my chest and a big grin appeared on my face as we heard him cry and got the all-clear from the doctors.

My son was born, and at 8lb 15oz he was another big one. The snip was booked in for the following month and that signalled no more fishing until the spring - and no more babies!

She was much more welcome than a snotty old bream.

Chapter 21 - Springing into action

This was to be my third spring fishing on Pingewood. After the last two, I felt I had to change my tactics to be more successful and to take advantage before they got hammered and returned to their normal pattern of being pigs to stick a hook in. Looking back over the results of the previous spring it was obvious to me that I could define what would be their downfall by the month, and for April, certainly the first three weeks of that month, zigs were a winner.

Never having been a fan of the method, I'd given it some serious thought and with April warming up, a lot of fly hatches occur, so I needed to make my hook bait mimic some sort of insect life. I'd got a good friend who fly fished to tie me up some imitation flies by cutting down some black foam and mounting it to the back of a hook.

I hoped that offering something more akin to what the carp were naturally slurping down in the upper layers, or off the surface, would give me an edge. Also, the fact that I had something that resembled a food item gave me the confidence to sit behind rods for long periods as opposed to using an alien square piece of yellow foam and fishing it half-heartedly, before winding it in and putting a bottom bait on for the night like I'd always done in the past.

Both big'uns, the Brute and Big Pecs, had fallen to black foam zigs the previous spring so it was a method I had to employ to the best of my ability. The other method that seemed to produce was fishing a chod rig over minimal bait. I'd chosen to start introducing my food bait straight from the off and apart from the Pearly Linear the previous April, I felt perhaps this was costing me fish. They weren't really getting on the bait and with all the abundant silkweed and fresh, short weed growth, that housed all sorts of snails and natural goodies, a choddy sitting on this natural larder could buy a bite quicker than a bait on a clean spot with a bed full of boilies. This sort of method had scored with the now elusive Silt Pit fish that had succumbed to a Brazil nut on a choddy over a scattering of particle fished among short weed growth, a couple of springs ago, for me, so now I was a man with a plan and it was up to me to put it all into practice.

The beauty of both these methods was minimal casting, as both methods could be fished effectively, pretty much whatever the bottom was like. As long as I knew what depth I was casting into for the zigs, which one cast of the marker would tell me, if I didn't already know from previous experience, I could tell what I was on just by feeling the lead down.

The Pingewood fish were very nomadic. A quick move could put me on fish and I could have all three rods out fishing in no time at all, sometimes in just three or four casts, thus reducing the chance of unsettling these spooky fish.

This year, Easter fell on the first weekend of April. On most lakes, and Pingewood was no exception, the bank holiday meant it was rammed as the weekenders took advantage of the extra couple of days available to them. The weather was also a negative factor as winter was still clinging on and it was far from spring-like just yet, so I left it until the Monday morning before loading up the car and hitting the M4.

I pulled into the car park mid-morning, and discovered that virtually everyone had apparently had enough and pulled off, leaving me to have the pick of the lake. I grabbed a bucket from the car, walked down the lawn bank and stood in the Lawn swim scanning the water. The wind was blowing southerly, normally quite a warm wind but this one was mighty chilly.

I wandered down to the Slipway swim where the wind was pumping in but despite the bitter chill to it, I'd have to grin and bear the cold if I wanted the best chance of getting an early bite. These fish worshipped a good blow on the water and never more so than early doors, so I left the bucket in the swim before doing a quick circuit, in the vain hope of spotting some fish. With nothing showing, the wind decided my swim choice.

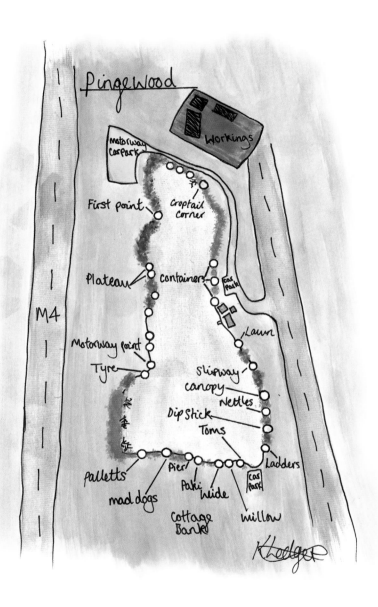

Pingewood

Workings

motorway carpark

First point

croptail corner

Plateau

Containers

car park

M4

Lawn

Motorway point

Tyre

Slipway

canopy

Nettles

Dip Stick

Toms

Ladders

palletts

Pier

car park

mad dogs

Paki

wide

willow

Cottage Bank

K Lodger

I now had something that resembled a food item.

I knew that Kev Wilson had caught on zigs from this swim, at range, the previous April and knowing that it was about ten feet deep out there, what with the water levels being high, a zig was tied at eight feet and standing at the top of the bank with the fly out behind on the grass I launched the 4oz lead out into the headwind. The 14lb fluorocarbon slowed the cast down, so I only managed about 90 yards, but with the wind making the waves lap into my bank I felt it was a good area for a carp or two to be milling around in.

I tied up another zig and this one was also punched out into the prevailing wind to the right, 80 or so yards out. Within a few minutes I had two rods fishing and the marker rod was still in the sleeve! Different fishing to what I was used to but with these carp being so mobile, as long as I could get my little black beauties in their zone I had a chance, and by not having to plumb an area I wasn't going to pee them off.

Old habits die hard so I had to fish one bottom rig over some bait. The Slipway can produce close-in on a southerly and with the Brute having slipped up a few times in this area, I knew a nice, clean silty spot to present bait, about 35 yards out. I pulled the marker float out of the dead weed and dropped it onto the silt, before sliding the lead back about five feet to the 'cleanest' area and popping the float up. I was then able to cast the rig just to the back of the float and with a nice dull thud felt through the line, I slackened off, hoping my chosen spot was a feeding area. Around 20 boilies were scattered in the silty channel before winding in the marker and it was all done in less than an hour, which is not like me at all!

Mid-afternoon came and I witnessed the first carp I had seen that year. A black head popped out, and what's more it was in front of me. It was a bit long, though, at about 120 yards but I could get close to it if I changed lines. A quick dig in my bag and I had one of my spare spools with 12lb mono which I had used on the Park Lake the previous month. So I quickly had the lead skipping along the surface and with the rig cut off, spools changed, the zig tied back on, and the rod held high above my head, I took aim at the first big tree where the fish had nutted out, and launched it high into the breeze.

The lead landed in the distance on the right lines so I was angling once more and felt fairly confident of early spring success. I'd made the decision that this month I'd keep at least one zig out at all times, so I left the long one out for the night, but I did wind the right-hand one in and changed to a bright yellow pop-up tied to a chod rig. I fished this over the sandy strip at 80 yards.

On investigation with the marker it appeared there was patchy silkweed covering the spot. Perfect for a choddy and with a good friend of mine, Paul, having caught the Brute from this spot a couple of autumns before, albeit from the Lawn swim next door, I was always confident fishing this spot. There was low pressure so I felt a night-time bite more likely to come fishing the bottom, but I had to have conviction zig-rigging, so my black beauty would fish all alone out in the middle zone.

As darkness fell, the motorway lights flicked on and the holiday traffic died down, as did the wind, and the lake took on a more tranquil look; the far bank was lightly illuminated by the street lamps that adjoin the hard shoulder. I snuggled down in the sleeping bag and drifted off, hoping to be dragged from my slumber by a shrieking buzzer.

As is often the case on Pinge, this failed to materialise and I woke at dawn to find that the southerly breeze had returned with a vengeance. After a call of nature in the fresh chill of the breeze, I whacked the kettle on before snuggling back into the warmth of the bag, and made the brew from there, all cosy.

Morning is always the prime time on Pinge, and Brute-time was usually between 9 and 11 o'clock so I would stay until 11.30am before heading home to spend the afternoon with the wife and kids. The days when all my waking thoughts were of how I was going to snare my target fish were well and truly over. My two young'uns were especially demanding on Daddy's time, so my fishing head (Worzel Gummidge-style!) would only switch on fully on the way to the lake; at home my time and thoughts were directed at them. It was a much more demanding scenario than in my younger, single days, but I wouldn't have it any other way. I'm sure most dads are nodding their heads at this.

At about 10am, a further fish did show in the same area as the day before, and the zig stayed out there until all was packed down and I wound in begrudgingly, biteless, at half-past eleven. I hoped that by the next Sunday the weather would have turned more spring-like, a bit of sun would trigger the fly hatches, and the zigs would be able to do some damage.

Well, the weather had changed the following Sunday to a cold northerly and it was feeling far from spring-like, but with the air pressure set to rise on the Monday, it was forecast to be sunnier and a bit warmer.

The motorway bank was the place to be on a north wind, so I drove straight round to the motorway car park, left the car there and went for a stroll with bucket in hand. The First Point is the first swim on this bank and as I stood at the front of the swim, the cold wind was certainly hacking in. It looked good but I wasn't sure so I carried on, stopping off at the Plateau for a look but nothing was showing so my next stop was Motorway Point and the bay.

The point was splitting the wind and it was pushing into the bay as well as the top end, so I decided, purely on the greater chance of the Brute coming out of the bay than up at the top end, to set up base camp in the Tyre swim on the side of the point which fishes into the bay. There was a bonus; no one else was on this bank so I could fish one rod off Motorway Point and two in the bay - carrying two nets and having remote alarms had their benefits. Also from the other side of the point I could have a good view of the top end and if fish did start moving up there, I was sure they'd give their presence away by showing, and a quick move could be executed up the bank.

Tactically, I once again fished one on a zig in the entrance of the bay, a bottom rig over a few baits in the middle of the bay, and on the rod fished off the point I cast a bright choddy over some fresh new weed on a spot where I'd caught Broken Rib, a couple of summers before. With the trees and bushes as cover, as well as having the bivvy side-on to the wind, I had a more pleasurable and comfy time out of the direct icy chill.

After an undisturbed night, I was up with the lark and with a hot cup of tea in hand I wandered between the three swims on the point, watching and waiting for a fish to show. Chances were, if I saw one show then there would be a few more in the close vicinity so, with a stream of fresh tea to keep me wide awake, I remained on the lookout for fish.

The only thing I noticed was Steve, moving from the left-hand Container to the right-hand of the three Container swims. I knew he was fed up with where he was and on my arrival the previous day he'd mentioned that he planned to move the following day. Either he was going for the easy move of just 20 yards, or so, or he'd seen fish in the top bay.

Richie came past with his gear. He'd spoken to Steve and found out that fish had been topping and slurping down flies off the surface in the top bay. Richie was off to the First Point, ruling that one out of the question. The Plateau could be an option as I could intercept fish as they travelled up to the top bay, or if they backed off the wind, I could then get them on the way out. I was now in one of those catch 22 situations. Did I wind in early and risk the chance of a bite or hang on for a bit and risk someone else turning up or moving up to the top end?

The weather was brightening up and the sun was nice and strong. Despite the cold north wind it was turning into a pleasant day so I decided to compromise and give it until 10 o'clock and then investigate the Plateau swim. I kept watch from my three vantage points but at 10am I headed up the motorway bank to investigate the Plateau swim. My mind was soon made up as within 20 seconds of standing in the swim, a decent fish came out halfway before sliding back down. With the marker rod propped against the tree and the swim claimed, I legged it back for a quick pack down, and then carried the made-up rods and pushed the rest of the gear, precariously balanced on the barrow, to the Plateau.

The Plateau is a short point and you can fish rods on the left- and right-hand side of it, so I chose to fish two to the left and one in the right. The first rod was an easy one and I would cast my zig out toward where the fish had shown, so I put

The Tyre swim.

the marker out first and finding it was eight-feet deep, I shortened my hook link down to six feet so my hook bait was two feet under the surface; one rod done and only two casts needed.

The second rod was a bit trickier as I wanted to put it on the very edge of the plateau itself. I found the slope and it felt clear with the marker, but after a few casts, with a light lead to reduce any disturbance, I kept on picking up silkweed. I'd tied up a bottom bait but with the silkweed likely to mask the rig, I whipped it all off and used a chod rig on a length of green leadcore, so I was able to fish the spot and be sure that my presentation wasn't affected by the clinging green stuff.

The third rod was fished short in the right-hand swim as I knew they travelled down this motorway bank quite close in, and Richie had told me about a small hard spot in front of this swim, so I fished a bottom bait over about 50 boilies.

All the time I was setting up, the odd fish was topping. The majority seemed to be in the direction of my zig rod but a bit further out. This spot was a bit of a Bermuda Triangle; you could fish it from the Plateau, First Point or the right-hand Container swim and it was probably about 45 yards from all three swims. I'd seen where Richie had put his hook baits and he wasn't fishing that area, but I wasn't sure where Steve had his.

The rest of the day remained fishless for all three of us but as the light faded, another couple showed on that same spot, and I was sure they were mouthing, 'catch me if you can'. Not wanting to disappoint them, I wound my zig rod in and taking aim, whizzed it out to the zone. It went a few yards further than I'd intended, so I whipped it back with the tip before the lead sank and softly touched down over light weed. Perfect! I laid the rod on the ground to sink the line as Richie wandered to the front of the swim. I didn't have a rod in my hand, so he was unaware that I'd recast. It was borderline water so as he wasn't fishing that area it would have been rude not to have put a bait there, don't you think?

The night was clear, the wind had dropped right off and a big moon lit the sky. With a few bats sounding off the buzzers now and again, the flies were obviously abundant and I dozed off, hoping that the activity below the surface would be as busy.

A short burst of bleeps and I was awake and down the slope to find the indicator on the zig rod jammed up against the alarm. Bending into the fish, I found it already with its head in weed. With the rod held high and adding pressure, I breathed easier as I felt it kick before moving right. I was in business and it felt like a good fish as it powered away, now with a clear run as it'd shaken the weed. The mirrors and commons seem to fight very differently in Pinge and this one felt like a powerful mirror.

I had no idea what the time was, but with only the odd car flying past behind me on the motorway and the moon now round in front of me I guessed it to be 2 or 3 o'clock. There was silence all around, so I could fully concentrate and it was a straight contest; Claridge versus carp, and only one could win. With only a 10lb hooklink I applied just steady pressure and after a few minutes she kited to the left. As I said earlier, the Plateau swim is on a slight point; to the left is a small, reed-fringed bay and this is where the carp headed, away from the other line. I was happy with this and treading into the waders I got into the water, in-close. It looked like netting was imminent!

The carp swung back and forth in front of me before all went solid. I clambered out of the margin to gain some height, pulled from above and from both sides, but it was stuck fast! I hate these moments. What now? I grabbed my phone and head torch and with the rod back on the rest and the clutch set, I rang Richie. He'd only got his bloody phone switched off! I gave it one more pull but it was still stuck fast, so with the rod back on the rest I legged it up to get him. It wasn't the fact that he could do anything but I knew he'd fished the swim before and he might have an idea if it was a snag of some nature, or was just weed.

A Cheryl Cole of the fish world.

Waking the ginger one, I legged it back and Rich was soon standing beside me. Richie was unaware of any snag so I tried pulling into it again - nothing. Richie then asked if I'd twanged it. Wondering what the hell he was on about, I said, "You what?" He said that by twanging the tight line, the vibration transmitted down the line would unsettle the fish and might force it to swim out. In for a penny in for a pound, and not the sort of strumming I was used to!

It was a good idea but it wasn't working. I shone the torch down the line and it appeared, by the angle, that it was closer than I'd thought, so I waded out until the water reached the top of my waders, stood on tiptoe, leaned out, and being over the top of fish, literally piled on the pressure and with that, up it all came, a ball of weed hitting the surface. I took a couple of steps backward, grabbed the net and scooped up the lot. I feared that the fish was long gone, but stuffing my hand in I felt a big back among the ball of weed. Relief or what!

The little black beauty had scored under the moonlight and it wasn't until we hoisted her out and parted the mesh that I realised what a stunning creature I'd captured. A 'Cheryl Cole' of the fish world; not the biggest, but one of the prettiest. I would have said 'the wife' but I know she wouldn't like to be compared to a carp, whereas I'm sure Miss Cole would be well chuffed!

I gently lifted her into the wet sling after I'd extracted my zig out of her lip and with the net pole as support we watched the needle spin round before settling at 31lbs 4oz.

She glowed orange in the springtime.

Well pleased with my start to the spring campaign, I let her rest up for a while and as soon as the light was reasonable and the sun peeked over the trees, we marvelled at one of, I'd say, England's finest traditional-looking old carp. It's right flank almost a full linear, and then you flip her around to reveal a half fully-scaled, still in her winter colours. She glowed orange in the spring sunshine and I couldn't have asked for a better-looking carp. The Pretty Linear swam away strongly and as this one only usually came out once a year, it was even more of a result to notch up on the bed chair post!

I fancied my chances of another bite as the odd fish still showed out in that area, but satisfied all the same, I pulled off about 11am and went back to family duties. I think it was that weekend when one of the regular good guys, Glynn, had the Brute out, and on a zig too. At just over 50lbs, the Colonel (liking the chicken) bowed out in style. It was now warming up, being mid-April, and the fish were being spotted just under the surface, enjoying the spring sunshine. Glyn capitalised on spotting the big girl among others down in front of the Ladders corner.

On the Sunday afternoon, I found the lake quite busy and as it was now warm enough for just a T-shirt, it was much more pleasant to wander round. The water was flat calm, with fish visibly cruising around, and I had visual aids for a change.

There were a fair amount of fish from the Slipway across to the Cottage Bank, but also a lot of pressure in this area. The mouth of the motorway bay, had one or two lurking about in it and with no pressure, I felt they would be likely to drift into the bay. The forecast was for hotter weather on the Monday, so it was either the Pier swim on the Cottage Bank or the Tyre swim in the motorway bay.

I chose the Tyre for two reasons; one, it was a bit shallower on this side and the second reason was that Big Pecs had been caught the year previously, at the same time, from the Tyre in very similar conditions - on a black foam zig, as well. I hoped that two plus two would equal four for me.

I chose to fish a firm area in the entrance of the bay on a chod and a zig at about 45 yards, where the water shelved up from 10 to eight feet deep. The third rod was on a silty strip tight to a gravel seam halfway across the bay to the right of the Pallets swim.

The Pretty Linear swam away strongly.

I didn't realise at the time how important this spot would prove for me in the future, but I was happy with my three areas and full of confidence after my result from the week before.

The night was clear and a bit nippy but that meant a cracking dawn, and the extra heat of the early morning sun brought the carp to life and a good fish showed. It was further into the bay and at the same range as I had my right-hand bait, but a good 10-15 yards to the right. A few rolls and a good amount of fizzing subsequently exploded on the surface intermittently. I felt it was close enough for a take as I had bait around that right-hand hook bait, but if nothing happened, then a bait would have to be moved over for the next day.

I wound in at 11-ish and scaled the tree on the other side of the bay to see if I could identify any of the fish that were about, but the light wasn't right to see out in the middle of the bay so I wandered down to the Paki swim, where Nigel Sharp had set up early that morning. He fired up the stove and over a couple of teas we swapped info on what we'd seen. From Nigel's position he could see right into the bay and had seen more in front of me than I could see from my swim as it had quite an enclosed opening. We had both seen a few in front of the Cottage Bank out in front of Nige, but he felt I was in pole position. I wasn't thinking of moving, and this just concreted my decision to stay put but I did want to move my left-hand rod and leapfrog it over the other two that I was happy with, and get it in the zone that the fizzing had come from.

On my return, I had one cast with the marker just to check out the bottom and also the depth. It was as weedy as I'd thought, but I checked the depth to be between eight and nine feet, so I knew a seven-foot-long zig would put me 18 to 24 inches below the surface. To get the fly in the 'hot' zone I had to wade out a few feet because of the trees, and with the zig floating on the surface behind me I sent it soaring to land about 40 yards out toward the willow on the far bank, the scene of the most activity that morning. The bottom bait was already clipped, so one cast and I was spot on, and the other rod on the zig was also done in a single cast. No sweat and tears today, getting the sticks out.

The only thing that I'd done differently with the zig link was that it went further into the bay and I'd changed over to the thinner 10lb Double Strength. As it was daytime in clear water, I felt the slightly thicker 10lb Kruiser might be more obtrusive. I was soon to find out if this had been a wise decision.

At 5pm, while siting with Richie and Ross on the point, just five yards from my own bivvy, my buzzer burst into life. As I raced down the slope, I could see the right-hand rod bent round and I was soon leaning into the bush on the left as I lifted into it. As with the Pretty Linear, the fish had dived straight down into the weed and was stuck fast. I took the opportunity to don the chesties and get the rod up in the air. I could feel something on the end and gained a couple of reel turns but the line was grating through weed the whole time. Jerking back, I was gaining a little and all I could think of was to keep it moving. It wasn't meant to be; the tip jerked back abruptly and I wound in half my hooklink. Whether there was anything in the weed or if it was just the weight and pressure of it, I don't know, but I was regretting my decision to tie the finer hooklink.

I retied my zig with seven feet of the thicker Kruiser line, cast it back to the zone and then sat and sulked for the evening, kicking myself because I'd changed hooklink. Fortunately, I didn't have to wait long for my next opportunity as in the early hours, the same rod hooped round in the rest and I stumbled down the bank and grabbed it, falling into the bush in the process. My priority was to get the fish moving and anyway, the bush was holding me up. With a few turns on the reel and the carp lunging on the end, I managed to regain my footing and with only a few yards gained, once again we hit stalemate as the fish plugged in the weed.

Cussing to myself, I got the chest waders on and waded out a couple of yards and tried to get it moving but unlike the week before, it was too far out to get an upward pull on it. I decided patience would be my best bet and I slackened off for about half a minute and then wound back down, and with the rod held high, I increased the pressure.

After a couple of seconds' pause, I felt a kick and with that movement she broke free and I was quickly gaining line. Just as I was feeling deflated, thinking that it had fallen off, the lead rose from the water, before the line cut to the left and I gladly back-wound as it tore up the margin. I gingerly played it out in-close and it kept creating big vortexes on the glassy, moonlit surface. It was just me doing battle with the fish; the hunter and the hunted in the middle of the night. They're always special moments for me as an angler.

Despite the long hooklink, and the 3.5oz. lead swinging about, which surprisingly had not discharged as the tail rubber was barely on, I had no drama netting the fish and once again, I could make out another mirror nestling in the net. I secured her, and then woke up Richie with the news that I'd got another one. He must have loved me for waking him up with such news two weeks running!

On the mat, it was another gorgeous linear, but it looked like it was a repeat capture for me. I checked the camera and it was indeed the same fish that I had caught on my very first night on the lake, but a bit bigger this time at 25lbs. It was a cracking fish, however, and added confidence to my zig rig approach. The hook had opened up slightly, so as it was only a size 10, I then put on a new Black Beauty tied to a size 8, and tied a new hooklink as well, what with the weed abuse that the last one had taken.

My head torch was dulling all the time and I couldn't quite see if my palomar knot on the hook had bedded down correctly, but I tested its strength and it appeared to be fine. Keen to get the rod back out, and get tucked up back in the bag as it was quite a cold night, I cast it back to the spot and snuggled back down until daylight.

No sooner had I done the pictures of the Baby Linear than this rod was away again, and the fish plunged into the weed. Once more, I hit stalemate and as I put on pressure something gave and I wound in minus my hook. I don't know if the knot was all right, I kicked myself because I hadn't retied it; a schoolboy error that I shouldn't be making with my experience. I gave myself a good rollicking, hoped it wasn't a whacker I'd made a silly mistake on, and made sure I had new batteries in the torch!

The following week and the lake was rammed. With a south-westerly hacking down the lake, I set up in the teeth of it in the Ladder swim right in the corner. Despite a carp rolling in close as I set up that evening, a quiet but gusty night followed. The wind had died out by morning and I had itchy feet and fancied a move. Ross was moving back on to Motorway Point from the Tyre Swim in the bay, so I gambled that I could repeat the previous week's success and made the long move round. Ross informed me that he'd seen the Brute show in the bay the previous evening so I was a bit surprised that he'd already moved back to the Point. I'd seen a fish show in the bay myself that evening, but it looked like a small common to me from the Lawn bank, so I was unsure what to make of this information.

Unfortunately, neither the Brute nor the small common came knocking and I disappointingly blanked that trip. With it being May the following week, I was starting to think more boilie-wise as nothing had been hooked on the zigs since my activity the previous week. In fact, apart from my four takes I think everyone else together had only mustered about four bites between them on the zigs, so it wasn't quite as prolific as it had been the previous spring.

I was back again on the Sunday and it was evident by the number of cars that the lake was busy once again. I phoned Lee and he informed me that he was in the Tyre swim but would be off in a bit. I enquired if Motorway Point was free and with the news that it was, I grabbed a bag and a bucket and made my way down the motorway bank. A strong north to north-west wind was banging into this bank so I felt somewhere along here would be the best place to go.

I dropped some gear on the point and nipped into Lee's swim to find out the latest goings on. It appeared there had been a fair few fish out from the Cottage Bank, and with the big guns out this week, that being Ian Russell in the Wide swim and Sharpy already set up in the Willow, this area was a closed shop. The two Richies were on the Avago Bank with Ginge in the Canopy and Scouse plotted up in the Slipway. I wandered round to the Cottage to see Ian and Nige and with Ian bigging me up saying I'd catch wherever I went after my recent success, I had the craic with them for a few minutes before returning to the car to get my gear with my ego massaged nicely by Mr. Russell. Brimful of confidence, I loaded the barrow and sped down to the Point.

Usually, I'd just lay the bed out and with my tackle boxes strewn over it, get the rods sorted, but the northerly wind was bloody freezing and very strong so with the bivvy set up side-on, I got inside and rigged up my rods sheltered from the bitter wind.

My plan was to fish all three rods out towards the middle as I hoped the wind and angling pressure would push the bulk of the fish closer to me and I could nick one from where they were currently showing out in front of Ian. I knew Scouse Richie only fished close in the Slipway so I'd still be miles short of him, even if I went halfway.

I knew exactly where my two outside rods were going. The left one 80 yards out toward the Canopy swim, a spot I'd caught Pearly Linear from the previous June, and the right-hand one was going 60 yards out toward the Ladder, from where I'd caught Broken Rib. I knew of an area that was a natural feeding spot at certain times of the year, out-long, and had witnessed fish tearing it up on this spot on more than one occasion. It's always too weedy to contemplate fishing it in the summer, though, because it's a good 90-95 yards out.

It was a cracking fish and added confidence to my zig rig approach.

I fancied a chod rig cast to this area could be a killer method and changing over to a limper, green-flecked 35lb leadcore, I spliced a heavy ring onto the end before tying my 4oz lead on with 4lb line and then PVA'ing it for the force of the cast. The lead would snap off out of harm's way should a fish tank off through the weed. I'd also got some different pop-ups with me that I'd added a bit of orange colour to, and some of my all-time favourite Scopex flavour, to give them an added dimension to my normal fishmeal boilies. They were still fairly not-in-your-face pop-ups and had come out more ginger colour than orange. This was ideal as they stood out from the freebies but were not too blatant.

On the third cast with a 15mm ginger one on, the fluorocarbon line spilled off the spool as good as gold and I feathered the lead at the last second and felt it drop down with a nice firm donk. The drop on the lead seemed a touch shallower than the water around it, so I was well chuffed with the cast as it was on a slightly pronounced mound out in the middle. I dotted around a scattering of big baits over the spot as darkness fell, and not only had the wind dropped but the dreaded feathered rats had disappeared off to roost, too. Giving it the big'un with the stick had them all dropping in the zone.

My plan was to fish all three rods out to the middle.

Soon after darkness had descended, the wind had blown itself out completely and all was still. It was now much more pleasant and I drifted off to sleep with my alarm set for 5.30am. A bream had me recasting my left-hand rod about 1am, but with the aid of the pole-elastic marker it was a relatively straightforward job getting it back on the money.

Forcing my eyes open as the alarm on my phone picked up pace, I poured some water in the kettle, from the comfort of the bag, and fired up the stove. With a steaming tea, I struggled out of the bag and went to stand at the front of the swim by the water's edge. It was a beautiful, clear, still morning and now the 4th of May, so there was no sign of frost and it looked set to be a nice day.

I scanned the water for signs of bubblers and was best part though my tea when the indicator on the long rod head-butted the blank and the line pinged from the clip. I was standing right next to it, so I quickly changed from china to carbon in my hand and bent into it. Even at range, this fish wanted to get as far away from me as possible and the spool was a blur as the power of it left me trembling.

It must have taken 30 or 40 yards and was well down in front of Nige and Ian. Fortunately, the lead snapped the weak link on the savage take, so the fish was staying mid-water. I began the long wind in, guiding it gently like a dog on a very long lead, and when it was about 40 yards out, I put on my chest waders, which were ready to step into and pull up.

By now, it was obvious that it was a very good fish. I threw the net out in front of me and waded round the corner as it kited into the mouth of the bay. It was now at the bottom of the shelf and it was just a case of keeping the rod high and letting the fish tire itself out against the absorbing carbon. I said to myself, 'please be one of the big two and not a repeat capture!' With a few 'come on baby' mutterings, I led it to the net and with a final cough of water, the sizeable mirror was engulfed in the mesh.

With a feeble, 'please be the Brute!' I peered into the folds of my net. It was certainly big but a check of the head revealed that it was normal. I rolled the mighty mirror on its side and was relieved not to see those little pearly scales again as that would have been a third capture! It took a few seconds for me to realise, but as the fish righted itself, facing away from me, its sheer width and bulk and the huge paddles that replaced normal-sized fins meant it could only be one fish - Big Pecs. Pingewood's number two was mine!

I staked the net safely, grabbed my phone and called Simon who was up on First Point. The gangly giraffe completed the two hundred yards in a couple of strides, and with big grins on both our faces we gazed at the immense carp that lay peacefully in the confines of my net.

"That's a 40 isn't it"? I enquired, and Si agreed. "It sure looks like it, mate!"

All the weighing gear was wetted and ready; I cut the line, rolled the net down and with the monster fins folded flat against the body I struggled to the mat and the needle spun round to 41lbs 10oz. It was my first 40 for a while so I left him to settle in the margins for a few minutes and gave Sharpy a ring. He already had a good idea of what I had, as he told me he'd watched through binoculars and had seen a huge pec come out of the water as I drew the fish over the drawstring. With Nige and Si both on the cameras I was sure to get some pukka pics and nothing less would do such a majestic carp justice.

I gave it another few hours before winding in and going round to the Cottage Bank for a social with Ian and Nige. Ginger Rich was also there and Ian and Nige were already ripping into him, and Rich was taking it as it was meant, in good humour. Even when he returned to his swim he couldn't escape as the pair of them were laser-penning him every time that little red head emerged at the front of the swim. It was good banter and I'd missed the big fish celebration times since I'd moved away from Yateley.

Hopefully, this would be a bit more of a regular thing because I'd taken the decision to accept a Car Park Lake ticket once again after my three-year exile. Heather had been more in my thoughts and as the month ticked by, I dreamed of a Heather celebration to come, once June arrived.

The huge paddles that replace normal-sized fins meant it could only be one fish – Big Pecs.

"That's a 40 isn't it?"

Beauties and the Beasts

Chapter 22 - Not to plan

A lot of the Pinge fish had been hooked so the remainder of May was less prolific, with just the odd fish tripping up, despite the never-ending pressure that the lake was now seeing. It's surprising what a 50-pounder can do! Everyone was cramming in the time.

The Car Park was a 9pm start on May 31st and it meant that because of the 48-hour maximum stay rule, everyone who'd done the opening night would be off on June 2nd, so this is when I planned to arrive. Pinge was only a quarter of an hour drive from Yateley, so I could get there for first light if I packed up from Pingewood early doors, and get a good choice of swim as well as witness some sort of fish activity. Heather the Leather was the driving force behind my returning quest and all my thoughts on bait and spots had been channelled in her direction.

I'd set up in the Slipway on June the 1st and with my soaked maples just coming to the boil on the stove, I received a phone call from my friend Lee.
"Got some bad news, mate," Lee exclaimed.
"Bloody hell, she's not been caught already has she?" I asked.
"No, worse than that. Heather's dead! She's just been dragged out and buried on Trumptons!"
Wow! You could have knocked me over with a feather and all my plans were blown out of the water.

It was obvious that the carp grapevine was working overtime. Richie wandered down from the Lawn and could tell by the look of shock on my face that what he'd just

409

heard was true. If I was told to choose a carp as the last one I'd ever catch, then my answer would instantly be Heather. That was how much she meant to me, and she was my reason for returning to the rock-hard Car Park Lake. I was gutted. Bollocks! What now? I still had three nights left so I could either stay on for the Brute, or as planned, nip over to the Car Park after one of my two remaining targets, Arfur and the Baby Orange.

I reflected on my options throughout the evening, between calls on the mobile about Heather's sad demise. Heather had always been the queen of carp to me, but I could change nothing now so all I could do was plough on and as I'd spent a lot of money on the ticket, I decided to go full steam ahead until Arfur was caught or had spawned.

The decision made, I decided to head on up to Yateley, but I'd leave it until after 10 o'clock as the Brute in the net would be the perfect way to rock up to the Car Park with that one's slime fresh on my shirt. That fairytale didn't come true, though, and after Brute o'clock I wound in and made the familiar drive back over to my old stamping ground.

The Car Park was still fairly busy and I nipped into the End Secret to see if I could spot anything; it was a good area for Arfur to bob about in the early summer sunshine. Immediately, I spotted three carp over the back of the weedbeds and despite them all looking like the stockies that had been introduced 18 months before, it was a good sign so I left a bucket in there and started a stroll round for the first time post-Heather.

There was a strange feeling to the place and as I bumped into people on the lake, some old faces, some new, everyone was down and a very melancholy atmosphere filled the banks. I didn't know most people; Mad Martyn, Turking Stick, who was off, and Gaz Fareham were the only anglers I knew and I didn't even get a cup of tea, on a complete circuit of the pond. It wasn't like the old days anymore.

With no sign of any of the big originals, I set up and did a couple of days in the End Secret. My spot was tiny and it took a few casts, seemingly landing on the same spot before it would bang down clean and hard. The stockies had a few recce trips over my particle and it looked favourite that I'd snare one of them. However, it wasn't to be; the old wise Yodas had taught their young Jedi well and as was the norm, the Car Park remained fishless, apart from a 33lb common that had come out from the Snags on opening morning.

Next trip, I set up in the Snags swim as there was a fish or two at this end. The next morning, from the top of the tall Bars tree, I spotted Arfur grubbing around on the middle bar and there were also a few commons and stockies about. Probably the majority of the lake's stock was up this end, but apart from Arfur I didn't spot any of the other four originals. I kept Arfur's whereabouts to myself, only confirming that there were a few stockies and commons to anyone who asked, as it was obvious there were carp about.

With a small in-line lead, I cast a single, balanced tiger and tiny PVA stick on the shiny gravel patch where I'd seen Arfur mooching. As it was only about two-feet deep, it was too shallow to feel the lead down so I eased it back to confirm that it was on the clear spot. It slid back immediately as I tightened up before the foam nugget popped out of the PVA stocking as that melted. With a fluorocarbon main line I slackened off and was relying on luck that my line lay over the bar was good enough not to spook them from the area.

The odd bubble and rocking on top of the bar happened late afternoon leaving me shaking in anticipation and excitement, but the only action I had was in front of the GMTV film cameras as the press had jumped on the Heather bandwagon and had come to do an interview about the great fish, to which I'd agreed. I hoped to give a more realistic angle on what Heather was to English carp history, and to the anglers who pursued her, and not the complete trash that appeared in The Sun newspaper claiming Heather had been caught a thousand times in her lifetime. That made it look like she'd been on the bank more than in the water! It was more like twice a year average and if you look at the calibre of anglers who caught her, and the amount of rod hours, it's clear she was no mug! Unfortunately, the papers painted the wrong picture to the public, and not the extreme effort and commitment that goes into catching a fish such as Heather the Leather.

"Heathers dead! She's just been dragged out and buried on Trumptons."

The End Secret; a good area for Arfur to bob about in the early summer sunshine.

I left the rig out in the shallow bar all night and it wasn't until about 9am that a fish head-and-shouldered out in the deeper gully and, as it was damp and overcast, I wound it in to cast to the showing fish. It felt perfect when I retrieved the rig so I can only assume I was sussed out in the shallow water, and not for the first time by these exceptionally clever carp!

The following week, I found Arfur straight away in the End Works. She was definitely working a spot that Sunday evening. Waddling up from a hole in the weed she'd circle before dropping back down into the hole. I thought the Dugout was free and was surprised to find Byron already set up in there. He'd noticed a fish tail patterning down to his right so I informed him that there were a couple of stockies down there. Well, I didn't want him prying too hard, did I?

With all my gear in the End Works it appeared that the big girl had drifted off, possibly due to Byron flicking a marker float about. Taking this chance, I got my own marker where I thought it needed to be and returning to my vantage point saw I was close, and just needed to go a couple of feet to the left and about six feet past. Using my float as reference, I cast a choddy onto the area as it wasn't clear, and 'pulted a few baits on top. My other rod was fished at the bottom of the shelf of the main bar. A tiger nut over a few spodfuls of particle completed this trap.

Once again I kept Arfur's whereabouts close to my chest and Byron packed up the following morning so he could get back the following day for another 48 hours. I can't remember who it was but someone came round and said they'd seen a big fish nut out at dawn. The area they described was my left-hand rod and so I surmised that Arfur had been back to the area.

With no fish present, I plumbed the spot in detail and found a dinner plate-sized clear spot which I eventually got my nut hook bait on, and followed it with half a dozen spods of particle mix, bang on top, which I hoped would encourage Arfur to forage and clear the spot. If nothing should happen I thought I could at least work the spot. Again, if she had returned that night, the cagey bugger got away with it, so I loaded the area with my remaining particle and hoped return to a glowing, clean spot. The spot was very awkward to cast to as it was round the corner and I'd even had to bungee back some branches to enable me to get a drop, so I hoped no one else would fish it in my absence.

The following weekend, Martin King was in the End Works so I dropped in the Dugout and booked the End works, as Martin was off first thing. Arfur had been seen in this area over the weekend so I hoped she'd been having it on my spot and would be prime for a bite.

The weather was hot and sunny that week so the weed had flourished and the spot was worse than the week before. I fished it with a light lead but I was gutted that my plans had backfired, and it certainly looked like Arfur had not fed hard there that week, as hoped.

The Big Orange was the first of the originals to make a mistake when Mad Martyn caught it out of the edge in the Back Bay. Martyn banked it at 39lbs at the end of June after plenty of prep work. It was a good capture, despite the disappointing weight for the fish that used to be mid-40s.

I missed the next week because I was away on my family holiday so my next chance came just after they'd spawned about mid-July in the Islands. Both mornings they fizzed up on 'Heather's Table' and with the odd liner and the occasional fish rocking in the weedbed behind, it looked a banker to rip off. Darren Miles popped down both mornings and right on cue they'd start bubbling as he sat his arse down on my chair. I was hoping he'd be my lucky charm but on the second morning, after the activity was dying down, the indicator crept to the top and held so I struck into it only for it disappointingly, to be a liner; another chance gone begging.

The glorious Car Park Lake was in fast decline.

The Big Orange was the first of the originals to make a mistake.

That week, Pearly Tail went the same way as Heather and another grave was dug for the old girl. We now had more graves than living fish and the prestigious line-up of nine was now down to a mere four.

What with Martyn having seen Arfur mooching in the Curly/Bars area, I chose to fish in the Bars on my next visit and as the evening was fast progressing I had a 'mare getting the short rod to crack down. Eventually, I got the desired drop and fortunately, the long rod went much smoother, out toward the V in the trees in the corner of the Back Bay. Pulling out of the weed, it went smooth before sliding over hard ground.

Martyn and Lee watched on as the light faded and I whacked out my fluorocarbon rig, this time with a barrel-shaped boilie, for the first time since back on, and as the rig landed bang on behind the float and cracked down, I bowed to my applause. Eight spods of boilie and mixed particle were dropped on the back of the float and that rod had proved plain sailing.

The swim resembled a bombsite, so I chucked everything under the bed, got the bivvy pegged down and got on with making the tea for a thirsty Lee. After a couple of brews and giving me the rundown on the goings on at Pingewood, where he was fishing, Lee headed off home, leaving me to get my head down, knackered from racing round and getting sorted before darkness interrupted my preparations.

After a quiet night, dawn broke and the long rod woke up. The indicator pulled up against the blank and I pulled into a solid resistance. Fishing so close to the weedbeds meant that the fish had got in there but with pressure I felt it start to move and keeping the rod at test curve I started to gain line. About halfway in I could see a bivvy-sized lump of weed heading my way and I was still unsure if there was a fish of some description hidden amongst it. The best way is just to net the lot and then go digging so as it came up to the spreader block, I engulfed the huge ball of vegetation and as I lay on my belly on the board and parted the weed, a carp's tail waved back at me.

I'd have liked it to be a knobbly old stumpy cut-off tail but this belonged to a much younger fish. I left it in the net and nipped next door to the Snags to grab John Elmer to give me a hand as it was sure to be lively after no scrap. With most of the weed dumped out, I had a much lighter net and lifted one of the new order of Car Park mirrors on to the mat. At 24lbs 4oz it was half the size of the one I wanted, but a good confidence booster on the first night having used a boilie.

The fish couldn't have been feeding alone as I'd seen a bow wave push away from the area when I'd had the take and, as it didn't take line, it must have been a different fish, probably another stockie, but it could have been one of the whackers!

I laid my traps in the Middle Secret.

The next evening my wife was looking on my Facebook page and said someone was asking Mad Martyn about his brace. I quickly scanned the screen and it looked like Big Carp Mart had indeed done the business. I sent him a text to find out if it was true and heard back from the man himself that he'd had the Big Orange again, just after I'd left, down even lower at 37lbs-plus, and followed it up with Arfur at 42lbs 8oz. This made it even more apparent that I'd been close, but Arfur had chosen to slip under the trees and dine on Martyn's pellets instead. Good angling, my friend!

Arfur was now nursing a sore lip and was well down in weight, so I decided to have a break and go back for her in the autumn when there might be a chance, and she'd had a chance to bulk up a bit. The Brute hadn't been out since April so she was well due and I looked forward to the next trip to renew my quest for the old warrior.

The very next morning I read a text that came through telling me that the Brute had just been out at 45lbs 8oz to Sean Leverett; both targets out of the game in less than 24 hours - bloody typical! Anyway, the plus side was that she'd gone back on the feed, after all the bad algae that had been affecting Pinge, and with most of the other mirrors to play for it would still be a better bet for catching than hammering away on the Car Park. Also, Sean who was not only a very good angler but also had a lot of time on his hands would be off the lake and so there'd be one less body to compete with. Game on!

Big Carp Mart had indeed done the business.

Chapter 23 - Back for the Brute

The Brute had only come out on the Thursday, so I was in no rush to return and spent my Sunday afternoon and night at home, instead of bombing up the motorway. As much as I love my time on the bank, with a big family I need to have some balance, so extra time with the children is a necessity, as well as pursuing monster carp.

After picking up Isabelle from nursery school and having had some one-on-one time with Ben, I loaded the gear, said my goodbyes and got to Pingewood just after lunch. Sean had caught all three of the big'uns in the previous couple of weeks so the lake was quiet. None of the other mirrors had been out, though, since the lake had become clouded up with algae. I could now see what Lee was on about. The normally crystal-clear lake was a horrible tea colour with lots of paint-like green algae on the windward bank's margin. All the weed had died off through lack of light, I guess, from the algae bloom, so I fancied the middle of the lake.

The two Richies were the only ones on. They were installed in the Slipway and the Canopy, the two swims from which Sean had caught his three mirrors. As the fish seemed to be coming on to the feed, I was surprised to hear that Richie was only using single hook baits. This had been Sean's tactic when he caught the Pearly Linear and the Brute. With this knowledge, I decided to do the opposite and give them a bit of bait as I was sure they would start to get hungry very soon.

I headed round to the Motorway Point and got the float out about 80 yards on the edge of the gravel hump that I'd caught Pearly from the previous year. I was going to spod out some hemp, corn, Partiblend and boilie so I wanted a bait hard on the bottom and this seemed the ideal time to try a new rig I'd tied up on the Car Park the week before. It consisted of a stiff material at the hook end that I could curve gently, chod-style and a 2½-inch section that I'd joined to a coated braid with an Albright knot. The middle part of the rig had the coating stripped off, creating a flexible hinge. With a soft hair trapped on the bend with a piece of silicone tube, the hook would dig in as soon as the stiff section tensioned to the lead. Also, if the fish attempted to blow out the bait, the very stiff section would be hard to eject.

The Brute had a very under-slung mouth so I felt that a bottom bait was the way to go, and although I had utter faith in my pop-up rig, I was starting to wonder if this was a contributing factor to my failure to catch the Brute, or some of the other 'bait' fish. I'd caught most of the rarer ones to visit the bank - only recently I'd had Big Pecs - but I was still to catch the more regular bank visitors; Popeye, the Toad, Cluster, Two Scales and, of course, the Brute. I hoped that a bottom bait might account for some of these other mirrors.

I had a bit of corn in the spod mix so I put in about 20 spods on the back of the float, not super-tight, but over an area the size of a family car, and added a piece of plastic corn to my 18mm boilie. Not only would this be a bit more visual in the coloured water, but also the added buoyancy would take the weight of the rig out of the equation. I fished the other two rods on short pop-ups out to where I'd caught Pecs from, over a scattering of bait. Old habits die hard!

I was all done by about half-past three so after a sarnie and a cup of tea, I decided to get my head down for an hour as I was exhausted. My son was still not great at night and I felt a quick power nap, snug in the bag, would pep me up. After an hour and a half kip I felt a lot better and sat at the front of the swim, taking in the summer's evening. Although I didn't see any carp show, I went to bed that night confident that I was in the right area. This was confirmed at 6am, when the rod fished over the bait with the bottom bait and new rig came to life, the bobbin kissing the Delkim as all was held up tight.

I pulled into the culprit, but it was coming in fairly easily with just the odd shake of the head felt down the line and I was unsure if it was a carp or a tench. At about 30 yards the rod pulled down firmly as it picked up pace and headed westbound up the motorway bank, forcing me to backwind. At least I knew it was a carp, so I played it with care. The tussle was non-spectacular, the fish just holding its ground and boring about down deep for a few minutes. I felt a common might be responsible as the mirrors normally charge about more, but I was more than pleased to see a mirror glide over the drawstring.

Ross, who'd set up for an overnighter on the Cottage Bank, came jogging into the swim to lend a hand and we both peered into the net to see which one it was. It looked an upper-20 and I was pretty sure it was the Toad. On the mat, I ran my hand along its flank, and could feel by its leathery bumpy skin that it was indeed the Toad, named for its textured flanks rather than looking like one! Ross read out 28lbs 2oz on the scales and after getting a few snaps done, I let her swim off in the bay. Not only was I chuffed because I'd caught on the first night back, but the new rig had scored on the first attempt and the bottom bait had snared one of the pack that I'd been unable to get among until now.

Back at work, I booked the following Wednesday off so I'd be able to do a rare three-night session. As I pulled up at the main gate on my return the following Sunday, I looked across the lake and the Point appeared to be empty. There was a westerly banging on to the Cottage Bank and after my success on the Point the previous week, plus I'd picked up bloodworm on my hook when I'd wound in, a natural feeding spot had to produce more bites if I could position my rig bang on.

The Point was indeed free and a chat with Ross in the Lawn revealed that not a lot had happened over the weekend, just a few showing in the middle. Music to my ears! Ross was just getting ready to pack up so I headed round to the motorway car park and with the barrow loaded, headed down to the Point with a spring in my step.

I hoped a bottom bait might account for some of these other mirrors.

I'd made up some more of my new bottom bait combi rigs before I'd packed up the previous week, so my intention was to fish two rods on this rig. As Ross wound his rods in, I dispatched the marker out toward the Slipway, which would put me on the far side of the Lawn long spot, a Brute area over the years.

As I found a glide of smooth silt I counted seven, 12" pulls before the float marked the spot. At about 70 yards it was a bit shorter than where the baited area would be but close enough should fish sit back off it, and I could imagine the Brute hanging back as his mates gorged themselves, but tempted to pick up the odd bait. With this in mind I scattered 20 boilies over the top and got the new rig with a straight bottom bait lying on top of the firm silt.

The Brute, as with most of the Pinge fish, has a very black mouth, a sure sign of a silt feeder. The right-hand rod went long onto my Pecs spot with a pop-up and again 20 baits dotted in the zone completed that trap. The middle rod, with a fake corn-tipped bottom bait, was dispatched onto the spot I'd banked the Toad from. My lines were still marked from the previous week and so made this quite straightforward. With the spod still clipped up, I soon had 25 spods of goodness over the top and as darkness fell, I could still see the spod landing, from the illumination of the M4 lights behind me.

I was up at 5.30am on the lookout for fish and did see one head pop out between my left and middle spots, and one longer again, not far from my right-hand rod's rig.

I could feel by its leathery bumpy skin that it was indeed the Toad.

Things looked promising and soon I heard, 'kettle on boyee!', ringing in my ears as my old mukka from Yateley, Simon Croft, came sauntering into the swim. Si had got down early and primed up his stalking spots before caning my tea supplies and we chatted for a few hours before he went off to check his spots, but my bucket lid stayed warm as another old Yateley pal in the shape of Darren Miles turned up. For those who don't know, Darren caught all the Car Park mirrors apart from Heather, many of them two or three times, in fact, but he hadn't fished for a while as he'd had a break and also got married. It seemed strange that five years before we'd only had carpy thoughts on our brains as we fell asleep at night, and now we both had a wife with whom to share our passions – and carp were often not at the top of the agenda!

Time was bombing on and a look at the clock revealed that it had passed 11am and so it looked like a chance of a take had also gone. A few minutes later, the left-hand bobbin crept to the top before dropping down an inch, and then back up.
"Bloody bream!" I cussed as I wound down and pulled into it.
"Bream?" enquired Daz.
"Not sure, mate," I replied.
Normally, you just wind them straight in but this had a bit of weight to it and although it was coming in, it was also kiting left. With the one buoy in the lake in this direction and the fish still past it, I got right over to the right-hand side of the swim and wound like mad to get enough line on the spool; I was sure by this time that it was a carp.

As it neared the buoy I could see a black line just under the surface, and assumed this was my lead core but in fact it was silty scum on the main line, and as I realised this, it was too late and the fish had made the back of the buoy. The buoy swung left as the fish pulled the line against the rope before coming back and snagging solid.

I kicked myself because I hadn't reacted sooner, and we were now in a 'what to do' situation. We phoned Tim to see if any of the bailiffs were about to come down in the boat, but as no one was available and I didn't want to risk my ticket in a boat, I pulled a bit harder and as the buoy bobbed it came free with a slightly opened-out hook, the fish having transferred the hook to the rope. Sometimes you wonder if they really have got hands!

Being so late in the morning, I just wished I hadn't messed up my chance of the Brute, which has a history of late-morning bites, but I was sure it would have given a more aggressive account of itself, and the fish I'd lost was probably a common. I took the opportunity to recast all three rods with fresh baits. After two takes in two nights, I had the new rig on all three rods, such was my confidence in it now.

I had to wait until dusk for the wind to ease and for the seagulls to sling their hooks before I could re-bait. Again, I put 30 boilies on the outside rods and another 10 spods of boilie and particle on the middle rod. Ross and Lee popped in that evening and on hearing of my loss, laughed and told me that's what I got for fishing the Lawn spot.

Admittedly, it was a bit left of my normal spot, but with no one in the Lawn I wasn't interfering with anyone. I argued that it was borderline water but they weren't having it.

Si was back in my plot, early doors, and after an uninterrupted night I was already up. I swear he'd heard me spark up the stove as he stuck his head round the corner of the bivvy as the first puffs of steam chugged from the kettle spout. With two sets of eyes scanning the flat calm surface, we ought to have seen any shows but it was unusually quiet. A couple of hours of chatting later, a south-westerly breeze started to ripple the lake and gently strengthened, pushing from left to right toward the Cottage Bank.

Fortunately, I didn't have to wait as long as the previous day for a take. At about 9:15am, while we were both standing at the water's edge, a Delkim blurted out a few bleeps. I hesitated for a couple of seconds as for some reason I thought it was the left-hand rod, before noticing the bobbin wedged into the buzzer on the long right-hand rod. The fish must have been lifting the backlead because as soon as I pulled into it, it was obvious that a good carp was pulling away from me. After the previous day's disaster, I was very aware of keeping it away from that buoy so keeping the pressure of the rod to the left, I hoped to encourage it to kite right and away from danger. I started to gain line and it was pretty much coming straight in.

At about 50 yards out, the tip flew back and my heart dropped "C**T," I shouted and no sooner had the expletive left my mouth than I was back in contact. What had happened I don't know, but Simon was laughing his head off and now relieved it was still fish on, I started to giggle as I could see the funny side of my sudden outburst.

With it being Brute time I soon had my serious head back on as it came close. Si started to pull up his trousers and took off his shoes and socks. I offered my chest waders, forgetting that the lanky giant has feet the size of a circus clown!

Although Si had dropped the tips of my other two rods, the fish still managed to pick up one of the lines as it hugged the lakebed under the tip. Si lifted the offending rod and rather unsuccessfully we tried to unloop it from my main line. All we seemed to be doing was making it worse so I told Si to leave the bail arm open and hold the tip up. I didn't want to take my eye off the ball and concentrated on wearing down

The big golden cluster of scales on her shoulder shone like jewels in the sunlight.

the leviathan attached. Soon the leadcore started to pop out of the water before burying back down.

A minute or two later, and we got a first glimpse – well, Simon did as he was standing out in the water. The water was coloured so it wasn't a clear view but I was a bit disappointed to hear the words, "Looks like a common, fella."
After one more dive for freedom, I turned her and led her over the drawstring and Si scooped her up. With a big grin, Si turned round to declare that it was actually Cluster. I'd never seen this one on the bank, so with the chesties on I marched out to have a butcher's and even in the muddy water, the big golden cluster of scales on her shoulder shone like jewels in the sunlight.

Once quite a friendly fish and one that I previously described as one of the bait fish, Cluster hadn't visited the bank for over a year and on the bank I was impressed how well my size 8 choddy was buried in the bottom lip. I don't know what the sudden tip jerk during the fight was all about, because there was no way that the hook had moved.

Cluster swung the needle round to 34lbs 9oz and we photographed her straight away. I was honoured and proud to hold aloft such a good-looking carp, Pinge had presented another of its stunners to me. She was my fifth mirror so far this year from the lake and the bottom baits were helping me to nail some of the different ones, and my quest for the Brute looked better than ever. Surely it would be soon. I just needed to get on her!

It was the August bank holiday the next weekend and the lake was shut for a memorial charity match so I wouldn't be fishing until the Monday. On the Sunday, while at work at the shop, I got a text saying that someone had caught one in the match and guess what fish it was...the Brute at 44lb 4oz, and guess where it was caught? You've got it, Motorway Point!

I only had 24 hours to fish so I thought I might as well go, and would try my luck up at the 'easy narrow end' after one of the two others I was after, namely the Croptail Linear and Nathan's Common, both fish liked to spend time up at the workings end.

I spotted Lee's car in the car park, and rang him to discover that he was round in Mad Dogs where Ross was still fishing, having fished in the match. I found Glynn and Lee huddled under Ross's brolly and on quizzing them about the Brute's capture (the only fish that was caught), I breathed a sigh of relief that it hadn't come off my long spots but had picked up matey's bait flicked in the edge to the right.

Ross and Glynn took great delight in informing me that the Brute had another fresh hook hold and someone must have lost it in the last few days. The smirks on their faces revealed it as a wind-up. Ha, bloody ha! They had me worried for a few seconds

and if it had been anyone else telling me I might have believed them, but these two jokers were far too transparent. I fancied giving the First Point a go, and on learning that it hadn't been pegged in the match, this made it even more attractive as I wouldn't be fishing over loads of uneaten bait. The change of scenery was nice but with the predicted north-easterly not coming to fruition I packed away to record my first blank since my return.

The next week I followed a similar plan of fishing the top end, but this time on the other bank, fishing the right Container swim. In fact, it was quiet and by carrying two landing nets I was able to fish two in the right and one in the middle Container. I found some lovely spots and again fished two on just boilies and one on boilies over particle and boilie.

The wind was really tanking up and as Ginger Richie was in the First Point, the two of us had this end to ourselves. Richie had caught the Thick-wristed Half Linear at lunchtime, so it really looked the end to be.

At dawn on the Monday morning, Scouse Richie turned up and asked me if I minded him dropping in the left-hand Container. It would have suited me more if he hadn't but it was an available swim which didn't interfere with my water so I told him if he wanted to go there, then crack on. Richie took a while getting his rods sorted and with the wind increasing, the waves were lapping up to my right.

At about 3pm, I'd just got all my rods sorted for the afternoon when I looked across to see Scouse with a fish on. It was just being washed in by the waves and not doing anything when it came up to the surface, and a big creamy mirror wallowed on top. I legged it back to my swim and grabbed my waders, and with them on and net in hand I half stepped, half fell, into the margins and as it bobbed in front I scooped it up. It was Richie's first mirror from the lake and what a mirror to start with! The Croptail Linear and over 37lbs!

Whether I'd have had a chance if Richie had not been there, I'll never know, but with that capture and no carp coming to me I returned down to the other end the following week with my tail between my legs; firstly in the Slipway and then the Canopy. The winds throughout this period were south-westerlies which are good for those swims, but it had gone stale and I hoped for a warm north-westerly as I felt the Motorway Bay had the potential to produce the big girl next. Crofty had caught it up against the motorway bank in the bay, poling across from the Pallets last October 1st. The previous couple of autumns, the Brute had been regularly in the bay, in and around the snag willow tree, an area of which she seemed particularly fond.

I tried my luck at the 'easy, narrow end'.

Bearing this in mind and with the lake quiet, before I left on the Tuesday I lugged a bucket full of hemp, pellet and boilie round, climbed out on the snag just up from the willow and deposited it off the end. That should give her a taster if she was in the area.

The following weekend, the wind had turned northerly but was bitterly cold and I texted Lee to find out if anyone had gone in the bay. Lee himself was in the Pallets but informed me that it was freezing cold and nothing had been out. On the Saturday I was well rough with bad guts and spent most of the morning curled up in pain and most of the afternoon with my head down the toilet.

I felt a bit brighter on Saturday evening so made it to work on Sunday morning, but I was still a bit fragile and as it was so cold and I wasn't up to rushing about, I decided to leave it until Monday and just go to Pinge for 24 hours. I dropped my little girl off at nursery school at 8.45am, intending to sort the gear out and head up to Reading, but I started to get pains in my guts again and then after a visit to the toilet with the runs, I thought I'd give the fishing a miss. Good job as a couple of hours later it was coming out both ends, just what I'd have needed on the bank.

I plumped for the Slipway and even had the house up by darkness – result!

The Croptail Linear and over 37lb!

Although it went through my whole family, the sickness was gone by the next Sunday and as it was the start of October and the new moon on Thursday, I felt this was my last chance before going back to the Car Park Lake. I'd tried to get the Wednesday off work but at short notice this wasn't possible so I just had two nights to get it right.

I managed to get away from home a little earlier and pulled up at the gate at 4.30pm. This gave me two hours to choose my swim and get the rods out. I was tempted to go in the bay but couldn't see anything and on learning that Frampton Martin had just done three nights in there and that the Slipway had not been fished, I plumped for the Slipway, and at least this way I could keep an eye on the bay. Having fished the Slipway recently I was able to get all three rods out relatively quickly and even had the house up by darkness – result!

I had a good night's sleep, got up at first light and with a hot tea in hand, sat by the water's edge on the lookout for any signs. At about 9am, I saw a head pop out, a bit longer than my two rods at the third tree, so I wasn't too far off. While staring at the spot, something caught my eye and I looked past it to where a big splash in the middle of the bay was subsiding. I missed the fish but it had put up a big spray so must have been a good one.

An hour or so later, another one showed long in the Slipway, but as the sun was getting up and the forecast was for it to be quite hot that afternoon, I wanted to check out the bay. It would be perfect conditions for the bay and I could only guess that Martin had seen something in there for him to do three nights in the one swim, because he's quite a switched-on angler.

My only concern was Richie looking in the bay before me, as Ross was snoring away in the Lawn. Richie was next door in the Canopy and I managed to winkle out of him that he was giving it until at least noon before he wound in. I wanted to leave the rods out as long as possible also, so at 11.50 I quietly wound the leads in, avoiding them skipping the surface so Rich wouldn't know I'd beat him for a look round.

I put on my Polaroids and made it clear that I was off to have a look in the bay as I fancied it, and off I went. If the Brute was in there, I reckoned it would be hanging around the willows snag in the corner, but as I walked into the Pallets it was clear that the water was far from that, with a thick layer of green, scummy, paint-like algae covering the corner. There was no way I could see through that, and there could have been every fish in the lake under it but you wouldn't see them. The clarity of the water itself was now very good so it was a shame the algae had scuppered my plans.

My line strung across the corner of the bay like an empty washing line.

I wandered round to the end bank as it wasn't as bad round there, and climbing a few feet up the tree I strained my eyes trying to see through the filmy algae that hung on the surface. It was under this tree that Crofty had caught the Brute a year before. After a few minutes, a bit of oil 'pinked' up like trout pellet being disturbed. Was it bait down there, or had a fish flanked on the bottom?

I couldn't see any dark shapes so after two or three minutes, a bit peeved, I slid down and as I headed off I stopped and looked back down the margin. With the noise of the motorway, you can't hear a thing, so I don't know what made me look back - something out of the corner of my eye perhaps, that or a sixth sense, but thankfully I did as there on the surface, ten yards down the bank, was a big frothy patch of bubbles with rings rippling away. Another ten seconds up the tree and I'd have seen it, another five seconds earlier and I'd have been on the path and missed it completely!

Quickly, I shinned back up the tree and as I did so a good common lolloped, a rod length out and bang in front of me. It might not have been the Brute but there were carp in the bay and I needed a better look so I raced round to the Pallets swim to climb the tree that gives a good view at this time of day and as I walked into the swim, Richie and Ross came up the path.

They asked me if I'd seen those two fish bosh on the tree line and I had to act fast. I admitted I had and said I was probably moving in and that I was just going to climb the tree. This had the desired effect and they said they'd let me get on with it and were off for a look up in the top bay.

There, in my vision, was that unique-shaped head that could only belong to one fish – my target, the Brute.

I pulled myself up the first part of the tree and then climbed up as high as possible. Immediately, I spotted three dark shapes over where the carp had just boshed out and after about ten minutes, they ventured a little closer where the scummy film had cleared. I could make out that one of the fish was significantly larger than the others. Was it the Brute? I couldn't tell, but with only 24 hours of my session left it had to be worth the gamble so I stripped off my sweatshirt, left this to claim the swim and ran back to pack away and move round to the Pallets. I was just pulling the bungee strap over a loaded barrow when Richie came along and started quizzing me about if I'd seen the Brute. I honestly didn't know if the bigger fish was the Brute, or not, but judging by past history, there was a chance - even though I'd seen fish show in the Slipway. I was there to catch the Brute, not just to catch.

The sun was climbing higher and the fish had ventured out into the middle of the bay on my return, so I worked in double-quick time because I wanted to get a rig poled up over on the end margin and with the fish out in the bay I needed this opportunity because I would have to wade in to get the rig in position. With just a 2oz bare lead on the line I whacked it across, but I overdid it a bit and it was too high. I cursed as the next cast landed short; I didn't want anything to alert the fish of my presence. Third time lucky, and it landed perfectly up against the bank next to the climbing tree. Armed with my rig and leadcore leader in my bait bucket, baiting spoon and handle and a long bankstick to 'pole' up to, I headed round to the spot as the fish were basking out in the centre of the bay seemingly oblivious to my activities.

When I got back round to the tree, I could see that the line had gone through the willow fronds as the lead had soared to the bank so I got hold of the line and gave it a few tugs but it wasn't pulling through and I just ended up pulling line off the clutch. A change of plan was called for so I wrapped the lead around the tree a couple of times and returning to the swim, I tightened up and pulled the line down. It wasn't having it so I opened the bail arm and flicked the line out so it was slack and dropping down vertically. I grabbed a seven-metre whip from the quiver and once again returned to the spot.

I fully extended the whip and waded out a few feet so I was able to drag the line back to me after a couple of attempts, and once the line was in my hand, I cut it off and now had a direct line to the rod tip. I then tied on my leader, placed the rig in the scoop and, keeping hold of the main line, fed it out into about five feet of water and bumped the spoon on the bottom until I found a hard patch. I then simply had to tip the rig out. With a small back-lead attached, I lowered this to the lakebed and with the line vertical from the back-lead I pushed in the bankstick and clipped the line tightly into the plastic line clip.

A few handfuls of pellet and a couple of dozen boilies completed the carefully laid trap. I pulled the cut-off line from the tree, returned to the Pallets with all my paraphernalia and tightened up to the clip by lifting all the line out of the water, which is not easily done with the surface tension restricting it, and being careful not to pull the line out of the clip. I put the rod on the rest with the tip skywards and my line strung across the corner of the bay like an empty washing line.

On scaling the Pallets tree again, I could see that the fish had moved a lot closer to my bank and as it was only 25 yards out, I could now see that there were four fish and yes, one was a lot bigger than his mates. I descended from the tree, grabbed my polarised binoculars and with these round my neck, I shot back up the tree. I got into a position where I could balance myself steadily, juggled the bins from round my back and holding them up to my eyes, I focused on the four carp below. With the focus wheel adjusted, I picked out the big one and my attention went straight to its head. There, in my vision, was that unique-shaped head that could only belong to one fish - my target, the Brute.

My heartbeat was racing and I knew this was my chance to catch it. Everything was falling into place; she was due out, it was only two days until the new moon, conditions were perfect for the time of year, and I had the whole bay and surrounding area all to myself. I couldn't afford to stuff this up so I decided I'd get the other two rods ready to cast out, but would wait as long as it took to be safe from spooking them away.

I attached lighter 2oz leads and would use smaller baits that I could catapult out with minimal splash and noise. I knew of a firm, silty strip to the far side of some gravel in the middle of the bay which I had fished from the Tyre swim on the other side. I worked out the angles and felt that I could find this spot relatively easy. I'd have to wait until either the fish moved out of the bay or back into the corner out of harm's way.

I took this time-out break to eat and drink and after another couple of trips up the tree, my chance came as they meandered out into the mouth of the bay. Firing the marker right over to the far margin to avoid spooking the carp with a big splash, I flipped the bail arm over immediately and wound it back along the surface to where I thought the back of the spot was. I let it sink on a tight line and got a nice 'dink' as it hit bottom. I dragged it back a rod length, over the smooth, firm bottom and as it hit the first tap of gravel I popped the float up to the surface. Perfect.

I tried to get an early night as I was quite drained from the afternoon's events.

With a piece of fake buoyant corn tipping my 14mm bottom bait, this would not only negate the weight of the hook but also, by using minimal bait it would act as a bit of a sighter. I tied on a three-bait stringer, parachute style, to avoid a potential tangle and with the odd back breaking the surface out in the mouth of the bay, I launched a 2oz lead to the marker. It went a bit long so I lifted the tip, swished it back and the lead swung down with a nice 'dink' - spot on, and with only one cast to the area. I quickly climbed the tree and could see that the Brute and his mates were relaxed out in the mouth, enjoying the autumnal sunshine. One at a time, I fired out a dozen 14mm boilies to the back of the float and even the seagulls left me alone today! Float in, and two rods down - one to go.

An hour later, the fish came back into the bay and began to mooch about between my two spots to the left. I launched the marker to the mouth, where they'd been hanging about, and finding a nice spot I got a rig out first cast again. I was just firing out some bait when Lee called in for a social. With the marker in, I filled him in on the day's events over a few brews. As Lee left I told him to leave his phone on because I felt it was my time to catch the Brute. Lee retorted that I wouldn't catch it as I was the Darren Miles of Pinge. Darren had caught all of the fish in the Car Park Lake apart from the queen herself, Heather the Leather, and Lee felt that I'd catch every other big one barring the Brute. Cheers for that, mate!

The only other person apart from the missus that I'd told was Si Croft, on the phone. As I said earlier, he'd caught the Brute from the Pallets on October the 1st the year before and today was October the 4th, 11 years to the day after I'd caught Bazil, still my personal best. Si was more gracious with his support and said I'd have it in the morning. I dearly wished that to be the case.

I tried to get an early night as I was quite drained from the afternoon's events in the sun, what with 'up and down' the tree over a dozen times and the adrenalin rush being 'on the Brute'! I can normally fall asleep sitting up, but tonight I was finding sleep elusive, partly because of anticipation but largely the bloody noise from the motorway. The Pallets swim was only about 60 yards from the hard shoulder and I'd never had a problem on the motorway bank, with the back of my bivvy to the M4, but tonight the traffic didn't want to die down and it must have been gone 11pm when it lessened and I dozed off.

Soon after first light, a bleep on the middle rod had me raising my head off the pillow. A poxy coot was over the area and so I was straight out of the bag. I grabbed a handful of boilies, skimmed a couple at the feathered robber and this had the desired effect as he scuttled off. I didn't know whether he'd picked up the hook bait or just brushed the line scrabbling on the bottom. Should I recast? The bay was flat calm and the rig in prime position, so I quickly dispelled this idea. The plastic corn would have prevented the boilie from being plucked off if the bird had indeed picked it up. I did 'pult out the half-dozen baits in my hand, though, just to top it up if he'd nicked any freebies.

It was time to stick the kettle on. As I sat on the edge of my bed, I scanned the water for signs and glancing over to the Slipway, I could see Richie, who'd moved in there after me, rod in hand playing a fish. Bollocks! Had I made the wrong choice? If this was the Brute, I'd be kicking myself for making the move. I told myself that I'd moved on to the Brute, so whatever Richie had on, I had to have made the move 100%.

After a few minutes, I could tell all was not well and by the look of it the fish had made the snag to the right of the swim. I saw Richie put the rod down and run up to Ross and then run back. Ross was soon in tow and after a bit of toing and froing, the rod got launched into the reeds and Ross melted off. Rich was not going to be a happy chappie.

I looked back out to my spot, had another slurp of tea, then all hell broke loose as the middle bobbin tried to snap the rod as it smashed up and the spool started

"I've got her, babe."

spinning, all to a one-noting Delkim. I grabbed the rod but wasn't able to get it above 45 degrees because it was stripping line off me at an incredible rate of knots. The angry beast headed straight to the far side of the bay and only turned due to the fact that it was running out of water. As it kited right out past the Tyre swim, I dropped the other line and stepped into my waders. With the net chucked out in front of me I waded down to the right, away from the other line and the various rubble and posts that adorned the margin to the left.

The carp stopped about 25 yards off the corner of the point. It felt bogged down and my heart seemed to stop momentarily because I couldn't move the fish, before it started kiting right again. There was no weed out there and I think it was purely using its weight to hold its ground, having a breather. For the first time in the fight I started to get some line but as I got 30 yards on the reel, it then took 20 back and slowly but surely, I got it coming closer and at about 30 yards, I saw a gold flash. I hoped it wasn't a common.

It dived back down to the bottom and took another couple of turns off me but seemed to be tiring and as I got it coming up in the water and the top of the five feet of lead core touched the surface, a big grey mirror came into view; the gold flash must have been its belly as it rolled over.

Under great strain I held the old warrior up for the cameras.

The leadcore disappeared again and I pushed the net into position in front of me. Another few yards closer and the leadcore rose out of the lake like Excalibur, and attached underneath was my obsession - the huge mirror with a big scale on its side. With my breath held and my butt cheeks clenched, I gingerly kept it on the surface, coming and coming, and with a step out toward it I engulfed it in the net.

"YEEEEEESSSSSSS!" echoed across the lake. As I pulled the net closer, there was a big, black, wide, crusty back and there was that unique-shaped head that I'd looked for each time I'd landed a big Pingewood mirror, but had not had the pleasure of seeing before. I inhaled a big lungful of air and at the top of my voice screamed, "BRRUUUUTTE!" above the drone of the rush hour traffic.

I secured the net over one of the scaffold poles at the front of the swim. I grabbed my phone, the emotion of fulfilling the dream washed over me, and as the phone rang before my wife Lynn answered, I felt quite choked. As Lynn spoke, I managed to stutter out, "I've got her, babe!"
Lynn was cheering and shouting to my kids that I'd caught the big one, and I must admit that I welled up a bit.

After 11 years and one day I finally had a new PB.

"How big?" she asked.

"I've only just netted her, babe. I'll let you know once I'm sorted."

There was no need to ring the other lads because I could see they were on their way and checking that the Brute was lying quietly at the front of the swim, I filled up the kettle and sparked up the stove.

I dug out the scales and wetted the sling as the lads came in to congratulate me.

"At least you know it wasn't the Brute you lost, mate!" I laughed to Richie. He said that he knew it wasn't but it was a good mirror. In this game, some you win, some you lose and there was no doubt that this glorious day belonged to me.

With the tea made we got the big girl out and my size 8 was well back on the floor of the mouth, firmly nailed. We slid her into the sling, hoisted her up and the scales confirmed that today I'd caught the biggest fish of my life at 48lb 2oz. After 11 years and one day since my capture of Bazil, I finally had a new PB.

I secured her in the margin while Richie went to get another mat, and Ross had to shoot off because he had a doctor's appointment. I phoned Lee, taking great delight in telling him that I hadn't done a Darren, and then Si to tell him that I had bagged the big girl, at last. When Richie returned we got her out and carried her down to the grassy Mad Dogs swim where the light was better, and under great strain I held the old warrior up to the camera lenses and basked in the glory of my moment. I managed to get a few return shots done and then with a thank you and goodbye from me, she waddled back out into the depths to make someone else's dream come true.

As I recounted the story of the capture to the two Richies, I texted the weight to my wife and several friends and when the tea was all gone, both Richies went back to their swims, leaving me alone to pack up. My time on Pingewood had come to an end and as I locked the gate for the final time, I shouted out a big "Thank you!" to the lake and to my new personal best. Made up or what! As Hannibal would say in the A-team, "I love it when a plan comes together."

Back into the depths to make someone else's dream come true.

Chapter 24 - A winter walk in the park

With the Brute caught, it was time to get back for Arfur, and as winter was fast approaching, I realistically had a month, which equated to about eight nights' fishing. As the nights began to draw in, it was all a bit of a rush on a Sunday afternoon and with only one or two hours of daylight to get the rods sorted, it gave me no time to look round on arrival. I was relying on Arfur to return to old form, so I concentrated on the top end and the Chair in particular.

After tripping up the Brute I was confident in my bottom bait rig and persisted with this. Often, fishing at least one rod in the margins enabled me to use bits and pieces, and some juicy white maggots and trout pellets formed part of my attack. All the captures of the originals had come out from the edge this season. They were used to finding bait in the margins so, as November and possible bad weather was not far away, I needed to fish areas that the Baby Orange and Arfur were likely to visit. I'd love to be able to tell you how I found Arfur troughing on one such spot, got a rig in and after a hectic battle lifted the net around the big, fat, wily, old sod but alas, the Car Park Lake did what it is best at, sucking you in, chewing you up and then spitting you out!

I packed up in the Curly in mid-November and it proved to be the last session of the year as the weather deteriorated drastically and the arctic conditions took hold of the whole country, freezing everything until well into January.

Despite everywhere thawing a week or so into January, I still had no inclination to sit on the bank freezing my nuts off. I'm older and wiser these days, and I needed to get a few jobs done at home and was enjoying spending my days off with my two little ones and the missus. The eldest three were at school and college, so that gave me some quality time with Isabelle and Benjamin, and my wife was enjoying having me home every night. Winter is the new close season!

I told Lynn that once I started back up I'd like to get back into the rhythm of every week so would wait for conditions to improve to a level when I felt there might be a chance. The kids were moving bedrooms, and I'd get all the rearrangements done, so that when the time was right I'd be able to concentrate my attention on fishing again.

There was a big south-westerly forecast for the second week of February, and my jobs at home were almost at an end so I arranged to meet the guy from whom I could buy a ticket for a local park lake. There were only five weeks of the season left and I hoped that they'd be waking up with the big winds coming in.

On the Sunday, I got a text from my mate, Liam, saying that he'd had two that day - a 29 and a 30. It looked like my timing was spot on and was going to coincide with them coming out of their winter slumber. Liam had a third later that afternoon, a small common and I had the necessary spring in my step as I walked up to the Dam Wall with my ticket in my pocket, to have a quick look round before nipping back home to grab my gear.

I fancied the Dug Out swim but as I wandered up the bank, I could see a barrow behind the swim. The Bus Stop was also taken, unsurprisingly as this was where Liam had caught his three the previous day. I found Mark Bryant in the Dug Out and he told me that he was off about 5pm, so I said I'd return later and drop in after him. This way, I could get the last of my jobs done at home and return for the night and be able to get a couple of baits near the diving board where the wind was pumping down.

I returned at about half-past four and noticed immediately that the wind had dropped and the skies were clearing; my first night back was set to be a cold one. Welcome back! Craig in the Bus Stop had caught a couple of low-30s so he was well chuffed and while I was waiting behind the Dug Out for Mark to pack up, I noticed Craig into another one. Alan was setting up in the Bus Stop and Craig's last rod, which was lying on the floor, had gone off. Luckily, Alan had spotted it before it water-skied off the dam wall and into the depths.

Craig was obviously into a good fish so I legged it round to where it was putting up a fine account of itself and eventually, it came close enough for me to scoop up with the net. It was a common, and a good one at that. I heaved it out onto the mat and between the two of us we lifted her up on top of the dam wall and over to some grass. It was a country park, so there were plenty of people about and among the usual public questions was "What are you going to do with it?" when you put it into a sling, but Alan got in first with, "You could do with some chips with that!" At 36lbs 6oz, it turned out to be the short, fat common and there were no leeches on it; these fish were well awake and more importantly, eating.

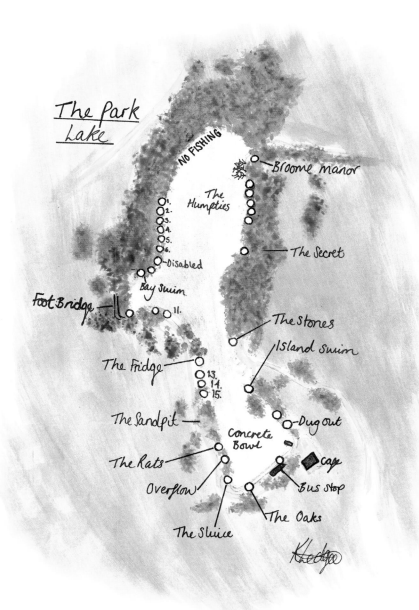

The Park Lake

NO FISHING

Broome manor

The Humpties

1.
2.
3.
4.
5.
6.
Disabled

The Secret

Bay Swim

Foot Bridge

11.

The Stones

Island Swim

The Fridge

13.
14.
15.

The Sandpit

Dug out

Concrete Bowl

The Rats

cage

Overflow

Bus stop

The Sluice

The Oaks

I got back round, once the fish was safely returned, a two- or three-man job on the treacherous slope of the dam wall, to find Mark packing down and so I got on and tied some baits on choddies, and managed to get all three out on dark. There wasn't a cloud in the sky; the park went quiet, the temperature plummeted and my first night back at the park lake was a frosty one. I fished through until about 4pm but had to leave then as my son had a parents' evening.

The cloudy and windy weather returned on the Wednesday, the fish continued to feed, and the Bus Stop was producing a fish virtually every day, and by my return on the Sunday, both the Dug Out and the Rats had produced fish too. They were down this dam end big style so choosing which part of the lake to fish was a no-brainer.

I arrived late on the Sunday and not only was it getting dark already but it was also pouring with rain. The Bus Stop had taken a hammering and nothing had been out of there since Friday morning, so I chose to fish the Rats. I'd fished this swim at the end of last season and liked the area it put me in where the fish drifted out into the middle of the deep and silty bowl end.

There was zero chance of getting a rod out before dark and the rain was steady so I chucked up the house and got the bed and other essentials in the dry before they

took a soaking, and there was no weed whatsoever to worry about so the rods wouldn't be too much trouble to get sorted. With two on chod rigs on long lengths of lead core, I blasted a white pop-up out long toward the Dug Out and an orange Tutti about 80 yards out and further to the right. I was going to fish the other one shorter and over a bit of bait.

The wind was hacking into the sluices to my right and so after a few casts I found a harder area and with my lead clipped at the right range, I walked it out on the grass and pushed in a bankstick. I then walked out my spod to just past the bankstick and by doing this I'd be able to get some bait the perfect distance in the wind and rain. I used the silhouette of the diving board as my horizon marker and first got the rig out with a stringer, then by just putting five boilies in the spod I was able to have a similar groups of baits on the area. I only wanted 20 baits out there so four casts and I was done. It had been raining all this time so I was glad to get the waterproofs off and fire up the stove for a warm-up and a cup of tea before settling down for the night.

Just before first light, one of the park's bream had me awake and with the hook point gone, I put a new chod rig on and a fresh Tutti and by the time I'd made a tea it was light enough to recast at the lifebuoy on the far bank. The 3oz lead soared out and at 80 yards I stopped the lead and felt it fall to land with a firm donk. Pukka. I felt more confident fishing the firmer areas and after slackening off, put the rod in the rests. Liam was setting up in the Bus Stop but apart from him we had the lake to ourselves and with only the odd early morning jogger and dog walker, I sat back and enjoyed the relative peace.

At 8.30am, the recast middle rod pulled up tight but didn't come out of the clip. As I pulled into it, it was evident that something far heavier than the previous bream had taken a liking to my Tutti. I dropped the other two lines to the lakebed and slowly but surely it made its way in. It stayed fairly deep the whole fight so I was unaware of what it was. I glanced up to see Liam running round but when a good common broke the surface, I could see that it would be ready for netting before he'd make it, so after one last dash down for freedom, I brought it back up and led it over the drawstring.

It looked a decent fish, although not huge and with the net secured, I got the other two rods back on to rests, by which time Liam was by my side, keen to have a look-see at what I'd caught. The weighing gear was out of hibernation and ready, I cut the line above the leadcore and with the net rolled down and her fins all flat against her body, I lifted out my first carp of the year.

The middle of the deep and silty bowl end.

It was certainly a good-looking common with a proper set of shoulders and its bronze scales glowed in the February sunshine. It looked about 24lbs but the quivering needle of the Reubens proved my estimation wrong and I was pleased to see it go to 25lbs 8oz. There was absolutely no one about so we carried her on the mat out to the grass behind and with good light got some nice pictures, before lowering her back into the murky depths and she disappeared from view as she waddled off.

Liam legged it back to his rods, and with another fresh rig and pop-up on I fired it back to the same spot. Luckily, I'd checked the line beforehand as about five yards above, there was a nasty scored section so I would have to be careful as there was obviously some sort of snag down on the bottom in front of me. Usually, you'd expect it to be a branch or something but on this place it could be a bike or shopping trolley.

At 12.45pm the same rod's indicator danced up and down and I was in again. The fight was a similar pattern to the common, just swinging left and right as it came in. With the snagged line on my mind I kept the rod high and tried to keep it off the bottom. As it came in close I could see it was a mirror this time and when it went in the net I could see it was of a similar size to the common. Quite a long fish but with no gut.

I rang Liam and he came straight round. As he arrived in the swim, I already had the fish unhooked and hanging from the scales - 26lb 2oz of February mirror carp. Once again, there were no leeches on it but the most obvious thing was its colour. The reds and pinks were stunning and it was my biggest park lake fish to date.

Liam and Craig had both caught three in a day, those first two days when they'd woken up eight days ago, so I was hopeful of another one but that was my action done for the day, and the next day I couldn't repeat it. Anyway, two mid-20s from a hard water in the middle of February was a right result so I was more than happy with my brace. My method of chods with glugged-up bright orange Tuttis were a winner, so I had that part of rig and bait sussed, and was happy with it. I just hoped I could get back on them.

I put on a new chod rig and a fresh Tutti.

The following Sunday, I managed to get back in the Rats and with half an hour of daylight remaining, I got three chods out and see where they landed before darkness descended. Again, I'd found the firmer patch with my lead and this time fished it as my right-hand rod with the middle rod at the same distance just to the left, and my left-hand rod was fished out in the middle. This time I'd make sure to pole-elastic marker my lines so I could recast the exact distances in the event of a bite.

Apart from a tench at first light, all was quiet and as it was a bit drizzly I watched the water from the comfort of the sleeping bag. The wind had eased from the previous week but a gentle south-westerly was still pushing on to the dam wall and there was complete cloud cover so the temperature was staying constant at about 8 degrees.

With most of the fish coming out on the sunny days it didn't look great, but at 11am the right buzzer howled and the indicator held tight against it. I'd hooked something but wasn't too sure of the culprit and as I got the fish in close, it pulled a bit and so I dropped the other two tips. The pressure soon told, a small common popped up and a couple of dives later it was sitting in the bottom of my net - not a monster, but a welcome sight and the third take off the spot in as many nights. I checked its weight at 16lbs 4oz, slipped it back and wasted no time in getting the rod back on the spot.

The rest of the day was quiet, not counting the hundreds of people walking past, a bit of a problem if you have a weak bladder, like me, waiting for a gap in the procession! I recast my left-hand rod a tad further to the right that evening and it definitely donked down on firmer ground.

At 8am, the repositioned left-hand rod was away. Even on a much longer line it felt a better fish and it kited left, which I was happy with, away from the other rods, and the underwater snag that had scored up my lines the previous week. The fish was kiting into my bank so I quickly gained line and at one stage it was under the brambles in my left-hand margin. A big yellow shape could be seen ghosting just below the surface as I steered it out from under the overhanging brambles, and even in the murky water I knew it was the best one yet, and this was evident as it went in the net.

A welcome sight and the third take off the spot in as many nights.

It turned out to be the Map fish.

It was just gone 8 o'clock so I grabbed my phone and rang Liam straight away as I knew he was passing on his way to work. He wasn't far away, so I unhooked her and on the scales she went 31lbs 12oz - a good one at last, and my biggest February carp. Liam soon arrived and I got her back out, and with my memories recorded on camera, including a few shots as she slipped off, another productive winter trip was over.

I kept in touch with the lake but nothing came out after my two that week. The weather was changing a bit, the wind had gone north-east and hence it was a bit colder, only five or six degrees daytime temperature and I was starting to think that perhaps they'd done the off from the bowl end.

Lynn and I were taking the two little ones to see Fireman Sam at the theatre on Sunday afternoon, so I knew I'd be setting up in the dark. It was a very enjoyable afternoon, the excitement and delight on their faces when it all started was worth every penny. I waited until they'd gone to bed and arrived at a now peaceful park lake about 8pm. With only Clive in the Sluices, I dropped back in the Rats, intending to move down to the other end if no action happened. The lines were marked, the wind was over my shoulder and I soon had all three rigs out spot-on. The change of wind direction made getting a dozen baits around each one much easier.

The last day of February turned out to be overcast. I'd felt all three leads donk down and the lines were pointing right in line with my far bank markers so I left them untouched all day. Having cork-plugged my pop-ups, I knew the buoyancy would be unaffected and as they were glugged, they'd still be emitting that fruity aroma. Just as I was starting to give up hope of adding to my tally, the long rod took off, even pulling out of the clip this time. I wound down and had to gain a few yards before getting direct contact as the fish kited. It was fighting quite hard at range and I willed it to be one of the big girls. As it neared my bank, I chucked the net in. A bit more plodding and the fight was typical of a lump, then the leadcore rose out of the water, a chunky mirror coughed air and with my 4oz lead and orange hook bait hanging from its mouth, I led her over the outstretched net. It was a good'un for sure but not a monster.

Liam was down in the Secrets so I rang him but couldn't get through. Clive, who'd moved over to the Dug Out, was winding his rods in so I was assuming he'd seen me net one. I heaved her out and it felt like it might go 30, and at 30lb 12oz it sure did. I held her in the sling and with Clive on his way round I tried Liam again but it was going to voicemail all the time, so I texted him.

A good one at last, and my biggest February carp.

"Come quick, it's the biggest fish in the world!"

With Clive on the scene, I got her back out and started to take the pictures, and when my phone rang I assumed it was Liam. He just made it round before I put it back and it turned out to be the Map fish which he'd caught the first day it kicked off just over three weeks before, so this one was definitely hungry.

In front of the usual park audience of Joe Public when a fish is on the bank, I held her aloft and tried to ignore the stupid questions but one lady shouted to her kids to come quickly, as it was the biggest fish in the world. That was quite nice! Not quite, but a February 30 was a worthy trophy.

With a new rig and pop-up on, I cast out to the left and found my elastic mark and then smacked out the rig. It landed tight on the clip and bumped down sweetly. With the line slackened off I put the rod on the rest and attached the bobbin, but each time I put it in the clip and looked back at the bobbin it was tight again. Surely not? I watched the bobbin as I paid off more slack, and as it picked up again I bent into the rod and felt a fish on, less than a minute after recasting. The carp god was shining his light on me today, for sure. The choddy must have only just settled before it was sucked in. This one came in a lot quicker and with the wet net chucked back in, a little golden common of just over 14lbs made it the second of the day. It appeared that the fish hadn't done the off after all.

It took a couple of casts to get it back to where I was happy, and with the aid of the wind I was able to get a dozen Tuttis out to the area on dusk. With fresh baits on the other two and them recast, it was dark again and on reflection it had been my best February by a country mile. I hoped that March would be as good!

It certainly started off well as by 5.30am I had another mirror in the bottom of my net, the left-hand rod bringing the action, and this was the first take to come in darkness. A short, dumpy mirror with nice golden scales recorded a weight of 25lb 12oz and as Liam had already left for home, I rang the missus, who drove over and obliged with the camera. This was the first fish Lynn had seen me catch and she shrieked like a girl when it flapped on the mat. Apparently, its beady eye was looking at her! Lynn did get brave enough to touch it though before I slipped it back.

The first fish Lynn had seen me catch.

With the rest of the day still ahead of me, there was still time for another one. I had until four and at just after three, the left-hand rod's line was out of the clip and straightaway, it pulled down hard; this was more like it. Liam was waiting to drop in behind me when I moved out, and he also remarked that it might be a good fish. This fish cut across to the right and with Liam sinking the other two lines I had no drama. At about 20 yards out I saw a big, long, ghostly shape about a yard below before it cut back up to the left, over the other two lines. I felt this was the big one and so I took it steady, especially as Liam was trying to take photos - pressure on!

Liam manned the net and this was the moment of truth as the leadcore rose out the lake. A three-foot common slid over the net and sunk to the bottom. As I peered into the net, I could see that the huge length was not backed up in depth and width and the 'Anorexic Common' was christened.

From believing I was attached to a 40, this chub-like common looked like it would struggle to make 20. The Anorexic didn't even do that and at 17½lbs, it turned out to be a bit of an anti-climax after the previous day, and with half an hour left I whacked it back onto the spot and then packed down the rest of the gear. Not surprisingly I couldn't repeat the same result two days running, and I wound in and left Liam to it.

The Anorexic Common was christened.

There were one or two big-breasted 'birds' around the Park Lake.

The season ended on March 14th which was a Monday and I took the last week off work so I could do a couple more trips before it shut. I knew the lake would get busy so I resigned myself to fish down the other end and with none of the really big ones getting caught, perhaps they were spending their time away from the bowl end which had done all the fish.

My power-steering pump went on the way to work that Sunday, but fortunately my mechanic was about and even better had a written-off car the same as mine at his yard, so after work we managed to swap them over and I was back in business. Cheers, James! Lynn shared a birthday along with little Isabelle on the Thursday, and by the time I'd got away and collected my wife's birthday presents, it was about 4pm and I called into the lake to see what the state of play was. The bowl end was indeed busy and not only was Bert in the Rats but there was also a loaded barrow behind ready to move in when he left. With the week ahead of me, I headed home and spent the rest of the day doing family stuff. I headed up to the lake after lunch on Monday. The bay was flat calm and the sun had been pitching on it all day, so it looked a good area.

I'd seen nothing but as the only carp I'd seen the whole time were the ones in the net it was no surprise. I decided on peg 7 which not only gave me the entrance of the bay but I could also fish the other two out long into the middle stretch of the lake.

I knew that a mate, Danny, had done well in this area a few winters before and I put a handful of baits around each rig, the spod needing to be employed with the long rods which were out about 115-120 yards out. The middle rod bleeped a few times before dropping and then climbing again at about 7.30pm that evening. A big slab was the culprit and with the temperature plummeting with a frost on its way, it took me a few casts before it soared out to land hitting the clip. With nothing else to go on, I stayed another night in the same swim just moving the rods around a little bit in search of fish but there was still no sign of them.

On the Wednesday morning I made the long walk back in the rain that had just moved in, and headed home. I planned to return on the Friday for the last three nights, after all the birthday celebrations were over. I was quite glad that I was at home that night. On my return, I heard that the police were all over the park that evening because some nutter had been running around with a knife and

threatening to top himself. Liam was shitting himself down in the Secrets, all alone! The park can be a lovely place sometimes, this just three days after the café wall was sledge-hammered as some toe-rags tried to break in. Fortunately, the anglers on the lake alerted the police who, for once, were on their toes and caught the culprits red-handed.

The only place, as far as I knew, that hadn't been fished at all and could often throw out the big girls was right up the far end and so on Friday I gambled and fished the main Humpty swim. As usual, three choddies were dispatched on to likely areas and again, the only thing to disturb the silence was a bream that night. I got up at first light but nothing was stirring so when I heard that the bowl end was almost deserted, Liam and I were soon packing up and driving up there.

With a light south-westerly and glorious spring sunshine I was very confident as I got back in the Rats and Liam dropped into the Bus Stop for the day. Within half an hour I'd caught a tench on the right-hand rod and then over the next two hours followed this with three bream, all off the same spot. As fast as I was retying new chod rigs, the bream were blunting them!

It looked cock-on for a carp, but by Monday I was still waiting with just the occasional bream tripping up. At 4pm I wound in, all done, and after the fireworks of February, March had fizzled out with only one small common getting caught since the two I'd had on March the 1st. The big'uns had made it and could now enjoy their three months lay-off.

As fast as I was retying new chod rigs the bream were blunting them!

Chapter 25 - Doggy Park

With the park lake shutting on March 14th and Pinge thankfully completed, I needed to find somewhere new for the spring. My two options were the mighty Burghfield after the best common in the land, as well as a few other crackers, or a much smaller local pit that held not many fish but among them were some real stunners, the big mirror going over 40 as well as one or two others that occasionally hit that mark. Also of particular interest was the gorgeous big common that resides in the lake which was also getting close to the magical 40 mark.

My biggest common was 36lbs 14oz, so this pristine fish would be a personal best for the species. Although the Burghfield fish was a much larger specimen and certainly a fish of a lifetime, the Dog Park common was a much more realistic target, the lake being much smaller and more local, as well as the fish being a much friendlier customer than the rarely caught Burghfield monster.

My Car Park ticket ended on March 31st so I had two trips left, but on March 15th I went, along with my little girl, Isabelle, for a look around Dog Park before deciding to purchase a ticket. I was armed with a bag of bread so that Isabelle could feed the ducks, plus her baby doll's pram which she soon got fed up with pushing and it was left to Daddy to drag it round. Thus, no tree climbing and looking for fish was possible but it gave me an idea of the swims and with the water crystal clear it looked like the weed would soon be flourishing. Although not the most stunning lake I'd ever fished, the carp that swam in its depths were stunners so as it was a cheap, local ticket it suited me for the spring.

Anyway, I had two trips left on the Car Park in the faint hope of catching Arfur. When I say 'faint hope', I don't mean that I'd given up hope of catching old Fatso but the fact was she had never been out at the back end of the season in all the time I'd fished the lake. It had only been out once in March, to my knowledge, and that was back in about 1998 when Oil-slick Rick caught her out of the Gate. The Baby Orange was a more realistic target in the winter months and as it was likely to be still over 40, it was a more than admirable prize to catch.

The clocks hadn't changed, and Sunday night was going to be a bit of a rush so with my lines on my fluorocarbon spools still marked up from the last time I'd fished the Car Park in the Curly Wurly swim, I plotted up in the Curly for the first night and knowing the swim like the back of my hand, soon had my two baits out. The closer rod was fished over a scattering of maggots - a particular favourite morsel for Arfur - casters, pellets and a few boilies, and over the long spot I scattered just ten baits around my pop-up. With Kingy in the Chair being the only other angler on the pond, I'd have the chance to move if I spotted any fish.

Giving it till midday with no signs, I then wound in and went for a mooch round to try to find some fish. Creeping into the Gate snag, I squatted down and after a couple of minutes could make out a carp sitting on the bottom, slowly wafting its fins. With the March light not the best, it was a struggle to make out which fish it was. It certainly was wide and Arfur-shaped but its fins looked too big for the old original. I knew one of the Italian stockies had spent a lot of time in the Gate snag last summer so when it turned and I could see a full tail, I knew it was that one.

There was another much smaller scaly fish in there as well, and a common turned up later after I'd done another circuit, but there was no sign of either Arfur or Baby O, so after a bit of deliberating I decided to stay put in the Curly as it had the potential to produce both my targets. When a tufty hooked itself on the long rod at about 10am I called it a day, but before I left I heaved in a bit of bait on the Gate margin spot. I felt it was only a matter of time before the Baby Orange got in there and would be catchable off that margin spot.

So that I wouldn't have to rush the next week, I'd booked the Wednesday off work so I could arrive on the Monday morning and do the full allotted 48 hours. With the Thursday being the last night, I hoped that a lot of people would do the last two nights, so my two nights would be quieter. On texting John Elmer on the Saturday, I discovered that he was in the Gate and he had seen the Baby Orange in there. At least my theory was right so now all I had to do was get the practicals right.

Monday morning was bright and sunny so I should be able to spot one or two. I backed the car up to the Gate swim and leaving a bucket in the swim, went round to check the snag. I couldn't see anything in there but often they didn't turn up until midday and as it was only about 11am, it gave me an hour to look round.

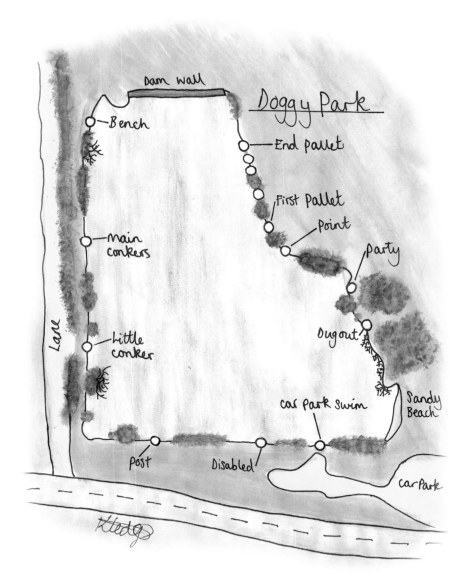

Kingy was in Trumptons and had caught the Pineapple, the elusive little fully-scaled. Fred had also had a couple of stockies out of the End Works so they were waking up, but would the originals? With the Dustbin dying in February after the thaw, there were only three left and the chances were that they'd all be together. From the End Secret I could see there were fish out between there and the Islands so I ran round to the Islands and managed to get a good vantage point in the tree, from where I could see what was swimming about, enjoying the March sunshine.

There were about eight fish and two of them were bigger. One was away from the pack and as it headed off out into the Middle Secret water I was sure it was the Baby Orange. The other one was definitely the pale and rather tatty Big Orange. The Big O was staying with the gang of stockies, but where was Arfur?

As I wandered backwards and forwards from the Secrets round to the Islands, a big fish waddled out from the trees and there was big fat Arfur looking clean and healthy. Right, I'd found the fish and now I had to set the traps, I was pretty sure the best interception point was the Middle Secret and having fished the swim in the summer, I was familiar with the spots. However, I soon found these areas weedy and it took me a lot of casts to get two baits out and then I still wasn't 100 per cent happy with them, but with the big'uns in the area, I couldn't afford to totally pee them off by thrashing the water to a foam.

After an uneventful night, I wound in about half nine and armed with the marker rod marched round to the Islands. If I was going to move then I'd have to move fast

in case anyone else turned up. I chucked out to the Islands spot and it was clean although not hard, as I'd have preferred it. Under the tree looked clean as well and with Arfur turning up not far off the tree line when I'd seen her, I felt more confident that my rigs were on better spots for what was to be my final night on the Car Park. The sun wasn't out, as it had been on the Monday, and I saw no evidence of fish and just had to hope the lake would give me a golden handshake.

As was usual, the lake put up two fingers instead and 24 hours later the gear was in the car and the net was dry. I would have to settle for six of the original mirrors to be my final tally and as I said my goodbyes to the lads on Trumptons, I briefly stopped at Heather's grave and said goodbye to the old girl. She'll always have a special place in my heart and I'd have loved her to have adorned the cover of this book, but it was sadly not meant to be, and with new challenges ahead, I shut the gate for the final time.

The water of the Dog Park Lake was crystal clear and with angler pressure increasing on the small stock, I put on fresh 12lb fluorocarbon lines on three spools. I planned to fish chods and zigs to any fish evident and travelled to the lake on Sunday evening hoping to have as good a spring as last year on Pingewood.

The weather was overcast and blowing a south-westerly and the lake looked fairly busy as all the main car park bank swims were occupied. As I walked up the bank, there was also a bivvy in the Party swim but with a familiar face looking out of the bivvy. I stopped for a chat with Taz, who's a customer at the shop and one of the regulars on Dog Park.

It appeared that my timing was good as Taz had seen a number of fish show out in front of him and with the wind pushing in it looked prime. Taz was off in the morning and this gave me an option if I couldn't get on fish that night; I swapped phone numbers with him so I'd know when he was going. The next swim, the Point, was also occupied so this left just the high bank step swims or the conker bank. As I made my way round I could see that there was one at each end of this bank as well. It was a bit busier than I'd wished for, but there had been three or four caught so far this year so all the rest were due out, and as the big one hadn't been out since May the previous year, everyone was keen.

As I walked round past the car park on the way to have another look at the small dug-out swim in the car park corner, I saw a big fish nut out about 40 yards out in front of the Point swim. I ran round and stopped at the Party to see if Taz had seen it but the tree on his right blocked his view.

A couple of friendly park inhabitants.

With the Point occupied, I went in the First Pallet swim and just managed to get two choddies and one zig out, all at 35 to 50 yards. The water was lifeless in front of me so at about half-past eight I packed everything on the barrow and pushed it down to the Party swim. Luckily, Taz was packing up so I'd be able to get in there sooner than I'd thought.

As Taz wheeled his barrow off, I whanged the marker out and after a couple of casts found a firm, smooth channel among tall weed stems. With a bright orange Tutti on my chod rig, I sent it beyond the float, pulled it back and as it hit bottom I got a nice thud from the 3oz lead. It felt 'right'! Making that the middle rod, I fished the right-hand one up to the weed, straight out about 45 yards, and checking the depth, I shortened my zig by a foot and cast that one out to the left.

With the bivvy quickly up and the bed stuffed under, I fired up the stove for a long overdue tea and a bacon sarnie. Once breakfast had been eaten I could sit and relax and watch the lake. Suddenly, the middle rod's hanger pulled up against the rod and stayed tight, and I legged it down the slope being careful not to end up on my arse. As I pulled into it the rod went straight over into battle curve and I felt that satisfying feeling of a hooked carp. It kited round a bit before plugging into weed.

There was a high bank behind me, so I used this to my advantage and from the top, applied pressure which soon budged it and as I gained line, I made my way back down the slope and dropped the other lines onto the lakebed. The fish was now

closer in so I simply had to let it tire and soon a chunky mirror was saying hello to the inside of my net.

With the waves lapping over it and in the clear water, it had looked a 30-pounder but once on the bank I wasn't too sure and at 28lbs 2oz, it was a lovely fish with which to open my account. The bloke on the Point came down to do the pictures for me and as soon as the fish was back, I got a new rig on and a fresh, cork-plugged Tutti, and getting a nice donk again got it back on the spot. The guys on the car park bank had seen me catch and it wasn't long before the bait boats started coming a bit further my way.

The wind was quite strong, pushing straight in, so with another night still to go there was no reason why they shouldn't stay in the area. The south-westerly blew all night and at 5.30am, when the same rod was off again, I was soon wide awake with a really powerful fish wrenching the rod round as it pulled left, thankfully away from the weedbed. The line was singing in the strong wind and I was forced to lower the rod tip to water level as it dragged me down the left-hand margin under a big overhang. As I inched it back, I was able to lift the rod and with the waders on I slipped into the margins and played it under the tip. No more dramas followed and soon it was beaten.

It looked a big fish but I didn't want to turn the torch on at the edge, as I didn't want those bait boats drifting into my water again. I grabbed a bankstick and secured the net, before cutting the line, and got the sling wetted and zeroed, the torch only being put on from behind the cover of the bivvy. With the net rolled down I struggled up the bank and there was no doubt that this one was well over 30, and felt closer to 40. I laid it on the mat behind the bivvy and with the torch on in the half light, a very big, fat mirror looked back at me.

By the scale pattern I could see that it wasn't the big'un so I transferred her into the sling, and with the aid of the net handle, the needle spun round to 35lbs 10oz, my third 30 of 2011. The hook had been buried in the bottom lip and was perfectly nailed. I secured her in the sling and phoned a mate to come down and do the photos. He said it sounded like Teardrop, the sixth biggest in the pit and he'd be about half an hour.

No sooner had I fired up the kettle than a mate, Alan, turned up, so I phoned back to tell Chris not to travel over as Alan would do the honours. We had a quick tea, then got her out where she was crapping out bait all over the mat so they were well on the munch. It was certainly a heavy old lump and its fat shape filled the frame in the photos. I got a rig back out on the spot but that, unsurprisingly, was my lot. It appeared word had got out in the area of my instant success and I started to hear all sorts of rumours as the tittle-tattle and Chinese whispers spread like wildfire.

It was a lovely fish with which to open my account.

Teardrop, the sixth-biggest in the pond.

The next Sunday, I returned and with it being red hot the lake was packed, not with anglers but people picnicking, barbecuing and even swimming. The Party swim lived up to its name with the public taking advantage of the hot weather. There was only one angler on, Dougie, and he was in the Point so with fish bow-waving about up at the narrow end, I chose the Big Conkers swim and fished two zigs and a choddy at the distances where they'd been cruising. I'd been tempted to wait and go back in the Party when the swimmers buggered off but I would have only been going on the previous week's results and not on fish sightings. I set my alarm for first light and got my head down for the night as the last of the groups of youths left on dark.

There were no interruptions in the night and I awoke to my phone bleeping so I hit the snooze button but managed to get up when it went off again. If I didn't force myself up and make a tea, I'd fall straight back to sleep. With a good view of the lake I wandered up and down, and keeping the tea on the go kept me awake. The only fish I saw show was out in front of the Party at about 7am and I told myself that if I saw another one I'd move straightaway. I kept watching, but the flat-calm lake surface was unbroken bar the odd tench or bream.

This one was well over 30, and felt closer to 40.

When the surface started to ripple and push into the Party I was packed down and whizzing round with the barrow in double-quick time, arriving in the swim by 8.30am. Obviously, the first rod out was back on to the hotspot and with no birds about I stuck out a handful of dark baits and a couple of bright Tutti sweets for good measure. I whanged out two zigs and sat back to see if anything else showed. It was even earlier than the week before when the pop-up was picked up and was out of the clip as I scrambled down the slope. I should have walked straight back up the high bank but instead I faffed about, dropping the other two tips.

By this time the fish had found sanctuary in the tough stalky weed stems that were about five-feet long. I got to the top of the bank and increased the pressure, but it was stuck. I eased off a couple of times and then tried again but after a few minutes the tip jerked back a few inches and then as it pulled free I had that gut-wrenching feeling as I realised it had got off. Although gutted, I was pleased. I must be doing something right as I'd now had three bites in as many nights and most people didn't get that many in a year. Apart from telling Taz, I kept my lost fish to myself because I was getting enough unwanted attention as it was and I didn't want to get invaded again when more anglers turned up.

The next week and the lake was rammed, all except the far end. There was a light easterly picking up and blowing up this end, and learning that nothing had been out

all week I headed right to the far end. With a bottom bait cast next to a big snag down the margin, I hoped one or two might have ventured away from the pressure.

I put a choddy out on a patch of silt and cast an 11' zig into 13' of water halfway across the bay. By the time I'd got them out it was dark so after a brew and a sarnie, I got my head down for an early start. Fortunately, my Delkim beat the phone to an alarm call and my zig had tempted a fish in the middle of the moonlit night. The fish had dived straight into weed but with a heavy 4oz lead, and the tail rubber only butted up to the clip, I soon had it moving as the line jerkily grated through before pulling free and effectively, I was now freelining direct to the fish. It came in quite easily now and with an 11-foot hooklink I had to lower the tip when the lead clip rattled into the tip ring, momentarily catching until I dropped the tip and back wound a few feet. I was now fully conscious not to let that happen again.

The fish plodded under the tip and I thought it would soon be in the net, but then it woke up and stripped 25 yards off me - not fast and furious, but steady and heavy. I was sure it was one of the big ones and as there was a full moon and the common had form of coming out on this moon, I felt it could be that one, or one of the other whackers. I got it back into my margin and it just bored about, hugging the bottom, going round and round. With a 10lb link and size 8 hook I couldn't give it too much pressure but even on stronger gear I wouldn't have played it any harder. I had all night and at this rate it looked like it was going to take that long.

After what must have been half an hour, it came up in the water and being careful not to get the lead clip stuck in the tip again, I eventually managed to bundle it over the draw cord. Keen to look at my monster I pulled the net toward me and peered in. It was a mirror, but what surprised me most was the size; it wasn't the expected whacker but a mid-20 with massive fins. I'd have put money on it being 35–plus and would have been devastated if it had come off.

Anyway, it was a stunning mirror and for the record it went 25lb 10oz. The 10oz must have been its massive paddle which had tricked me into imagining its size. Taz came round at first light and took the pictures for me and as it was my third capture in as many trips, it would at least give the locals something to gossip about. Top of the list of gossip I heard was that my wife was about to have another baby and that was why I was fishing locally. I'd have to have words with her as I'd had the snip 18 months before! Where people dreamed that up from I have no idea. The other one I heard was that I was heavily baiting the lake with Tuttis as loads had been found in the margins. The fact that I'd caught on singles meant that they were clutching at straws and just making up stories, for whose benefit I have no idea. Anyway, I stayed put as the odd fish showed down to my right.

The flat-calm lake surface was unbroken bar the odd tench or bream.

On the Tuesday morning, I had a visit from Dougie asking for my help as the Big Male had been caught but was not well and kept rolling on its side. I wound my rods in and grabbing my waders, I legged it down to where I found the Male being held in the captor's net. I'd had a similar experience on Farmhouse when Jamie Woods had the male from that lake and it had taken us ages to get it going.

Without being held he'd just roll over so, holding the wrist of the tail, I kept him upright and moving the wrist from side to side in a swimming motion, tried to get his whole system going. I did this for about five minutes and then holding the gills open, rocked him gently to try to get lots of clean, oxygenated water through his gills. The others were rightly worried but I was fairly confident he'd be all right and already he was staying upright, although staying on the surface the whole time. I was just gently keeping him working, and then noticed a stream of bubbles come out of his gills and with that his gills started to become regular, he then sank to the bottom. Result. Trapped wind had been his problem.

I told him he owed me one and to visit my net soon.

It wasn't the expected whacker but a mid-20 with massive fins.

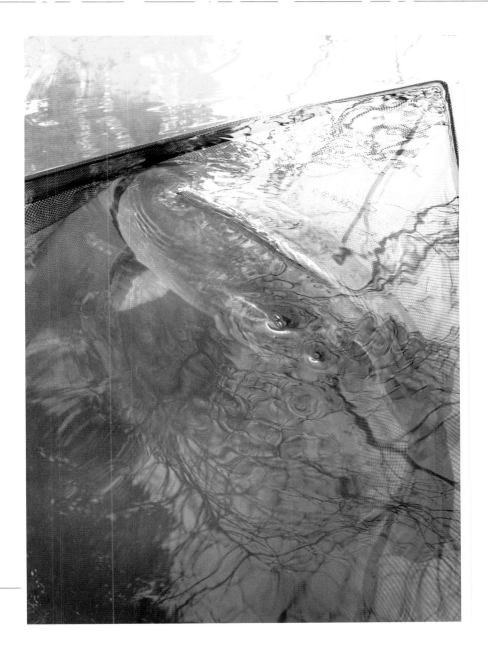

After a few minutes, and making sure he was strong and pulling, I let him go and hugging the bottom, he waddled off down the shelf. I told him he owed me one and to visit my net soon. With that I returned to pack up, pleased with the outcome as big old fish like that have to be looked after and I hoped that the lake would pay me back for saving one of its residents.

My next three trips were a bit frustrating. The common had been out at 38lbs 6oz, as well as the Moonscale mirror on the same day. The lake was busy and there was the added problem of three full-timers hogging the main swims, despite there supposedly being a 72-hour limit in a swim, which was being blatantly abused. The 40 now hadn't been out for over a year and the prospect of it being a big weight kept me plodding away.

I turned up on Sunday evening, May 22nd. The wind was blowing south-westerly, forecast to get even stronger and the lake looked quiet. The road bank was empty, the first time I'd seen that and I walked round to the Party expecting to find Dougie. As I neared the swim, I could see a barrowload of gear at the back and as I rounded the corner, I could see Dougie folding down his bivvy. He was off and with no one else on I could finally get back in the Party swim.

I ran and got my gear and as Dougie departed I had the lake to myself. I also had a secret weapon to try as I had the first batch of my new bait that I'd been working on for Richworth. After five months, I'd got the bait how I wanted it and rolled a mix of both 14 and 20mm baits by hand. I had what I hoped would be the winning recipe.

I found my hot spot and it was still presentable despite the increase in weed growth. With the spod clipped to the range, I put six spods of mixed-size boilies of the prototype mix bang over the top of my chod hook bait. I also cast a Tutti on the chod about 20 feet to the right at the same range.

The left-hand rod went a bit further and more to the left in a silty gully where I'd seen carp show on a previous trip. This also saw a few spods of the new mix. The wind was strong and pushing in so I set the bivvy a bit more side-on and further back than normal, the big bush to the right acting as a bit of a windbreak.

The wind continued throughout the night and in the morning it was even stronger, and had swung a fraction more, now battering my swim directly. I saw one fish near my left-hand rod but it was the middle rod, as usual, that at 12.20pm pulled up and line ticked off the clutch.

Not a bad morning's work!

A more perfectly proportioned big common you couldn't find.

Learning from the last loss in this swim, I made my way up the bank and with the extra height I kept it moving and it slowly came toward me and left a bit. As it got to about 20 yards out I made my way back down and dropped the left-hand line out of the way and stepped into my waders. As I pulled them up, I tightened back down fully and the fish bogged down straight out at about 15 yards; at this close range, and with the rod held high, I literally lifted it out the weed.

As it made its way left, I followed it down the margin away from the other lines. The leadcore popped out and I saw a big flank flash over under the waves. Up it came again, and there was a big, fat fish covered in common carp scales, like coins of gold.

It could only be the big common and the treasure I longed for, but it was not beaten yet and I gingerly played it for another five minutes as each time it would rise up to the top before thrashing its tail, spraying water into the air before diving deep again. As it surfaced and rolled over, I pulled the rod behind me and with the waves washing the big common over the net, I blurted out a "Yesssss!" as I engulfed her.

What a stunning-looking fish, and a more perfectly proportioned big common you couldn't find. I staked the net securely and when everything was ready, staggered up to the mat with my biggest-ever common. She wasn't fat like I'd thought, so as it had been 38lbs 6oz five weeks ago, I wasn't expecting her to go 40 and the scales recorded 39lbs 6oz, just ten ounces short, but I didn't care. I'd caught one of my two main targets, it was my biggest-ever common and I'd done it all in just 15 nights.

In the last eight months I had caught myself two new personal bests - a Beast of a mirror and a true Beauty of a common! Oh, and the new bait had produced this magical carp in less than 18 hours since it hit the water. Not a bad morning's work!

Thanks for reading. I hope you enjoyed it and that you've been inspired to catch a Beauty or a Beast for yourself.